Issues in the New Europe
Graham Drake

University of

Hodder & Stoughton

A MEMBER OF THE HODDER HEADLINE GROUP

Acknowledgements

The author and publishers would like to thank the following for permission to reproduce copyright materials in this book. Every effort has been made to trace and acknowledge all copyright holders but if any have been overlooked the publishers will be pleased to make the necessary arrangements.

BBC Wildlife Magazine, 1983; Belhaven Press, Rural Policy & Planning, A W Gilg, Fig 5.22, The Geography of Europe's Futures, Figs 7.20, 7.21, Immigrants & the Social Geography of European Cities, Fig 6.14, The Channel Tunnel; Blackwell Publishers, Patterns of Residential Segregation in Budapest, J Ladanyi; British Petroleum, Fig 6.21; Energy Policy, Vol 19, No 8, Oct 1991, pp756–7 Fig 8.14, Vol 21, No 3, Mar 1993, pp284–295 Fig 8.16, Vol 20, No 12, Dec 1992, pp 1186–97 Figs 8.18–9, reproduced here with the permission of Butterworth-Heinemann, Oxford, UK; Central Statistical Office, Social Trends, 1993, Fig 4.4; Commission of the European Communities, The Week in Europe, Background Reports, Figs 3.5, 3.24; Department of the Environment, Urban Air Quality in the UK, Whitelegg, Figs 6.19, 6.22, 6.23 ; © The Economist, Figs 2.12, 2.16, 2.21, 7.8; The European, Figs 2.5ab, 2.6, 2.7, 2.14, 2.19, 2.20, 3.19, Europe Braced for Migrant Invasion, L Walker, N Comfort; Eurostat Publications, Portrait of the Region, Fig 10.15; Faber & Faber, The Demographic Revolution, Jane McLoughlin, Fig 4.12; The Financial Times, Figs 3.25, 4.20; Food and Agriculture Organization of the United Nations, FAO Yearbook, Production Vol 44, 1990, Fig 5.3; The Geographical Association, Geography, Figs 6.8, 6.10, 7.4, 7.7, 9.7, 9.9; The Geographical Magazine, Figs 3.2b, 3.22, 3.27, 8.5, 10.7; The Guardian, Figs 2.8, 2.9a, 3.8b, 3.14, 4.17, 4.19, 4.21, 4.22, 4.23, 4.25, 5.8, 5.11, 5.12a, 5.21, 6.11, 6.12, 6.17, 6.20, 7.19, 8.3, 8.6, 8.14, 8.15; The Independent, Figs 6.26, 6.28, 8.11, 8.13, 10.5; Granta Publications, The State of Europe, Ivan Klima; International Waterfowl and Wetlands Research Bureau, Integrated Management & Conservation of Wetlands in Agricultural & Forested Landscapes, Ed M Finlayson, Fig 9.5; Kogan Page, Doing Business in Poland, Fig 5.23; Journal of the Regional Studies Association, Developments and Impacts in Regional Studies, J Tuppen, Fig 7.6; Leading Edge Press, High Speed Trains: Fast Tracks to the Future; Longman Group UK, a table from Smith: The Nationalities Question in the Soviet Union; MAFF, © Crown Copyright, ADAS Cartography, Fig 5.20; National Geographic Society, Albania Opens the Door, Dusko Doder, Europe Faces an Immigrant Tide, Peter Ross Range, East Europe's Dark Dawn, Jon Thompson, Fig 4.16; New Hungarian Quarterly, Fig 9.1; New Scientist, Bank to Bale out Bulgaria's Reactors, Debora MacKenzie, Fig 8.12; New Statesman & Society, Tom Nairn; The Observer, Figs 5.10, 9.2; Office for Official Publications of the European Communities, Figs 3.16, 3.17, 3.18 (Linguistic Minorities in the EEC 1990), 5.4 (Agriculture: Statistical Yearbook 1990), 7.2 (Community Support Frameworks 1989–91), 7.22 (Statistical Bulletin, No 2, 1992), 10.15 (Portrait of the Regions Vol 3 1993); Oxford University Press, Agricultural Change in Great Britain, B Ilbery, Figs 5.14, 5.16; Penguin Books Ltd, Rebirth of History, Misha Glenny; Philip Allan Publishers, The Politics Review; Philips Geographical Digest, Fig 4.1; The Planner, Fig 6.15; Routledge, Geography of the EC, J & F Cole, Fig 2.13; Royal Society for the Protection of Birds, A Steppe in the Right Direction, Figs 5.17, 5.18, 5.20 (Case Study of European Farmland 1991), 5.7 (J P Taylor, J B Dixon); Copyright by editrice La Stampa SpA, Turin, Italy; The Sun, Fig 10.6; Town & Country Planning Association, There is an Alternative, Linda McAven; United Nations Publication, Demographic Yearbook, various years, Fig 4.13, Statistical Yearbook 1990–91, Fig 10.14; University of London Examinations and Assessment Council, Fig 5.13; Unwin Hyman Ltd, Inequality and Development, A Reed, Fig 4.2ab.

Cataloguing in Publication Data is available from the British Library

ISBN 0 340 60755 6

First published 1994

Impression number	10	9	8	7	6	5	4	3	2	1
Year		1999	1998	1997	1996	1995	1994			

Typeset by Serif Tree, Kidlington, Oxford.
Printed in Great Britain for Hodder & Stoughton Educational, a division of Hodder Headline Plc, 338 Euston Road, London NW1 3BH by St Edmundsbury Press Ltd.

The author and publishers also thank the following for permission to reproduce photographs in this book:

J Allan Cash, pp. 61, 110, 124, 203, 230, 238, 242, 252; Architectural Association, pp. 118, 211; Associated Press Photo, p. 87; British Telecommunications, p. 261; Robert Harding pp. 7, 10, 116, 156, 205, 219, 243; Impact, pp. 61, 126; Life File, pp. 13, 170; David Money, p. 163; Oxford Scientific Films, p. 207; J Jose Pascual, p. 106; Popperphoto, pp. 102, 166; Select, pp. 135, 14; Frank Spooner, pp. 7, 80, 98; Still Pictures, p. 160; Sygma, pp. 42, 214; Topham, pp. 12, 14, 15, 44, 51, 61, 62, 70, 72, 85, 90, 92, 141, 152, 174–5, 183, 186, 188, 194, 221, 235, 256; Tony Waltham, p. 246; Wolfgang Kunz, p. 143.

All other photos supplied by the author.

Chapter 1 opener: Lloyds of London, Robert Harding; Chapter 2 opener: 1993 European Council, Corfu, Frank Spooner; Chapter 3 opener: child in small community outside Burrel, Albania, Impact; Chapter 4 opener: Albanian refugees at Bari in Italy, Topham; Chapter 5 opener: Northern Spain peasant woman, Topham; Chapter 6 opener: Les Halles shopping centre, Paris, Architectural Association; Chapter 7 opener: Avlona, Albania, Zita-Sygma; Chapter 8 opener: Grimethorpe colliery miners leave after last shift 30 October 1992, Topham; Chapter 9 opener: River Acheloos Dam Project, drought on wetlands, Katz Pictures; Chapter 10 opener: TGV Sud-Est trains, Gare de Lyon in Paris, J Allan Cash.

Contents

KEY IDEAS

1.1 Europe can be defined in different ways. For the purpose of this book Russia and Turkey have been excluded.

1.2 Europe is experiencing rapid and unpredictable change. Europe in the 1990s is a very different place to the Europe of earlier decades.

1.3 Although links between most European countries are being strengthened, Europe is a continent of enormous environmental, social, cultural, political and economic diversity.

FIG 1.1   *The Countries of Europe*

1.1 Defining Europe

Europe has been traditionally defined as the part of the Eurasian land mass to the west of the Ural Mountains in Russia. For most purposes this definition is not very useful. There has also been a tendency in some western European countries, at least until recently, to use the word 'Europe' to refer to western Europe or even the European Union (EU). This was perhaps understandable when there was relatively little contact through the Iron Curtain dividing eastern Europe from western Europe, but it is not acceptable in the 1990s.

For the purposes of this book Europe is defined as all the countries to the west of Russia. Russia is generally excluded on the basis that many of the issues facing that country stem from the fact that much of its land area lies within Asia. Nevertheless, it is referred to when it is of direct relevance to Europe. Turkey is also excluded for the same reasons.

Another problem of definition is the regional divisions of Europe. For most purposes in this book Europe is divided into western Europe and eastern Europe, with eastern Europe including the former Communist countries and the countries which were part of the Soviet Union until 1991. The term central Europe, which is often used to denote the region including Poland, the Czech Republic, Slovakia, and Hungary, is not generally used in this book. The terms southern Europe, meaning the countries bordering the Mediterranean, and northern Europe are used where appropriate.

The Europe of the 1990s has two important characteristics:

− it is experiencing rapid change;
− it is a region containing enormous variety.

1.2 Rapid Change

Since the end of the 1980s Europe has experienced rapid and profound changes. Europe in the 1990s is a very different place to the Europe of the 1980s − hence the term 'The New Europe'. Despite the international tensions of the Cold War, Europe showed considerable stability for four decades. Few people dared to predict, even as late as 1988, the dismantling of the Berlin Wall, the anti-Communist revolutions throughout eastern Europe, the collapse of the Soviet Union and the unification of Germany − all of which had happened by the end of 1991. The disintegration of Yugoslavia into warring ethnic factions was not surprising once Communism collapsed, but the brutality of the three-way civil war in Bosnia shocked Europe and the rest of the world. It destroyed the myth that Europe had progressed beyond such national hatreds.

By the end of 1992 Europe had seen the creation of 14 new countries and the disappearance of the former Soviet Union, Yugoslavia, East Germany, and Czechoslovakia. Many of the longer-term impacts of these changes are still far from clear, and many countries are facing an uncertain future.

Even in relatively stable western Europe the future no longer seems quite so predictable. Within the European Union moves towards greater co-operation and unity, in particular the Maastricht Treaty, have been thrown into doubt by disagreements within and between countries. International economic problems and a growing feeling that the current policies of the Union have become outdated in post-Cold War Europe have all contributed to this doubt. Large-scale migration, the rise of extreme right-wing political groups, particularly in Germany, and the strengthening of nationalism seem to threaten the political stability which has been a feature of most western European countries over recent decades.

These important political changes are altering the geography of Europe, but they have tended to push other equally significant trends into the background. Environmental issues are likely to become increasingly important over the next decade. The uncertain future of energy production, growing concern over the environmental impact of traffic, the deterioration or urban environments, and worries about the effects of capital-intensive farming are typical of the environmental issues which European societies have to tackle. The fact that Green Parties have failed to attract significant support in most European countries does not mean that environmental issues will not become a potent political force.

Other equally important issues which are rapidly changing the social and economic geography of Europe include declining birth rates and ageing populations, de-industrialisation, the development of telecommunications and investment in high-speed transport networks.

The following chapters in this book highlight these and other issues which are likely to continue to affect the economic, social, environmental and political geography of Europe for the next decade and beyond.

1.3 A Continent of Variety

There was a tendency within western Europe, particularly during the 1980s, to emphasise the common cultural characteristics of the region in order to emphasise the desirability of greater European integration and co-operation. In fact, despite growing economic and political co-operation between most countries, Europe is a continent of bewildering variety. Including the tiny principalities of Gibraltar, Andorra, Liechtenstein, Monaco, Vatican City and San Marino, there are 42 countries and a far greater number of languages. There is a surprising variety of cultures, religions and ethnic groups reflecting a wide variety of historical backgrounds.

There are enormous environmental variations, from the tundra of northern Scandinavia, where average January temperatures are below $-10°C$, to the Mediterranean region, where average July temperatures can exceed $25°C$. In terms of relief there are the mountainous regions including the Alps, the Pyrenees, Norway and the Carpathians – the highest mountain being Mont Blanc in the Alps at 4807 m above sea level. At the other extreme are flat low-lying regions, such as the Netherlands, some of which lies below sea level, and the North European Plain covering northern Germany and much of Poland.

The economic variations are, in terms of economic policy, less pronounced than they were in the 1980s. All European countries are now embracing free market economics to a greater or lesser extent. Yet levels of wealth vary enormously, from the extreme rural poverty of parts of Albania where people are dependent on foreign aid, to the wealth of urbanised and industrialised regions such as Lombardy in northern Italy, the Paris region and parts of western Germany.

Politically, the variations are far less pronounced than they were before the collapse of Communism. Almost every European country is now a multi-party democracy, yet the emergence of nationalism as a strong politcal force in some countries is creating new political tensions.

So while it is true that there are ethnic, cultural, political and social characteristics which distinguish Europe from the rest of the world it is important not to play down the diversity of Europe. This diversity should be seen as a strength and something to encourage. It certainly makes Europe an interesting continent, and the following chapters aim to highlight some of this diversity and to capture much of this interest.

Montmartre, Paris (top), Hydra Port, Greece (bottom)

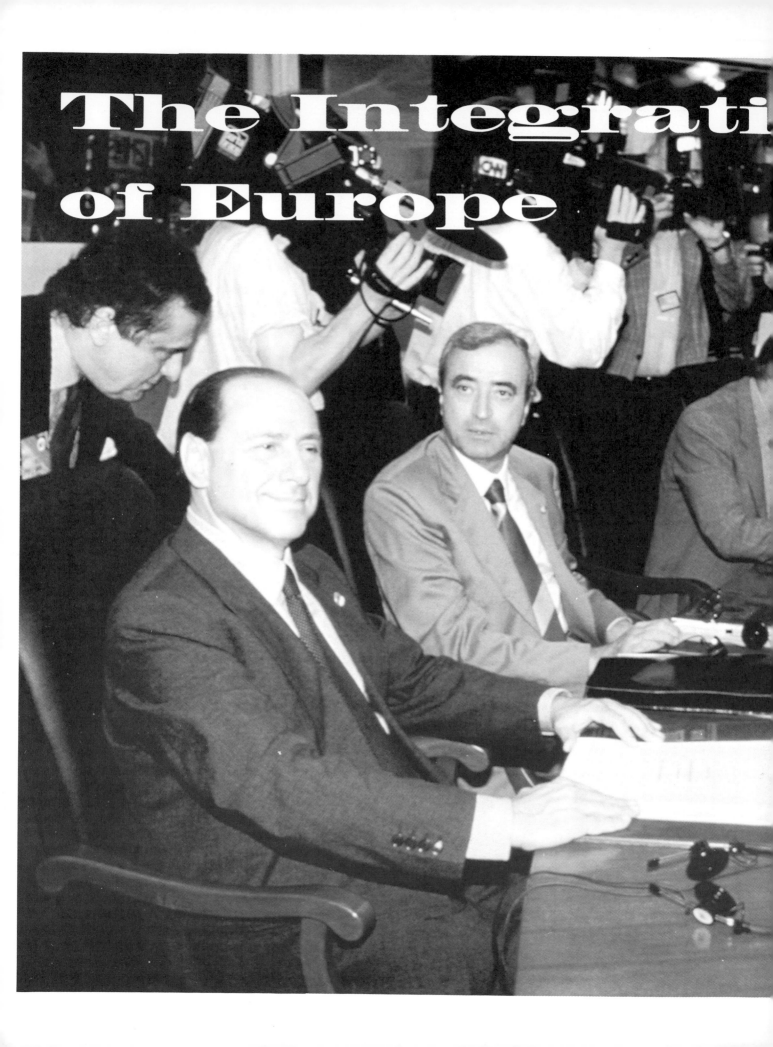

The Integration
of Europe

KEY IDEAS

2.1 Europe is experiencing two processes which are apparently contradictory. On the one hand many countries are strengthening economic and political links between each other. In other words, they are economically and politically integrating. On the other hand, some countries are experiencing fragmentation. In other words, they are showing signs of breaking up into smaller units.

2.2 For four decades Europe was divided by the Iron Curtain into two opposing blocs threatening each other with nuclear destruction. When Gorbachev became President of the Soviet Union rapid changes began throughout eastern Europe. These changes led to the collapse of Communism throughout the region between 1989 and 1991.

2.3 The post-Communist governments in eastern Europe are seeking to strengthen economic and political ties with western Europe.

2.4 Most eastern European governments continue to face problems in trying to establish western European-style free market economies and democracies.

2.5 The problems of integrating western and eastern Europe are highlighted by the problems Germany is facing in integrating its western and eastern regions.

2.6 In order to aid the transition to western European-style democracy and free market economics the western countries are giving a considerable amount of aid to eastern Europe. This is because western Europe is concerned about eastern Europe becoming unstable if the transition is a failure.

2.7 Within the European Union there is a trend towards greater integration. The European Exchange Rate Mechanism (ERM) and the creation of the Single Market were designed to strengthen integration.

2.8 The Maastricht Treaty is designed to further strengthen integration of the European Union. It aims, among other things, to create a single European currency for all countries in the European Union.

2.10 A number of additional European countries want to join the European Union. By the year 2000 the EU may be considerably larger than it was in the first half of the 1990s.

2.1 Integration versus Fragmentation

'Integrate: 1 To combine or form into a whole
2 To bring or come into equal membership of a community'

The Oxford Paperback Dictionary.

Europe is experiencing two contradictory processes – integration and fragmentation. On the one hand Europe, as a whole, is now more united than at any time since 1945 and there are signs that ties between many countries could grow stronger over the next decade or so. On the other hand nationalism and separatism are leading to the break up of some countries into smaller units – the most recent example being the break up of Czechoslovakia into the Czech Republic and Slovakia. There are signs that other countries could break up

The Berlin Wall During the Cold War

into smaller units in the future – for example Belgium, Italy and the Ukraine. It is impossible to predict whether one of the two processes will gain the upper hand in the long run or whether both processes will continue to operate at the same time.

Chapter 3 looks in more detail at the issue of fragmentation, while this chapter examines ways in which Europe is integrating.

Three main trends can be identified which are leading to stronger links between European countries:

– as the former Communist countries of eastern Europe continue their transition to democracy and **free market economics** they are becoming increasingly tied into the international economy. There are growing commerical and financial links between western Europe and eastern Europe. Europe is also seeing the formation of new international political organisations comprising both western and eastern

European countries – one example of this is the Conference on Security and Co-operation in Europe (CSCE), with 52 member countries;

– closer links are being forged between EU member countries – particularly the formation of the single market at the beginning of 1993, the implementation of the Maastricht Treaty since 1993 and moves towards European **Monetary Union** in the late 1990s;

– plans are well advanced to enlarge the EU – it is likely that additional countries will join the EU during the second half of the 1990s or during the following decade.

This chapter looks at each of these trends in more detail.

2.2 The Ending of the Cold War

The first pictures of the Prague demonstration of 17 November 1989 were of young girls placing flowers on the shields held by riot police. Later the police got tough, but their furious brutality failed to provoke a single violent response. Not one car was damaged, not one window smashed during daily demonstrations by hundreds of thousands of people. Posters stuck up on the walls of houses, in metro stations, on shop windows and in trams by the striking students called for peaceful protest. Flowers became the symbol of Civic Forum (the main opposition group opposed to the Czechoslovak Communist government). It is only recently that we have seen the fragility of totalitarian power. Is it really possible that a few days of protest – unique in the history of revolutions for their peacefulness – could topple a regime which had harassed our citizens for four decades?

Ivan Klima, in The State of Europe, Granta.

The collapse of **Communism** in eastern Europe in 1989 and in the Soviet Union in 1990 led to revolutionary changes in Europe. The collapse was unexpected and happened with remarkable speed. To understand the changes which have occurred it is necessary to have some knowledge of how the original split between Communist eastern Europe and Capitalist western Europe developed after the end of the Second World War in 1945.

Nazi Germany finally surrendered in May 1945 when Soviet forces invading from the east and Allied forces (mainly US and British) invading from the west met in central Germany (see Fig 2.1). Germany was divided into four zones administered by the USA, Britain, France and the Soviet

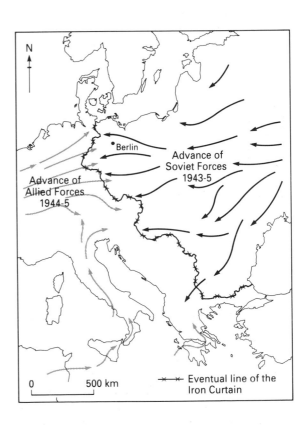

FIG 2.1 *Central Europe at the End of World War Two*

11

Union. The former capital of Germany, Berlin, which now lay inside the Soviet zone was also split between the four powers (see Fig. 2.2).

In the western countries, which had been liberated by the Allied forces, democratic governments were restored. Meanwhile, in eastern Europe, which was under the control of the Soviet Union, Communist governments were installed between 1946 and 1949. In Germany the western zones under the control of Britain, USA and France effectively became the state of West Germany (or the Federal Republic of Germany) and the eastern zone became Communist East Germany (or the German Democratic Republic). Berlin was similarly divided, with West Berlin linked to West Germany by air, rail and road corridors.

By the end of the 1940s political conflict between the USA and western Europe on the one hand and the Soviet Union and eastern Europe on the other was developing into a bitter Cold War – the name given to the competition between the two **power blocs** to acquire superior weapons and to obtain the upper hand in regions throughout the world. The two power blocs had completely different ideologies – the west supporting the ideals of **democracy**, individual freedom and **Capitalism** or the free market, the east supporting the ideals of Communism including equality, state ownership of property and **central planning**.

FIG **2.2** *Allied Control Zones in Occupied Germany 1945–49*

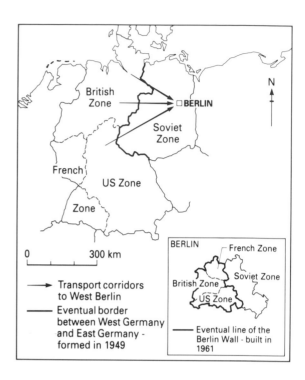

A Czech Protestor Taunts a Soviet Tank, 1968

The frontier between western and eastern Europe became the focus of the Cold War. Two military alliances faced each other across the increasingly fortified border which became known as the Iron Curtain. The armed forces of much of western Europe, along with the USA and Canada, were integrated into the North Atlantic Treaty Organisation (NATO) alliance while the eastern armed forces were integrated into the Warsaw Pact. Although the Iron Curtain was the focus of the Cold War the conflict was dominated by the two superpowers – the USA and the Soviet Union (see Fig 2.3).

Berlin was the location for one of the most serious crises of the Cold War. In 1948 the Soviet Union blockaded the road and rail corridors linking West Berlin to West Germany in an attempt to force the western allies to hand over control of West Berlin to the Communists. The Allies managed to overcome the blockade by supplying the city by air – about 900 flights a day delivered food, fuel and other vital supplies in what became known as the Berlin Airlift. In 1949 the Soviet Union accepted failure and ended the blockade, although occasional disruption of the land corridors continued.

Perhaps it was only the threat of nuclear weapons that prevented the outbreak of war in Europe during the 1950s and 1960s. But they did not prevent armed conflict between allies of the two superpowers elsewhere in the world. Nuclear weapons were seen as a deterrent – discouraging either NATO or the Warsaw Pact from attacking the other side. This concept of **deterrence** became known as Mutually Assured Destruction (MAD). In other words, if one side launched a nuclear strike they would immediately be attacked by the enemy's nuclear weapons and such a strike would guarantee complete destruction of the country and its population.

By the 1970s both alliances had enough nuclear warheads to destroy the entire globe many times over. Some of these weapons were strategic (that is, capable of being launched from within the territory of the USA to reach targets within the Soviet Union, or vice versa) while others were either targeted on Europe or were tactical weapons designed to be used during an armed conflict confined to Europe. Massive conventional forces also faced each other across the Iron Curtain. NATO claimed that they could only resist a Warsaw Pact tank attack on western Europe for a few days before they would have to resort to nuclear weapons.

By the early 1980s many feared that the concept of MAD was breaking down as weapons technology improved. The USA's Star Wars programme (involving the development of satellites which would be designed to shoot down enemy nuclear missiles) encouraged some military strategists to discuss the possibility of a 'winnable' nuclear war. Growing fears of a slide into nuclear conflict or of a **pre-emptive nuclear strike** by one side led to the emergence of a large and influential peace movement in western Europe in the early 1980s.

The Iron Curtain was a barrier to the movement of people, goods, information and ideas. The frontier was fortified by the Communists largely to prevent people from the east migrating to the west to take advantage of the higher standard of living and greater personal freedom the west offered. The most well-known part of the Iron Curtain was the Berlin Wall, although

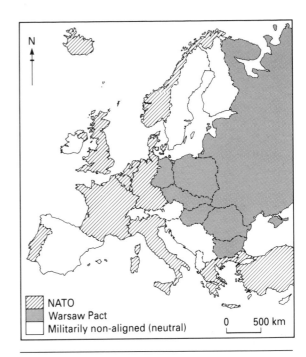

FIG 2.3   *The Military Blocs of the Cold War 1989*

the wall was in fact inside eastern Europe and separate from the rest of the Iron Curtain. The wall was built in 1961 by the Communist authorities. Anybody attempting to cross the wall was to be shot on sight. Many people did die in the attempt. Although the rules banning the movement of people across the wall were gradually relaxed over the following decades the two halves of the city developed completely separately (see Section 6.5). The situation was similar elsewhere along the Iron Curtain. No continent has ever been so completely divided and even in the mid-1980s it was difficult to see how this division could ever end. Eastern and western Europe developed along totally separate lines – each

McDonalds in Prague, a Western Company in an Eastern City – this would have been impossible during the Cold War

had their own economic and trading organisations – the EU in western Europe and *Comecon* in eastern Europe, with very few links between the two. European integration seemed to be a utopian dream.

There were countries in Europe which refused to ally themselves with either NATO or the Warsaw Pact (see Fig 2.3). In western Europe, Switzerland, Austria, Sweden, Finland, Ireland and Spain remained militarily neutral or non-aligned. With the exception of Spain (which until the death of President Franco in 1975 remained relatively politically isolated from the rest of Europe), their economies were strongly linked with the rest of western Europe. Ideologically they were similar to the rest of western Europe. By 1960, for example, all with the exception of Spain and Ireland had joined the European Free Trade Association (EFTA), a western European trade organisation.

In eastern Europe, Communist Yugoslavia refused to ally itself with the Warsaw Pact. Yugoslav Communism developed along different lines to the rest of eastern Europe. Under President Tito the country developed economic links with western Europe and became a major destination for western tourists. Albania developed a particularly strict form of Communism. In 1961 the Albanian Government broke off relations with the Soviet Union. In 1968 the country left the Warsaw Pact believing that the other Communist countries were failing to develop true Communism. The country became totally isolated from the rest of Europe.

Celebrating the Opening of the Berlin Wall

Poor Living Conditions in Tirana, Albania

The Soviet Union dominated eastern Europe and prevented any liberalisation of Communism in the region. In Hungary in 1956 people demonstrated against the presence of Soviet troops in the country, against the activities of the secret police and in favour of free elections. The uprising was crushed by the Soviet Army. In 1968 the Czechoslovak Communist Party introduced a series of reforms, including the lifting of censorship, known as the Prague Spring, but again Warsaw Pact armies intervened and restored censorship. From 1980 onwards opposition to the Communist Party in Poland was organised very effectively by the free trade union called Solidarity despite government repression. Although Communism in eastern Europe would continue for another ten years Solidarity in many ways marked the beginning of its end.

In the mid-1980s Gorbachev became President of the Soviet Union. He launched the radical policies of *glasnost* (political openness) and *perestroika* (economic restructuring) aimed at breathing new life into the ailing Communist system which was showing increasing signs of economic failure. The whole situation in eastern Europe changed. The Soviet Union was now prepared to allow the eastern European countries to develop in their own way and made it clear that they would not intervene in their affairs. This liberalisation released the forces of democracy and nationalism which by 1991 had brought about the overthrow of Communism throughout eastern Europe, the disintegration of the Soviet Union into 15 independent states (see Section 3.2) and the removal of the Iron Curtain. In most cases the Communist collapse was peaceful, although in Romania gun battles rocked the capital during the Christmas of 1989. The peaceful overrunning of the Berlin Wall earlier in 1989 symbolised the end of the Iron Curtain and was probably one of the most dramatic events in European post-war history. European integration now seemed a realistic goal.

By the standards of western Europe the Communist economies had performed badly. The system of central planning had proved to be extremely inefficient and unable to provide enough goods for people. While the aim of greater equality had been achieved, at least to some extent, it was equality at a relatively low level. Data produced by the World Bank suggests that income per capita in Hungary and Yugoslavia, two of the more prosperous eastern countries, was only half that of Greece, the second poorest EU country.

2.3 Old Enemies Make Friends: the Integration of Western and Eastern Europe

In three years the countries of eastern Europe have transformed themselves from **command economies** *to something that is more than half way to capitalism. It seems unlikely that this achievement will now be overthrown.*

The Economist, 13 March 1993.

All the former Communist economies of eastern Europe are in a period of transition. Some are moving more quickly and successfully than others towards a free market economy, but all the eastern countries have a broadly similar goal – to create a free market economy similar to those found in western Europe and to privatise much of their state-owned industry. (See Fig 2.4).

One of the effects of these changes is to strengthen economic ties between western and eastern Europe because:

– western European companies are investing in eastern Europe;

– trade between western and eastern Europe is growing. Goods are mainly flowing from west to east but even as early as 1992 exports from eastern Europe to the EU rose by 17 per cent in one year;
– eastern European governments and firms have turned to western Europe for advice on operating a free market system.

Initially, with the collapse of Communist central planning all the eastern countries experienced a savage fall in industrial and agricultural output. Real wages fell sharply, unemployment climbed steeply and the patterns of trade established by Comecon were seriously disrupted. De-industrialisation became a major problem (see Section 7.3).

FIG 2.4   *The Transition from Communism to Capitalism in Eastern Europe*

Eastern European Communism

The state, and not private companies, own and run the means of production – i.e. factories, farms, shops, banks, and transport.

The state subsidises key industries.

Belief that society is more important than the individual. Individual freedom should be limited in order to benefit society as a whole.

Collective living should be encouraged – i.e. individuals should be encouraged to contribute to society by membership of political and community organisations set up by the state.

Differences in the amount of wealth owned by individuals should be minimised.

Individuals should serve the state. Criticism of government policy should not be tolerated. The Communist Party alone should run the country. Criticism would undermine the aims of Communism.

Producing consumer goods (e.g. cars, videos, freezers) is less important than producing capital goods (e.g. trucks, tractors, machine tools).

All people should have access to the same level of state subsidised social services. All adults should have paid employment.

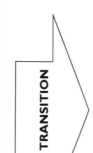

TRANSITION

Capitalism + Democracy

Wherever possible private firms or individuals own and run the means of production although in most western European countries the state continues to own some industries.

Individuals can buy shares in private companies.

The individual is important. Society is a collection of individuals. Individual freedom should be maximised as long as it does not lead to unacceptable conflict between individuals.

The state is there to serve society and individuals.

There should be minimal state interference in the ownership of individual wealth.

All adults should be able to vote for the political party of their choice in elections.

The production of consumer goods to satisfy demand is important.

Individuals should be free to buy education and health care if they wish.

Unemployment is tolerated as an unfortunate consequence of market forces.

However, there are now signs that the worst of the economic disruption is over, at least in some countries. In 1994 of those countries outside the former Soviet Union, only the Romanian economy is expected to still be in decline.

In Poland Gross Domestic Product (**GDP**) grew by two per cent in 1992 and 1993, (despite repeated strikes and five prime ministers and four different governments since 1989), and was expected to grow by four per cent in 1994. All the largest political parties in Poland now support the **privatisation** programme, including former Communists. Policies on controlling subsidies to state industries and removing restrictions on private firms have been remarkably consistent. By late 1993 1.7 million private firms accounted for 45 per cent of the country's GDP.

The Czech Republic is doing particularly well. By 1995 many economists expect the Czech Republic and Hungary to be the leading eastern economies but they also expect the Czech Republic to pull ahead of Hungary in the late 1990s. The Republic earns more from tourism than Hungary and is not as dependent on the struggling agricultural and steel and engineering sectors. The Czech economy is already stronger than the Greek economy – the second poorest in the EU. Thanks to large inflows of foreign investment the country has one of the lowest unemployment rates in the world. By the end of 1993 unemployment reached ten per cent but is predicted to fall to four per cent during 1994.

Many economists are even optimistic about the future of Romania – a country that suffered particularly badly under an extreme form of Communism enforced by President Ceausescu. Now under new laws foreign investors are allowed to own up to 100 per cent of firms, property or land and they are offered tax incentives to invest. Between 1990 and 1993, 30 000 foreign companies set up in Romania with capital investment totalling £600 million.

The state-owned portions of the economies continue to shrink – in Poland it now produces less than half of the country's GDP. Much of the privatised industry is being bought by foreign investors and many western companies are investing in new plants in eastern Europe. Between 1990 and 1992 total foreign investment in eastern Europe grew from about £1.5 billion to £7.5 billion. Hungary has attracted half of all foreign investment in the region. Foreign investors, mainly from western Europe, bring in new management techniques, new technology and access to new markets. In effect they help to integrate the economy into the international and European economies. The Hungarian travel firm, Ibusz, became the first eastern company to be sold on a western stock market when its shares were put on sale in the Austrian stock market in 1990.

The eastern car industry is a good example of the pace of change. In the Czech Republic total car production is expected to rise from 200 000 in 1992 to more than 350 000 by the end of the decade. In Hungary production is expected to rise at an even greater rate. These predicted trends are based on the recent investment by Volkswagen, Opel and Suzuki in the region. This investment is largely aimed at increasing output of western European models, such as the Astra and Cinquecento, but at the same time taking advantage of cheaper labour in eastern Europe. One eastern make which is benefiting from western investment is Skoda. Skoda, bought by Volkswagen in 1991, will have benefited from £3.3 billion of investment by the end of the 1990s.

Foreign investors, particularly those from western Europe, are interested in eastern Europe for two main reasons:

- the region offers cheap skilled labour. Many firms intend to produce in eastern Europe and then export products to the more prosperous and sophisticated markets in the west;
- the region is likely to offer a rapidly growing market over the next decade or so, assuming the transition to free market economies is successful. The EU has a population of about 325 million people and a total GDP of about £3500 billion. Eastern Europe (160 million) and Russia (148 million) together have a population almost as large. If eastern Europe and Russia were to achieve GDP levels similar to those in the west an enormous additional demand for goods would be created.

FIG 2.5a *The European, 12 August 1993*

Some of the state-owned industry is being bought by ordinary east Europeans. The former Czechoslovak Government, for example, gave every adult a voucher that could be used to bid for shares in state firms in an attempt to create a 'share-owning democracy'. More than a million people used their coupons. In the first round of privatisations ending in December 1992, 2000 firms worth £4.5 billion were transferred to private ownership in this way.

However, very serious economic problems remain:

- governments are facing serious financial crises as their revenues from taxes fall. At the same time people continue to want the expensive state benefits which were available under Communism;
- there is no widespread tradition of private enterprise to provide the dynamism behind a free market economy. It will take time to create the new attitudes needed to run a free market economy successfully;
- many within eastern Europe are unhappy about the way in which the privatisation programme is being handled. For example, when a Greek firm, Forum Maritime, bought 51 per cent of the shares in the main Romanian shipping company, Petromin, for £230 million a Romanian court declared the sale invalid. Their decision followed accusations that the company had been undervalued and that corruption was involved;

Poles fear invasion of the asset-strippers

POLAND'S privatisation programme has been attacked by union leaders and opposition parties as a charter for foreign asset-strippers. The programme has become a serious issue as the country heads for parliamentary elections on 19 September.

The centre-right parties and the Solidarity trade union claim that many of the 2,250 state enterprises already sold have been disposed of too cheaply to investors – mainly from EC countries – with insufficient guarantees for employees.

Solidarity is opposing President Lech Walesa's plans for a pact of national unity and has criticised its former leader for drifting away from the ideals of the original Solidarity movement. The minister in charge of the privatisation

programme, Janusz Lewandowski, maintains that foreign companies who have bought into Polish industry are pledged to invest in modernisation which will ensure the future of the country's industrial base and employment prospects for its workers.

His critics claim that the terms of the sales give foreign investors a key advantage in the market place over locally owned concerns, which could lead to closures and redundancies.

In one of the largest and most controversial privatisations since the start of the programme in 1990, major shareholdings in two cement works were recently sold to the Belgian cement conglomerate CBR for more than 1,000 billion zlotys ($60 million). CBR bought 42 per cent of shares in a financially ailing and outdated

cement works at Strzelce Opole and, as part of the same deal, 30 per cent of the shares in another modern and profitable factory at Gorazdze.

Privatisation represents a major part of the $4 billion in foreign equity investment in Poland to date. Lewandowski – who is becoming accustomed to bands of demonstrators wherever he goes – says the latest deal was necessary to save the Strzelce Opole factory from closure. "The two factories continue to pay taxes to the Polish treasury and employ Poles living in the region," he said.

Altogether no fewer than 30 Polish companies, as well as Solidarity, have complained about the way the privatisation programme is being carried out. Local businesses claim that the sell-offs are an invitation to asset-

strippers.

A senior member of the Confederation for an Independent Poland party, Krzysztof Krol, this week attacked the Gorazdz deal as scandalous.

"It is hard to understand why such a modern cement works was sold when at the same time a decision has been made to build a network of motorways in Poland which will mean significant new cement contracts," he said.

Krol said foreigners would reap the benefits. He was also concerned that the price of cement would be dictated by foreign concerns. The union has been promised that ten per cent of shares in the cement works will be given free to employees and the rest will go on the stock exchange to be bought by domestic investors.

- the eastern economies have also been hard hit by the collapse of Comecon and the loss of markets in the former Soviet Union. Trade with ex-Comecon countries now acounts for only 20 per cent of the region's total trade;
- unemployment, caused largely by de-industrialisation, stands at 15–20 per cent in most eastern countries and is set to grow over the next few years. This threatens attempts by governments to cut their spending because they have to spend more in social security benefits. Also, with high unemployment ordinary people are less likely to support further economic reform.

Other problems facing eastern European countries attempting to steer a smooth course through the transition process are outlined in the next section.

FIG 2.5b *The European, 19 November 1993*

- Study Fig 2.5a on page 17.
  - **a)** What do you think is meant by 'asset-strippers'?
  - **b)** Summarise the reasons why some Poles are concerned about the privatisation programme.
  - **c)** What examples of strengthening economic or financial links between eastern and western Europe are mentioned in the article?

- Study Fig 2.5b below.
  - **a)** What evidence is there in the article that western European consumer products are in great demand in eastern Europe?
  - **b)** What evidence is there in the article that western European firms are investing in eastern Europe?
  - **c)** What impacts is greater economic integration between western and eastern Europe having on eastern cosmetics firms?

- Study Fig. 2.6. Outline the economic trends highlighted by the graphs. Are the trends encouraging or discouraging for the people of eastern Europe?

Poland's sweet smell of success

TO HEAR Ronald Lauder tell it, the decision to open a high-profile boutique in Warsaw was nothing more than another of the intuitive moves that have made his family-owned **Estée Lauder** Companies a global force in the cosmetics and personal care products industry.

"We never did any market research", the former US Ambassador to Austria said at last week's ribbon cutting in the city's shopping district. "Polish women are spending money on cosmetics and they understand quality and that's the right combination for us."

The Lauder store joins established company-operated boutiques, including Dior and Guerlain, in brightening up the grey streets of Warsaw. Domestic distribution companies are highlighting balance sheets on sales of perfume, lipstick and eye and hair products from Scandinavia, Italy and the UK. Already entrenched firms like Germany's Henkel, the Dutch Unilever and Procter & Gamble of

the US are adding more personal products to their lines of soap and washing powders. L'Oreal of France is investing more than $6.7 million to produce hair care items from the collective Polish Pompadour.

According to the US Foreign Commercial Service in Warsaw, imports made up more than half of the estimated $110 million which Polish women spent last year on cosmetics. That figure is expected to increase despite high tariffs and competition from lower priced domestically produced creams, face powders and toiletry items.

"A bigger percentage of the Polish population is buying luxury cosmetics than in France", said Epa Kostecka of the US office. "But retail prices here are higher than they are in Austria." This is because of heavy taxes on imports. In addition to a 45 per cent custom duty importers pay 25 per cent more in excise fees and 22 per cent Value Added Tax.

Given that the taxes are compounded, an ounce of perfume that sells for $100 in the

west reaches more than $221 by the time it hits a Polish counter. Nevertheless demand is rising.

"We expected a 20 per cent growth in sales over last year and that trend should continue for the next several years", said Bozena Rodak, a manager for the PolKaufring distribution company that handles products from Lancôme, Helena Rubenstein, Ralph Lauren and Guy La Roche.

Pressure from imports has thrown domestic producers into a scramble to retain their market shares and bring their products up to the standard of manufacturers in the West. Further still, those firms have had to cope with a loss of markets to the East. Poland was a leading cosmetic manufacturer among countries of the former Soviet Bloc.

The result has forced some collective producers out of the market while others have formed strategic partnerships with western companies.

"The influence of international companies is bery big and it is becoming more competitive all

the time", said Dariusz Grabowski, whose Cosmex firm rang up $2 million in sales last year.

"Packaging has become more important and companies that have money to advertise will put themselves in a better position."

Vehicles for advertising have grown up quickly in Poland's market transition with a variety of specialised magazines targeting women. A flip through *Twoj Styl* (Your Style) and *Pani* (Lady), two popular titles, reveals that they are laden with cosmetics advertisements. Rodak said her advertising budget was spent almost entirely on print with only two per cent allocated to radio and television.

To promote its boutiques, Estée Lauder offered free lipstick to customers and supermodel Paulina Porizkova was among the Lauder entourage who met the press at a lavish buffet luncheon.

According to Kostecka, at the US commercial office such affairs will become more common as Poland's market economy grows.

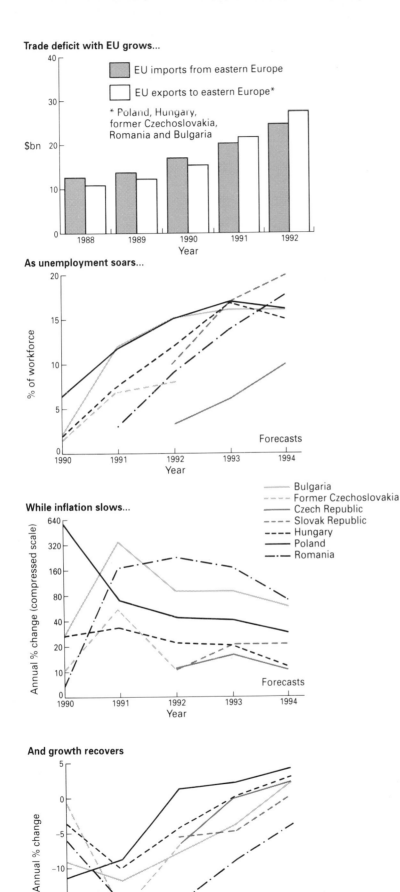

Trade deficit with EU grows...

Legend:
- ☒ EU imports from eastern Europe
- ☐ EU exports to eastern Europe*

* Poland, Hungary, former Czechoslovakia, Romania and Bulgaria

(chart: $bn vs Year, 1988–1992)

As unemployment soars...

(chart: % of workforce vs Year, 1990–1994, Forecasts)

While inflation slows...

(chart: Annual % change (compressed scale) vs Year, 1990–1994, Forecasts)

Legend:
- Bulgaria
- Former Czechoslovakia
- Czech Republic
- Slovak Republic
- Hungary
- Poland
- Romania

And growth recovers

(chart: Annual % change vs Year, 1990–1994, Forecasts)

FIG 2.6 *Economic Trends in Eastern Europe, The European*

Political Integration

Nearly all the eastern states now have a system of **parliamentary democracy** similar to that found in western European countries, and with the exception of Hungary they have all had at least two parliamentary elections since 1989. In many cases the key figures in government are former leaders of the underground opposition to Communism before 1989. Vaclav Havel, formerly a key figure Civic Forum, which co-ordinated opposition to the Czechoslovak Communist Party, was elected as President. Lech Walesa, the charismatic leader of the Polish Solidarity union also became President of his country. All the governments are keen to develop stronger links with western Europe and take an active part in European integration.

The recent changes in the international political and military organisations in Europe indicate the extent of the changes in Europe and the moves towards greater integration. The Warsaw Pact has disappeared while NATO, although still in existence, now sees its role as one of co-ordinating western responses to threats wherever they may appear in the world. There is even a possibility that Poland, Hungary, the Czech Republic and Bulgaria could join NATO before the year 2000. However NATO is concerned not to upset the Russian Government by admitting eastern countries without Russian agreement.

A new organisation, called the Conference on Security and Co-operation in Europe (CSCE), and which comprises almost all the countries in western and eastern Europe as well as the former Soviet states in Asia, has been formed to try and develop military and political co-operation across Europe. Such an organisation would have been impossible before 1990.

The best indication of growing European integration is probably the determination of some east European countries to eventually join the EU. The prospects for an enlarged EU are examined in Section 2.9.

2.4 Obstacles to Change in Eastern Europe

We are not in a market economy at the moment and we are not in a socialist one either. It is a time for changing the attitude of our people. They are learning but I think it is going to take five years. It will take another 10–15 years for the real economy to adjust and to become competitive.

Thedor Stolojon, Prime Minister of Romania.

As the previous section outlines, all the former Communist states in eastern Europe and the newly independent Soviet states are in a process of transition to democracy and free market economics. However, there are a number of obstacles in the way of a smooth transition. These obstacles could seriously disrupt the process of transition during the later part of the 1990s.

Economic Collapse and Low Levels of Economic Development

… I soon discovered that it would take years, perhaps generations, for Albania to catch up with the modern world … I saw three schoolchildren, no more than ten years old, standing by the side of the road and stopped to pick them up … Unable to speak their language, I offered each of them a banana. They giggled nervously and declined to eat. I doubt if they had ever seen the fruit before. It was also my impression that they had never been inside a car … As soon as I stopped the car and opened the door and let them out, they scampered down the mountainside as if they had just escaped from a spaceship. The towns I passed through had a gaunt, untidy look; the shops were shabby and virtually empty. In one store all I found was two sacks of potatoes, four mouldy cabbages, and a few cans of fish … I entered Tirana just as the capital city was waking from its long sleep. Amid the faded grandeur of the main squares and streets, hopeful people talked of little else but politics. Loggers, factory workers, students and clerks stood in the middle of the street, chatting as if to make up for all the lost time.

Dusko Doder, Albania Opens the Door, National Geographic, July 1992.

No one can image how living standards can drop further – but they will. Even to survive will be tough. It will be difficult for the people not to react.

Genc Ruli, Albanian Minister of the Economy and Finance.

While some countries such as the Czech Republic and Hungary have relatively healthy economies, others are not so healthy. Albania, Europe's poorest country, is probably facing the most serious problems.

Albania, with a population of 3.4 million, is Europe's only predominately Muslim country, other than Bosnia. Enver Hoxha ruled Albania from 1944 until his death in 1985. Under his dictatorship the country became totally isolated from the rest of Europe and hardly changed over four decades. In 1991 there were only 6000 telephones in the entire country. All foreign business was forbidden, religion outlawed, criticism of food shortages banned, beards made illegal and the wives of disgraced Communist Party members could be ordered to divorce their husbands. Foreign tourists were unwelcome. The secret police were likely to victimise the families of anybody who broke the law or criticised the Party.

Albania was the last country to overthrow Communism in Europe following demonstrations, strikes and riots during 1990 and 1991.

By 1992 the inflation rate had reached 400 per cent, industry was at a virtual standstill due to a shortage of raw materials, and agriculture was in chaos. Schools, offices and factories were also often forced to shut down because of a lack of fuel for heating. More than 50 per cent of the workforce was idle even though they were receiving 80 per cent of their wages. Crime had increased dramatically. The average wage was £5 a month and much of the 3.2 million population depended on foreign aid distributed through an inadequate rationing system. People in the countryside were hoarding the food they grew instead of sending it to urban areas. Many people died in riots following attempts to break into food warehouses.

In 1992 the Albanian Government launched a series of reforms in an attempt to stop further economic collapse. The social security payments which gave people 80 per cent of their wages even when they were out of work were ended and price controls were relaxed. While these measures may have been necessary if a new economy was to emerge they threatened the ability of Albanians to even feed themselves.

The problem for Albanians is that the state sector of the economy has been virtually destroyed but a free market has not yet emerged. Many Albanians have a defeatist attitude following years of repression and believe that the only way to improve their standard of living is to emigrate.

Albanians sell blood for a living

"I WISH the government could see that there's nothing here for us," says Lulzim, proprietor of a greengrocer's store in Kukës, in mountainous north eastern Albania, looking at the people shuffling past, buying nothing. "I wish they could move us somewhere else."

"We have been forgotten about," says Lulzim, whose business brings him about $3 (Ecu2.6) a week. "Tirana doesn't care about us, even though we are on the front line if Serbs come this way. We are too far away for the rest of the country to count."

He is one of the luckier people in Kukës. Most are unemployed – especially since equipment shortages mean the nearby chromium mines operate only part-time – and rely on paltry unemployment benefit which ends after a year. Selling blood to hospitals, on a regular basis, has become a commonplace means of scraping a living.

The break-up of the agricultural collectives last year led to a sub-division of land that in these mountainous conditions allows little more than subsistence farming.

As a result, much of the town's food comes in the form of aid packages or is sent by road from Tirana. After the removal of state subsidies and controls, prices are high. Some shops offer only EC rice for sale; others a few expensive cans or beer or cola from Greece.

Although Kukës is a bone-shaking, often precipitous six-hour drive from Tirana, it has not been entirely off the beaten track in recent times.

There was recently a visit from the BBC World Service Publicity Bus, which, with Albanian and British staff, was travelling around the country promoting the newly restored twice-daily Albanian service. And the town's hotel is regularly host to the EC Monitoring Group. Since February these unarmed, white-clad personnel have scrutinised the border with Serbia for "irregular activity", reporting back to headquarters in Zagreb.

Guy Sheriden, head of the EC Monitoring Group in Albania, visited several areas late last year as part of a reconnaissance. According to him, many villagers had not had a western visitor since 1945.

"I simply could not believe such a thing was possible in Europe in the late 20th century," said Sheriden.

FIG 2.7 *The European*

Privatisation dream 'a sham'

THREE years after their anti-communist revolutions, the countries of eastern Europe face economic catastrophe, mass unemployment and social and political breakdown as their remaining state enterprises fall deeper into debt, in many cases terminally, according to a report on their economies published today.

Hopes that privatisation would be achieved in four or five yeas have turned out to be "wildly optimistic", according to the authors, Paul Reynolds and Peter Young. At the present rate, they say, it will take Poland, Czechoslovakia and Hungary an average of 28 years to privatise only half of the state companies still in their hands.

The report, entitled Eastern Promise and published by the Adam Smith Institute in London, is one of the most thorough and pessimistic appraisals of eastern Europe since the collapse of communism in 1989. It is sure to raise concern in Western capitals about the efficacy of World Bank policies, and of bodies such as the British expertise fund set up by Margaret Thatcher three years ago to help promote free-market economics.

"The existence of Western advisers has not led to a general reassessment of privatisation and reform programmes," the reports says. "In effect, there is a serious mismatch between the need for advice and the supply of advice available.

"In this, foreign aid fund providers must share the blame ... Many tens of millions of dollars have been spent in each country. But still East European governments are unable to put together any kind of [privatisation] strategies and programmes," the report says.

Western advice, the authors suggest, should not necessarily be taken. Rather, the example of east Asian enterprises should be examined for ways of competing successfully in international markets.

With every passing year, the authors warn, radical reform is made more difficult. After two years, living standards are still declining for most people. "If it hasn't worked after five years, they will turn to other solutions."

Foreign investors are beginning to show an interest in Albania's scenic beaches and mountains as a new tourist destination, and in the country's oil, chromium and copper reserves. However, massive investment is needed in the infrastructure – even roads are few and far between and in a poor state of repair. The sheer scale of the country's problems are an obstacle to Albania integrating with the rest of Europe over the next decade.

- List the social and economic problems facing the region of Albania described in Fig 2.7.

While Albania is undoubtedly an extreme case, other eastern states face severe economic problems. The Ukraine is in economic and political crisis as it struggles to pay for imports of increasingly expensive Russian oil and gas, and to cope with high inflation, low wages, strikes and a growing division between nationalist western Ukraine and the more pro-Russian eastern Ukraine. In mid–1993 90 per cent of the country's coal mines and many other enterprises were on strike. In August 1993 the currency collapsed falling from 6000 karbovanets (the Ukrainian unit of currency) to the US dollar to 19000 to the US dollar (at the time the minimum monthly wage was 20000 karbovanets). By the end of 1993 an

FIG 2.8 *The Guardian, 19 October 1992*

inflation rate of more than 2000 per cent indicated the beginning of hyperinflation. The rate of industrial decline seemed to be accelerating with GDP down nine per cent in the first half of 1993 compared with the same period in 1992.

The Baltic states of Lithuania, Latvia and Estonia also face severe problems. All three suffered a disasterous drop in industrial output and high inflation in the years following their independence.

An opinion pole conducted in 1992 indicated that people in other eastern European countries were also very concerned. More than 75 per cent of Poles thought things were 'a lot better' under the Communists and 70 per cent of Hungarians felt that there 'was no reward in working harder for a living'. In contrast, only 12 per cent of Czechs believed life was better under Communism.

- Read Fig. 2.8.
  a) In the light of all the information in this article and the previous section does the Adam Smith Institute report on eastern Europe seem to be accurate or over-pessimistic?
  b) The report states that if the transition to free market economies 'hasn't worked after five years, they will turn to other solutions'. What do you think the 'other solutions' might be?

Institutional Obstacles

Firms seeking to set up in Poland find themselves battling with a lethargic and incompetent bureaucracy, out-dated and obstructive laws and inexperienced or greedy officials. While many struggle on and succeed, others give up or go elsewhere.

Patricia Clough, The Independent, 20 April 1992.

In many eastern countries the transition to free market economics and economic integration with the rest of Europe is being slowed by institutions which are finding it difficult to adapt to the new economic system. Problems include:

- some officials, perhaps former Communists, may be unhappy about the transition to free market economics and try to stop any changes;
- officials and managers are inadequately trained and have little experience of operating in a free market;
- laws are out-dated and not designed to meet the needs of a free market economy;
- corruption frequently prevents resources being allocated effectively.

The type of problems facing western investors is illustrated by the case of eight British farmers who received a grant of £750 000 from the EU to set up an agricultural institute near Kaliningrad in Russia. They have introduced new varieties of potato and grain, have helped farmers to dig wells and to treat cattle disease and have built a new creamery. But former Communist officials in the area saw the farmers as a threat and tried to prevent the creamery from opening. Seed potatoes have been stolen and local Russians working for the project have been threatened.

Protectionist Policies in Western Europe

Eastern European countries are increasingly angry about restrictions imposed by the EU on importing goods from eastern Europe. The EU imposes high **tariffs** on imports and agricultural and manufactured products in order to protect industries in the EU. This in turn prevents eastern countries selling their products to some of the wealthiest markets in Europe. In 1989 the balance of trade between western and eastern Europe was roughly balanced, but by mid-1993 the EU was enjoying a trade surplus of $3.6 billion thanks to a 22 per cent increase in EU exports to the east in 1992. This trade imbalance is expected to continue growing. This trend is helping the western Europe industries hit by recession, but is unhealthy for eastern economies. Trade is most heavily restricted in the products eastern Europe is most competitive in producing – steel, textiles, chemicals, footwear and farm products. In a conference held in 1993 to discuss the issue the EU refused to lower tariffs. Instead they encouraged eastern countries to rebuild trade links with the former Soviet states which had been lost when the Soviet Union disintegrated. However, even if this could be achieved the potential market would be much smaller because of the low standard of living in those countries. The eastern countries accuse the EU of hypocrisy – on the one hand, they argue, the EU encourages the eastern countries to develop a free market and on the other hand they intervene to protect western European industry.

Teething Troubles with Democracy

… Almost everywhere, the new democracies seem fragile. Semi-authoritarian regimes masquerading as democracies in Serbia and Romania. Czechoslovakia split in two despite clear public opposition in both parts. Instead of consolidation, there is fragmentation: 67 parties fought Poland's most recent general election, 74 Romania's. At the extreme, it is possible to argue that democracy is only an outer crust. Necessary institutions are missing … Where institutions exist, they do so without public support or understanding.

Order Disguised As Chaos, The Economist, 13 March 1993.

There is concern that although all the eastern countries have now elected parliaments, democracy is not strong enough and may not last. Democracy has not existed in any of these countries since before the Second World War and few people have any real experience or understanding of it. The populations tend to blame the governments for the economic and social problems their countries are facing and there is widespread apathy. In the Hungarian local elections of 1992 only 34 per cent of the electorate voted.

There is evidence that people still strongly support **Socialist** or Communist values. In opinion polls 70 per cent of the east European electorate stated that they believed it is the responsibility of the state to provide jobs, health, housing, education and other services. In the 1993 Polish election 20 per cent of the votes went to the former Communist Party – now called the Democratic Left Alliance.

It can also be argued that the proliferation of political parties threatens democracy. In Poland 29 parties have seats in parliament. The result is instability as the parties continually change allegiances, and coalitions collapse. Poland had three different governments in 1992 and five different ministers for privatisation between 1990 and 1993.

However, while these political problems are undoubtedly slowing down the economic and political transition in eastern Europe, the general view is that the transition has now gone too far to be reversed. In many countries, such as Hungary, the Communist Parties are now pro-free market, pro-competition and pro-reform, and are more similar to the British Labour Party than to the former Communist parties. Also, although the parliaments may appear chaotic, policies have been pursued effectively considering the scale of the problems being tackled. This is because although there is a large number of political parties they share many common beliefs and policies. The six parties in Hungary and the Czech Republic are closer in many of their policies than the Labour Party and Conservative Party are in Britain. All, for example, want membership of the EU, privatisation and currency convertibility (that is, the ability to buy and sell their currency in the foreign exchanges). The transition to a free market and greater integration with western Europe is likely to continue regardless of which parties have the most power.

2.5 Disillusion in the East: the Integration of West and East Germany

The Wessis are deliberately forcing all our businesses to the wall so they can take over everything and have a free rein. They are just out to make profits from us.

I've got a video and so on, but what does that matter when half of Leipzig is unemployed.

Disappointment, anger and bitterness run deep in eastern Germany.

Comments made by East Germans.

The problems of integrating western and eastern Europe are seen particularly clearly in Germany, where Communist East Germany merged with Capitalist West Germany in October 1990 following the opening of the Berlin Wall. The following extract illustrates the optimism which accompanied the creation of a new united Germany:

41 years of division was ended yesterday when Germany was reborn as a united country. Vast crowds gathered at the rebuilt Reichstag in the centre of Berlin to watch the hoisting of the black, red and gold German flag … In a nationwide television broadcast, Helmut Kohl, who became the first Chancellor of a democratic, unified Germany since Hitler's takeover in 1933 said a 'dream' was being realised. 'After more than 40 bitter years of division, Germany, our Fatherland, is being united again. This is one of the happiest moments of my life.'

The Week in Europe, The European Commission, 4 October 1990.

However, the problems of uniting the two Germanies have been greater than most people expected. They include:

– the massive cost of renewing eastern Germany's relatively run-down and out-dated infrastructure. This in turn worsened the depth of the recession in Germany in 1993;

- rapid de-industrialisation in eastern Germany (see Section 7.3);
- high unemployment in eastern Germany;
- disagreements over social policy in the new Germany. For example, East German law allowed abortion on demand, while the law in West Germany restricted abortion to situations where the woman's physical or mental health could be harmed by having a child. East Germany had free nursery education for all children while in West Germany provision was more limited. New policies had to be devised and generally western policy has been adopted;
- widespread disillusion and anger in eastern Germany that the German Government has failed to protect the population from growing unemployment and poverty. Most feel that there has been a takeover by West Germany rather than a merger of the two countries. They feel that many of the good things about life in East Germany, such as free nursery education, cheap entertainment, cheap and frequent public transport and low rents for housing, have been lost while many cannot afford the benefits offered by the West;
- widespread anger that professional qualifications obtained in the former East Germany are no longer recognised in the new Germany;
- less serious but nevertheless unwelcome changes have also taken place. For example, in East Berlin, without any consultations with local people, many street names have been changed when they refer in any way to the former Communist system;
- other social problems such as crime, prostitution and drug-taking are now rising in eastern Germany;

- under the terms of the unification treaty West Germans are reclaiming property which was legally theirs before being taken over by the state in Communist East Germany. This has often been done even when an East German family has lived there for a considerable time and they are afraid that the change of ownership could lead to them becoming homeless. Delays in settling property claims is also slowing economic investment. Over 1.2 million people were laying claim to 2.6 million properties in 1993 and only 22 per cent of all claims since unification had been settled;
- widespread racism, particularly in eastern Germany, sparked by the rapid changes in eastern Germany (see Section 4.8).

In many people's minds Germany is still not united because the two parts of the country continue to be so different. People talk about *Wessis* and *Ossis* (westerners and easterners) as two separate groups and many still think of the two parts of the country as being very different. Although the Berlin Wall and Iron Curtain no longer exist Germans refer to the 'wall inside peoples' heads' to describe the continuing social, psychological and economic division of the country.

- Read Fig 2.9a.
    a) List the grievances of the steel workers.
    b) Is there any evidence in the article that these workers have benefited from the unification of Germany?

FIG 2.9a   *The Guardian, 28 April 1993*

Defiant east German workers prepare to strike

DEFIANT but uncertain of their future, east German steel and engineering workers yesterday turned out in force to vote in a union ballot that could trigger the first massive industrial action in the east for more than 60 years.

"This is not how we envisaged political change. We were taken for a ride under communism for 40 years, and we are now being duped again," said Harry Uhlmann, aged 49, an electrical worker as he left the Oberspree cable works in east Berlin.

Married with six children, he takes home DM1,700 (£680) a month. His wife collects unemployment benefit of DM780 (£312), most of which goes to pay the rent.

A 38-year-old colleague with two children and take-home payof DM1,500 (£600), added: "We are ready to vote for another revolution. We can't afford the public swimming pool, we never go out at weekends, and for holidays, we go to the Czech Republic as we always used to."

Both men were aware that a crippling strike would almost certainly lead to more job cuts. "We have no experience with strikes and we may be out of a job as a result, but this is to show we won't be mucked about any longer," said Mr Uhlmann.

Strikes were banned by the Nazis in 1932 and disallowed in

eastern Germany during the years of communist rule.

The Hennigsdorf steelworks, a sprawling grey mass just north of Berlin, last had a strike in 1928. "We are united to a man for strike action," said a shop steward at the plant, which is among the successes of the transition to the market economy.

Eastern Germany's steel and engineering workers feel deeply aggrieved over the bitter row that began as a pay dispute. This turned into a confrontation about union rights after employers cancelled a wage deal promising a rise of up to 26 per cent this year to bring east German wages up to western levels.

"Our workers feel if they don't strike now, they'll still be here in 10 years on 50 per cent of western pay," said Manfred Foede, a union official at the cable works.

Almost three years after east and west adopted monetary union, the workers feel they must make a point. They know the real unemployment rate in the east is 35 per cent, that short-time work is increasing, that productivity is declining and that, on average 20,000 east Germans a month still leave to settle in the west. But they are fed up with working longer hours than their western colleagues, for less money and little security, while prices rise relentlessly.

Disneyland Communism

A German businessman, Frank Georgi, hopes to make money out of the growing nostalgia felt by many eastern Germans for the stability of life in the former Communist East Germany. Georgi wants to create a theme park around the site of the military compound north of Berlin where Erich Honecker, the former East German leader, had his secret nuclear bunker.

The park will recreate certain aspects of life in East Germany. He believes that while few people would want to go back to the Communist era, many miss the predictability and strong community spirit which often characterised life under Communism. He also believes that the increasing numbers of younger people who do not remember life under Communism, and tourists from other countries, will be interested.

Attractions in the theme park will include.

1 Jackbooted guards manning searchlights in watchtowers around the edge of the park.

2 Secret agents mingling with the crowds. Visitors overheard making jokes about Communism or complaining about queues will be 'arrested', searched and 'imprisoned' for a short time.

3 Interrogation cells manned by people pretending to be members of the Stasi secret police.

4 Shops will sell poor quality or damaged fruit and vegetables.

5 Visitors will be able to hire Trabant cars (small and basic cars made in Communist East Germany) to drive around the park.

6 Pubs will sell East German beer and an East German Coca-Cola substitute.

7 An actor posing as Erich Honecker will tour the park in a chauffeur-driven large black car.

8 There will be two hotels. One will be very basic. The other will be luxurious but will only accept western currency.

Not everybody is happy about the plan. People who were punished by the Communist authorities or suffered from repression see it as a sick joke. Residents of the nearby village of Prenden are worried that large numbers of tourists would disrupt their lives.

- Read Fig 2.9b.
  a) List the aspects of life in Communist East Germany which will be reproduced in the theme park.
  b) What do the proposals for a Communist Theme Park tell us about the view many East Germans have about the former Communist system?

FIG 2.9b *Disneyland Communism*

- Using the information in this section and sections 4.8, 7.3 and 7.4 write a 500 word evaluation of the short-term success of German unification.

2.6 West Helps East: Aid for Eastern Europe

Western governments are keen to see a successful transition to democracy and free market economics in eastern Europe. They realise that if the new democratic governments fail to provide their people with an acceptable standard of living then they may be overthrown and replaced with dictatorships or extreme nationalist governments. This could pose a threat to western countries or, at least, slow down or prevent the strengthening of links between western and eastern Europe. The European Bank for Reconstruction and Development, based in London, has the job of distributing funds for economic development in the former Communist countries.

The EU is spending large sums of money in eastern Europe.

One scheme called *Phare* aids east European countries and another called *Tacis* aids Russia and the other former Soviet states. Tacis and Phare together supply about 70 per cent of all technical aid (in other words, advice and know–how, rather than cash) going to former Communist countries although some of the money is also used for material aid such as food or medical equipment. In 1993 Phare assistance totalled £800 million and Tacis £390 million.

The money is used to pay western experts to give advice on running private enterprises, banks or farms or on issues such as the environment or reforming the civil service. In Hungary, for example, Phare has funded advice centres for small businesses, a new share trading system, a new land registry to speed up privatisation of land ownership, and equipment for measuring air pollution.

Unfortunately, both Phare and Tacis have been criticised for being slow and bureaucratic, and for giving too much advice and too little material aid.

Russia has received by far the largest amount of western aid. In April 1993 leaders of the western industrialised countries agreed on an aid package worth £28 billion. This massive sum included cancellation of Russian debts, money to support Russian industry, funds to help support the rouble in foreign exchange markets and export credits (that is, assistance in buying goods manufactured in eastern countries). £18 billion of the funding was to come from the International Monetary Fund (IMF) and the World Bank.

2.7 Ever Closer Union: Integration within the European Union

The Benefits of Economic Integration

It is generally accepted that if countries become more interdependent and their economies more integrated through the promotion of trade then their economies will benefit and so the standard of living in those countries will improve. It is also generally agreed that the most effective way of encouraging trade is to remove tariffs on imports – in other words to allow **free trade**. Since 1947 The General Agreement on Tariffs and Trade (GATT) has tried to encourage global free trade by urging all 195 member countries to lower tariffs and promote free trade. Most European governments have also been keen to encourage free trade within Europe, although between 1945 and 1989 the Cold War meant that two separate **trading blocs** were created with very little trade between western and eastern Europe.

There are three main reasons why international trade is seen as something to encourage.

1 It is argued that trade encourages competition between industries or farmers in different countries. This then encourages them to become more efficient.

2 It allow economies of scale because each producer has a much larger potential market which includes both the home market and foreign markets.

3 The less efficient producers are driven out of business and this in turn is likely to encourage each country to specialise in producing those goods which it can produce most efficiently and cheaply.

There are four possible levels of economic integration. The first two levels are designed to boost trade, while the second two are designed to promote additional economic links between countries. (The economic justifications for third and fourth levels are more complex and are dealt with later in this section (see The Single European Market) and in the section on the Maastricht Treaty (Section 2.8)).

1 Free Trade Areas

This is where two or more countries agree to remove **tariff barriers** to trade between themselves while maintaining their own tariff barriers against countries who are not in the free trade area. The European Free Trade Association (EFTA) is an example of this level of integration. In 1993 EFTA comprised Austria, Switzerland, Finland, Norway, Sweden and Iceland.

2 Customs Union

This is where tariff barriers to trade between the members of the union are removed and a common external tariff is agreed against imports from countries outside the association. For much of its life the EU has been a customs union.

3 Common Market

This is similar to a customs union, but in addition the union allows the free movement of factors of production including capital and labour. The creation of the Single Market in the EU at the beginning of 1993 allowed it to become a common market.

4 Economic Union

In an economic union a common market is created but in addition the member countries have the same financial and taxation systems and a common currency. The Maastricht Treaty is designed to bring about economic union in the EU.

The Beginning of the European Union

The Treaty of Rome which created the EU was signed in 1957 by six countries – France, West Germany, Italy, Belgium, the Netherlands and Luxembourg. The EU was initially called the European Economic Community (EEC) and more recently, until late 1993, the European Community (EC). The aim of the EEC was to promote the economic integration of its members by:

– the gradual reduction of tarifffs and other barriers to trade between the six countries;
– the setting up of a common external tariff barrier – that is, all six countries would levy the same tariffs on imports from countries outside the EEC;
– the promotion of free movement of factors of production including labour and capital;
– harmonisation of policies on transport, industry, energy and agriculture.

FIG 2.10   *How Does the EU work?*

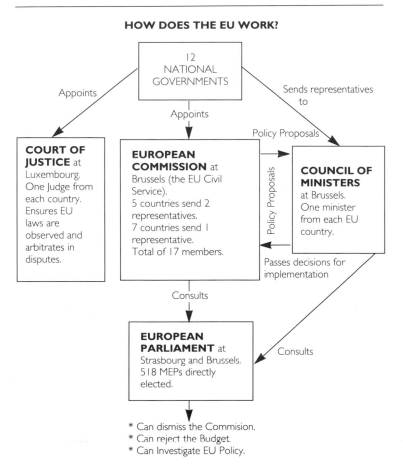

HOW DOES THE EU WORK?

The treaty also made it clear that the members would strive for 'ever closer union'. Despite the economic emphasis of the treaty, the EEC's overriding purpose was to promote peace in Europe by improving international co-operation and promoting prosperity. The treaty was signed only 12 years after the end of the Second World War. To tie West Germany into an economic union was seen as an important guarantee of future peace.

In 1973 the UK, Ireland and Denmark joined the Community, followed by Greece in 1981 and Spain and Portugal in 1986 (see Fig 2.17).

Throughout its history the EU has been heavily influenced by what became known as the 'Franco-German Axis' – in other words, France and Germany, the two wealthiest countries in the EU, have been able to influence EU policies more than any other country. Britain and Italy, the other two largest and wealthiest countries in the Community, have generally been in a less influential position. Britain has often shown a reluctance to commit itself strongly to the EU. The Italian Government has rarely had the stability or strength to have a major role in influencing the direction of EU policy.

How is the EU Run?

There are four main institutions within the EU which control EU policy.

1   The Commission – there are 17 Commissioners from the 12 countries, aided by a large civil service. They propose EU policy and legislation. The Commission is based in Brussels, Belgium.

2   The Council of Ministers – this is the main decision making body. It has to decide whether to accept or reject the policies and legislation proposed by the Commission. Each of the 12 member countries has a representative minister on the Council. The presidency of the Council is held for six months by each country in turn.

3   The European Parliament – this is a parliament directly elected by the population of the EU. It has 518 Members of the European Parliament (MEPs) who are supposed to represent the views of their electors on EU policy. Its powers are limited although it could, in extreme cases, dismiss the Commission. It can reject a budget proposed by the Council of Ministers or conduct a detailed investigation of any EU policy. Its main role is to debate policy and to make recommendations to the Commission. The Parliament is based in Strasbourg, France, although a new parliament building has been built in Brussels to allow some sessions to be held there.

4 The European Court of Justice – this comprises one judge from each country and its role is to ensure European laws are observed and to arbitrate in disputes between countries.

Fig 2.10 on page 27 summarises how the four institutions relate to each other.

The EU Budget

In 1992 the total budget of the EU was £50 billion, a huge amount although it was equivalent to only one per cent of the total GDP of all the EU countries. The sources of this money and the way in which it was spent are shown in Fig 2.11.

- Fig 2.12 shows which countries benefit the least and the most from the EU budget.
  - **a)** Can you suggest the reasons why some countries are net contributors while othes are net recipients?
  - **b)** Does the allocation of EU funding seem fair? Explain your answer.

FIG **2.12** *Contibutions to and Receipts from the EU Budget 1989*

	Contribution (C)	Receipt (R)	Balance (R – C)	Gain or loss ECU* per head
	Millions of ECU* in 1989			
West Germany	11 110	4580	–6530	–106
France	8623	5677	–2946	–53
Italy	7606	6177	–1429	–25
Netherlands	2700	3830	+1130	+76
Belgium	1807	683	–1124	–114
Luxembourg	73	8	–65	–163
UK	6568	3214	–3354	–59
Ireland	371	1712	+1341	+383
Denmark	871	1045	+174	+34
Greece	566	2565	+1999	+200
Spain	3575	3544	–31	–1
Portugal	458	946	+488	+47

* In late 1993 £1 = ECU 1.3

FIG **2.11** *The EU's Income and Expenditure 1992, The Economist, 8 February 1993*

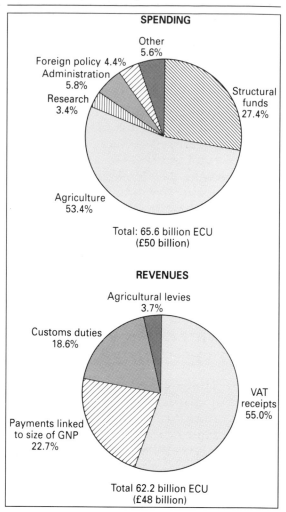

SPENDING

Other 5.6%
Foreign policy 4.4%
Administration 5.8%
Research 3.4%
Structural funds 27.4%
Agriculture 53.4%

Total: 65.6 billion ECU (£50 billion)

REVENUES

Agricultural levies 3.7%
Customs duties 18.6%
Payments linked to size of GNP 22.7%
VAT receipts 55.0%

Total 62.2 billion ECU (£48 billion)

Moves Towards Monetary Union

A decision was made by the original six members of the EU to move towards monetary union in 1972. Five years later the European Monetary System (EMS) was set up as the first stage towards full monetary union. The most important part of the EMS was the Exchange Rate Mechanism (ERM).

What are Exchange Rates?

An exchange rate is the price at which one currency is exchanged for another currency, although this price may constantly fluctuate. On 17 September 1993, for example, £1 cost $1.53, or DM 2.46 or F8.55. In a floating exchange rate system (that is one where the market in foreign currencies is allowed to operate without any government intervention) the exchange rates constantly change in response to the changing supply of and demand for a currency. If the supply of a currency rises then its value will fall. If the demand for a currency rises its value will rise. In that sense currencies are no different to any other commodity.

The supply and demand for currencies varies for a number of reasons.

– If British importers want to buy, for example, German goods then they need to sell pounds for German Marks because a German producer would only accept payment in Marks. In this particular instance both the supply of pounds and the demand for Marks would increase.
– If British investors want to invest capital in Germany (for example, to set up a new factory) then they would have to buy Marks by selling Pounds.
– A British investor may want to transfer funds from a British bank to a German bank to take advantage of higher interest rates. Again, they would have to sell Pounds to obtain Marks.
– Investors may also transfer funds from one country to another to take advantage of the fact that one economy may be healthier or more stable than another and so give their funds more security.

The problem with floating exchange rates is that constant fluctuations create uncertainty.

1 Uncertainty is created in international trade and international investment. It is more difficult to plan or to sign long-term contracts if the actual cost of imports or the earnings from exports are likely to vary.

2 The competitiveness of industry will vary. For example, a decline in the value of the Pound against other currencies will lower the price of British goods abroad but raise the price of imports. This would improve the ability of British firms to compete with foreign competitors.

3 It allows **speculators** to make enormous profits by buying and selling currencies at the right time. If for example a speculator can buy Pounds when their value is low and then sell them again when their value recovers they have made a profit. Massive sums are being moved around the globe each minute of the day by speculators. These movements in turn affect the supply and demand of currencies causing greater fluctuations in their value.

What is the ERM?

The EU is determined to remove the uncertainties and obstacles that floating exchange rates create for trade between member countries. It is argued that there cannot be a truly single EU market or integrated EU economy as long as exchange rates vary.

Under the ERM each participating country (Greece has never joined the ERM) agreed to maintain exchange rates with all the other participating countries within 2.25 per cent of an agreed rate against the ECU (or six per cent in the case of Spain and Portugal). If there was a danger that a currency may move outside this 2.25 per cent band then the central banks of each country were obliged to intervene. They can do this by:

– selling their reserves in a particular currency on the foreign exchanges in order to artificially increase its supply;
– buying a currency to artifcially increase demand;
– attempting to attract funds to a particular currency by raising interest rates in that country.

However, the UK refused to join the ERM until 1990. This effectively delayed any further progress towards full monetary union. The UK was reluctant to join at the time because of the instability of the Pound on the foreign exchanges. The government believed that the weakness of the Pound would make it too expensive to maintain its value. Also, the British Government was reluctant to lose its freedom to use exchange rates as a tool of economic policy.

The ERM did have a certain amount of success in promoting exchange rate stability but in September 1992 the ERM came under severe pressure from currency speculators. Massive buying and selling of currencies caused currencies to move outside the agreed 2.25 per cent band. Governments were reluctant to spend the enormous sums needed to try and maintain the agreed exchange rates. First Italy was forced to leave the ERM. Then despite spending billions of Pounds from its reserves, the Bank of England failed to adequately defend the value of sterling and so the British Government decided to leave the system, having joined it only two years earlier.

A second crisis hit the ERM in August 1993 when international speculators 'attacked' the French Franc forcing its value downwards and outside the 2.25 per cent band. The Danish and Belgian currencies also hit the bottom of the agreed band. The EU had to respond by virtually disbanding the ERM and widening the agreed band from 2.25 per cent to 15 per cent. The EU's dream of creating a single currency by removing variable exchange rates had suffered a serious blow.

What is the ECU?

The EMS also created the ECU (European Currency Unit). The value of the ECU is calculated using a very complex formula which takes account of the average value of all EU currencies. It is used as the unit of money by EU institutions when allocating funds to its various programmes such as the Common Agricultural Policy or the European Regional Development Fund. It is also used to settle debts between member countries and to buy each others currencies.

The Single European Market

In 1986 the EU member countries signed the Single European Act agreeing to create a single market within the EU by the beginning of 1993. Between 1986 and 1993 EU governments had to remove as many barriers to trade as possible (in other words, to liberalise trade) and to 'harmonise' rules which affect the movement of goods, people and capital between countries. Measures taken included:

- removal of exchange controls (that is, any restrictions on the quantity of currency which can enter or leave a country);
- harmonising product safety standards, so that products produced anywhere in the EU will conform with safety standards throughout the EU;
- harmonising the size of food cartons and other packaging so that food can be more easily sold throughout the EU;
- reduction of frontier controls to remove delays on the movement of goods between countries;
- reduction of differences in taxation between countries so that high taxation in one country does not affect the competitiveness of products exported to that country;
- reduction of qualification barriers so that educational or training qualifications gained in one country are valid throughout the EU.

All of these measures, and many others, were designed to integrate the EU more fully and to create a genuine single market. In other words, a British manufacturer, for example, can export their products to any part of the EU and be sure that rules and regulations will not reduce the competitiveness of their product. In the same way, a British worker can move to any other part of the EU without rules and regulations preventing them from obtaining an appropriate job. Examples of more specific measures include the removal of limits on the amount of alcoholic drink that a British holidaymaker can buy in France and bring back to Britain (as long as it is for personal use and not for resale), or the removal of controls of British banks or insurance companies opening branches elsewhere in the EU.

In reality not all barriers to the movement of goods, people and capital have yet been removed. For example, the issue of border controls has not yet been fully settled. Nine out of the 12 EU countries (excluding the UK, Ireland and Denmark) agreed to remove all border controls such as passport and customs checks by 1994, under what became known as the Schengen Agreement. The countries reluctant to withdraw controls are very concerned that the effect would be to make life easier for drug smugglers, international criminals, terrorists and illegal immigrants. The UK in particular was concerned that the agreement would remove the advantages of being an island when attempting to control illegal movements into the country.

2.8 Towards a United States of Europe?: the Maastricht Treaty

Negotiations on a new treaty to strengthen the integration of EU contries began in 1991. For many in the EU Commission the Maastricht Treaty which emerged over the following two years (its proper name is the Treaty on European Union) is the next logical stage in creating 'ever closer union' between the 12 member countries. The treaty has been extremely controversial in almost all the EU countries. At one extreme the treaty has been criticised for taking away too much power from

national governments and handing it to unelected bureaucrats in the EU Commission – some fear that it is another stage in the creation of a 'United States of Europe' with an EU government and only limited power delegated to national governments. At the other extreme the treaty has been praised, for exactly the same reasons. Unfortunately the treaty is so complex, and the negotiations have been so long and confusing, that few people in Europe understand what the treaty is really about.

The main aim of the treaty is to strengthen the political and economic links between the EU countries. Because the treaty significantly reduces the control national governments will have over their own economies, few governments have approved the treaty without first having to overcome a great deal of opposition. In some countries a referendum was held so that the whole adult population could express a view. For example, in Denmark the people narrowly rejected the treaty in a referendum in 1992, but narrowly approved it in a second referendum in 1993 following some changes to the treaty. The British Government decided that a referendum was not necessary but the debates in parliament caused splits within the Conservative Party.

By the end of 1993 all EU countries had ratified the treaty and it could be implemented. However, Britain and Denmark in particular have negotiated a number of opt out clauses which means that the treaty will have different effects in different countries.

What Effects will the Treaty have?

1 The treaty sets a deadline of 1999 for complete monetary union (see below). This would abolish individual currencies like the Pound, the Mark and the Franc and they would be replaced by the ECU.

2 All citizens of member countries will also become citizens of the EU (the treaty changed the name from the Economic Community to the European Union). In fact this will have little effect on most people other than that they will have the right to take any complaints they have against the EU to a new EU Ombudsman (a neutral official who will decide whether the individual has a justifiable complaint).

3 The Treaty's Social Chapter aims to harmonise laws on living and working conditions throughout the EU. This includes minimum wages, maximum working hours, levels of social security and health and safety at work. One of the main purposes of the Social Chapter is to prevent unfair competition from countries where industry could pay low wages, cut safety standards or exploit workers in other ways. The British Government has opted out of this part of the treaty because it believes it involves unacceptable government intervention in industry and unnecessarily raises industry's costs.

4 The Treaty encourages co-operation between EU countries on justice and home affairs – that is, issues such as drugs, refugees and immigration, international crime and terrorism. For example, a European police force (called Europol) is to be set up to tackle international crime. These policy areas are referred to as separate 'pillars' of the treaty because although they support European integration they lie outside the responsibility of the main EU institutions. The emphasis is on encouraging co-operation between national governments.

5 The treaty also urges greater co-operation between governments on foreign and defence policy. However, as in item 4 above, the treaty does not propose that EU institutions should take over any responsibility for foreign or defence policy. An organisation called the Western European Union (WEU) is given the job of trying to co-ordinate EU defence policy and acting as the European section of NATO. Nor does the treaty propose the setting up of an EU army or military alliance to replace NATO despite the fact that a few EU governments are in favour of the idea. Germany, France, Belgium and Spain formed the 'Eurocorps' in 1993 (a 40 000 strong armoured force) for peace-keeping missions organised by the EU. No other country has shown any interest in the idea.

6 The treaty shifts some power from the EU Commission to the Council of Ministers and in particular to the European Parliament. In reality this is likely to make very little difference, but it is an attempt to deal with the criticisms that the EU is not democratic.

7 The treaty proposes a new Cohesion Fund of £12 billion for Spain, Portugal, Greece and Ireland, to strengthen EU regional policy and to counteract some of the bad effects monetary union could have on the poorer countries (see Section 7.7).

What is European Monetary Union?

As explained above, European Monetary Union is one of the main measures included in the Maastricht Treaty. EMU involves two important changes.

1 The creation of a single currency (the ECU) to replace the existing national currencies like the Pound, Mark, Franc and Lire.

2 The setting up of a European Central Bank which would be independent and outside the control of National governments or the EU Commission. This Bank would be responsible for European monetary policy (that is, control of interest rates, exchange rates with non-European currencies and the quantity of money in circulation).

It would be catastrophic for most European economies if a single currency was created immediately. The treaty states that the EU economies must become more similar to each

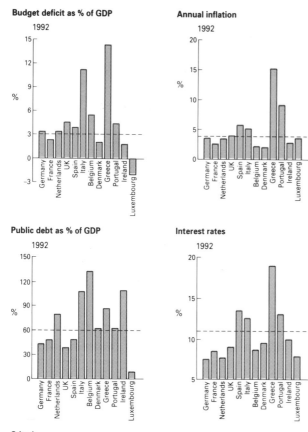

Budget deficit as % of GDP

1992

Annual inflation

1992

Public debt as % of GDP

1992

Interest rates

1992

Criteria

1 Budget deficit as % of GDP: permitted maximum is 3%.
2 Annual inflation: permitted maximum of 1·5% points above average of three lowest national inflation rates.
3 Public debt as % of GDP: permitted maximum is 60%.
4 Interest rates: permitted maximum of 2% points above average of three lowest national inflation rates.

FIG 2.13   *EU Economies and the EMU Convergence Criteria, The European*

British Anti-Maastricht Treaty Demonstrator Celebrates the First Danish Referendum Result

What are the Problems with Maastricht?

… The big mistake at Maastricht was to assume that by hastening political and economic integration, the EC could somehow protect itself from the impact of outside events. In reality, the upheaval to the east had already begun to change the very nature of Europe … the social, political, economic and moral priority is to bring the countries of eastern Europe into a much closer relationship with the EC. To achieve that, a two or three-speed Community may be necessary. To build Europe by excluding a part of it is impracticable as well as indefensible.

Maastricht is Obsolete, The Independent.

It might as well have been Mars, so far as millions of ordinary Europeans were concerned. The Maastricht Treaty on European Union has since seemed an almost insulting irrelevance, given the televised Balkan horror-show and the growing worries over jobs.

The EC: Back to the Drawing Board, The Economist, 3 July 1993.

Public disquiet about the treaty … lends support to the claim that European integration is an elite-led process, viewed with indifference or hostility by the people of Europe.

Philip Lynch, Europe's Post-Maastricht Muddle, Politics Review, November 1993.

other before their currencies can be replaced by the ECU – the process of making economies more similar is called 'convergence'. A number of criteria are set by the treaty which economies must meet before they can take part in EMU (see Fig 2.13).

At present only France and Luxembourg meet these criteria. Also, by the end of 1993 the virtual collapse of the ERM and the resulting instability in exchange rates (see Section 2.7), combined with the effects of the recession in western Europe, made it look increasingly unlikely that the timetable set by the Maastricht Treaty for convergence and EMU was a realistic one. The chances of Greece and Portugal ever achieving convergence are extremely slim.

So what will happen if convergence is not achieved? As Fig 2.14 shows, in 1996 the EU will decide whether the majority of member states meet the four criteria. If they do, then the Third Stage of monetary union will be implemented. If they do not, then the timetable for EMU will have to be delayed or it will have to be scrapped completely.

In any case, both Britain and Denmark have negotiated opt out clauses which allow them to decide not to take part in EMU at any time up to 1997.

- Read the three extracts above and explain in your own words why the writers believe the Maastricht Treaty is unsuitable for the 1990s.

The criticisms people have made against the treaty can be summarised as follows.

- It proposes an unacceptable loss of **sovereignty** from national governments.
- It increases the responsibilities and powers of EU institutions which are undemocratic.
- It will try to reduce the political, social and cultural diversity within the EU by imposing unacceptable common laws and standards on countries.
- The Social Chapter will increase the costs facing industry and will make it more difficult for European industry to compete with the USA, Japan and the rapidly growing Pacific economies such as Taiwan, Singapore and South Korea. There is already evidence that Europe's competitiveness is declining. The EU's share of world manufactured exports fell by 20 per cent between 1980 and 1993. Between 1979 and 1990 productivity (output per worker) rose by five per cent in Japan, four per cent in the USA, but only three per cent in the EU. Imports of high-technology have increased much more rapidly than exports.
- European Monetary Union will cause major problems for the poorer regions of the EU (see Section 7.7). Individual countries will no longer be able to use exchange rates or interest rates to make their economies more competitive because they will have to conform to rates met by the European Central Bank.

- The convergence criteria which have been set to achieve EMU (see above) are totally unrealistic.

The problems facing the Maastricht Treaty grew in 1993 as opinion seemed to turn against the idea of strengthening the EU. A number of factors caused this change in attitude even amongst many traditionally pro-EU groups.

- The convergence criteria demanded by EMU have been made even more unrealistic by the slow-down in the EU economy. The only way in which most countries could achieve these criteria is by implementing economic policies which would have major social costs – particularly even higher unemployment. Even Germany, faced with the massive costs of integrating eastern Germany, seemed to be in economic trouble.
- The virtual collapse of the ERM in 1993 dealt a major blow to the EMU timetable. It seemed to make convergence and EMU even more difficult to achieve.
- The inability of the EU to even agree on the best response to the civil war in Bosnia (see Section 3.2) seemed to make the treaty's aim of a common EU foreign policy over-optimistic.
- But perhaps most important of all was the realisation that events in eastern Europe had overtaken the Maastricht Treaty. Growing demands from the new democracies in eastern Europe to be accepted into the EU seemed to make the aim of integrating only 12 western European countries increasingly obsolete.

- Summarise the main patterns and trends in public opinion shown in Fig 2.15 on page 34. Does public opinion support the EU? Do the graphs provide any evidence that the Maastricht Treaty has reduced confidence in the EU?

- Summarise what the opinion poll results in Fig 2.16 on page 34 tell us about the level of support for the current policies of the EU.

Growing opposition to the Maastricht Treaty and the prospect of EU enlargement has strengthened the hand of those people who argue that the EU should no longer aim to have uniform policies throughout all the member countries. To some extent they have already won the argument because Britain has opted out of the Social Chapter of the Treaty

First Stage 1 JANUARY 1994	European Monetary Institute formed to: a) co-ordinate monetary policies of member countries; b) develop the use of the ECU; c) supervise the production of ECU banknotes.
Second Stage 31 DECEMBER 1996	Deadline for EU to determine whether a majority of countries are ready to adopt a single currency and whether full monetary and economic union should be proceeded with.
1 JANUARY 1998	Deadline for British Government to decide whether it wants to join European monetary union.
Third Stage 1 JANUARY 1999	Full economic and monetary union. European Monetary Institute replaced by European Central Bank. ECU becomes common currency in all participating countries.

FIG 2.14 *The Maastricht Timetable*

and both Britain and Denmark have reserved the right to opt out of EMU. Also, even if the EMU timetable is adhered to, some countries, such as Greece and Portugal, are unlikely to be part of EMU. But some argue that a two or three-speed Europe should emerge with some countries integrating more rapidly than others. Another term which policy-makers are now using is a 'variable geometry' Europe, or an 'a la carte' Europe. In other words, countries should be free to pick and choose those aspects of EU policy which they want to adopt. Some people believe that such an approach is the only way of guaranteeing the survival of the EU in the first decade of the twenty-first century.

Others worry that such an approach would create second division countries unable to effectively compete with the rest of the EU.

Fig 2.16   *Opinion Poll Results*

QUESTION	ANSWER	UK %	FRANCE %	GERMANY %
Do you think the process of economic and political integration should be:	Accelerated? Slowed Down? Don't Know?	15 58 27	45 31 24	39 45 16
Do you think those countries willing to proceed with integration should go ahead, or should all countries proceed together?	Those willing should go ahead. All should move together. Don't know.	22 56 22	35 53 12	28 61 11
If there were to be a referendum on the Maastricht Treaty would you vote:	In favour? Against? Don't know?	24 34 42	— — —	64 24 12
Are you in favour or opposed to the creation of a single European currency to replace the Pound, Frank and Mark?	In favour. Against. Don't know.	27 59 14	64 29 7	34 57 9
Do you agree that EU institutions are too busy creating long-winded directives and rules?	Agree. Disagree. Don't know.	72 7 20	79 13 8	75 8 17
Are you in favour or opposed to the EU ensuring the same employment rights in all member countries?	In favour. Against. Don't know.	61 21 18	81 14 5	50 39 11
Are you in favour or opposed to a single defence force for the whole of the EU?	In favour. Against. Don't know.	46 32 21	83 12 5	62 26 12
Are you in favour or opposed to the integration of East European countries into the EU?	In favour. Against. Don't know.	45 27 28	57 32 11	66 23 11
Should an EU humanitarian force have intervened in Yugoslavia and Somalia?	Yes. No. Don't know.	62 19 19	85 11 4	70 20 10

Based on an opinion poll in October 1992 conducted by ICM for The Guardian, CSA for La Croix, and Forsa for RTL plus.

Fig 2.15   *Public Opinion on Maastricht and the EU, The Economist, 3 July 1993*

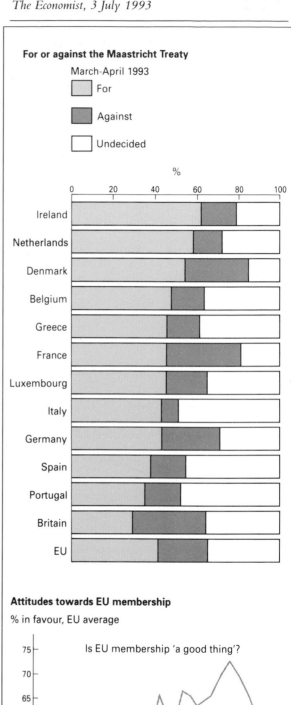

For or against the Maastricht Treaty

March-April 1993

For

Against

Undecided

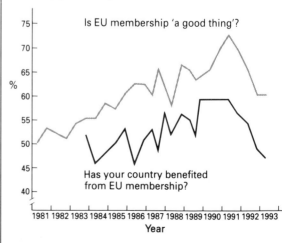

Attitudes towards EU membership

% in favour, EU average

2.9 Knocking on the Door: Enlargement of the EU

As Section 2.8 has shown, the EU has been putting most of its energies into the process of deepening and not into enlarging. In other words, into strengthening the links between existing members and not into increasing the number of member countries. However, increasing numbers of influential people within the EU believe that this is a dangerous mistake. They argue that the EU is acting as though the end of the Iron Curtain and of the Cold War has not happened. They believe that it is becoming increasingly unrealistic for the EU to act independently from the rest of Europe and that the priority should be now to enlarge membership to include other western European countries and the former communist countries of eastern Europe. The alternative is, they claim, a dangerous division of Europe into a prosperous and integrated western Europe (with some western European countries excluded from the mainstream) and a poor and unstable eastern Europe – a situation as potentially dangerous as the Cold War.

Western European Countries

We want to contribute actively to building a strong and coherent European Union, devoted to peace, freedom and democracy, to economic growth and social progress, to a clean environment and cultural diversity.

Ulf Dinkelspiel, Swedish Minister for European Affairs.

The EU demands that any new member country must:

a) be European;
b) have a democratic government;
c) have a government which respects human rights.

By 1993 negotiations were underway to expand the EU from 12 to 16 countries by admitting Finland, Sweden, Norway and Austria before 1996. These countries could be accepted into the EU without fundamental changes to the Union's structure. All are relatively wealthy and have a small population – collectively they would contribute more than £2 billion to the EU budget from a total population of only 25 million.

Their entry into the EU, which is subject to a referendum in each country, would create some problems. The economic, political and cultural diversity of the EU would be further increased and this inevitably creates additional stresses on the organisation. For example, they would add an additional three languages which would complicate the work of the European Commission. At present EU interpreters and translators have to be used for 72 possible language combinations. With the four additonal members this would increase to 132 combinations – this significantly increases the cost of EU administration and can slow down negotiations within the Community.

There are also problems for the prospective new members. Switzerland, Norway and Finland give particularly high subsidies to their farmers to compensate for the mountainous or sub-Arctic and Arctic environments which dominate their territories.

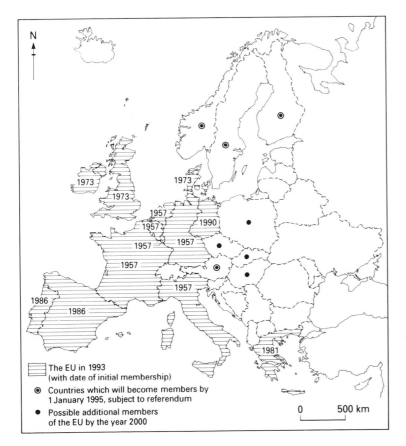

N

1973
1973
1973
1957
1957
1990
1957
1957
1957
1957
1986
1986
1981

The EU in 1993
(with date of initial membership)

⊙ Countries which will become members by
1 January 1995, subject to referendum

● Possible additional members
of the EU by the year 2000

0   500 km

FIG 2.17   *The Expansion of the EU*

Frightened of ghost villages

A HOLIDAY in Austria's westernmost state of Vorarlberg rewards the visitor with stunning scenery at any time of the year. But although transient tourists from all over Europe – whose money is vital to the local economy – are warmly received by their hosts, federal state law prevents them from buying land or property for holiday homes.

The original law, which dates back to 1962, flies in the face of single market regulations which prescribe the free movement of people, goods and services within the community.

With an Austrian referendum on EC membership due in 1995, Brussels is pressuring the state of Vorarlberg to abandon the restrictive laws. The Vorarlberg government has reacted with a compromise, agreeing to relax the conditions for purchase of a "second home". The amendment to the law will be introduced next year when permission to buy a second home will be granted, regardless of nationality, to anyone who has lived permanently in Austria for at least five years.

But citizens of Vorarlberg see this as a bad sign. Some predict that the next step will be to scrap all restrictions as a condition of entry to the EC. Residents in the most popular Alpine areas in western Austria fear that this would mean an invasion of wealthy EC citizens whose purchasing power would push up prices and force Austrians out.

In the idyllic Vorarlberg village of Schrüns, with a population of 4,000, locals fear the effects of EC expansionism. Helga Salzgitter, who runs a guest house with her husband Hubert, worries about the future of the tourist industry there. "I hope our politicians are sensible enough to realise what they will do to Schrüns if the property restrictions go for good. If rich foreigners buy homes here they will be elsewhere for most of the year. The village will empty in no time and the money will stop coming in."

FIG 2.18   *The European, 19 August 1993*

Sober thoughts on ending drinks controls

IF AND when Sweden joins the European Community, the nation's drinkers will be among the first to raise their glasses.

Strict curbs on alcohol consumption have long been a pillar of this health-conscious social democracy. But they are certain not to survive – or at least be watered down – under Brussels' rules on free competition.

The Swedes operate a highly restrictive policy on alcohol. Wine, strong beer and spirits may be bought only in state shops, the Systembolaget. Exorbitant taxes ensure that prices are stiflingly high, and outside major towns there are virtually no pubs at all. When you do find one, a 0.5 litre glass of beer can cost up to Skr50 (Ecu5).

Puritan attitudes to alcohol date back to the 18th century when agricultural workers received part of their wages in vodka and schnapps. Drunkenness was endemic and rationing was imposed early this century. It remained until 1955 when the *Systembolag* monopoly was founded. The shops' opening hours are restricted and they must close at weekends.

EC membership could change all this. The government's cry that the alcohol monopoly is vital to the nation's health has fallen on deaf ears in Brussels. The Commission has said that health goals could be fulfilled by less restrictive means; for instance, improved education. Commercial monopolies, it said, run counter to the Treaty of Rome.

Sweden is considering a seven-year transitional period to phase out the state monopoly. This has raised the ire of teetotallers and, although most Swedes loathe the monopoly, the temperance movement is powerful. It has threatened to mobilise its 500,000 members to vote No to EC membership if the government caves in.

At first sight, the public health argument appears reasonable: Sweden has one of Europe's lowest death rates for cirrhosis of the liver.

But more than 3.5 per cent of Swedes are classed as alcoholics, and it is estimated that smuggling and illegal alcohol production almost doubles the official level of alcohol consumption. Police battle to clamp down on illegal distillation. Recent figures suggest the amount of *hembränning* (home distilling) has nearly quadrupled in the past 15 years.

Swedish brewers await the outcome of EC entry negotiations with bated breath. The advent of the single market could, at last, give them something to smile about.

Many Norwegians in particular fear job losses in farming if membership goes ahead. Their government guarantees all farmers an annual income of £14000 and farm subsidies represent two per cent of the country's GDP. They fear that despite the high subsidies allowed under the Community's Common Agricultural Policy (see Section 5.2) they would still lose out because under EU regulations they would not be allowed to receive higher subsidies than farmers in other countries.

- All of the countries which have applied to join the EU will have to make changes to some of their national laws so that they conform with EU laws. Read Figs 2.18 and 2.19.
  a) Summarise the legal changes described in the two articles.
  b) Do you consider the changes described to be beneficial or harmful to the countries involved? Explain your answer.

The Finns are particularly keen to join. The collapse of the Soviet Union poses challenges for the future of the country. After the Second World War, during which Finland had been invaded by the Soviet Union, the Finns had to sign a Treaty of Friendship, Co-operation and Mutual Assistance with the Soviet Government. This effectively forced

FIG 2.19   *The European, 19 August 1993*

Finland to be militarily neutral and to be partially tied economically to the Soviet Union. With the collapse of the Soviet Union the Friendship Treaty was no longer valid. Fearing economic instability in Russia and in the new Baltic republics on their doorstep, and fearing the possible emergence of an aggressive Russian Nationalist Government in the future, the Finnish Government is keen to tie itself much more closely with western Europe.

The end of the Cold War has also encouraged the militarily neutral countries of Sweden and Austria to join. Both countries are already strongly linked to the western European economies – 75 per cent of Sweden's exports, for example, go to western Europe. Norway has applied to join the EU before, at the same time as the UK joined, but the Norwegian people rejected membership at that time in a referendum.

Cyprus, Malta and Turkey have also applied to join the EU. In the case of Cyprus, controversy over the longstanding partition of the island between Turkey and Greece is likely to delay membership for a considerable time. The EU believes that Turkey would not be able to meet the demands of EU membership, at least at the moment, mainly because of its relatively poorly developed economy.

Switzerland may put the issue of membership to its population in a referendum in 1995 or 1996 but its confederate government system (each state or *canton* has considerable independence) could make it very difficult for the country as a whole to harmonise its laws with EU laws. The Swiss population has already rejected membership of the European Economic Area. The European Economic Area came into effect at the end of 1993, and is designed to integrate the EU and EFTA to create a customs free zone of 400 million people, while at the same time side-stepping the issue of the EFTA countries becoming full members of the EU.

As it turns out the concept of the Economic Area could be overtaken by events if the other EFTA countries become full EU members.

Another potential member of the EU is Iceland, but at the moment it sees no advantage in joining because it would lose its right to keep other countries out of its fishing grounds and its economy is dependent on earnings from fish exports.

Eastern European Countries

The treatment the European Community has reserved for those nations of central and eastern Europe that have been most successful in their emancipation from communism appears designed to keep them at arm's length from western markets. Rather than being treated as new member-states of Europe, they are regarded as potential economic rivals to rich western Europe.

Jacques Attali, President of the European Bank for Reconstruction and Development.

All the former Communist states of eastern Europe (Poland, Czech Republic, Hungary, Slovakia, Bulgaria, Romania and Albania) are keen to join the EU. Of the seven, Poland, the

Czech Republic and Hungary could most realistically become members by the end of the decade because their economies are showing the most progress.

The eastern governments see EU membership as a way of ensuring political and economic integration with western Europe and as a way of gaining access to the wealthy markets in the west.

The eastern governments are, at the moment, unhappy about the way they have been treated by the EU. Their trade with EU countries has been restricted by EU trade barriers designed to protect the Union's industries and farmers from competition from the east.

By the end of 1993 no timetable had been agreed by the EU to even discuss membership of eastern European countries.

The EU is reluctant to admit eastern countries for a variety of reasons.

- Membership would remove barriers to migration. EU governments are worried that this would open the flood-gates to large-scale migration by people seeking a higher standard of living in western Europe (see Section 4.4).
- EU countries are worried that low wages in the east would encourage EU industries to move to the east causing higher unemployment in western Europe.
- The EU argues that the eastern economies are not yet ready to join the Union. They are poorer than Greece and Portugal, the two poorest EU members, and they could not possibly meet the 'convergence criteria' agreed in the Maastricht Treaty (see Section 2.8). Industries in the east could be destroyed by western competition.
- Existing EU institutions could not cope with so many additional members without major reorganisation.
- It would be very expensive for the EU, particularly because of extra demands on the European Regional Development Fund (see Section 7.7) and the Common Agricultural Policy (see Section 5.2). It has been estimated that the EU budget would have to rise by 20 per cent if the three most prosperous eastern countries became members.
- The EU has been concentrating on greater integration between its existing members and additional members would confuse this process.

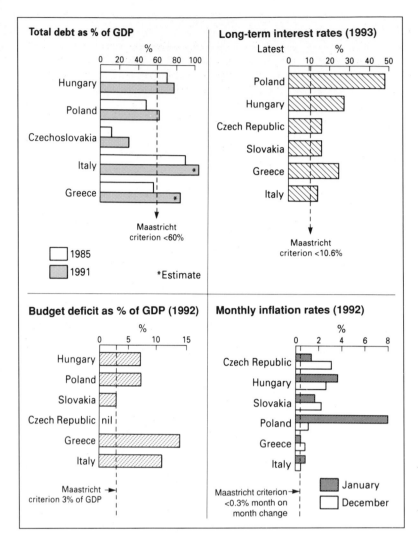

Total debt as % of GDP

Long-term interest rates (1993)

Budget deficit as % of GDP (1992)

Monthly inflation rates (1992)

- Study Fig 2.20. Does the data in the graph support the argument that the eastern countries should not be admitted to the EU because they cannot hope to meet the economic criteria laid down in the Maastricht Treaty? (See also Section 2.8).

- This section lists six reasons why the EU is reluctant to grant membership to the eastern countries:
  a) Which two reasons appear to be contradictory?
  b) Draw up a list of arguments in favour of these countries joining the EU. You may need to use information on eastern Europe from elsewhere in this chapter to help you.

Of the other eastern countries, Slovenia may be in a position to join later this decade, but all the other former Yugoslav states are far too unstable. Similarly, the former Soviet states are either too poor or too unstable to be serious contenders for EU membership before the year 2000.

FIG 2.20 *Eastern Europe and the Maastricht Convergence Criteria, The Economist, 13 March 1993*

1 'European integration is ocurring more rapidly in the 1990s than at any time since 1945'.

Using evidence from this chapter discuss the extent to which you agree with this statement.

2 'The ending of the Cold War was probably the best thing to happen to Europe since 1945. On the other hand, it has brought major problems which need to be tackled during the 1990s.' Discuss the extent to which you agree with this statement.

3 Why has the Maastricht Treaty proved to be so controversial and why may the treaty fail in achieving its main aims?

4 Evaluate the advantages and disadvantages of enlarging the European Union.

5 Using information in this chapter, and Chapters 6 and 7, evaluate the success of German unification.

Glossary

capitalism	A social and economic system in which economic activity (such as factories and shops) is controlled and owned privately and not by the state. Supply and demand, or the free market, decide what and how things are made and the price charged for commodities.
central planning	The running of a command economy where the state plans the economy and makes all the important economic decisions.
command economy	An economy in which all economic activity (such as factories and shops) is controlled and owned by the state and not by private individuals or companies. All important economic decisions are made by the government.
communism	A social system in which all property is owned by the state and the individual is seen as being less important than society as a whole. Each member of a communist society is supposed to work for the good of society as a whole.
democracy	A government system where all adults can vote in elections so that the population chooses representatives for a national assembly or parliament. The political party or parties which have the largest number of representatives form the government.
deterrence	A system of defence which relies on the threat of force to discourage other countries from starting a war. Nuclear deterrence is based on the belief that no country will start a war because of the fear of being destroyed by nuclear weapons in retaliation.
free market economics	An economic system where supply and demand, or private firms and consumers, make all important economic decisions (see capitalism).
free trade	International trade without legal or financial barriers. Countries are free to export goods to any other country and no tariffs are imposed on imports.
GDP – Gross Domestic Product	A measure of the total value of goods and services produced by an economy during one year. It is an indicator of the amount of wealth produced in a country.
monetary union	Where a group of countries share a common currency and important financial decisions are taken jointly by all the countries involved.
parliamentary democracy	See democracy.
power bloc	A group of countries which form a military alliance. For example, NATO and the Warsaw Pact were the two main power blocs in Europe during the Cold War.
pre-emptive strike	A military attack carried out by one country on another in the belief that the other country was planning to attack first.
privatisation	The process of selling state-owned industries to the private sector.
socialism	The belief that important industries should be owned by the state and run for the benefit of society as a whole.
sovereignty	The power and freedom to run a country without external interference.
speculator	A person who buys and sells currencies in order to make a profit.
tariffs, tariff barrier	A tariff is a tax levied on imports. Tariffs may act as a barrier to international trade.
trading bloc	A group of countries which encourage trade with each other by removing tariffs and other trade barriers.

The Fragmen
of Europe

KEY IDEAS

3.1 Europe is a patchwork of ethnic, linguistic and cultural groups. Most states in Europe contain more than one such group. Many of these groups are demanding greater autonomy.

3.2 The fragmentation of Yugoslavia, the Soviet Union and Czechoslovakia during the early 1990s resulted from tensions between different ethnic, linguistic or cultural groups.

3.3 Some states in Europe, such as Spain, could fragment into smaller political units during the 1990s as a result of tension between ethnic, linguistic or cultural groups.

3.4 A number of states, such as the UK and Italy, contain groups campaigning for greater regional autonomy or greater recognition for their cultural differences.

3.5 Some ethnic, linguistic or cultural groups may fail to maintain their distinctive identity despite having achieved a degree of autonomy.

3.1 The European Patchwork

There will be more borders in this future world, not fewer – more kinds of division, a cacophony of contrasts and conflicts previously repressed or distorted … Is this a new order, or a new disorder?

Tom Nairn, Does Tomorrow Belong to the Bullets or the Bouquets?, New Statesman, 19 June 1992.

Since the nineteenth century, Europe has consisted of a number of countries or **nation-states** each with its own clearly defined territory and government. However, the term nation-state can be misleading. Many so-called nation-states include two or more nations.

A nation can be defined as a group of people with their own distinctive ethnic origin, language or culture and who belong to or identify with a particular geographical area. If a nation or ethnic group feel that their interests are being ignored by the government, nationalist political groups may emerge. Such groups may demand greater **autonomy** or complete independence. This process can be called separatism or nationalism. Nationalism and separatism can therefore lead to the break up or fragmentation of existing countries.

Most countries in Europe provide a home to indigenous **linguistic**, ethnic or cultural minorities. Many of these minorities have called for some degree of autonomy.

A Corsican Nationalist

FIG 3.1   *States Created Since 1990*

Growing support for nationalist and separatist movements is leading to far reaching changes in Europe. Between 1990 and 1993, 11 new countries appeared in Europe as a result of separatism. But it is not just the map of national boundaries which is changing (see Fig 3.1). All over Europe people are increasingly identifying with a particular region rather than with their country as a whole. Regionalism, where people feel regions within a country should be given more power, is gaining strength.

It is far from clear what the end result of a strengthening of nationalism and separatism will be. There are literally hundreds of areas with distinctive cultural or ethnic characteristics scattered across Europe. If all of these demanded autonomy there would be a complete collapse of the system of nation-states currently seen as 'normal'. There would be a complex patchwork quilt of independent regions. In some cases these regions would be very small. Many people believe that this would be a recipe for chaos and conflict.

Others see a 'Europe of the Regions' as an idea to be welcomed. Each region would have a large amount of autonomy, but all the regions would be bound together by a powerful and expanded European Union. Such a system, they argue, would give people more influence over government decisions.

FIG 3.2a   *Linguistic and Cultural Groups Associated with Demands for Greater Autonomy*

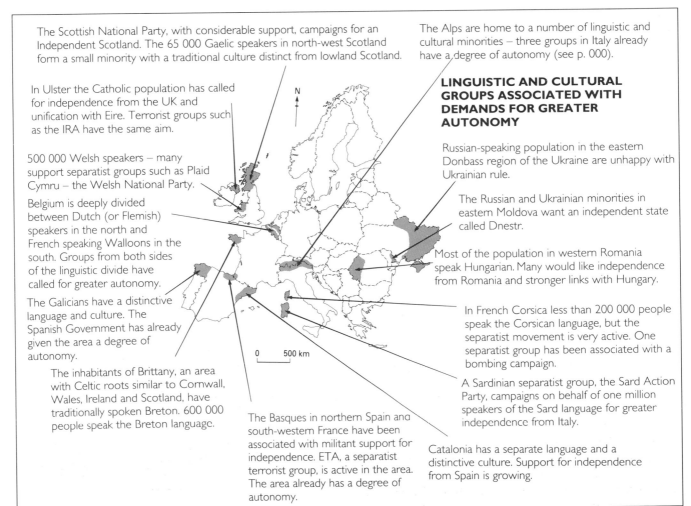

The Scottish National Party, with considerable support, campaigns for an Independent Scotland. The 65 000 Gaelic speakers in north-west Scotland form a small minority with a traditional culture distinct from lowland Scotland.

In Ulster the Catholic population has called for independence from the UK and unification with Eire. Terrorist groups such as the IRA have the same aim.

500 000 Welsh speakers – many support separatist groups such as Plaid Cymru – the Welsh National Party.

Belgium is deeply divided between Dutch (or Flemish) speakers in the north and French speaking Walloons in the south. Groups from both sides of the linguistic divide have called for greater autonomy.

The Galicians have a distinctive language and culture. The Spanish Government has already given the area a degree of autonomy.

The inhabitants of Brittany, an area with Celtic roots similar to Cornwall, Wales, Ireland and Scotland, have traditionally spoken Breton. 600 000 people speak the Breton language.

The Basques in northern Spain and south-western France have been associated with militant support for independence. ETA, a separatist terrorist group, is active in the area. The area already has a degree of autonomy.

The Alps are home to a number of linguistic and cultural minorities – three groups in Italy already have a degree of autonomy (see p. 000).

LINGUISTIC AND CULTURAL GROUPS ASSOCIATED WITH DEMANDS FOR GREATER AUTONOMY

Russian-speaking population in the eastern Donbass region of the Ukraine are unhappy with Ukrainian rule.

The Russian and Ukrainian minorities in eastern Moldova want an independent state called Dnestr.

Most of the population in western Romania speak Hungarian. Many would like independence from Romania and stronger links with Hungary.

In French Corsica less than 200 000 people speak the Corsican language, but the separatist movement is very active. One separatist group has been associated with a bombing campaign.

A Sardinian separatist group, the Sard Action Party, campaigns on behalf of one million speakers of the Sard language for greater independence from Italy.

Catalonia has a separate language and a distinctive culture. Support for independence from Spain is growing.

Why is Fragmentation Happening Now?

There are a number of reasons why nationalism and separatism have gained in strength since the 1980s.

1 Sociologists have suggested that people feel alienated or insignificant in an increasingly complex industrial society. People need to develop a sense of community based on local **culture** and traditions. This gives them a greater feeling of belonging and gives them a clearer identity. This is similar to the desire many people have to show a strong allegiance to their local football club or a strong feeling of pride in their home town.

2 People living in peripheral or remote areas may feel that the government is ignoring their needs. Within the United Kingdom, for example, many Scottish people feel that the London-based government is ignoring the needs of Scotland. This is particularly likely to be the case during periods of economic recession such as the early 1990s. Peripheral areas often suffer from high unemployment.

3 All countries are finding that they have less control over their own economies as the global economy becomes increasingly integrated and complex. Giving greater power to smaller regions can be seen as a way of counteracting the power of global economic organisations such as multi-national companies.

4 The strengthening of the EU has also encouraged many nationalist groups to believe that their regions stand a better chance of competing economically with their much larger neighbours. Nationalists in Wales and Scotland, for example, have made much of this arguement over the last few years claiming that EU membership would give them more influence in Europe despite their small size.

Man Stands on Soviet Union Flag – Demonstration Supporting Ukrainian Independence

What is nationalism?

NATIONALISM is an off shoot of the eighteenth century doctrine of popular sovereignty. It preaches the idea that any group that thinks of itself as a nation has the right to 'self-determination' – the recognition by others of its uniqueness and its claim to independent statehood, or at the very least, to a wide measure of cultural and political autonomy within another state. Nations and states are not the same thing, though they are often treated as much. A nation can be described as a pre-political community. A state is a legal and political unit with the power to require loyalty and obedience from its citizens. States can be democratic, autocratic or totalitarian.

Surprisingly, Joseph Stalin's definition of a nation is quite widely used. He said a nation should have four characteristics – a common language, a common territory, a common economic life and a common mental make-up.

The latter probably has to include a sense of solidarity, a common culture and a historic sense of being a nation.

Fig 3.2b *The Geography Magazine, July 1992*

5 The collapse of Communism in eastern Europe unleashed a wave of nationalism, particularly in Yugoslavia and the former Soviet Union. Communism claimed to have eradicated nationalism. All working class people were supposed to have common interests which would make divisions on ethnic or cultural lines irrelevant. Nationalism was believed to be a Capitalist disease. In reality Communism simply suppressed nationalism and it went on simmering below the surface. When Communism collapsed nationalism re-emerged.

- Read Fig 3.2b. Using Stalin's definition do you think the UK can be called a nation? Can England be called a nation?

- Summarise Fig 3.3 by completing the following sentences.

  a) Nation-states may be too small because …
  b) Nation-states may be too large because …
  c) EU integration is, paradoxically, encouraging fragmentation because …

The End of the Nation-state?

NATIONALISM and the nation-state bind people together but they also separate one part of the world from another and, thereby, one group of people from another. But after 300 years the nation-state may be coming to the end of its shelf-life, its rationale undermined, paradoxically, because it is both too small and too big. It is too small because sharp spatial demarcations are becoming irrelevant to the dynamics of a world economy of multinational corporations and global markets. It is too large because most governments and politicians are too distant from the everyday experience of ordinary people.

The nation state is too small to deal with world pollution and too big to cope with neighbourhood waste disposal. It has become a spatial anachronism, too small to have the necessary global consciousness and too large to be sensitive to the needs of localities.

There are moves away from nationalism. In one direction is the globalism which sees the need for world solutions to what in reality are world problems of war and peace, poverty and plenty, sustainability and ecological harmony. In the other direction is the localism which aims to solve local problems and avoid the easy option of only talking and worrying about ecological issues in the abstract or if they occur on the other side of the world. The slogan '*Think global, act local*' is an attempt to join the two. In Europe we are beginning to see the geopolitical consequence of these trends. On the one hand there is the inexorable move towards European integration and the creation of a European super-state which will eventually override the sovereignty of existing nation-states. And, on the other hand, there is the disintegration of existing nation-states as smaller, more localised loyalties and allegiances begin to emerge. In Spain, for example, Andalucia, Castille and Catalonia have always existed in uneasy harmony. When the power shifts from Madrid to Brussels they no longer need to speak to one another. In Britain the Scots have remained in the Union for the want of any other alternative. But when money is doled out from Brussels rather than London there seems little point in staying with the English. Nation-states were always a compromise, a point of tension between competing interests. In the different world of the next century they may become an irrelevance.

FIG 3.3 *Geography Review*

- Copy Fig 3.4a showing the reasons why fragmentation is occurring and write a sentence in each box summarising each reason.

- Europe can be divided into a Core area which includes the wealthiest and most developed areas, and a Periphery which includes the poorer and less developed areas. Study Fig 3.2a which locates many of the groups in Europe demanding greater autonomy and compare it with Fig 3.4b. Is there any evidence in the two maps that peripheral areas are more likely to demand autonomy? Try to explain your answer.

- Nation-states try to encourage a sense of national identity or patriotism among their people. Which geographical area do you identify with most strongly? Copy and then fill in the matrix below by putting a tick in the appropriate boxes. Compare your answers with those of the rest of the group.

FRAGMENTATION

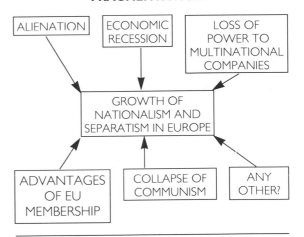

FIG 3.4a *The Causes of Fragmentation*

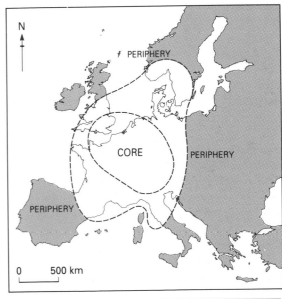

FIG 3.4b *The European Core and Periphery*

	IDENTIFY WITH:				
	NOT AT ALL ◄—			—► VERY STRONGLY	
YOUR HOME CITY, TOWN OR VILLAGE					
YOUR COUNTY					
YOUR REGION					
ENGLAND, WALES, SCOTLAND OR NORTHERN IRELAND					
THE UNITED KINGDOM					
EUROPE					

EU regions where there are demands for autonomy*	GDP per person (EU average =100)
SPAIN	
Galicia	64
Catalonia	84
Basque Country	89
FRANCE	
Corsica	77
Brittany	89
WALES	
Clwyd, Dyfed, Gwynedd, Powys	87
SCOTLAND	
Dumfries, Galloway, Strathclyde	94
Highland, Islands	99
Grampian	125
Rest of Scotland	102
ITALY	
Sardinia	76
Friuli-Venezia Giulia	116
Trentino-Alto Adige	118
Vallée d'Aosta	134

*Data for Belgium, and for the regions of Wales where support for autonomy is limited, has been excluded.

- Using the data in Fig 3.5 construct a bar graph showing GDP per person in the regions listed. Indicate the EU regional average GDP per person on your graph. To what extent does your graph support the hypothesis that 'regions suffering from economic problems are more likely to demand autonomy'?

FIG 3.5 *Autonomy and GDP*

3.2 The Fragmentation of the Soviet Union and Yugoslavia

The End of an Empire: the Break Up of the Soviet Union

1991 saw the collapse of the Soviet Union and the emergence in its place of 15 separate states in eastern Europe and Asia. Even as late as 1990 few people would have predicted such a rapid collapse of one of the world's two superpowers. The policies of *Glasnost* (which introduced greater democracy) and *Perestroika* (which aimed at improving the efficiency of the economy) introduced by President Mikhail Gorbachev in the late 1980s had led to a reduction of central government control. One of the consequences of this was the emergence of previously banned nationalist organisations. It was these organisations which helped to bring about the collapse of the Communist Government in Moscow and led to the emergence of the new states. In theory these states had existed within the Soviet Union. In reality they had had little effective independence and were controlled from Moscow.

The Baltic states of Estonia, Latvia and Lithuania were the first to achieve independence between 1989 and 1991. They had become part of the Soviet Union in 1940 having enjoyed 20 years of independence after 1920. The Baltic states did not regain their independence without bloodshed. In January 1991 Soviet paratroopers attacked crowds in Lithuania who were demanding independence, killing 14 people. In the same month four people died when Soviet Black Beret troops occupied government buildings in Latvia.

Each state has its own language and individual history, although each is also home to a Russian minority. In the case of Latvia only 53 per cent of the population are ethnic Latvians and in Estonia only 62 per cent are ethnic Estonians. This continues to cause friction. Many of the Russians were unhappy about independence and now feel that they are being treated as second class citizens by the new governments. Under Latvian law **citizenship** is automatically given only to people who were citizens of independent Latvia between 1918 and 1940. Only 40 per cent of Russians, Ukrainians and Jews have managed to gain citizenship in Latvia. Without citizenship they cannot vote, even though more than 90 per cent of these minority groups have lived in Latvia for 16 years or more. In some cases they have lived there for their whole lives.

Russia (or more precisely the Russian Federation since it includes a number of semi-autonomous areas of its own), Belarus, Ukraine and Moldova emerged later from the ashes of the Soviet Union following the failed coup by Communist Party hardliners in the summer of 1991. (Eight other newly independent states were formed further east in the Caucasus and Asia but these lie outside the area covered by this book.)

Russia, with Moscow as its capital and with 147 million of the Soviet Union's 287 million people, had always dominated the Soviet Union. The new states continue to worry about being dominated by their much larger neighbour. The new Russian President, Boris Yeltsin, attempted to form a loose **confederation** of independent states (called the Commonwealth of Independent States or CIS) which would share an army and co-operate over economic matters. In fact, fear of Russian domination and enormous cultural, political and economic differences between the states meant that the Commonwealth has been largely ineffective.

The future of these newly independent countries is still very uncertain. They are all making the traumatic transition from centrally planned Communist economies to market economies and face enormous economic problems (see Chapter 2). Some, particularly Russia, include ethnic minorities which in their turn are now demanding greater autonomy. In 1992, for example, the Crimea declared independence from the Ukraine. Sixty per cent of the Crimea's population is Russian and they are unhappy about being politically and geographically separated from the rest of Russia. The 1990s could see a continuing, possibly violent, fragmentation of the Russian federation.

Other countries face separatist movements too. The Russian and Ukrainian minorities in Trans-Dnestr in the east of Moldova are demanding their own fully independent state and in 1992 a civil war erupted between the Moldovan Government and Dnestr separatists. Many Russian speakers in the east of Ukraine, a region called the Donbass, are demanding greater autonomy.

There are also a number of political disagreements between these new countries and it is feared that these disagreements could, at some point during the 1990s, lead to war. Such wars have already broken out in the Caucasus between ethnically divided Armenia and Azerbaijan. The consequences of such conflicts are impossible to predict.

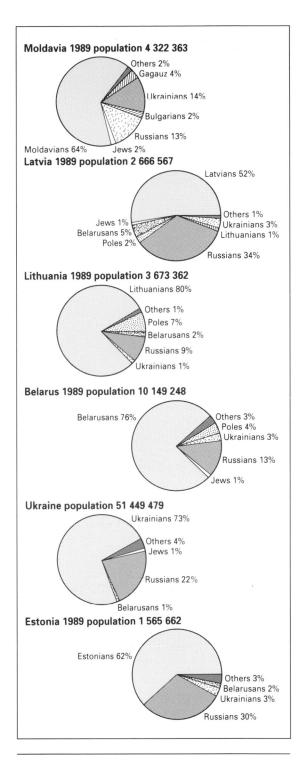

FIG 3.7 *The Ethnic Composition of the Former European Soviet Republics*

FIG 3.6 *Development Indicators – Former Soviet Republics*

	Students in Higher Education (per 10 000 people)	Demographic Factors			Personal Income % with monthly earnings	
		Birth Rate	Death Rate	Natural Increase (per 1000)	<75 roubles	>200 roubles
Russia	200	17.1	10.5	6.6	6.3	22.0
Estonia	151	16.0	11.7	4.3	3.9	33.6
Latvia	164	15.8	12.1	3.7	3.2	28.3
Lithuania	178	16.2	10.1	6.1	3.6	24.0
Ukraine	166	14.8	13.6	3.4	8.1	14.2
Belarus	179	16.1	9.9	6.2	5.0	19.5
Moldova	126	21.8	9.6	12.2	13.0	11.0

- Look at the data in Fig 3.6. Devise a method of ranking the states according to their level of economic development using the indicators in the table. Also devise a method of weighting the more useful indicators.

- Study Fig 3.7. Which states are the most ethnically homogenous and which are the least ethnically homogenous?

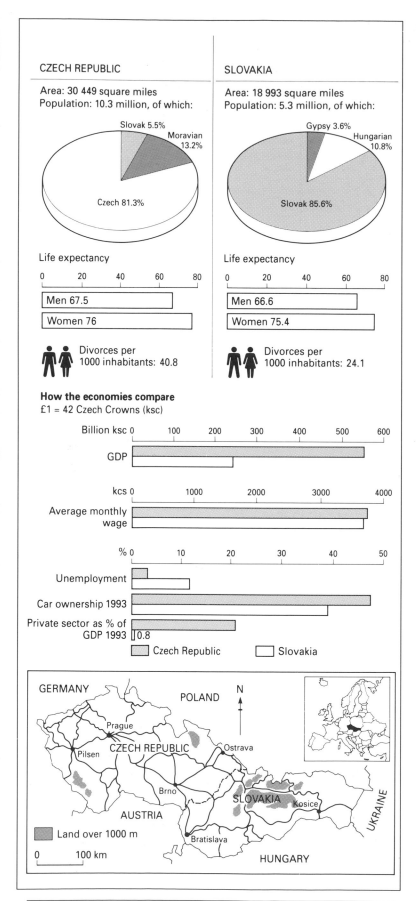

CZECH REPUBLIC

Area: 30 449 square miles
Population: 10.3 million, of which:

Slovak 5.5%
Moravian 13.2%
Czech 81.3%

Life expectancy

| 0 | 20 | 40 | 60 | 80 |

Men 67.5
Women 76

Divorces per 1000 inhabitants: 40.8

SLOVAKIA

Area: 18 993 square miles
Population: 5.3 million, of which:

Gypsy 3.6%
Hungarian 10.8%
Slovak 85.6%

Life expectancy

| 0 | 20 | 40 | 60 | 80 |

Men 66.6
Women 75.4

Divorces per 1000 inhabitants: 24.1

How the economies compare
£1 = 42 Czech Crowns (ksc)

Billion ksc | 0 | 100 | 200 | 300 | 400 | 500 | 600 |
GDP

kcs | 0 | 1000 | 2000 | 3000 | 4000 |
Average monthly wage

% | 0 | 10 | 20 | 30 | 40 | 50 |
Unemployment
Car ownership 1993
Private sector as % of GDP 1993 0.8

☐ Czech Republic   ☐ Slovakia

GERMANY
POLAND
N
Prague
CZECH REPUBLIC
Ostrava
Pilsen
Brno
SLOVAKIA
Kosice
AUSTRIA
Bratislava
Land over 1000 m
0   100 km
HUNGARY
UKRAINE

FIG 3.8b *Czechoslovakia: the two halves, The Guardian, 28 December 1992*

N
(FINLAND)
Gulf of Finland
Tallin
ESTONIA
(Population 1 570 000)
Baltic Sea
Riga
LATVIA
(Population 2 680 000)
• Moscow
LITHUANIA
(Population 3 700 000)
Vilnius
RUSSIAN FEDERATION
(Population 147 390 000)
Kaliningrad (part of the Russian Federation)
Minsk
BELARUS
(Population 10 200 000)
(POLAND)
• Kiev
UKRAINE
(Population 51 700 000)
MOLDOVA
(Population 4 340 000)
• Kishinev
Sea of Azov
(HUNGARY)
(ROMANIA)
Black Sea
(BULGARIA)
0   500 km

FIG 3.8a *The New Countries of eastern Europe*

- On the basis of the data you have analysed in the questions on page 47, which states do you think are more vulnerable to social unrest?

- Using Fig 3.8a as evidence, suggest why the new states feel vulnerable to any future Russian aggression.

- Czechoslovakia was another country which disappeared as a result of fragmentation. At the beginning of 1993 it split into two separate countries: the Czech republic and Slovakia. Study Fig 3.8b:
  a) Why do you think Czechoslovakia split? Suggest ethnic, social and economic reasons.
  b) Which country seems to have most benefited economically and socially from the separation?

An Ethnic Kaleidoscope: the Break-Up of Yugoslavia

From the Alpine comfort of Slovenia to the dusty poverty of Kosovo, Yugoslavia does not consist of only six republics and two Socialist Autonomous Provinces attached to the Serbian republic: it contains also dozens of different cultures and languages, three major religions and a feast of historical vendettas. Most East European countries have one national conflict to solve. … In Yugoslavia a kaleidoscope of historical patterns, soiled with liberal coatings of blood, is confusing the country's attempt to transform itself into a democracy − a feat that is almost beyond comprehension.

Yugoslavia is about to collapse − one can only hope that it will do so peacefully.

Misha Glenny, The Rebirth of History (1990).

Sadly, Misha Glenny's hope of a peaceful collapse was far too optimistic. In 1991 civil war erupted in Croatia and in 1992 Bosnia was torn apart by a brutal three-sided civil war.

Yugoslavia was created in 1918 as part of the settlement at the end of the First World War. Since the end of the Second World War Yugoslavia had been a Communist country. Under the leadership of Tito it had followed an independent course, refusing to be part of the Warsaw Pact (see Chapter 2), and at the same time becoming a popular destination for tourists from western Europe. Behind its successful image, however, ethnic rivalry and disputes continued to ferment. At times Tito had to use repressive methods to control these disputes and after his death in 1980 the break up of the country looked increasingly inevitable. The disintegration, when it occurred in the early 1990s, was rapid and violent generating the worst conflict seen in Europe since 1945.

When Slovenia, in the north of Yugoslavia, declared independence in 1991 conflict was avoided, largely because there were few ethnic complications − 95 per cent of its population is Slovene. When Croatia declared independence in the same month the ethnic conflict between Serbs and Croats boiled over into civil war as the Serbs, with the backing of the Serb-dominated Yugoslav army, tried to create autonomous Serbian areas within Croatia. In 1992 United Nations troops were deployed in an attempt to restore peace, but Serb militias continued to terrorise Croats living in Serbian held areas as part of so-called 'ethnic cleansing' operations (a term used to describe attempts to use terror to force ethnic groups to leave in order to create ethnically pure or homogeneous areas).

Macedonia declared independence later the same year. In 1992 Bosnia-Herzegovina voted for independence but again civil war broke out as Serbs fought Muslims and Croats for the creation of autonomous Serb areas within Bosnia. Then in 1993 the informal alliance between Croats and Muslims broke down and the Croats also started to fight the Muslims in order to create independent Croat areas within Bosnia. Atrocities became commonplace and millions of people were forced to become refugees. Few people even at the beginning of the 1990s would have predicted the degree of hatred and brutality which emerged in Bosnia in 1992.

FIG 3.9   *Regions in the Former Yugoslavia*

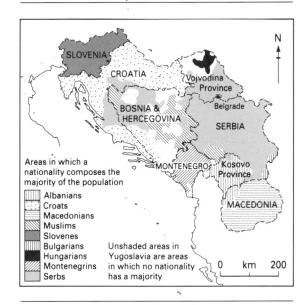

FIG 3.10   *Ethnicity 1991*

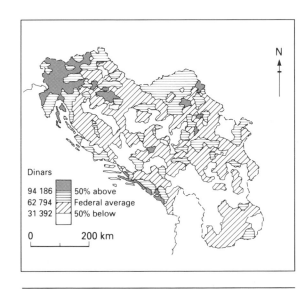

FIG 3.11   *Per Capita National Income 1991*

The break up of the country is almost complete (only tiny and ethnically homogeneous Montenegro has voted to remain with Serbia) but the conflict within and between the newly independent countries is far from over and the borders between each country may well change. In 1993 a peace plan, known as the Vance-Owen Plan, was put forward by international negotiators. The Plan proposed a division of Bosnia into independent states along ethnic lines, but the Plan failed. Muslims felt Serbians were gaining too much from their aggression. Some Serbians will not be satisfied until a 'Greater Serbia' has been

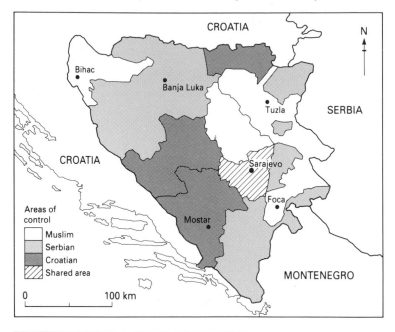

FIG **3.13**   *The Vance-Owen Plan for Bosnia 1993*

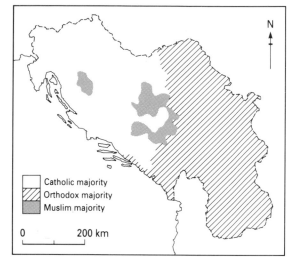

FIG **3.12**   *Religion 1991*

FIG **3.14**   *The Guardian, 18 May 1992*

Ethnic terror stalks Croatia's village streets by night

THE old Ilok peasant desultorily took his switch broom to the dusty yard around his cottage and explained: "There is a saying that he who's afraid flees. He who stays gets a beating."

As the ethnic map of this part of eastern Croatia has been redrawn over the past year of war, Andrija Matus has stayed on in this little Danube river town on the Serbian-Croatian border where he was born.

Like the dwindling number of non-Serbs who remain in Ilok, he, a Slovak, lives in fear – fear of beating, fear of murder, fear of explusion, fear of having his house, land and belongings seized by Serbian newcomers.

For centuries the region has exemplified central Europe's heady ethnic brew, home to Serbs, Croats, Hungarians, Slovaks, Ruthenians and Germans. Until last year Ilok's 10,000 inhabitants were 60 per cent Croat, 20 per cent Serb, and 20 per cent Slovak.

Now to be a non-Serb in the territories wrested by the Serbs from Croatia is to be an alien in your own country, nervously awaiting the knock on the door. It usually happens in the dead of night.

When the curfew descends every evening on this war-ravaged area, the armed thugs who have a licence to terrorise come calling on the non-Serbs left behind, nearly all old men, women or children. The thugs suggest that the non-Serbs would probably like to leave, and offer a paper for signature "voluntarily" relinquishing their property and livestock, according to United Nations officials in the region.

The deportees are then herded into buses, minibuses, or cars, and driven a few miles up the road to the death trap that is the Serb-Croat frontline.

Those expelled, according to the officials, are dumped in the middle of the no-man's land in the dark. To their rear are the Serb gunmen shooting over their heads to egg them on. Before them sit

Croatian troops nervously wondering who is coming and whether they should shoot. To the right and left of the road, the lush cornfields of Slavonia are generously laced with lethal mines.

Diane Lubin, a civilian affairs officer at the regional UN centre in Erdut, north of Ilok, says… "There were deaths in the cornfields before we arrived.

"If they stay in the cornfields, they are mined. In the dark they might be shot. It's a no-win situation. Some of them with an instinct for self-preservation lie down in the no-man's land and feign death until light breaks."

Ms Lubin's team has compiled evidence of at least 400 such evictions in the area over two weeks in April. UN refugee workers say about 1,200 non-Serb villagers have been forcibly expelled in the area in the past two months.

International aid agency workers say that since the beginning of the year, about

20,000 Serbs, most of them refugees from Croatia, have moved into the area to take over the houses of Croats and Hungarians driven away by the war.

In the past few weeks UN workers have looked on helplessly as old women clung to the doorknobs of their houses in a vain attempt to avoid the bus trip to no-man's land. Grenades get thrown through the windows of houses which newly arrived Serbs covet but owners refuse to vacate.

The vast majority of Ilok's 6,000 Croats have gone, driven out last year before the UN arrived. They have been replaced by Serbs kicked out of Croatia.

"It's a well-organised expulsion machine," Ms Lubin says. "They have lists. They know which houses they're going for. As soon as they're empty, they are reoccupied."

"The harassment, the intimidation, the threats, the waiting every night, who can live like that," Ms Lubin says.

created encompassing all the Serbian areas within Croatia and Bosnia. The present war is adding to the hatreds and desire for revenge which have soured relations in the region throughout the twentieth century.

- Study Figs 3.9 to 3.12.
  a) Summarise the spatial patterns revealed in the maps.
  b) Evaluate the following hypotheses.
   i) Yugoslavia should never have been created as a nation-state. Its eventual break up was inevitable.
   ii) The break up of Yugoslavia was totally a result of ethnic divisions.
  c) Imagine you are working for a European Union committee which has been asked to propose long-term solutions to the conflict. Prepare a short report summarising your proposals

and then compare and discuss your proposals with other people in your group. Can you achieve a consensus view in your group?

- Does the Vance-Owen Plan shown in Fig 3.13 look as though it could be a long-term solution to the conflict? Explain your answer.

- **a)** How would you define the word nationalism?
  b) How would you define the word racism?
  c) What is the difference between the two terms?
  d) Read Fig 3.14. Are Serb policies in Croatia nationalist or racist?

3.3 The Basque Country: the Fight for Greater Autonomy

More than one in four Spaniards speaks a language other than Spanish. In the regions of Galicia, Catalonia and the Basque country, which each have their own distinctive language, linguistic and nationalist issues are important.

In the north of Spain and in the extreme south-western corner of France, between the Pyrenees, the Bay of Biscay and the River Ebro, lies the home of the Basques. The Basques speak a unique language called Euskara which is totally unlike any other European language. There is disagreement over the exact size of the Basque Country. Many Basques believe it should include four provinces in Spain (Vizcaya, Guipuzcea, Alava and Navarra) and three provinces in France (Labourd, Basse-Navarre, and Soule). In reality the French provinces and Navarra are usually excluded (see Fig 3.15).

Basque nationalism has had considerable support since the 1930s. In 1936 the Spanish Government gave the Basque region autonomy but in 1937 the government was overthrown by Franco during the Spanish Civil War. Franco, who was to remain Spain's leader until 1975, executed or imprisoned thousands of Basque nationalists. The teaching of Euskara and its use in publications was made illegal, and all Basque names were banned.

In 1959 a new nationalist organisation called *Euskadi ta Askatasuna* (ETA: Euskadi and Liberty) was formed. In the late 1960s they declared war on the Spanish state. Their campaign included killing members of the police and other security forces and bombing government buildings. They said armed struggle would continue until a socialist independent Basque country was created comprising both the Spanish and French Basque provinces.

Farm in the Basque Country, France

FIG 3.15 *The Basque Country*

Although ETA and its political wing, called *Herri Batasuna*, continue to attract considerable support, the *Partido Nacionalista Vasco* (PNV) is now the most important nationalist party. The PNV aims for the greatest possible autonomy but is happy for the Basque Country to remain part of Spain. It condemns the use of violence.

In 1979 the Spanish Government held a referendum on autonomy for the Basques and the result was a massive majority in favour. The Basque country became one of Spain's new autonomous communities. A new Basque parliament was created, and a Basque police force and television station were introduced.

The Basque region is not the only part of Spain with a strong nationalist movement. Support for autonomy is particularly strong in Catalonia although in Galicia, despite the healthy state of the Galician language, support for separatism is small. The present Spanish constitution, dating from 1979, recognises the cultural and linguistic diversity of Spain. There are now six Autonomous Communities which have Spanish and at least one other language as their official languages. These communities have varying degrees of autonomy, with Catalonia and the Basque Country having the most independence.

Nationalist parties have a majority in both the Catalan and Basque parliaments.

The Basque Autonomous Community excludes the province of Navarra and has a population of about two million. Navarra is a separate autonomous community.

Basque nationalists see the Euskara language as the most important sign of Basque identity and the regional government is putting considerable effort and resources into encouraging greater use of the language. This is not an easy task, particularly as only a third of the representatives in the Basque parliament can speak Euskara fluently.

The ETA has continued its violent compaign since its aim of a socialist Basque country including, the French provinces, has not been achieved. Hundreds of people have died in bombings and shootings during the last 25 years.

- Study Fig 3.16 which shows the location of the bilingual Autonomous Communities. Describe and suggest reasons for the spatial distribution of the Communities.

FIG 3.16 *Autonomous Communities, Spain*

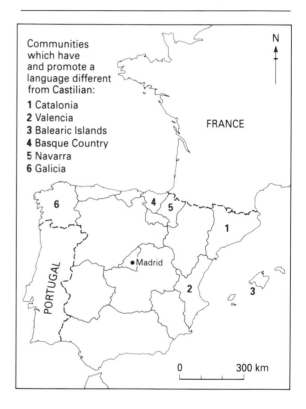

FIG 3.17 *Local Languages in the Different Autonomous Communities*

	Population over 2 years old	Native speakers		Speak the language		Understand the language		Do not understand the language	
Catalonia (Catalan)	5 856 425	2 986 776	51%	3 747 813	64%	5 287 200	91%	550 878	9%
Valencia (Catalan)	3 677 957	1 471 182	40%	1 802 198	49%	2 734 928	74%	943 029	26%
Balearic Islands (Catalan)	663 485	424 630	64%	469 880	71%	593 620	89%	69 865	11%
Basque Country (Euskara)	2 089 995	508 543	24%	513 824	25%	877 940	42%	1 212 055	58%
Navarra (Euskara)	501 506	49 741	10%	60 180	12%	75 225	15%	426 281	85%
Galicia (Galacian)	2 726 294	1 499 461	55%	2 453 664	90%	2 562 716	94%	163 578	6%
All Communities with own language	15 470 867	6 940 333	45%	9 047 559	59%	11 341 529	72%	3 384 033	22%
All Spain	37 280 743								

- Study Fig 3.17. Construct a graph to show the extent to which Euskara is used compared with Galician and Catalan in their respective communities. What conclusions can you make about the 'health' of the Basque language?

Territory	Population	Do not understand	Some knowledge	Understand and speak
Alava	262 407 (100%)	77%	14%	8%
Vizcaya	1 153 844 (100%)	64%	19%	18%
Guipúzcoa	675 654 (100%)	39%	18%	43%
Whole of Basque Country	2 091 905 (100%)	57%	18%	25%
Navarra	483 867 (100%)	84%	5%	10%

Population Census 1986 – Population over 2 years

FIG 3.18   *Basque Country and Navarra – Knowledge of Euskera*

- Study Fig 3.18 and the map showing the Basque provinces. To what extent does the data support the following hypotheses?
  - **a)** Euskara is strongest in the provinces where there is less likely to be regular contact with Spanish-speaking areas.
  - **b)** Physical barriers, such as mountain ranges, help to protect minority languages.

- Read Fig 3.19. What conclusions can you make from the articles about:
  - **a)** the extent of support in the Basque Country for ETA?
  - **b)** the political, social and economic impact of ETA?
  - **c)** the success of ETA as a separatist movement?
  - **d)** the success of the Spanish Government's policy of creating Autonomous Communities as a way of undermining calls for autonomy or independence?

FIG 3.19   *The Guardian*

Basque threat halts railway

SPAIN'S railway system was returning to normal yesterday after being brought to a standstill by threats from the Basque terrorist group, ETA. Some 200 000 people starting or ending their holidays on the busiest weekend of the year had their journeys cancelled, delayed, or re-routed after ETA warned that it had put bombs on four specified lines. Only two devices exploded. One went off on the line between Madrid and Seville; the other on the line linking Madrid to the northern city of Palencia. No one was hurt in either blast. But they showed that ETA retains its capacity to strike outside the Basque country.

Saturday's events will be particularly worrying to the promoters of the high-speed rail link between Madrid and Seville. The track is due to be opened early next year, in time for Seville's Expo 1992.

5 August 1991

Police jailed for Basque deaths

TWO Spanish police officers last night received prison sentences of 108 years and eight months each for their involvement with 'death squads' operating against Basque exiles in the south of France.

But, crucially, the judges acquitted the state of any responsibility for the two anti-terrorist detectives' actions. This was despite the admission, at a preliminary hearing by the then chief of the Spanish police, that money they used to make contact with mercenaries had been drawn from public funds.

21 September 1991

ETA deaths lead to Basque riots

HUNDREDS of Basque nationalist demonstrators put up barricades and burned vehicles across the region yesterday in protest at the death of three ETA guerrilla suspects in a gun battle with police.

The Red Cross said 17 people suffered minor injuries in clashes with police in the coastal resort of San Sebastian, where ETA supporters set fire to two cars.

The ETA suspects were shot dead 24 hours earlier during a four-hour gun battle in San Sebastian in which two Civil Guards were seriously injured. The victims, and 11 other suspects detained in simultaneous raids in other Basque towns, are believed to have formed the deadly Donosti Commando of ETA, which has been blamed for more than 60 terrorist attacks since 1989, causing 15 deaths and 50 injuries. This year alone, the commando has killed six people, including a 17-year-old girl, and injured a further 37.

19 August 1991

3.4 Power to the Regions

A Threat to the United Kingdom?: Welsh Nationalism

To exterminate a nation is a tragedy next in seriousness to exterminating humanity and to exterminate a nation's language is the next in seriousness to exterminating a nation, because a nation ceases to be a nation sooner or later after losing its language.

Emrys ap Iwan, 1907.

The houses were burned with great sadness. We are not ferocious men. It is an act of despair.

From a letter to HTV Wales from Meibion Glyndwr, a militant Welsh nationalist group.

This targeting of individuals – a sort of ethnic cleansing, Celtic-style, smacks of methods once used by the British National Party and the National Front.

Paul Wilkinson, Professor of International Relations, St Andrews University.

The UK has a population of about 56 million. 5.1 million (nine per cent) of this total live in Scotland and 2.7 million (five per cent) in Wales. Welsh independence effectively ended in 1277 but Wales was not formally united with England until 1536. Scotland's independence ended in 1707.

Until the 1960s the UK was often portrayed as a textbook example of a homogeneous society with a single culture and a common set of values. Large-scale immigration from Commonwealth countries in the 1960s effectively ended this image but it had never been an accurate picture of British society. Significant differences between different regions of the country, not least in Wales, Scotland and Northern Ireland (collectively known as the Celtic Fringe), had always been present but had often been ignored.

It is probable that the UK is one of the most centralised states in western Europe. It does not have a **federal** or regional government structure and since 1979 much of the power of local councils has been transferred to central government.

It would be wrong to suggest that the British Government does not recognise the distinctiveness of Wales and Scotland. Both regions have their own government department with their own minister. Scotland has, in many respects, its own legal and education systems. However, many would argue these are only cosmetic differences. Certainly most Scottish and Welsh decision making responsibilities lie in London.

Sixty-three per cent of the Welsh people live in the southern, relatively industrialised and urbanised, counties of West Glamorgan, Mid-Glamorgan, South Glamorgan and Gwent. The other 37 per cent live in the rural counties of

south-west, mid and north Wales. The same rural counties include most of the 19 per cent of the population which speaks Welsh. This basically north-south division has an important impact on the nationalist movement in Wales.

Plaid Cymru (meaning the Party of Wales), the Welsh nationalist political party, was formed in 1925 but it received little publicity until the late 1950s when a proposal to flood the Tryweryn Valley in Mid-Wales to provide water for Liverpool aroused considerable local opposition. Plaid Cymru saw it as a clear case of the English authorities exploiting the Welsh landscape and Welsh natural resources. In the 1959 election Plaid Cymru attracted five per cent of the votes in Wales. By the 1970 election this had increased to 12 per cent although it declined to nine per cent in the 1992 election.

One of the main problems for Plaid Cymru is that its membership and support mainly come from the Welsh speaking rural areas in mid and north Wales. The English speaking population in the southern valleys see little relevance in the party's policies.

The party has attempted to widen its support by putting less emphasis on linguistic and cultural issues and greater emphasis on economic and environmental issues but most of its electoral support is still in the rural areas.

While Plaid Cymru has adjusted its policies to win wider support other more militant nationalist organisations have emerged. In 1962 Cymdeithas Yr Iaith Cymraeg (The Welsh Language Society) formed to campaign for greater recognition and use of the Welsh language. It has used non-violent direct action to further its aims (such as occupying buildings or obliterating English words on signposts). More recently, in the 1980s, a shadowy group called Meibion Glyndwr (The Sons of Glyndwr) claimed responsibility for hundreds of arson attacks on second homes owned by English people, on government offices and on estate agents who have sold houses to English people. They have also threatened individual English people who have settled in Wales and who they claim are 'anti-Welsh'. In a recent opinion poll 57 per cent of Welsh speakers said they sympathised with Meibion Glyndwr's arson campaign. The group is named after Glyndwr who led a revolt against English rule in the early fifteenth century and defeated the English King, Henry IV. In 1413 Wales was reconquered by the English.

The Welsh language has certainly been under tremendous pressure. As well as the problems facing most minority languages, such as the fact that most television, radio, magazines, newspapers and advertising are in the dominant language, Welsh speaking communities in North Wales have had to withstand mass tourism and the purchase of houses for use as holiday homes. Under such circumstances Welsh speakers can become a minority in their own village, especially in the summer months.

While Welsh autonomy is still only supported by a minority, support for the Welsh language has grown enormously. It is now actively encouraged by most local councils and the government. Gwynedd Education Department's language policy, for example, states that '*children who identify themselves with the Welsh way of life have the moral right to an education which gives due standing to the Welsh language and the traditional Welsh heritage*'. The Welsh Channel 4 (S4C) broadcasts many of its programmes in Welsh and Radio Cymraeg provides a Welsh language service. It now seems much more likely that the language has a long-term future. However, it is generally agreed that the survival of the language still depends on continued action to encourage its use.

Welsh nationalism also has a strong sense of place and of landscape as indicated by this extract from the 1992 Plaid Cymru manifesto:

Our nationalism starts with the love of the actual territory of Wales, the fields and mountains, the lakes and streams. In the past Wales has been ravaged by slag heaps and coal tips, drowned by reservoirs, sterilised by coniferous forest, shelled by army tanks, polluted by nuclear fall-out. Now even the atmosphere we breathe is a threat. Today, more than ever, our love of Wales demands a fight for survival.

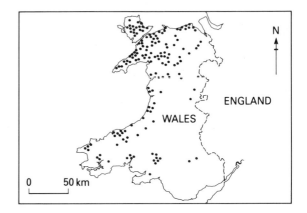

FIG 3.21   *The Distribution of Meidion Glyndwr Arson Attacks, Geographic Magazine, March 1990*

- Use the data and a copy of the base map in Fig 3.20 to construct a choropleth map showing the spatial variations in the support for Plaid Cymru in the 1992 General Election.

- Is there any correlation between your choropleth map and the pattern of Welsh language use shown in Fig 3.20?

- How do you think a Welsh nationalist would define the differences between being Welsh and being English?

- Comment on the distribution of arson attacks shown in Fig 3.21.

- Summarise the shifts in the geographical location of decision making being proposed in Plaid Cymru's resolution in Fig 3.22 overleaf.

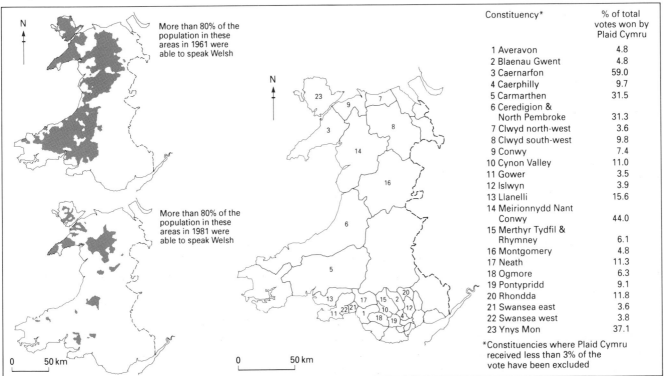

More than 80% of the population in these areas in 1961 were able to speak Welsh

More than 80% of the population in these areas in 1981 were able to speak Welsh

Constituency*	% of total votes won by Plaid Cymru
1 Averavon	4.8
2 Blaenau Gwent	4.8
3 Caernarfon	59.0
4 Caerphilly	9.7
5 Carmarthen	31.5
6 Ceredigion & North Pembroke	31.3
7 Clwyd north-west	3.6
8 Clwyd south-west	9.8
9 Conwy	7.4
10 Cynon Valley	11.0
11 Gower	3.5
12 Islwyn	3.9
13 Llanelli	15.6
14 Meirionnydd Nant Conwy	44.0
15 Merthyr Tydfil & Rhymney	6.1
16 Montgomery	4.8
17 Neath	11.3
18 Ogmore	6.3
19 Pontypridd	9.1
20 Rhondda	11.8
21 Swansea east	3.6
22 Swansea west	3.8
23 Ynys Mon	37.1

*Constituencies where Plaid Cymru received less than 3% of the vote have been excluded

FIG 3.20   *Spatial Variations in Support for Plaid Cymru*

Plaid Cymru Conference Resolution

THE Conference further declares that the nations and historic regions should have their own direct representations in the EU institutions. We call for the establishment of a new second chamber by 1995, to be called 'The Senate', whose members would be appointed by the national or regional assemblies. Appropriate sub-committees of the Senate would be responsible for 'regional' issues of concern to limited number of members, e.g. the North Sea. Both the Senate and European Parliament would have power to initiate and scrutinise legislation and would gradually take over the powers and the political and executive functions of the Council of Ministers and Commission, and this process should be completed by 2000. For legislation to be enacted, the agreement of both the Senate and the European Parliament would be required. An enlarged council of Ministers based on nations and historic regions could remain as a consultative body if this is deemed of value and the Commission would act as the civil service to the new legislative body. After 1995 European Commissioners would be nominated by national/regional parliaments in rotation, and appointed by the European Senate. The European Community shall be a free association from which any nation or historic region would be able to exercise the right of withdrawal. Nations and historic regions would be the units within this system in place of the present nation-states.

WELSH PARLIAMENT

A Welsh Parliament when established would assume responsibilities for all legislative and executive functions not carried out by the European Parliament and Senate and would be consulted by those bodies on all primary and secondary legislation affecting Wales. The Welsh Parliament would take its part in the social, cultural and economic developments in Europe, and would support moves to enshrine the values embodied in policy statements such as the Social Charter.

FIG 3.22   *Plaid Cymru Conference Resolution*

- Read Fig 3.23. Produce a table summarising the costs and benefits of independence for Scotland. Do you think Scotland has a stronger case than Wales for independence?

Wealthy Regionalism: Northern Italy

Before unification in 1861 Italy consisted of a number of separate states. Despite political unification Italy has continued to be an economically, and in some respects a culturally, divided country. Fig 3.24 gives an indication of the extent of the north–south divide. The south, which is home to about 20 million people, forms 41 per cent of Italy's land area but only produces 24 per cent of its GDP and accounts for only 27 per cent of national consumption.

FIG 3.23   *The Independent*

Big enough, rich enough, but…

Should Scotland become independent? Up to now the main economic debate has been over whether it gains or loses from the union in narrow public finance terms: does it pay more in tax than it gets public spending? There has to be that debate, for if Scotland is to be independent, there needs to be a deal on North Sea oil revenues. But other things matter more: size, wealth, efficiency, flexibility.

Anybody who thinks Scotland is not big enough is wrong. As an independent country it would be number 30 in the world in terms of its gross national product, behind Saudi Arabia and Turkey but ahead of Poland, Iran and Venezuela. It would have a somewhat smaller GNP than the Nordic countries Norway, Finland and Denmark, to which it is often compared. But it would be much larger than Greece or Portugal and more than double the size of the Republic of Ireland.

Anybody who thinks it isn't rich enough is wrong. True, it has a slightly lower income per head than the UK. But it would still be a relatively rich country: number 23, slotting in between Australia and New Zealand.

The real issue is whether it would become more efficient, which in turns means more flexible. If the world has learnt anything from the divergent performance of such countries as Korea and Poland, it is that being nimble matters more than having a big steel industry.

Were Scotland on its own it would, objectively, have a number of assets that would serve it very well. It is strong in energy and financial services. Aside from being an oil exporter, it is also an electricity exporter from its hydro and particularly nuclear power industries. (Scotland would be second to France in the European Community in terms of the proportion of power generated by nuclear reactors.)

It would have a strong financial services industry, with two large independent banks, half a dozen large insurance groups, and Britain's main investment trusts head-quartered there. (Edinburgh is thirteenth in the world financial centres in terms of funds managed, behind Los Angeles but ahead of Chicago.)

Scotland does not, contrary to popular opinion, have a particularly large manufacturing sector: proportionately, its manufacturing is smaller than in the UK as a whole. That may in fact turn out to be a strength rather than a weakness, if manufacturing throughout Europe is squeezed over the next decade – but that is conjecture.

On the debit side, though, Scotland creates proportionately fewer new businesses than England. As a result it is dependent on large businesses, usually with their headquarters elsewhere. It is not just key political decisions that are taken outside Scotland: key commercial decisions are too. it is difficult for an economy to be flexible if such decisions are being taken at a distance – and political independence would not automatically lead to commercial independence.

On the other hand, Scotland ought to have an extremely flexible workforce, for it certainly has a relatively well-educated one: 77 per cent of 16-year-olds staying in education against 63 per cent for the UK as a whole.

Objectively then, Scotland appears a competitive country – with pluses and minuses, as one might expect. But to argue that it would be better off on its own, one has to believe that independence would bring its own dynamics: that the economy would become more adaptive and flexible were the Scots to control their own political destiny.

The broad conclusion is that Scotland and the rest of the UK would be roughly square in terms of their public finances. One could certainly construct a deal to see that they *were* square without too much difficulty.

But at the end of the day it would not matter that much. Two or three years of good growth would more than compensate for a poor deal on North Sea revenues: oil revenues in the coming year will be perhaps £2bn; two years' growth at 4 per cent would add more than £3bn to Scotland's GNP.

And getting that higher growth is the hard part: taking an efficient but not particularly flexible economy and turning it into a much more nimble one. It is not clear that the Scottish National Party appreciates this need. But only people in Scotland can guess whether such a transformation would follow independence – not even people of Scottish ancestry who spend most of the year south of the border.

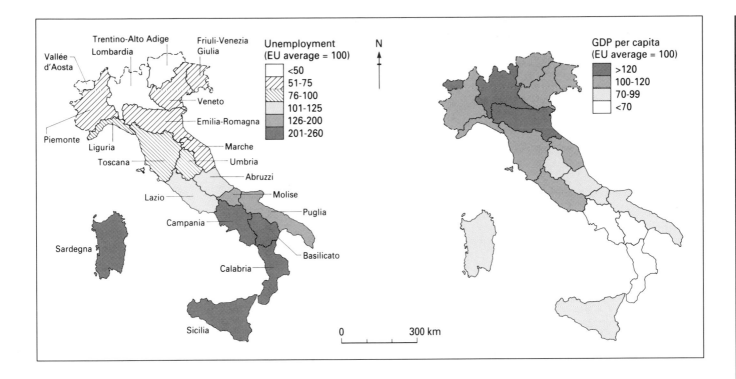

FIG 3.24 *North-South Divide, Italy (above)*

FIG 3.25 *The Financial Times, 30 March 1992*

Lombard warrior sets out to slay giants

THE MESSAGE of the Lombard League is brash and combative.

The populist movement, certain to disrupt the traditional voting pattern in northern Italy in the April 5 general elections, has chosen as its symbol a 12th century Lombard warrior brandishing a sword. Every poster mixes demands for autonomy with defiance of the Christian Democrat-led government in Rome.

"They are all ruffians in Rome," says Mr Luigi Moretti, one of the League's two Euro-MPs and secretary for the Bergamo region. "We want to make the Christian Democrats die of fright in these elections," he adds, echoing the bellicose contempt of the Italian political establishment shown by the league's leader, Mr Umberto Bossi.

Throughout Italy's hard-working northern industrial belt in cities like Bergamo the League has emerged as a big new force and is certain to remove votes not just from the Christian Democrats but across the traditional party spectrum. Nationwide, it could get 10 per cent of the vote.

Although Mr Bossi, the League's 50-year-old leader, is being ignored by the national media, his abrasive, emotional speeches decrying corruption of the traditonal parties and demanding greater regional autonomy have struck a chord among workers, the professional classes and small businessmen.

Typical of Mr Bossi is a comment in a written interview for the FT. "The league has threatened a campaign of non-payment of taxes to show the state that those producing the nation's wealth are exasperated: that they will no longer agree to work for a political class which sustains its absolute power enriching and swelling the numbers of its clientele; that they will no longer work for a free-spending state which survives by devouring its own citizens like Saturn devouring his children."

The son of a textile worker who moved from a small northern town near Barese to Milan, Mr Bossi, like many of his generation, was the first to experience higher education and grow up with the industrialisation of the north. A poor student, he gravitated into local politics formally founding the "Autonomist Lombard League" in 1984. On this ticket he was elected a senator for Varese in the 1987 general elections.

The initial stamp of the league was distinctly "autonomist" with a platform of demands having parallels with that of the Scottish Nationalists' calls for greater independence from parliament in Westminster.

Mr Bossi encouraged the formation of "autonomist" leagues in other regions of the North – in Emiglia Romagna, Liguria, Piedmont, Tuscany and the Veneto. Together in February 1990 these formed with Lombardy the Northern League as a federal movement, and subsequently leagues have been added covering central Italy and the south.

Thus while the movement is popularly referred to as the Lombard League it consists of a number of associated autonomist groupings headed by Mr Bossi.

He is proposing a radical constitutional shake-up of Italy into three blocks – the North, Centre and South. "The league wants a federal constitution with a central parliament that co-ordinates the activities of the parliaments of the three [blocks] which have a degree of autonomy which will be modelled on the experience of the Swiss, American and German models...to avoid the current damaging experience of centralism."

The essential aim is to ensure that northern savings cease to finance the nation's huge public sector deficit, much of which goes on ill-controlled transfers to the south.

Its most seductive slogan is "further from Rome and closer to Europe". This underlines Mr Bossi's threat to found a republic of the north, linked to Europe but separate from the rest of Italy, if the Rome politicians fail to reform their ways.

The gap between the north and the south widened during the 1980s as northern Italy became one of the wealthiest regions in Europe. The south suffers from a number of environmental and historical handicaps:

- low rainfall with high evaporation rates in the summer makes agriculture difficult;
- a mountainous terrain and poor soils add to the problems facing farmers;
- for centuries absentee landlords dominated the region. They made little effort to improve farm productivity;
- the lack of raw materials and the region's remoteness from the main European centres of population have hindered industrial development.

Between 1950 and 1987 the south (or *Mezzogiorno*) was aided by a special government development fund called *La Cassa del Mezzogiorno* – its brief being to narrow the economic gap between the north and the south. Incentives were offered to private companies to locate in the south. After 1971 80 per cent of all investment in state-owned industries had to be in the south. The Cassa has also funded infrastructure improvements and tourist developments. The north-south motorway, the *Autostrada del Sol* was an early example of the attempts to integrate the Mezzogiorno into the northern economy. Policies aimed at agricultural reform were also implemented to reduce inefficiency in southern agriculture. Between 1950 and 1975 £20 billion was spent by the Cassa (some of this money coming from international agencies such as the World Bank). This was equivalent to £1000 per inhabitant of the Mezzogiorno. After the closure of the Cassa, smaller and more specialised aid projects were implemented. The region has now become dependent on EU regional development funds.

Some of the schemes designed to help the south were successful but the results were largely disappointing. The southern economy remained very weak and self-sustained growth did not happen. The economy continued to be dependent on aid from the north. Between 1955 and 1980 more than five million people migrated from the south to the north, although this was offset in the south by a high rate of natural increase. However, despite growing prosperity in the north, the decline of traditional industries during the 1980s has meant that northern cities are no longer the magnet they once were.

Little has been achieved in narrowing the social divide between the two parts of the country. In his book *The New Europe*, Minshull commented that *'south of Rome there is a clearly identifiable atmosphere of dessication, impoverishment, lack of activity and an indefinable impression that this part of Europe is very different'*. Many southerners who have moved to the north, or second generation migrants, find difficulty in integrating into northern society, and yet also find that if they return to the south they are no longer readily accepted back into the communities there. In an opinion poll in 1988, 41 per cent of northerners thought southerners were 'backward' and many believe that southerners are 'lazy'. Such views are reinforced by the strong regional pride which has always been a feature of Italian life. In some cases the views held about people from the other half of the country are blatantly racist.

One of the most important factors contributing to this failure to integrate the country socially and economically, has been widespread corruption and organised crime. The Christian Democrats, who were the ruling party in Italy for decades until 1994, became increasingly linked with corruption. Public money has been used to extend political influence or to grant favours (a system of **patronage** known as the *sottogoverno*). Some politicians have been in league with the Mafia. In 1992, following the murder of a judge by the Mafia, public opposition to this corruption reached a new peak. 1993 saw more and more leading politicians charged with corruption offences. It is an accepted fact that much of the money spent by La Cassa del Mezzogiorno passed into private or Mafia hands. In some cases potentially successful industrial development schemes were undermined by the Mafia (or the *Camorra* in Naples) in order to protect the industries they controlled.

A new political force, called the Northern League, has emerged in northern Italy. Their support is based on peoples' dissatisfaction with bureaucracy, inefficiency and corruption in the national government. Many also believe that wealth created in the north is being used to 'prop up' an inefficient and corrupt southern economy and a bureaucratic central government in Rome. In 1993 the Northern League won control of most of the main towns and cities in the north including Milan. It obtained eight per cent of the votes in the 1994 general election and a much higher proportion of the votes within northern regions such as Lombardy. It is now the fourth largest party in Italy and the second largest in Lombardy, the northern region centred on Milan. It has members in all levels of government including two MEPs in the European Parliament.

The Northern League is an umbrella organisation for leagues in the northern regions of Piemonte (Piedmont), Liguria, Lombardia, Toscana (Tuscany), Veneto (Venice) and Emilia-Romagna, but it is the Lombard League, formed in 1984, which is dominant. Lombardy (population nine million) is the wealthiest region in Italy, with Milan being the country's financial and industrial centre. During the 1980s the region's economy grew by eight per cent a year, the highest regional growth in Europe. The League wants to form a federal Italy with three regions (North, Central and South), each region having a considerable degree of autonomy. The central authority would be responsible for defence and foreign policy but all other decision making powers would be devolved to the autonomous regions.

The League espouses the view that Lombardy is a nation in its own right with its own distinctive culture (but not its own language), and it is significant that the League's MEPs are members of the same parliamentary group as the Scottish National Party. Lombards, according to the League, feel they have more in common with the French and Swiss than they do with southern Italians. The League also opposes migration from southern Italy and from outside the EU which has led to accusations against the League of racism. The League strongly denies such accusations claiming that they are merely protecting regional identity. The League's leader, Umberto Bossi, has said *'we don't want our money to go to the south because if it goes to the south it goes to the Mafia.'* Without *'the burden of the south'* Bossi believes Lombardy could be as wealthy as Switzerland. He has also commented that *'it would take a government of the Lombard League a year maximum to purge the stench of the mafia from Milan'*.

Italian politics are changing so rapidly that it is difficult to predict the extent to which the League may affect future policies in Italy. It fought the 1994 election in alliance with the new ruling *Forza Italia* party and so the government may well be influenced by League policies. The League is certainly a major force within northern Italy.

- 'Italy is split into a wealthy north and a poor south.' Is this an accurate statement according to the information in Fig 3.24?

- Read Fig 3.25. What evidence is there in the article that:
  a) the Northern League is a separatist organisation?
  b) the League is a racist organisation?

- Using the two maps in Fig 3.24 and an atlas as evidence, construct a map showing the possible extent of the three regions proposed by the League.

- 'The League is encouraging northerners to be selfish.' To what extent do you agree with this statement?

3.5 Can Minority Cultures Survive?: Alpine Minorities

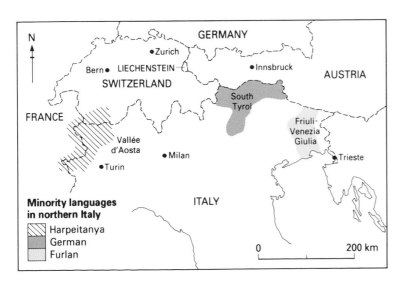

FIG 3.26 *The Italian Special Status Regions*

The Alps are home to a number of linguistic and cultural minorities which are largely unknown outside the region. For thousands of years waves of migrants or invaders have moved through the area and for hundreds of years the mountains have formed a border zone dividing territories or states and so the Alps have been subject to many different cultural influences. The terrain has also helped to preserve minority cultures with valley populations divided by impassable mountains. (See Fig 3.26).

One of these groups, the Harpeitanians, is found in the areas including Haute Savoie in France, Valais in Switzerland and Vallée d'Aosta in Italy. The Harpeitanians living in the Vallée d'Aosta are also known as the Valdaostans or Le Valdotain. Their language, called Harpeitanya, is a hybrid (or mixture) of

French and Provencal, the old language of southern France. The Vallée d'Aosta in Italy forms one of three special status or semi–autonomous regions in northern Italy.

The other two special status regions are the German speaking region of South Tyrol and the Furlan speaking region of Friuli Venezia Giulia. Furlan is another little-known minority language.

By giving these regions a degree of autonomy the Italian Government has recognised their cultural and linguistic distinctiveness.

- Using evidence from the article in Fig 3.27 evaluate the following hypotheses.
  a) Attempts by central governments to eradicate minority cultures in fact increase support for nationalism.

b) Widespread support for separatism is necessary before central governments will grant a region its autonomy.

c) Economic development and prosperity are the main threats to European cultural minorities in the 1990s.

- Assuming Vallée d'Aosta became fully independent what policies do you think the new government would need to introduce to:
  a) protect the cultural identity of the people?
  b) conserve the environment?

- To what extent would the measures you have proposed in the second question threaten the economy of the area?

FIG **3.27** *Geographical Magazine, October 1990*

Le Valdôtain – An Endangered Species?

When Augustus Caesar marched triumphantly into the Aosta Valley in 23BC, he founded the town of Augusta Praetoria and compelled the indigenous Salassi to erect a monument in his honour. The inscripton reads: "The Salassi, for a long time, defended their home – they succumbed" Three hundred years later, the Roman legions had withdrawn and Augusta Praetoria, now Aosta, was once again in the hands of the Salassi.

Today's Valdaostans have shown the same intractable resilience as their ancestors. This century, the first major threat to the Valdaostans' distinct identity came in the 1930s with Mussolini's policies of cultural assimiliation. Both Harpeitanya and French were banned and place-names were changed to their Italian form: Aoste to Aosta, Villeneuve to Villa Nuova and Saint Pierre to San Piero. Even family names were forcibly Italianized. But as with the Salassi, cultural repression merely served to strengthen the resolve of the Valdaostans. In the latter years of the Second World War, the region was one of the hot-beds of dissent against Italian fascism and the Nazi occupation.

In the post-war years, while Italy was drawing up a constitution for the new republic, the status of Vallée d'Aoste was being decided. Extremists advocated separatism or restoring of the region's historical links with the French Savoy. The hypothetical 'État Montagne',

which also included the Swiss Valais, would have played the role of a neutral buffer-state between two European powers. These ideas, however, were limited to a small intelligentsia and never made any significant political headway. Eventually, as a form of compromise, Vallée d'Aoste was granted autonomy in 1948. Names were changed back to their original French forms and the teaching of the French language was resumed.

In recent decades the increasing affluence in western Europe and the attractive recreational environmental of Vallée d'Aoste have brought a new threat to the mountain culture – mass tourism. In the commune of Courmayeur, the 'normal' population is boosted from 5,000 to 25,000 in the peak winter season, and to 40–50,000 in August. The scale of the tourism has necessitated a vast expansion of local services and an imported workforce to man them, the majority of which originate from the Italian south, expecially Calabria. The rising level of second-home ownership, particularly among the inhabitants of Piedmont, Lombardy and Liguria, has resulted in a boom in the local construction industry.

These changes are bringing great wealth into the region but they are also posing a serious threat to the indigenous culture – as the proportion (presently 65 per cent) of 'vrais Valdôtains' decreases and intermarriage increases, the language and traditions are being lost. Socio-

economic change in Vallée d'Aoste has been accelerated by the opening of the Grand-Saint-Bernard tunnel in 1964 and the Mont Blanc tunnel in 1965. Whereas previously cross-border traffic had to rely on the seasonally operational passes of the Petit and Grand-Saint-Bernard, the construction of the two tunnels made the region immediately accessible to Switzerland and France all year round. Stimulated by the growth of the EEC, these tunnels have become major communication routes linking Italy with the whole of western Europe.

The increase in commercial traffic is having an adverse effect on the environment: peaks of 3–5,000 trucks a day on the valley's inadequate road system create congestion, noise and air pollution. Atmospheric lead levels are now higher in Aosta than in the centre of Rome. An underground motorway, presently under constuction, may alleviate the congestion but will do little to reduce pollution levels.

The environment is also under pressure from tourism: skiing and the expansion of pistes has resulted in deforestation which has led in turn to the loss of natural habitat and soil erosion. The increased run-off, which is aggravated by urban expansion in the Doire Valley, creates hydrological problems. These have necessitated extensive canalization of the Doire and many of its tributaries, which merely 'exports' the flood hazard downstream.

As other Alpine minorities have realized, regional autonomy has done little to prevent the loss of language and the destruction of the environment. Cultural absorption into Italy is not being checked due to the vast economic rewards associated with these changes. Despite the declining usage of their Harpeitanian patois, the Valdaostans' sense of identity is still very strong – but many communities have allowed themselves to be thrust into the 20th Century and into the heart of Europe.

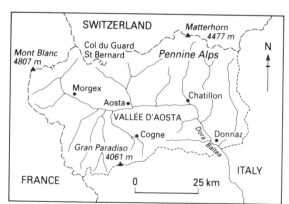

ESSAY

1 'Wales, northern Italy and Yugoslavia are each associated with separatist groups. However, the causes of separatism are very different in the three areas.'

Discuss the extent to which you agree with this statement.

2 'Until the end of the 1980s the possibility of nuclear war between East and West was the greatest threat to peace in Europe. Now the greatest threat to peace is nationalism.'

To what extent do you agree with this statement?

3 Nationalism can be defined as a desire to protect a distinctive culture or to obtain political power for a particular cultural group. Racism, on the other hand, can be defined as a hatred of other cultures or a belief that one culture is superior to others.

Using evidence from around Europe to what extent do you think nationalists are also racists?

4 Does it matter if minority cultures or languages in Europe die out?

5 'Separatism and nationalism have already changed the map of Europe more rapidly since 1990 than at any time since 1945. They are likely to cause further changes to the map during the rest of the 1990s.'

To what extent do you agree with this statement?

Farming in The Alps

Manorbier, Dyfed, Wales

Bilingual Sign in Gwynedd, Wales

Glossary

autonomy	Independence. The freedom to make decisions without outside interference.
citizenship	Having full legal rights as a resident of a country.
confederation	A group of countries, states or regions which co-operate closely with each other.
culture	The customs, lifestyle and beliefs held by a group of people or a nation.
federal	A system of government where a number of states or regions share a central government but retain a considerable amount of independence. The USA, Australia and Germany, for example, have federal systems.
linguistic	Connected with language.
nation-state	A country with its own government and borders. The term is usually used to refer to a country which is dominated by one cultural, ethnic or linguistic group.
patronage	Support given to a favoured person. Appointing people who agree with you for important jobs.

The People of
Population an
Migration

Europe:

KEY IDEAS

4.1 Europe is seeing a number of important demographic changes which together form a 'second demographic transition'. Birth rates are falling throughout Europe. Southern Europe has seen a particularly rapid fall. By the end of the first decade of the twenty-first century most of Europe will be experiencing population decline.

4.2 Life expectancy is rising in most of Europe.

4.3 Due to declining fertility and rising life expectancy European countries are seeing an ageing of their populations and this is likely to have important implications for future social policy.

4.4 Since 1945 Europe has been a destination for a large number of international migrants.

4.5 Germany in particular has received large numbers of migrant workers over recent years but very few have been given German nationality.

4.6 Immigration from less developed countries outside Europe is becoming a major issue in some European countries. This flow of migrants could well increase over the next decade.

4.7 Migration from eastern Europe has also become a major issue. Germany in particular has attracted many of these migrants.

4.8 Europe has seen increasing activity by racist right-wing groups in recent years. These groups are violently opposed to immigration.

4.9 In the 1990s a number of European countries have taken steps to reduce immigration.

4.1 A Second Demographic Revolution?: the Decline in Birth Rates

About 500 million people live in Europe but Europeans form a decreasing proportion of the world's population. In 1950 16 per cent of the world's population lived in Europe. By 1990 this had declined to nine per cent and by 2025 only six per cent of the world's population will be European.

Europe, compared with less developed countries, has a low death rate, a low birth rate and a low population growth rate. In fact, current projections predict that by 2005 western Europe's population will start to decline and by 2010 this decline will extend to southern Europe. Only in northern and eastern Europe will the population slowly grow.

The decline in the share of the world's population living in Europe is caused by the fact that by the second half of the twentieth century Europe had passed through what is known as the **demographic transition** (see Fig 4.1a). Most less developed countries, on the other hand, have barely begun this process (see Fig 4.1b).

FIG 4.1a *The Demographic Transition, Developed Countries*

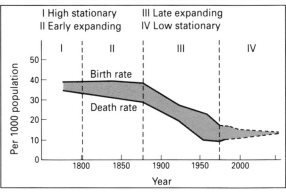

FIG 4.1b *The Demographic Transition, Less Developed Countries*

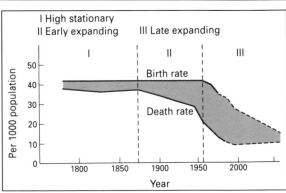

Country	Millions 1990 Population	2000 Population
Albania	3.25	3.80
Andorra	0.05	0.05
Austria	7.58	7.61
Belarus	10.30	*
Belgium	9.85	9.83
Bosnia & Herzegovina	4.44	*
Bulgaria	9.01	9.07
Croatia	4.68	*
Cyprus	0.70	0.76
Czech Republic	10.30	*
Denmark	5.14	5.15
Estonia	2.70	*
Finland	4.98	5.01
France	56.14	58.15
Germany	79.48	76.96
Gibraltar	0.03	0.03
Greece	10.05	10.19
Hungary	10.55	10.53
Iceland	0.25	0.27
Ireland	3.72	4.09
Italy	57.06	57.20
Latvia	2.70	*
Liechenstein	0.03	0.03
Lithuania	3.70	*
Luxembourg	0.37	0.38
Macedonia	2.09	*
Malta	0.35	0.37
Moldova	4.40	*
Monaco	0.03	0.03
Netherlands	14.95	15.83
Norway	4.21	4.33
Poland	38.42	40.37
Portugal	10.29	10.59
Romania	23.27	24.35
Serbia & Montenegro	10.39	*
San Marino	0.02	0.03
Slovakia	5.30	*
Slovenia	1.94	*
Spain	39.19	40.67
Sweden	8.44	8.56
Switzerland	6.61	6.76
Ukraine	51.80	*
United Kingdom	57.24	58.39
Vatican City	0.001	0.001
Countries not totally European		
Russian Federation	148.00	*
Turkey	58.69	66.79
TOTAL	498.37	510.02

* : 2000 estimates n/a

FIG 4.2 Populations of European Countries

- The demographic transition is a model of population change.
  a) Why is it called a model?
  b) What are the benefits of using models to help explain real processes?
  c) What are the drawbacks of using models to help explain real processes?

- Study Fig 4.3. Describe, and attempt to explain, any differences between the age-sex structures of the populations in Europe and those outside Europe.

The timing and rates of the changes comprising the European transition varied from country to country but the pattern was broadly similar across Europe. At the beginning of the nineteenth century both birth or **fertility rates** and death or **mortality rates** were high. During the nineteenth and first half of the twentieth centuries mortality rates fell in response to improvements in medicine, incomes, sanitation, education, housing and diet.

The decline in birth rates followed during the twentieth century. Fertility rates started to decline rapidly between 1890 and 1920 almost everywhere in Europe.

Industrialisation played a part in this decline by reducing the importance of the family as an economic unit. Children were less likely to be needed as a source of family labour and large families were more likely to be seen by parents as a threat to the family's prosperity. The spread of literacy and universal education also helped to change traditional attitudes to children and to the role of women. Increasing use of early forms of contraception also played an important part although this was rarely approved of in public. In fact in 1920 the French Government made family planning publicity illegal. Early forms of contraception included vaginal sponges soaked in spermicides such as vinegar or lemon.

Only in the two decades following the end of the Second World War was the decline in fertility interrupted, with birth rates reaching a new peak in many countries in the mid-1960s. Since 1965 the original downward trend has returned.

The demographic transition model assumed that fertility would stabilise at replacement level resulting in zero population growth (see Fig 4.1a). The **replacement level fertility** rate is 2.1 – that is, each woman having an average of 2.1 children during her life. In reality fertility has continued to fall to below replacement level. A lower than replacement

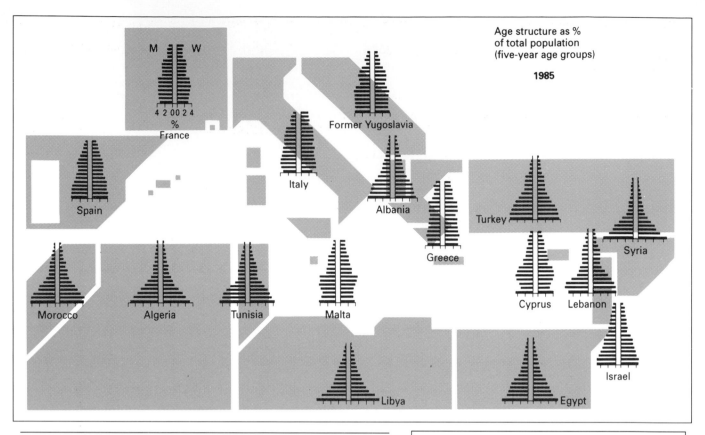

FIG 4.3 *Age Structure in Mediterranean Countries 1985*

level fertility rate does not mean that the total population starts to decline immediately (due to complexities in the population's age structure) but if this trend is maintained population decline in the early twenty-first century is inevitable. Some experts believe that Europe is entering a 'second demographic transition' – a stage beyond the original transition. It is quite possible that the 'natural' level of fertility in modern European societies is below replacement level.

In Britain, fertility has been below replacement level since 1973. Official statistics predict a gradual population increase from 56.1 million in 1991 to 59.6 million 2027. The population will only begin to decline from 2030. By then, three or four decades of below replacement level fertility will have occurred and the decline is likely to continue for some time whatever happens to fertility after 2030.

- Redraw Fig 4.1a to incorporate Europe's second demographic transition.

- Study Fig 4.4. Why do you think so many of the growth rate percentages in the table are positive if population decline is likely throughout western and southern Europe by 2010?

Some European governments have shown concern over the prospect of declining or stabilising population. During Chirac's presidential campaign in France in 1988 he expressed the view that *'Our population can be the biggest in Europe in a few decades as long as we have a policy that encourages families.'* A number of

Selected countries/areas	Population (millions)		Growth rate (percentages)
	1990	2025	1990–2025
Europe	498.4	515.2	3.3
European Union			
Belgium	9.8	9.4	–4.3
Denmark	5.1	4.9	–4.1
France	56.1	60.4	7.1
Ireland	3.7	5.0	26.0
Germany (West)	61.3	55.1	–11.3
Greece	10.0	10.1	1.0
Italy	57.1	53.0	–7.7
Netherlands	15.0	16.8	10.7
Portugal	10.3	10.9	5.5
Spain	39.2	42.3	7.3
United Kingdom	57.2	59.7	4.2
Other Western Europe			
Austria	7.6	7.3	–4.1
Finland	5.0	5.1	2.0
Norway	4.2	4.5	6.7
Sweden	8.4	8.6	2.3
Switzerland	6.6	6.8	2.9
Eastern Europe	113.2	122.9	7.9

FIG 4.4 *Population Growth Rates 1990–2025*

eastern European Communist governments attempted to boost fertility by offering financial incentives to parents.

Trends in fertility rates since the 1960s follow a broad geographical pattern:

– northern and western Europe: fertility had declined to below replacement level by the 1970s although the rate of decline slowed or even reversed in the 1980s. West Germany had the lowest rate in Europe until the 1990s. Sweden is a notable exception in this region with above replacement level fertility being reached in 1990;

– southern Europe: the decline in fertility started slightly later here but the pace of decline was maintained throughout the 1980s and rates are now below replacement level. Some countries in this region have experienced a very rapid decline – particularly Spain and Italy. Italy now has the lowest rate in Europe with an estimated rate of 1.27 in 1991. In other words on average each woman will have 1.27 children during her life;

– eastern Europe: fertility rose in parts of this region during the 1970s but decline followed. Only in Poland, Romania and Albania is fertility above replacement level.

FIG 4.5 *Fertility Rates*

Country (ranked by 1990 Fertility Rate)	1970	1980	1990
European Community			
Irish Republic	3.87	3.23	2.17
United Kingdom	2.45	1.89	1.84
France	2.48	1.95	1.80
Denmark	1.95	1.55	1.67
Netherlands	2.57	1.60	1.62
Luxembourg	1.97	1.50	1.62
Belgium	2.25	1.69	1.61
Germany (West)	2.02	1.45	1.50
Portugal	2.76	2.19	1.48*
Greece	2.34	2.23	1.43
Spain	2.84	2.22	1.30*
Italy	2.43	1.69	1.29
Other western European countries			
Sweden	1.94	1.68	2.14
Norway	2.24	1.72	1.93
Switzerland	2.10	1.55	1.59
Austria	2.29	1.65	1.45
East European countries			
Albania	5.16	3.62	2.96*
Soviet Union	2.42	2.24	2.26
Romania	2.89	2.45	2.19
Poland	2.20	2.28	2.04
Czechoslovakia	2.07	2.15	1.94
Yugoslavia	2.30	2.12	1.88*
Hungary	1.97	1.92	1.79
Bulgaria	2.18	2.05	1.73
Germany (East)	2.19	1.94	1.40

* = 1989 figure

- Summarise the trends indicated in Fig 4.5.
- Explain what the graph in Fig 4.6 indicates about fertility trends.

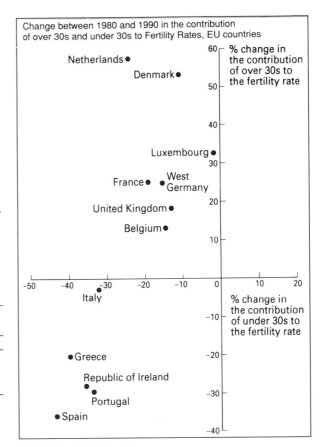

FIG 4.6 *Age and Fertility Rates, EU Countries*

The Decline in Fertility in Italy

By 1991 the fertility rate in Italy had declined to 1.27 – the lowest in the world. Having only one child or no children has become the norm. So why has fertility fallen so dramatically? Many of the reasons are similar to those causing the fertility decline in the late nineteeth and early twentieth centuries.

– The standard of living in northern Italy has improved considerably over recent decades and greater affluence usually leads to a decline in fertility. On the other hand this does not adequately explain why the decline has gone further than in other countries.

– Between 1971 and 1991 the number of men in the workforce remained constant but the number of working women rose by over 40 per cent. This is not an unusual trend in Europe but it can be argued that Italian working mothers face more difficult problems, partly because state and private child minding facilities are generally poorly developed and partly because male attitudes to working women are more traditional and conservative. So women who choose to work are more likely to delay having a family or choose not to have children in favour of their career.

Average family size in Italy by major geographic region 1951–1991

	1951	1961	1971	1981	1991
North	3.7	3.4	3.1	2.8	2.6
Centre	4.1	3.7	3.4	3.0	2.8
South	4.2	3.9	3.7	3.3	3.1
Italy (Total)	4.0	3.6	3.3	3.0	2.8

Fig 4.7 *Average Family Size, Italy 1951–1991*

– Italian society has become more materialistic and individualistic over recent decades and more people are choosing not to have children in order to protect their spending power and freedom of choice.
– The influence of Catholicism has declined, particularly in northern Italy, and this has led to a change in attitudes to the role of women in society and to contraception.
– Contraception has had a major impact on fertility throughout Europe. In particular the pill and the IUD, both launched in the 1960s, have allowed women to consciously plan family size.

This decline in fertility will have important repercussions on the structure of the Italian population. By 2001 25 per cent of all households will consist of one person and 30 per cent of two people. 50 per cent of single person households will be over 65 years old. The traditional Italian family with three or more children will be rare.

● Summarise the trends indicated in Fig 4.7.

4.2 Living Longer: Rising Life Expectancy

The changes in mortality over recent decades have not been as dramatic as the changes in fertility but they have been significant. In the 1960s the long-term mortality decline in most western European countries suffered a temporary halt. Worsening rates of heart disease and lung cancer were partly to blame. Since then the decline has resumed and improvements have been particularly large in southern Europe. In 1960 life expectancy for Portugese females was about eight years less than for Dutch females. The male life expectancy differed by ten years. By 1989 these differences had been reduced to two years for females and two and a half years for males despite the rise in life expectancy in the Netherlands. Italy now has one of the longest life expectancies in Europe (see Figs 4.8 and 4.9).

There is certainly no clear correlation between national income and mortality. Even among poorer countries there are variations which suggest that factors other than prosperity are important. Spain and Greece both have a life expectancy of 77 but their per capita GNPs are £5160 and £3190 respectively. The typical Mediterranean diet with a low meat and fat content but a high fish, salad and cheese content is thought to be at least partly responsible for the lower levels of heart disease in these countries.

Life expectancy in eastern Europe has been slower to improve. In fact some Communist countries have experienced a decline in life expectancy. Male life expectancy in Hungary fell by more than one year during the 30 years after 1960. East Germany saw a decline during the 20 years before unification of two years for men and one year for women. A number of factors have been blamed for this deterioration including:

– severe levels of atmospheric pollution;
– poor diet;
– poor housing;
– poor working conditions;
– alcohol abuse and high levels of smoking;
– low priority given to investing in health care.

FIG 4.8   *Life Expectancy*

Life expectancy at birth for selected countries 1960 and 1989

	1960		1989	
Country	Males	Females	Males	Females
Denmark	70.4	74.4	72.0	77.7
Netherlands	71.5	75.3	73.7	80.2
UK	67.9	73.7	72.4	78.0
Portugal	61.2	66.9	71.2	78.2
Italy	67.2	72.2	73.2	79.7
West Germany	66.9	72.4	72.2	78.7
East Germany	67.9	72.9	70.0	76.2
Hungary	66.8	71.3	65.4	73.8
Poland	65.8	71.0	66.8	75.5
Austria	66.5	73.4	72.5	79.0

Most experts believe that life expectancy could continue to improve over the next few decades throughout Europe. The United Nations has predicted a life expectancy in some European countries of 78 for men and 83 for women by 2025.

- Suggest reasons for the improvement in life expectancy in western Europe since the 1960s.

- Are there any additional reasons you can suggest for the continuing improvement predicted by the UN?

- What factors could have the effect of reducing the predicted improvement over the next three decades?

FIG 4.9   *Projected Age Structure in the EU, 2010*

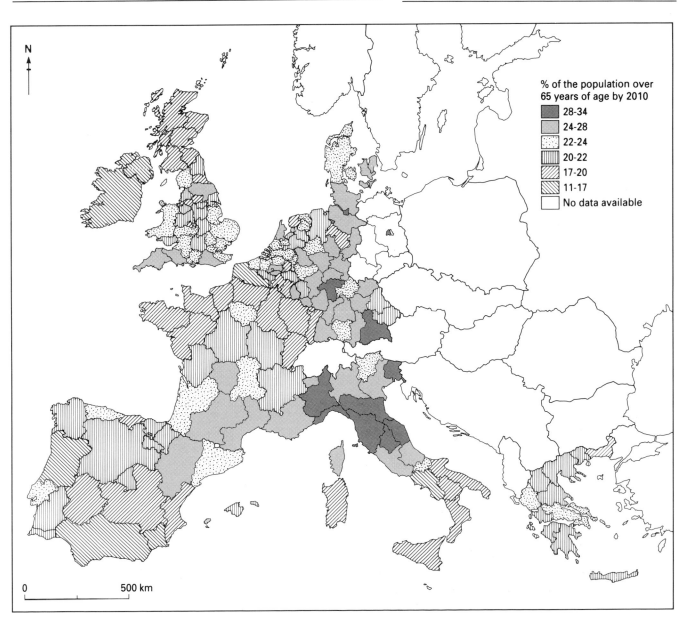

% of the population over 65 years of age by 2010

- 28-34
- 24-28
- 22-24
- 20-22
- 17-20
- 11-17
- No data available

0   500 km

4.3 The Greying of Europe: the Number of Elderly People Grows

Elderly Russian Woman

As the case study of Italy in Section 4.1 indicates the decline in fertility and marriage rates are having an impact on household structure. Increasing numbers of households consist of one or two people and fewer consist of four or more. As important as the apparent decline of the traditional family may be for European social policy a more significant trend is probably the ageing (or 'greying') of the population. Declining fertility combined with rising life expectancy are together causing a decline in the proportion of the population made up of young people and a growth in the proportion made up of older people.

The numbers of elderly people will continue to grow over the next few decades. Within the EU, for example, the percentage of the population aged 60 or over rose from 16 per cent in 1960 to 20 per cent in 1990 and is predicted to rise to about 30 per cent by 2020. These figures disguise the fact that within this age group an increasing proportion of people are aged over 75 – an age where many become highly dependent on state or family help and the cost of health care is high. In Britain, for example, there were about 3.5 million people aged 75 or over in 1991. By 2027 it is predicted that this will have risen to about five million.

Again Italy can be used as an example to illustrate this trend. In the early 1990s it had the fourteenth highest proportion of elderly people in the world. By 2000 it will have the highest proportion thanks to its record-breaking low fertility rate and rising life expectancy (see Fig 4.9). Out of a population of about 57 million nearly ten million will be over 65.

- Describe the spatial pattern revealed in Fig 4.9.

- Describe the trends revealed in Fig 4.10.

Throughout Europe policy makers are beginning to ask how elderly people will be supported in the future. In 1993 the EU launched the rather clumsily entitled 'Year of Older People and Solidarity Between Generations' – a recognition of the need for European society to recognise more fully the problems facing older people. More than £6 million was allocated by the EU to fund conferences and other events designed to encourage discussion of the issues (see Fig 4.11). A lot of people believe that the elderly have been **marginalised** in many European societies and face discrimination when trying to contribute to or take part in society.

Fig 4.10 *Age Structure in Western Germany 1910–2030*

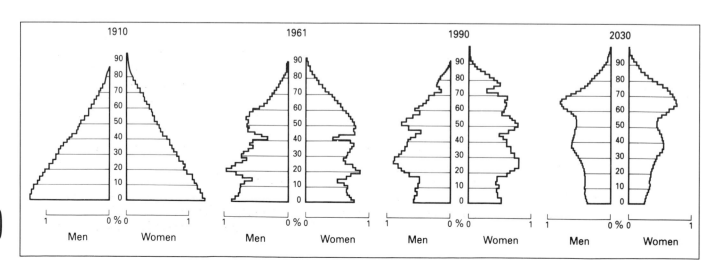

Leeds City Council

European Conference and Exhibition Fayre

(Hosted by Saga Holidays)

OLDER PEOPLE IN THE NEW EUROPE — POSITIVE IMAGES

HILTON INTERNATIONAL HOTEL

Leeds, United Kingdom — 28t·30th July, 1993

1993 has been designated 'European Year of Older People and Solidarity between Generations.'

This three day seminar is being hosted by Leeds City Council which coincidentally celebrates the centenary of its City Charter in 1993.
The Conference aims to:

* Raise awareness of the positive contribution and potential of older citizens within the European Community.
* To assist in countering the effects of ageism.
* To emphasise the positive aspects of ageing and the contribution older people can do and make to their communities.
* To facilitate the exchange of ideas, information and experience throughout the European Community.

Throughout the three days there will be presentations and contributions from prominent European speakers as well as workshops and local initiatives.

FOR FURTHER DETAILS AND INFORMATION PLEASE CONTACT:

Pamela Smith
Conference Co-ordinator
(Press & PR Unit)
Department of Social Services
Sweet Street
LEEDS LS11 9DQ

Tel: 0532 478730.
Fax No: 0532 440096

EUROPEAN YEAR
OF OLDER PEOPLE AND
SOLIDARITY BETWEEN GENERATIONS
1993
EuroConf.tam

LEEDS
1893 1993

FIG 4.11 *Leeds City Council Advertisement*

The elderly, because they are largely excluded from the job market and are dependent on private or state benefits, are particularly likely to be living in poverty. A survey in 1985 estimated that 20 per cent of pensioners in the EU (8.5 million people) lived in poverty. Poverty was defined as having to live on an income less than half the national average.

A new term has recently entered the vocabulary of policy makers in Europe – the 'demographic time bomb'. The term stems from the fact that current trends in fertility and life expectancy ensure that fewer and fewer people will be of working age in the coming decades and so fewer people will be making a net contribution to European health and welfare systems. At the same time rising numbers of elderly people mean that state pension and health systems will be in greater demand. Some governments are now worrying that existing pension and health systems could break down under the strain. Payments in the form of taxes will simply not cover potential expenditure. Some experts, on the other hand, argue that the problem is being deliberately exaggerated by some governments as an excuse to cut public expenditure and to reform welfare systems.

● The advertisement in Fig 4.11 refers to 'ageism'. Devise a definition of ageism.

Governments throughout Europe are looking at a number of options to deal with the potential problem:

– raising the retirement age. This has the benefit of reducing the proportion of the population entitled to state pensions but is likely to have the effect of raising unemployment in younger age groups;
– increasing the tax contributions paid by people in work to finance greater welfare expenditure;
– encouraging workers to make their own private pension arrangements or even ending state pensions for all but the poorest pensioners.

The Italian Government delayed making reforms to its pension system for fear of the resulting unpopularity, but at the beginning of the 1990s it finally announced that:

a) the minimum period over which pension contributions have to have been paid in order to be entitled to a pension would increase from 15 to 20 years;
b) incentives would be introduced to encourage private pensions;
c) the retirement age for men and women was to change from 60 to 65.

In the UK pressure from the EU to end the inequality of differing retirement ages for men (65) and women (60) meant that the government looked seriously at three options:

1 lowering the retirement age for men to 60;

2 adopting a common retirement age of 62 or 63;

3 raising the retirement age for women to 65.

The third option would clearly be the cheapest. This was the option that was adopted in 1993, despite the fact that three million people were unemployed at the time. In order to reduce popular opposition to the proposal the change was to be phased in over a number of years. Other countries are still discussing how to deal with the problem.

Pensioners in eastern Europe face a more serious problem. Pensions are not seen as a priority by the new governments striving to create market economies and payments are not inflation-linked. Their real value is rapidly falling with the current high rates of inflation.

FIG 4.12   *Ageing Populations*

- What do you think will be the main social impacts in Europe of an ageing population? Read Fig 4.12 to give you some ideas.

THE middle-aged and old in the 1990s and beyond are quite different people from previous generations at the same ages. Their expectations and lifestyles may have been defined by money – or more likely the lack of it – but in the 1990s their circumstances are completely different. As a large proportion of the population with financial and political clout, they no longer have to play roles dictated by more powerful age groups.

From now on, these newly visible age groups will also have a political voice which will force a change in the balance of power in deciding society's approach to the way we live. If America is anything to go by, the old will become a lot more militant in demanding political recognition and new rights. The American Association of Retired Persons has twenty million members, and showed its political teeth by forcing the Reagan administration to abandon plans to cut the social security budget. As pensioners realise that they have the power to demand quality of life, the American indications are that self-confidence follows. While competitiveness is minimised at work as the hierarchical office disappears, and male domination tumbles under the weight of working women's numbers, the last bastion of one-upmanship may well be the older person's state of preservation. The aim is not to look young, but to look in control. We will see a new age-assertiveness. The old want to be seen to be able to do and achieve as much as possible within a peer group. The lifestyle they evolve will have a knock-on effect on the way everyone else lives.

4.4   The European Magnet: Migration Since 1945

People may migrate to find work, to obtain a better quality of life or to escape war, political instability or persecution. Since 1945 the majority of migrants entering Europe or moving within Europe have been seeking jobs and higher incomes.

Albanian Refugees at the Port of Bridisi, Italy

However, the outbreak of ethnic conflicts in eastern Europe in the 1990s has forced large numbers of **refugees** to flee their homes looking for peace and safety. The affluent countries of western Europe have been a magnet for migration from poorer and more unstable areas.

By 1993 migration had become one of the most urgent issues facing Europe's politicians. In Germany particularly the country's post-war stability seems to be threatened by massive immigration. It also looks increasingly likely that economic crises in eastern Europe and Russia, and growing poverty in less developed countries could drive millions more to seek a better life in western Europe over the next decade or so. Should western Europe agree to accept these people or should it turn itself into a fortress designed to repel immigrants and refugees?

It is possible to identify three waves of migration into western Europe since 1945, although the actual pattern and dates vary from country to country.

Wave One – Migration of single men from less developed countries and southern Europe between the 1950s and early 1970s.

Wave Two – Migration of families to join husbands already living in western Europe in the late 1970s and early 1980s. This period saw a slower rate of migration.

Wave Three – Migration of **asylum** seekers from the less developed countries and eastern Europe in the late 1980s and 1990s.

Wave One

Between the 1950s and the early 1970s the main reason for immigration into western European countries was the demand for unskilled labour in these countries. A high proportion of the migrants were single men particularly from Italy, Spain, Greece, Portugal, Yugoslavia, Turkey, and Morocco.

A number of factors influenced where the migrants came from and where they went to. Links of language, culture or history usually played a part. Special ties between the UK and the **Commonwealth** countries, for example, meant that most of the UK's immigrants came from India, Pakistan, Bangladesh or the Caribbean. Language and historical links meant that France attracted people from north and west Africa. Western European countries often actively recruited workers from less developed countries into unskilled jobs which were unattractive to their own workforce. Many of these immigrants initially had little intention of staying in Europe. Most hoped to 'make their fortune' and then return home.

Wave Two

When the economies of western Europe slowed down after the 1973 oil crisis, unemployment grew and there was no longer a demand for foreign labour. Most countries imposed new immigration controls to restrict the flow of new immigrants. These new controls were often in fact a response to political and social pressure to control immigration as much as a response to the reduced need for unskilled labour. However, in most cases countries continued to accept the families of immigrant workers who were already in Europe and so the second half of the 1970s was a period of immigration of women and children and family reunification. Family reunification meant that fewer and fewer migrants seriously planned to return home. In some cases new restrictions on migrants returning to their country of origin temporarily and then re-entering their country of immigration encouraged family reunification as the only way of maintaining the family unit. By the 1980s family immigration was slowing down as the number of workers who had not been joined by their families diminished.

The growing numbers of immigrant couples meant that increasing numbers of children were being born in Europe to immigrant parents. These second-generation immigrants form an increasing proportion of the ethnic minority populations in western Europe. Second-generation immigrants usually have much weaker links with their parents' country of origin and

are more likely to adopt aspects of the culture and way of life of the European country.

Wave Three

The late 1980s and early 1990s have seen the growth of new types of immigration and an increase in the rate of immigration after the slow-down in rates during the 1970s and early 1980s. There has been a growth in illegal migration particularly from less developed countries into southern Europe and a growth in the number of asylum seekers from eastern Europe and less developed countries searching for a new life in western countries. Asylum seekers are migrants who want to be granted permission to enter a country on humanitarian grounds but have no legal right of entry. Some are genuine refugees who have been forced to leave their home countries by war or repression. Others are economic migrants who are fleeing from poverty and unemployment. In addition there has been an increase in ethnic migration with the disappearance of the Iron Curtain. Large numbers of ethnic Germans, for example, have been migrating to Germany from Poland, Romania and elsewhere over recent years.

One of the most notable changes during this third wave of migration has been the changing role of Portugal, Spain, Italy and Greece. During the first two waves, migrants left these relatively poor countries to find work in north-western Europe. By the late 1970s these countries were becoming destinations for migrants from less developed countries. Besides the growth in asylum seekers and illegal migration the 1980s also saw a growth in the migration of highly skilled technical, managerial and professional workers partly within western Europe but also from and to North America and Japan. Much of this migration is only short-term and based on temporary work contracts.

Most European countries collect data on migration on the basis of **nationality**. In other words, they distinguish foreigners from nationals. Foreigners or foreign nationals are people who are legally citizens of another country while nationals are legally citizens of the country concerned. Using these definitions it is possible for a national to be an immigrant or a foreigner to have been born in the country concerned.

The UK uses a different method. Statistics

are collected on the basis of the country of birth rather than on the basis of legal concept of nationality.

In all countries the most important ways in which foreign nationals can acquire citizenship of their new country are through naturalisation (i.e. obtaining legal recognition as citizens of the country) or by marriage to a national (in other words, a mixed marriage).

These different definitions can confuse the picture. For example, ethnic Germans migrating to Germany from Poland are automatically regarded as having German citizenship or nationality by the German Government. As a result they are not classed as immigrants by the German Government even though they are foreign born. On the other hand, somebody with British citizenship who was born, for example, in India and who decided to migrate to Britain would be classed as an immigrant simply because they were foreign born.

- Study Fig. 4.13. To what extent does the graph show the following:
  - **a)** an increase in immigration during the 1950s and 1960s (Wave One)?
  - **b)** a slow down in migration during the 1970s and early 1980s following the introduction of immigration controls (Wave Two)?
  - **c)** an increase in immigration in the late 1980s (Wave Three)?
- Study Fig 4.14.
  - **a)** What evidence is there in the data that a high proportion of foreign nationals in many countries are from adjacent countries?
  - **b)** Which countries, both in and outside Europe, appear to have been an important source of migrants?

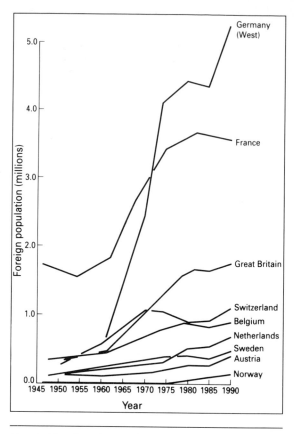

FIG 4.13 *Population of Foreign Nationality 1945–90*

  - **c)** Is there any evidence that historical or cultural links may play a part in determining the destination of migrants?
  - **d)** Why do you think migrants to Britain from the Caribbean, Pakistan or Bangladesh do not appear in the table?
  - **e)** How could the data be shown diagramatically?

FIG 4.14 *Most Frequent Countries of Foreign Nationality 1990*

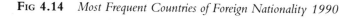

Most frequent countries of foreign nationality 1990 % of all foreign nationals in each country

Country of foreign nationality	Country of residence					
	Belgium	**France**	**Germany**	**Italy**	**Luxembourg**	**Netherlands**
Most numerous	Italy (26.7)	Portugal (17.9)	Turkey (32.0)	USA (10.2)	Portugal (33.0)	Turkey (29.4)
2nd most numerous	Morocco (15.7)	Algeria (17.2)	Yugoslavia (12.4)	Germany (7.5)	Italy (19.6)	Morocco (22.7)
3rd most numerous	France (10.4)	Morocco (16.2)	Italy (10.5)	UK (5.5)	France (12.3)	Germany (6.4)
4th most numerous	Turkey (9.4)	Italy (7.0)	Greece (6.0)	Greece (5.1)	Germany (8.7)	UK (5.6)

Country of foreign nationality	Country of residence				
	Norway	**Spain**	**Sweden**	**Switzerland**	**UK**
Most numerous	Denmark (12.0)	UK (17.8)	Finland (24.7)	Italy (34.4)	Ireland (27.5)
2nd most numerous	UK (8.2)	Germany (10.9)	Yugoslavia (8.5)	Yugoslavia (12.8)	India (8.5)
3rd most numerous	Sweden (8.2)	Portugal (8.8)	Iran (8.1)	Spain (10.6)	USA (6.4)
4th most numerous	Pakistan (7.9)	France (7.0)	Norway (7.9)	Portugal (7.8)	Italy (4.6)

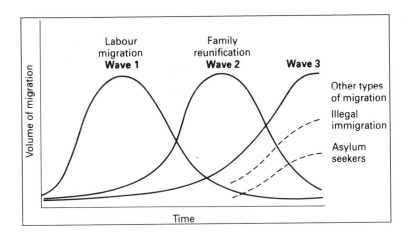

FIG **4.15**   *Model of European Immigration*

- Make a copy of Fig 4.15 and attempt to add a scale to the horizontal axis with the help of information in the text.

4.5 Visitors or Citizens?: Guestworkers in Germany

Deepening recession and rising unemployment are affecting all Germans but in western Germany it is the 'guestworkers' or *Gastarbeiter* who are affected the most. The economic slow-down is helping to generate a wave of racism against guestworkers and other immigrants (see Section 4.8).

The original Gasterbeiter were typical of the first wave of European immigration referred to in Section 4.4, although they are not confined to that period and continue to form an important proportion of foreign nationals in Germany. Most Gasterbeiter were male, unmarried and unskilled, although the term is now also used to describe their partners and children. Most were from Turkey. By 1993 there were 1.8 million Turkish nationals living in Germany. In fact in the late 1980s, before the large-scale immigration of East Europeans in the 1990s, Turks accounted for about a third of all foreign nationals in Germany. In Berlin they formed 45 per cent of the foreign population. About 70 per cent of foreigners in Germany could be classed as guestworkers at that time.

Germany considered these migrants to be temporary guests and most of the migrants probably had little intention of staying. They were given contracts for a year or two by German employers who often provided them with hostel accommodation. In the 1960s the policy of *Konjunkturpuffer* (or buffer against economic fluctuations) used migrants on short-term contracts as an army of workers which could be recruited or dismissed according to the current state of the economy.

This protected German workers from unemployment during periods of recession or slow economic growth. It was also cheaper for Germany because the immigrants did not receive many state benefits. Following a ban on the recruitment of foreign workers in 1973 the late 1970s saw the introduction of the more liberal policy of *Auslanderpolitik* which allowed the families of guestworkers to move to Germany and which aimed to give guestworkers greater civil rights. These changes encouraged many guestworkers to stay.

However, in 1983 the government passed the Return Migration Assistance Act which offered to pay guestworkers to return to their home country and removed their right of return to Germany. It is doubtful if many guestworkers who would not have returned to Turkey anyway took advantage of the grants offered by the government, but the measure did encourage a feeling of insecurity in the guestworker population and an impression that they were no longer welcome. This measure, along with a growth in unemployment, led to a decline in the guestworker population after 1981 and 1982.

Fig 4.16 shows the fluctuations in the guestworkers population in one German city and indicates:

- the high rate of departures throughout the period reflecting the temporary nature of many of the migrants' work contracts;
- the impact of German Government policies;
- the role of job availability in influencing the rate of immigration.

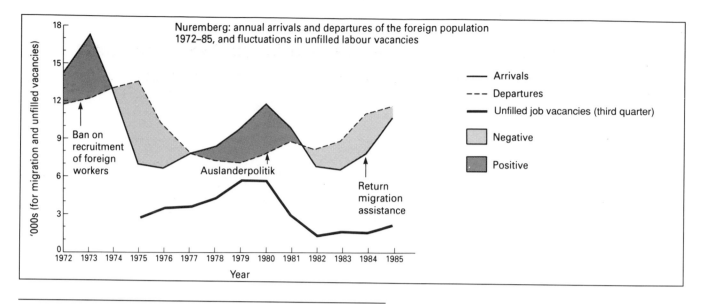

FIG 4.16 *Arrivals and Departures of Foreign Nationals in Nuremberg, West Germany*

The guestworker issue has declined in importance with the arrival in recent years of massive numbers of eastern European asylum seekers but nevertheless the problems remain. Much of the current concern over the issue stems from the rise in racist attacks against guestworkers (see Section 4.8) but there is also more general concern over the way in which Germany treats its guestworkers. It is almost impossible for guestworkers, or other foreigners, to obtain German nationality or citizenship. Yet by 1993 the 6.5 million foreigners in Germany formed eight per cent of the population. Of this total 1.85 million were Turkish nationals. Many have lived in Germany since the 1960s and 1970s. Of the total 6.5 million foreign nationals 60 per cent have been in Germany for at least ten years, nearly 50 per cent for more than 15 years and 25 per cent for more than 25 years. Surveys have found that 83 per cent of Turks want to stay in Germany and 90 per cent of young people want to apply for **dual nationality**. Every year about 30 000 Turkish children are born in Germany, and more and more Turks are second or third generation immigrants, yet they are not granted citizenship. Guestworkers are not allowed, for example, to vote in German elections regardless of how long they have lived and worked in Germany.

There is no doubt that guestworkers have made a vital contribution to the phenomenal success of the German economy since the 1950s and they continue to do so. Eight per cent of jobs are held by them. It has been estimated that businesses set up by self-employed guestworkers have created 125 000 jobs, contributed nine per cent of the country's GNP and account for seven per cent of the government's tax revenue. Guestworkers contribute far more in tax than they receive in welfare benefits.

The Turkish community is becoming more varied. A Turkish middle class has become established with a growing number of doctors, teachers and social workers. Thirty-six per cent of the Turkish population is aged under 18. 45 000 Turks own their own home in Germany and a further 135 000 are saving for a mortgage with a building society. 13 000 are students in German higher education institutions.

Some believe that a number of the problems now facing migrants could have been avoided if they had been granted German nationality and invited to integrate more fully into German society. In 1993 the government's Commissioner for Foreigners recommended that measures should be introduced to make it easier for foreigners to obtain dual nationality. She proposed that children of foreigners whose parents live in Germany should have an automatic right to citizenship and that other foreigners should be entitled to German nationality or dual nationality after eight years. Some members of the ruling Christian Democrat Party have suggested a period of between 10 and 15 years, but the majority of them continue to oppose any moves towards permitting dual nationality. In fact regulations on applying for German citizenship were eased in 1991, leading to a five-fold increase in applications to 10 000 during 1992. Following racist attacks and the resulting disturbances in 1993 Chancellor Helmut Kohl did voice greater support for the idea of making it easier for foreigners to apply for dual nationality.

- Why do you think the German Government is reluctant to grant dual nationality to Turks?

- Why do you think many Turks would prefer dual nationality to German nationality?

- List the likely benefits for **a)** Germany as a whole; **b)** the Turkish community stemming from foreign national groups like the Turks, being granted German citizenship.

4.6 The Poor are Breaking in: Illegal Migration from Less Developed Countries

Western Europe [is] bracing itself for its greatest challenge of the Nineties – a surge of migrants from lands bordering the Mediterranean that threatens to dwarf the growing influx from eastern Europe.

L Walker and N Comfort, Europe Braced for Migrant Invasion.

You can have a policy of stopping immigration but you won't really stop it. The border is a door that you open and close, but it's always porous. When people are hungry for freedom and hungry to eat, there's nothing you can do. The west is like a great beacon in the night and all the birds of the night will come to it. What we have to do – through development aid – is to make the beacon shine in a much greater circle. Then the birds can stay where they are.

Kofi Yamgnane, French State Secretary for Integration.

Fig 4.17 shows that less developed countries have been a major source of migrants over recent decades. Britain has traditionally been a destination for Indians, Pakistanis, Bangladeshis and migrants from Caribbean countries. France has large numbers of migrants from North Africa. In both cases links dating from colonial times when Britain and France controlled large areas of less developed countries have influenced the pattern of movement. What is different about much of the migration in recent years is its illegality. The affluence and stability of western Europe has acted as a beacon to migrants determined to find a better standard of living and to escape the poverty of their home countries.

There is growing concern that rapid population growth and lack of adequate economic development in developing countries will increase the numbers of people desperate to enter Europe from less developed countries in any way possible. The countries of North Africa are facing population growth rates of between two per cent and four per cent per annum. Egypt, for example, added 1 125 000 people to its population between 1985 and 1990 alone. The borders of less developed countries lie just across the Mediterranean and to the people of North Africa the southern European countries are the gateway to Europe. Italy in particular is experiencing a growth in illegal immigration from North Africa and other less developed countries. Morocco, Senegal, Egypt, Ethiopia, Somalia, Iran, Pakistan, the Cape Verde Islands, India and the Philippines are among the countries of origin. Many have entered as tourists and then illegally stayed on to become

FIG 4.17 *Numbers of Migrants from Developing Countries in EU 1990*

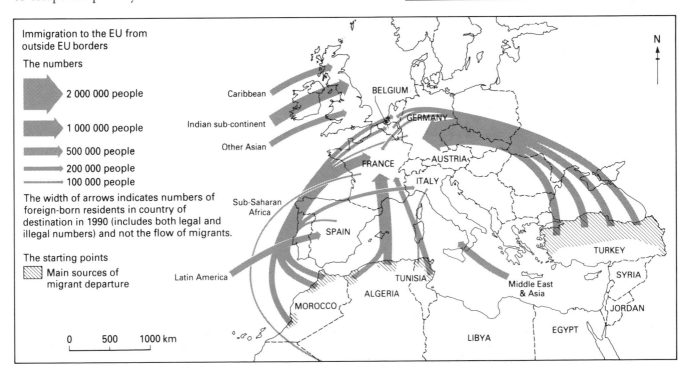

hotel or restaurant workers, domestic servants, street hawkers and farm workers – usually earning well below the legal minimum wage.

Italy has traditionally been a country of net emigration and was probably less well prepared than other countries for the wave of immigration which has followed its rapid economic growth during the 1980s. An estimated one million people have entered Italy in the last ten years increasing its population by about 1.5 per cent. Precise figures are impossible to obtain simply because much of the immigration is illegal. Many of these immigrants are found in seasonal jobs in farming, or as street traders in tourist resorts, or as domestic servants. The immigrants have become an important issue in Italy at a time when the Italian economy has entered a recession, and unemployment among Italians is growing.

Many Italians blame the immigrants for rising crime rates and drug dealing. When, in 1990, the police cleared Rome's main railway station of homeless migrants, many moved to a squatter camp in an abandoned factory. Within two months the camp housed 2000 Moroccans, Bangladeshis, Sri Lankans and others. About a year later the police decided to clear the camp but the squatters set fire to the factory before they left, attracting the media attention which the authorities were trying to avoid.

Some migrants seek to move further north into Europe. There is a thriving black market in smuggling illegal immigrants across the Franco-Italian border. Smugglers, known as *Passeurs*, charge migrants fees for guiding them over mountain trails which avoid border controls.

As well as illegal immigration there has been a growth in the number of asylum seekers from less developed countries seeking entry to EU countries. These are people who are, or claim to be, fleeing political repression or war in their own countries. In 1992, 557000 asylum seekers applied for permission to stay in the EU (although it has been estimated that only a third are genuine political refugees whose lives or freedom would be in danger if they returned home. Many are in fact economic migrants desperate to find a home in a prosperous country). Of this, 104000 were from Africa (19 per cent), 64000 from Asia (12 per cent), 25000 from the Middle East (five per cent) and 7000 from Latin America (one per cent). It can take up to two years before a government decides whether a claim for asylum is genuine or not and until 1993 most European governments have been reluctant to deport 'fake refugees' even if they can be found.

- Read Fig 4.18. Why do you think the success of the very small minority of migrants like Maria de Lourdes Jesus is so significant in the migration process?

France does not have such a serious problem of illegal migration but it has been a destination for African migrants during the last few decades. Between 1945 and the mid-1970s France's rapidly growing economy benefited from the cheap labour of migrant Algerians, Moroccans, and Tunisians from the Maghreb (the name for Arab North Africa). After establishing themselves many of the migrants were joined by

their families and many French cities acquired large Black or Arab North African populations. Many of these migrants have become concentrated in ghettos, often located in the high-rise suburban estates built since the 1960s (see Chapter 6). Ethnic tensions in many cities have helped to increase support for the racist National Front Party. The southern port city of Marseilles, because of its proximity to North Africa, has proved to be particularly attractive to North African migrants. The following account highlights the cosmopolitan nature of the city:

> ... *If they are looking for a glimpse of Africa without leaving Europe's shores, they won't get much closer than the warren of streets around the Port d'Aix in Marseilles, gateway to the Orient or, as the Marseillais often joke, the first African city on the Paris-Dakar rally. For centuries, Marseilles has also provided the first taste of Europe for hundreds of thousands of immigrants of every ilk ... More recently the city has taken in economic migrants from France's former colonies in Africa and Indochina.*

Half a million North Africans travel to Marseilles each year – some will remain legally and others illegally. Out of the city's total population of 800000, ten per cent are known to be North African muslims – the real figure is probably higher.

- Read Fig 4.19. In what ways do foreign nationals hope to guarantee the right to stay in France according to the article?

Some migrants from less developed countries are now trying to enter Europe by more complex routes. One route which uses Russia as a **transit country** has recently come to light. According to official Russian Security Ministry figures 242000 people, mainly Africans, Asians and Turks, applied to leave Russia in 1992 despite the fact that there was no record of them having arrived in the country. The migrants are hoping to travel to the United States, Germany, Scandinavia, and Britain, and are in fact merely travelling through Russia.

Highly organised crime rings are involved in this illegal trade in migrants but the KGB does not have the resources to adequately control the problem. The migrants are given false passports in return for £3000.

DO YOU SINCERELY WISH YOU WERE HERE?

CONCRETE solid and blackened with age, Mediterranean Marseille offers its worst face to the traveller arriving by boat.

Air travel has long overtaken the boat in popularity. In 1990, three quarters of the 950 000 foreigners who arrived in or left France by Marseilles travelled by air.

The new arrivals disappear as soon as they arrive in Marseilles. The motorway to the north for some, the Boulevard des Dames for the others, converging on the Porte d'Aix, a fake Roman triumphal arch and a beacon for immigrants.

Whether they are Algerians, by far the most numerous to enter here at La Joliette and Marignane, Tunisians, black Africans or Comorians, they rarely arrive by chance. In 1990, 440 000 Algerians, 50 000 Tunisians and 16 000 Moroccans came to Marseilles on tourist visas.

A tourist visa is the sole official means of entering the country since the closure of the borders to immigrants. Visitors join their families or, failing this, compatriots waiting to meet them. In the flats in the northern part of town, or the rooms of a discreet furnished hotel in Belsunce, there will be a little less space tonight. Visas, three months maximum, usually for less than one month, are issued on condition that friends and families confirm in writing that they can put the visitor up.

The registration office for foreigners is not very welcoming. The police who run it tend to inspire fear rather than confidence. However, this is where one has to come to make the official request. But first, prospective residents go to one of the numerous associations in Marseilles, or to the Maison de l'Etranger, where during the day claims for residence permits are discussed in Arabic, Turkish, Portuguese.

Greek, Italian, Spanish or English, Some 20 000 foreigners come here every year to find out the best way to circumvent the administration. Most are tourists or residents who want to extend their stay or are trying to reunite the family, but there are increasing numbers seeking political asylum.

In 1990, the prefecture of police registered 1140 such requests, of which half were made by Turks who had entered France overland. With out of date visas or expired residents' permits, life in the shadows begins. Most illegal foreigners fall into this category. A police check means immediate return back across the Mediterranean, after a spell in Arenc. Arenc prison, they call it here. Despite attempts to make it more acceptable, this bleak detention centre for foreigners awaiting repatriation, situated near the port, remains Marseilles' antechamber for expulsion. In 1990, 1105 illegal aliens passed through here.

The migrants enter Russia in a variety of ways. For example, visas are not currently needed between India and Uzbekistan or between Turkey and Azerbaijan. This allows Turks and Indians to enter these former Soviet republics without special documentation. It is then relatively easy for

FIG 4.18   *National Geographic, May 1993*

… Many foreigners live in fear of a sudden police check and summary deportation. "The police say, 'If you talk to journalists, we'll send you home," one African woman told me furtively. She had worked in Rome for ten years as a professional nurse but maintained a low profile and implored me not to use her name.

Other immigrants have overcome their fears, and a few have risen to prominent positions in Italian society. Maria de Lourdes Jesus has become one of the most visible foreigners as the anchor of a weekly television show on immigration called *Nonsolonero – Not Only Black*. Maria left her home in the Cape Verde Islands off the coast of West Africa when she was a teenager. For almost a decade she worked for Italian families, cleaning their homes and minding their children but always nurturing the dream of someday returning home to start a family of her own.

"It wasn't exactly slavery, but I was very frustrated," Maria said as she showed me around a studio of the Italian television network RAI Due. "There was no chance to improve my life. After six years I saw that even people who stayed ten years couldn't improve their situation. Nobody realized the dream. Nobody returned home. So I tried to better myself. I went to school."

She also improved her Italian and met Massimo Ghirelli, the producer of *Nonsolonero*. He told me he was impressed by her straight-forward way of speaking and her dignified manner. "She's real, and she knows the problems," he said. "She does not reflect the image of the poor immigrant in the street."

Today Maria's show has almost eight million viewers.

FIG 4.19   *The Guardian, 14 June 1991*

them to enter Russia. They then buy their new identities and travel to Europe where they hope their new identities will be enough to obtain permission to stay.

The numbers of migrants from less developed countries are now being dwarfed by the numbers from eastern Europe but they nevertheless represent a large migration of people. In any case, unless major civil wars break out in eastern Europe and Russia there is a likelihood that migration from eastern Europe will slow down. Meanwhile rapidly growing populations and poverty-stricken economies in less developed countries are likely to force ever greater numbers of people to try and seek a home in affluent Europe.

- Should migrants from less developed countries be prevented from entering Europe? To answer this question write,
  a) a list of the arguments which could be used against the policy;
  b) a list of arguments in support of the policy. Which set of arguments do you think is the strongest?
- What could European governments do to control the flow of migrants from less developed countries in the future?

4.7 In Search of Affluence: Migration from Eastern Europe

Border Guards Preventing Migration from the East, The Guardian, 14 June 1991

As the Iron Curtain fell four years ago, Hungary tore down the watchtowers and barbed wire it had built to keep its people in. Within months, though, Austrians built towers to keep newcomers out.

'We catch maybe half of those who try,' Raimund Wrana, an Austrian lieutenant, told me as we walked along this frontier one sunny afternoon. 'They're often in very bad shape. We give them some food and send them back. Yet even those poor devils often try again two or three times.'

Peter Range, Europe Faces an Immigrant Tide, National Geographic,
May 1993.

This extract highlights an irony resulting from the changes in Europe during the 1990s. During the Cold War western Europe and its allies opposed a Communist system which refused to allow its citizens to travel to the west. Having won the Cold War, and having welcomed the disappearance of the Iron Curtain and the ending of travel restrictions imposed on East Europeans, western Europe is now building barriers to prevent East Europeans moving to the west. Because the western Europeans see the new freedom of movement in the east as a threat a new 'iron curtain' is being enforced.

In the decades following the Second World War there was relatively little migration because of the travel restrictions imposed by the Communist governments. Between 1945 and 1989 ten million moved from eastern to western Europe.

Three and a half million of this total comprised movement of East Germans to West Germany before the building of the Berlin Wall in 1961. Other relatively small movements included political refugees after the uprisings in Hungary in 1956 and Czechoslvakia in 1968. Yet immediately after the collapse of Communism in 1989, 1.2 million moved from east to west, many within the new united Germany. In 1991, 187 000 eastern Europeans applied for asylum in the west. In the following year 800 000 people migrated from eastern Europe. Of these about 430 000 were asylum seekers – most of these were from Croatia, Bosnia, Romania and Bulgaria. During the first five months of 1993 there were 200 000 asylum seekers, mainly from Romania – a rate 30 per cent higher than the previous year.

The vast majority of these migrants (about 75 per cent) wanted to enter Germany. Germany is a particular attraction to migrants partly because of its relative affluence but mainly because of its liberal immigration laws. Until 1993 the right of asylum formed part of the country's constitution and the process of checking asylum claims could take up to two years in which time a migrant could find a job and settle. In February 1992 alone Germany received 38 000 asylum seekers and in the year as a whole the country received 438 000. About 75 per cent of these came from eastern Europe.

It is possible to divide the East European asylum seekers into three categories.

1 Economic migrants who are leaving countries like Romania and Bulgaria because of the poverty and economic chaos which has worsened since the end of Communism. These people are not genuine asylum seekers since asylum is usually only granted where people's lives are endangered if they are sent back to their home country. Ninety-five per cent of asylum applications in this category are eventually rejected. Economic migrants probably form the largest category although reliable figures are impossible to obtain.

2 Refugees from the war in the former Yugoslavia – particularly Bosnian Muslims whose homes have been destroyed or endangered by Serbian and Croatian forces or who have been forced out by ethnic cleansing. About three million people have been made refugees in this way although the majority of these remain within Croatia, Serbia, Bosnia and Slovenia. By the end of 1992 about 235 000 had been accepted by Germany. A number of other countries including Sweden, Switzerland, Austria and Hungary had accepted between 50 000 and 75 000. Britain had officially accepted about 2000. These people represent the biggest single human tragedy in Europe since the end of the Second World War.

3 People who have suffered persecution in their home country. This is probably the smallest category but again the numbers of genuine cases is impossible to determine. It includes Gypsies who have continued to face discrimination in Romania and elsewhere in eastern Europe.

Ethnic German Migration

Not all the migrants moving from eastern to western Europe are asylum seekers. Germany is accepting large numbers of ethnic Germans who until the end of the 1980s were 'trapped' in eastern Europe.

In 1989 alone 377 000 ethnic Germans (or *Aussiedler* as they are known) entered West Germany from Poland, Romania, Czechoslovakia, Yugoslavia, Hungary and the Soviet Union and the movement is still taking place. Their return attracted far less publicity than the 347 000 East Germans who crossed the newly opened frontier into West Germany – a movement which no longer counts as international migration with the unification of Germany.

These ethnic German communities have a long history. German-speaking people began moving eastwards in the twelfth century. Some reached as far as the Volga River in what is now Russia. Descendants of these migrants still live in eastern Europe and many still speak German as their main language.

Some experienced persecution, for example in the Soviet Union under Stalin and in Poland immediately after the Second World War.

The current picture is complex. In Romania Germans formed the third largest minority after the Hungarians and Gypsies with 300–400 000 people. Even before the end of Communism 140 000 moved to West Germany in the 1980s, their right to move reputedly purchased by the West German Government for £3500 a head. Romanian Germans continue to migrate to Germany in large numbers with the spread of ethnic violence in recent years. In contrast 200 000 ethnic Germans in Hungary enjoy a relatively high standard of living and are fully **assimilated** into Hungarian society. Very few expressed a wish to migrate to Germany.

The problems created for the German Government by the migration of ethnic Germans can be illustrated by outlining the migration in Poland. In the first two years following the disappearance of the Iron Curtain 300 000 ethnic Germans left Poland. Many of these found it difficult to prove their Germanic origin and about 20 per cent were refused entry to Germany. The German Government was concerned that only genuine ethnic Germans were accepted and that economic migrants seeking a better standard of living did not falsely claim German status. In fact, the German constitution stated that citizenship should be granted to all people proving German origin. It is estimated that in 1989 and 1990 30 000 Polish nationals bought forged documents claiming to prove German origin.

It should also be pointed out that any discussion of international migration to Germany is bound to exclude the migration of thousands of people from what was East Germany into western Germany. This movement has now slowed but has often created similar issues and problems to movement from outside Germany.

In addition to the asylum seekers and legitimate ethnic German migration it is estimated that in 1991 alone between 100 000 and 200 000 illegal immigrants entered western Europe.

The potential for further migration is enormous. Estimates of up to 20 million have been made for the number of migrants likely to leave the area of the former Soviet Union alone. There may be another two or three million ethnic Germans with the right to move to Germany.

Migrants readily find jobs

THE LEAN, weatherbeaten men tramping the roads of Epirus, their possessions kept in a cloth bag slung over one shoulder, are immigrants from Albania. They can be seen at any hour of day or night, travelling in twos and threes to look for work.

The trickle of Albanians crossing the border in north-western Greece has turned into a flood over the past year. There are thought to be over 200,000 Albanians – about 6 per cent of the country's population – in Greece. Among them are former diplomats and university professors. But an overwhelming majority are young men who enter Epirus illegally across the mountainous border.

As part of its commitment to improve relations with Albania's democratic government, Greece has adopted an attitude of *laissez faire* tolerance towards the immigrants, who do not ask to be treated as refugees.

In fact, it would require draconian measures to keep them out. Greek commandos patrol the border, but villagers on the Albanian side make a living out of guiding immigrants to out-of-the-way footpaths leading into Greece.

A senior police officer in Ioannina, the provincial capital, says: "Most days, we pick up about 500 Albanians in Epirus who don't have valid visas in their passports, and bus them back to the border. But there are probably more than that number coming across."

Greece issues visas to Albanians of Greek descent, most of them Greek-speakers from the North Epirus region of southern Albania, adjoining north-western Greece. Over 40,000 North Epirots and their families are now legitimate residents. In addition, Greece has agreed with the democratic government in Tirana to accept another 30,000 Albanians as short-term migrant workers.

It says something about the size of the black economy in Greece that Albanian immigrants have little trouble in finding jobs, however temporary. Albanians are in much demand as casual workers in agriculture and construction, as they will accept a daily wage of Dr3,000 (£9). While this is less than half the basic rate for Greeks, it is equivalent to almost a month's salary in Albania.

The flow of arrivals looking for seasonal work increased dramatically after Albania's democratic government launched a tough economic reform programme in July, in return for a stand-by loan from the World Bank, freeing food prices and cutting unemployment benefits.

With the aim of slowing the immigration rate, the Greek government is preparing a medium-term aid and development programme, to be focused on southern Albania.

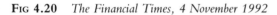

FIG 4.20   *The Financial Times, 4 November 1992*

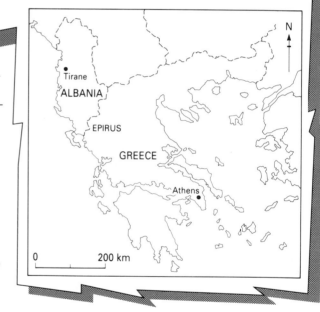

- With the help of information in this section and elsewhere in the chapter draw up a list of reasons why Germany in particular has attracted large numbers of migrants in recent years.

- Read Fig 4.20.
  a) Describe the migrant flow referred to in the article.
  b) Why is Greece, the poorest member of the EU, attracting Albanian migrants? List as many reasons as you can.
  c) How does the Greek Government intend to control the flow of immigrants?

4.8 The Violent Response: the Rise of the Extreme Right

Most Germans are disgusted by anti-foreigner violence. Yet most tend to agree with the right-wing slogan, 'the boat is full', meaning Germany has too many foreigners.

The Economist, June 1993.

One of the most disturbing trends in Europe in recent years has been the growth of violent racism sponsored by extremist neo-nazi organisations. The term 'neo-nazi' means that these organisations have very similar beliefs to those of the Nazis in 1930s and 1940s Germany. The ideology of the Nazis, or National Socialists, was based on nationalism, a belief in the concept of racial purity and the view that the state was more important than the individual. Many of the members of the present far right groups may not call themselves national socialists but they do believe in racial purity, they do believe that other ethnic groups (including black people, Jews and Gypsies) and minorities (including homosexuals) are naturally inferior and should be 'removed', and many do regard Adolf Hitler as a hero.

What has particularly disturbed many in Europe is the fact that the far right seems to be particularly strong and violent in Germany. Inevitably parallels have been drawn with the

ond World War. In the decades
Hitler in 1945 Germany had
eradicated support for nationalism and
strong and stable **liberal democracy**.
question just how stable and strong this
German society has really changed as
ight.

it-wing terrorism and the emergence of
is not confined to Germany. In fact at
ents in Germany has hidden equally
where in Europe.

One of the most shocking events was the attack on a hostel for Romanian asylum seekers in the eastern German city of Rostock in 1992 even though nobody was killed. (see Fig 4.21).

- What three aspects of the events in Rostock (see Fig 4.21) do you think particularly worried or frightened many people both within and outside Germany?

FIG 4.21   *The Guardian, 25 July 1992*

The following examples are typical of other racist attacks in a number of European countries.

In November 1992 three Turks – a ten year old girl and two women aged 20 and 51 – died when two houses were set on fire shortly after midnight in Mölln south of Lübeck. Nine people were injured including a nine month old baby and a 82 year old woman. A man phoned the police and fire brigade after the two fires and ended the call with the words *'Heil Hitler'*.

In May 1993 two women aged 27 and 18 and three girls aged 13, 9 and 4 died when the home of a Turkish family was burned down in an arson attack in Solingen near Cologne. The families involved in both the Mölln and the Solingen incidents had lived in Germany for more than 20 years.

In November 1992 swastikas, abuse and slogans were daubed on gravestones in a Jewish cemetery in the Austrian town of Eisenstadt. *'Heil Haider'* was scrawled on

Cheers as neo-Nazis set refugee hostel ablaze

RIGHT-WING extremists set fire last night to a building in Rostock, east Germany, that had housed 200 Romanian asylum-seekers, in the third consecutive night of racist violence in the city.

The building had been evacuated before neo-Nazis set fire to it with firebombs. German television reports said that during the violence most of the police retired from the scene to head-quarters and only one fire engine was brought in.

Several hundred bystanders egged on the rioters, shouting "Germany for the Germans". As one firebomb hit a balcony of the hostel and exploded in flames, spectators cheered and applauded.

The violence heightened fears of a new wave of violence by right-wing extremists fomenting unrest in eastern Germany. The extremists are making use of local prejudice and are calling in supporters from outlying areas.

The violence began on Saturday. According to the Mecklenburg police chief, Siegfried Kordus, neo-Nazis drove to the Baltic coastal city from Berlin, Hamburg and other cities in convoys and used citizens' band radio to co-ordinate their attacks.

"They were very well organised," he said yesterday. The Rostock riot was the worst

outbreak of racist violence since extreme right-wing gangs laid siege to an apartment block for asylum-seekers in September 1991 in the east German town of Hoyerswerda.

After violence flared on Saturday night, Germany's main television news predicted a second night of clashes, thereby alerting neo-Nazi militants all over the region. On Sunday speedily organised convoys increased from 150 to 500 the number of hardcore radicals hurling paving stones and firebombs at the home for Romanian asylum-seekers, most of them Gypsies.

"That news item to me bore the character of an invitation to violence," said a senior official of Hamburg's Verfassungsschutz, the counter-intelligence service which monitors extremism.

While the media had to do their job, the police should have matched the threat by taking tougher measures, he said.

The counter-intelligence ser-vice, the equivalent of MI5, believes that neo-Nazi activities are still operating "at regional and local levels through individuals" rather than having a "classic communication network" at their disposal.

News of future trouble spots is passed from mouth to mouth, at

rallies and football matches, and sometimes by telephone.

However, the Hamburg-based Chaos Computer Club, which made headlines in 1990 by "hacking" the computers of the US space agency Nasa and passing the information on to the KGB, does not share such an innocent view of Germany's 6,000 neo-Nazi activists and their tens of thousands of supporters.

"They operate not only with citizens' band radio, but also have their own data banks and electronic mail boxes through which information is spread," a spokesman said.

Once the right-wing radicals learnt of the simmering discontent among Rostock's burghers, disgusted by the "intolerable conditions" in a hopelessly overfilled asylum home in the middle of a residential area, the rest was easy. "They were protected by the local population like fish in water, and dived into the crowd for cover from the police," said a local journalist who was covering the violence.

The deputy mayor of Rostock, Wolfgang Zoellick, said it had been terrifying to see elderly local people cheering on the rioters with applause, Nazi salutes and chants of "foreigners out". Germany's Jewish community yesterday

described the popular backing by a thousand people as a challenge to democracy.

"These bystanders and their support is a reminder of the guilty behaviour of those who some 60 years ago made it possible for National-Socialist babarism to emerge," it said. "If you want to call me a Nazi, call me a Nazi," one red-cheeked citizen said, adding that "something had to be done" and that it was a good thing that the radicals' violent protests had succeeded in moving the 200 asylum-seekers to the outskirts of the east German port.

"I'm not against foreigners, but this goes against every German norm," said another local man.

Rostock's considerable neo-Nazi community, reinforced by a militant Hansa Rostock football fan club, had for months watched the growing discontent.

An anonymous caller told a local newspaper three days before that rightwing protests were planned to coincide with a "peaceful" demonstration by local people.

As long as there was no political solution to the "explosive mix" of an ever-mounting asylum problem, coupled with a growing neo-Nazi appeal among the young, the next outburst would only be a question of time.

GABRIELE S had made her mind up: "As soon as I come out of hospital I'll start a new life." She had not forgiven the racist yobs who beat her partner to death. Their son bears the name of the father he never saw, Amadeu Antonio.

"When I went to register the birth they asked me if I had any proof of the father's identity, any papers. Of course I hadn't. Who in the world imagines they could die two weeks before their son is born?" At home, an unpleasant surprise awaited her: "On the landing written in big letters, there was "Germany for the Germans" and on the neighbour's door there were swastikas." While she had been away, the social services in Eberswalde-Finow had allocated a flat in the same block to Tristan Dewitz, a known local neo-Nazi activist.

The town's mayor did not see any difficulty. "Dewitz assured me that he wanted to break away from the group and that he'd been threatened by his former companions," he said, in an attempt to justify the incident. Proof to the contrary came just four days later when the flat adjacent to Gabriele's was attacked by Dewitz and his friends. it belonged to a young left-wing couple.

Gabriele fled. Later, she got a new flat and some friendly advice from the mayor suggesting that "the best thing you can do is leave Eberswalde and go to Berlin or some other western part of the country". As far as the local authorities were concerned, the way to put a stop to the neo-Nazi attacks on foreigners was for the foreigners to go away.

Gabriele stayed. it wasn't long before Tristan Dewitz was her neighbour again. The psychological terror continued. "One day, the baby's pram was covered in Nazi swastikas. The next day it had been destroyed." In the street, where various friends of Dewitz's now lived, she was jeered at and humiliated with taunts of "black bitch".

Gabriele managed to live with the danger until she agreed to give an interview to a regional television station during the preparations for the trial of her partner's five attackers. Contrary to what had been agreed, the programme went on air without her face and voice being disguised. The death threats came immediately.

She fled to Berlin where an anti-racism organization found her somewhere to live in secret. But that was no way to live. At the end of the year, she plucked up her courage, packed her bags and went back to Eberswalde with little Amadeu.

At the trial of her husband's murderers in Frankfurt, four received prison sentences of three to four years, and the fifth a two-year suspended sentence.

FIG 4.22   *The Guardian, 27 October 1992*

many of the desecrated gravestones. Jorg Haider is a leader of the right-wing Freedom Party who is demanding a halt to all immigration, the deportation of illegal immigrants and limits on the numbers of non-German speaking children in Austria's schools.

Two hostels in Rome for North African immigrant workers were burned down in May 1993. No one was seriously injured although a number of Moroccans had to be taken to hospital. The destruction of the hostels left 1000 immigrants homeless and destroyed all their belongings.

In May 1989 a bomb exploded in a refugee centre in the Norwegian town of Eidsvoll.

In May 1993 a Turkish-owned electronics factory in Lyons in France was burned down after the walls had been daubed with swastikas.

The majority of racist attacks are less dramatic and attract little if any media attention but they are just as serious. Fig 4.22 outlines one example of the frightening persecution to which some migrants are subjected.

It is difficult to accurately assess the scale of support for violent racism. Germany's internal security service (the OPC) monitors extremist political groups. The OPC estimates that 40 000 Germans belong to far right groups or parties and 4200 to openly violent neo-Nazi gangs – 3000 of these in eastern Germany.

The growth in support for stricter controls on immigration is not confined to militant or violent racist groups. Right-wing parties which campaign for an end to immigration and the repatriation of immigrants have gained support in a number of countries. The French National Front led by Le Pen is probably the most well-known and the party has obtained up to 40 per cent of the vote in some deprived urban areas in the cities of Lille, Lyons, Marseille and Paris. Other parties which attract much smaller levels of support include the Nederlands Blok in the Netherlands, the Vlaams Blok in Belgium and the German Peoples' Party (DVU) and the Republikaner (REP) in Germany. The Freedom Party (FPO) in Austria gained 23 per cent of the vote in Vienna in 1991 after campaigning on an anti-foreigner platform. Opinion polls suggest the party has the support nationally of 17 per cent of the electorate.

Support for extremist organisations and the more moderate anti-immigration parties seem to come mainly from the young and the unemployed. Researchers in eastern Germany have found that 25 per cent of young people are of the opinion that *'we must keep Germany clean and prevent racial mixing'*. The majority of the voters who support the right-wing German Republican Party are under 30.

It would be easy to exaggerate the importance of these far right organisations. On the other hand, there is no doubt that in Germany they have had a destabilising effect. In May 1993, for example, the killing of four Turks in Solingen during an arson attack on their home led to angry demonstrations by Turks against racism and what they believed was a failure by the authorities to take adequate action. Some of these demonstrations ended in riots in the town. It is also probable that their activities helped to accelerate the speed at which some governments introduced new measures controlling immigration in 1993 (see Section 4.9).

German Neo-Nazis

A number of groups have been active in campaigning against racism, such as SOS Rassismus in Germany, and many German towns and cities have seen massive demonstrations opposed to racism. There has been widespread revulsion in Germany to violent attacks on migrants. Not surprisingly, minority groups are feeling increasingly vulnerable. Turks in Germany are losing confidence in the ability or willingness of the police to protect them and are resorting to self-defence or retaliation against neo-nazi groups (see Fig 4.23).

The Causes of Racist Terrorism in Germany

A number of factors may account for the growth of racism in Germany:

- the massive influx of immigrants from eastern Europe at the end of the 1980s and in the 1990s (see Section 4.7);
- the growth in the numbers of foreign nationals from outside Europe living in Germany (see Section 4.5);
- the collapse of the Communist system in the eastern part of Germany (see Chapter 2). People in eastern Germany have seen all the communist values and institutions they grew up with discredited and swept away. This has created a sense of failure, inferiority and lack of direction. Membership of far right groups may give young people in particular a sense of identity and importance as well as an ability to 'fight back'.

Turks go on the offensive

MORE and more Turks living in Germany are buying arms to protect their families or to go on the offensive against alleged neo-Nazis in response to continuing arson attacks on lives and property.

Turkish community leaders said yesterday that people were buying not only fire-extinguishers and ladders in case of fire-bombings but also gas-pistols and heavier weapons as they had lost confidence in the will of the police and state to protect them.

Many Turkish men, middle-aged as well as militant youths, have warned in the wake of the murder of five women and children in Solingen 10 days ago of their determination to escape the fate of German Jews under Hitler.

Evidence of this increasingly aggressive self-defence confirms security experts' predictions that racist violence between native Germans and foreign immigrants will get worse. Four more arson attacks on immigrants were reported yesterday.

FIG 4.23 *The Guardian, 9 June 1993*

FIG 4.24   *The European, 24–27 June 1993*

— the failure of the German Government to deliver the promised economic and social improvements in eastern Germany (see Chapter 2). The impact of de-industrialisation and high unemployment in the eastern part of Germany has been deepened by the feeling that promises made by the government have not been honoured. Instead of standards of living in the east rising to those in the west many feel that they are considerably worse off than they were under a Communist government. They believe immigrants are making the situation worse by attracting scarce resources for housing and social security and by reducing the chances of Germans finding a job. Immigrants also provide a convenient scapegoat to blame for the severe social and economic problems faced by eastern Germans;

— the recession in the whole German economy which began to seriously deepen in 1993. Many of the concerns felt by eastern Germans are now growing in the western part of the country as unemployment rises and public spending is curtailed. The wealth which West Germans have come to take for granted in recent decades now looks less secure. Large-scale migration can be seen as an additional strain on the economy and community. In the early 1990s the German Government was spending £4 billion per annum on caring for asylum seekers in addition to the costs incurred by ethnic German migrants.

It can be argued that while the last three factors are important, the far right would have attracted little support without the first two.

● What point is the cartoon in Fig 4.24 trying to make?

4.9 The Strengthening of Fortress Europe: the Government Response to Immigration

Since 1992 European governments have introduced a range of measures to reduce the flow of immigrants into western Europe. Both national governments and the EU have made it clear that they intend to strengthen 'Fortress Europe' against the further waves of immigrants from eastern Europe and the less developed countries expected during the second half of the 1990s.

In February 1992 the Polish Government introduced new measures affecting migrants from Romania, Bulgaria, the former Yugoslavia and the former Soviet Union who travel through Poland on their way to Germany. The measures were in anticipation of the German immigration reforms which were to be introduced in 1993. The Polish Government was worried that migrants turned back at the Polish-German border by the German authorities would remain in Poland. Under the new measures migrants travelling through Poland would have to prove they had been invited by a Polish citizen. The Polish citizen would also have to guarantee to cover any costs incurred by their guests.

In November 1992 the ministers with responsibility for immigration from the 12 EU countries agreed to aim to amend their national laws on immigration by the start of 1995. The amendments will give governments the power to:

– speed up the expulsion of asylum seekers when it is found that their claims for asylum are not justified;
– demand proof from asylum seekers that they have done everything possible legally in their own country to protect themselves from persecution;
– refuse asylum status to people fleeing from civil war – a measure clearly aimed at refugees from Bosnia.

In May 1993 the German Government tightened the country's asylum laws by amending the constitution to restrict access to refugees. The German constitution introduced in 1949 guaranteed that all migrants would be admitted to the country while their application for permission to stay was processed. This could take up to two years. Following the 1993 reform the authorities can turn back most asylum seekers at the border. The German Government also agreed to help finance more intensive border patrols by Polish, Czech and Slovak authorities to discourage migrants trying to get to Germany through those countries.

German Government officials argue that genuine refugees fleeing repression are not affected.

- Read Fig 4.25 on page 88.
  a) What second measure was the German Government considering at this time?
  b) Why, according to evidence in the article, were the protesters opposed to the reform?
  c) Why, according to evidence in the article, did the government believe the reform was necessary?

In June 1993 the French interior minister, Charles Pasqua, announced that France no longer welcomed immigrants and intended to aim for 'zero immigration'. He presented new legislation which would reduce the rights of immigrants living in France to apply for French nationality, including removing the right of automatic citizenship for French-born children of immigrant parents and

Turkish Demonstrators in Mölln, Germany, The Guardian, 30 November 1992

Bonn Defies Protestors to Curb Asylum Rights

GERMANY'S parliament yesterday defied thousands of demonstrators and tightened the country's asylum laws in a move that critics say will help create a "fortress Europe" against a growing tide of migration from countries stricken by poverty and war.

After 15 years of debate and mounting public resentment against the refugee influx that last year exploded in a wave of far-right terror against asylum-seekers, parliament, ringed by police and protesters, last night amended the constitution to restrict refugees' access to and presence in Germany.

The 521–132 vote to dispose of the guaranteed right of all foreigners to seek asylum came after 13 hours of heated debate that mirrored the tumult outside the parliament.

Four thousand police erected razor wire around parliament, temporarily housed in a former waterworks, to keep 10,000 demonstrators at bay. A number of ministers and MPs arrived by helicopter or ferry across the Rhine to attend the session.

After approval tomorrow in the upper house, the measure will become law on July 1.

Officials said the law, which would turn back most refugees at Germany's borders, would protect those threatened with political repression while keeping out economic migrants.

With 70 per cent of the population demanding some kind of action, Hans-Ulrike Klose, the Social Democratic leader, said, "unregulated immigration endangers the stability of democracy and only serves rightwing rabble-rousers".

Under Germany's 1949 constitution, any foreigner can seek asylum and remain for the months or years it takes for the application to be evaluated.

Germany pays about 10 billion marks (£4 billion) a year to care for asylum-seekers. A second bill under consideration yesterday would cut by 25 per cent the benefits paid to refugees.

From dawn protesters blocked streets around parliament. At an open-air church service demonstrators carried banners proclaiming "asylum rights are human rights" and "no repetition of history".

They later refused to allow MPs, office workers and journalists through to the government quarter and brought traffic to a halt. At one point some 300 hooded anarchists broke away from the overwhelmingly peaceful crowd and tried to storm the police cordon, but were driven back with batons.

Inside parliament, speakers said it was a "black day for democracy" if MPs had to shut themselves off behind police barriers. Protesters, who set up mock border posts and a ply-wood replica of the Berlin Wall, said they wanted MPs to be as beleaguered as refugees would be under the new legislation.

Wolfgang Schaüble, the parliamentary leader of Chancellor Helmut Kohl's Christian Democrats (CDU), and an architect of the asylum compromise agreed with the opposition Social Democrats (SPD), and said the new legislation was needed to preserve social peace in Germany.

"Our citizens are frightened by the unchecked refugee influx," he said. "We owe them a social order that allows Germans and foreigners to live peacefully side by side."

Rudolf Seiters, the CDU interior minister, rejected demands from SPD MPs to make last minute changes to the legislation. Responding to their concern that refugees from so-called "safe countries" – all countries bordering Germany – would be sent back and refused legal redress, Mr Seiters said: "This is the central plank of the new legislation. If you change that you open the floodgates to refugees."

Last year saw a record influx of 440,000 asylum-seekers, mostly from eastern Europe. But despite the liberal entry policy, Germany has one of the lowest recognition rates for refugees, with only 4 per cent of arrivals granted political asylum.

FIG 4.25 *The Guardian, 27 May 1993*

making the acquisition of citizenship by marrying a French citizen very difficult. The legislation would also slow down family reunions, speed up expulsions of illegal immigrants and would legalise random police checks to identify illegal immigrants. He was quoted as saying, '*France has been a country of immigration and no longer wants to be. We don't have the means. If we don't hold this line firmly public opinion will harden and the country will drift to the extreme right*'.

The legislation was met by widespread opposition. The Chairman of the government's International Migration Office resigned in protest, arguing that intensified police action in immigrant housing areas would raise tension and would give credence to the idea that immigrants were the cause of the country's problems. Many immigrants or ethnic minorities, it was argued, would see such police action as racial harassment. The Catholic and Protestant Churches also opposed the measures with one joint letter from 70 religious groups referring to the proposals as 'poisonous and destabilising policies'. Other groups including human rights organisations, judges and trade unions also expressed their opposition.

At a number of meetings in 1993, EU ministers agreed to take more action against illegal immigrants and to fine airlines bringing in passengers who do not have proper passports or visas. They also allocated more resources to immigration departments dealing with asylum applications located in the main refugee-exporting countries and agreed to classify most parts of the world as safe enough for asylum seekers to be returned to without thorough investigation of their cases. More controversially, they agreed to limit the rights of Bosnian refugees in western Europe who have been raped or interned in concentration camps to be joined by their families. This was despite appeals to the EU from the United Nations High Commissioner for Refugees that the families should be allowed to migrate.

- Make a list of reasons why European governments want to reduce the scale of immigration.

- Most of the measures described above are being taken by western European countries. What do you think will be the attitude of eastern European countries to large-scale migration to western Europe?

ESSAY

1 'Declining birth rates and increasing life expectancy pose an economic and social challenge for European decision makers.' Discuss.

2 Analyse the causes and effects of declining birth rates in Europe.

3 Assess the political impact of large-scale immigration into western Europe.

4 'The German Government's approach to dealing with immigration has encouraged the growth of racism'.
　Discuss the evidence for and against this statement.

5 'Western Europe is turning itself into a fortress.'
　Analyse the accuracy of this statement in the context of immigration policy.

6 Why are so many migrants determined to enter western Europe?
(You may also need information from Sections 2.4, 7.3 and 7.4).

Glossary

assimilation	To be absorbed into the majority population by adopting many of the same cultural characteristics.
asylum	To be granted permission to stay in a country in order to avoid persecution in a person's country of origin.
commonwealth	The countries which used to form the British Empire until they were granted independence. The New Commonwealth comprises those countries which have gained independence from Britain since 1945.
demographic transition	The name is given to the reduction in birth rates and death rates which has occurred in developed countries since the Industrial Revolution.
dual nationality	Being a legally recognised citizen of two countries.
fertility rate	The average number of children each woman gives birth to during her lifetime.
liberal democracy	A country or a system of government where power is held by a freely elected government, where all adults can vote in elections and where there is considerable individual freedom.
marginalised	Forced out of the mainstream of society. Deprived of many of the benefits received by the majority of people.
mortality	Death rate. The proportion of the population who die in one year.
nationality	The country in which a person is a legal citizen.
refugee	A person who unwillingly migrates, usually as a result of war, persecution or natural disaster.
replacement level fertility	The fertility rate which would maintain zero population growth.
right-wing	Those who believe in more conservative or traditional policies. Right-wing politicians usually support free market economic policies.
transit country	A country being used as a temporary home by migrants who intend to travel on to another country.

Agriculture: the Need for Reform

KEY IDEAS

5.1 The problems and issues facing agriculture in western Europe differ to those facing agriculture in eastern Europe. In the west farmers have become so efficient that the supply of food exceeds demand. In the east inadequate investment or poor management means that food supplies are unreliable or inputs are used inefficiently.

5.2 In western Europe, particularly within the EU, there is general agreement that agriculture should receive state support. The EU's Common Agricultural Policy (CAP), the system through which support is provided, has created a number of problems and the policy is in need of reform.

5.3 In 1992 EU member countries agreed to reform the Common Agricultural Policy in an attempt to tackle the problem of over-production and to control costs.

5.4 The EU's agricultural policies pose an environmental threat.

5.5 Conservationists believe that the environment must be given much greater priority in agricultural policy.

5.6 Agriculture in eastern Europe is experiencing a variety of problems. Some of these problems stem from policies implemented by the previous Communist governments while others are caused by instability following the collapse of Communism and the transition to market economies.

French Farmer

Olive Grove in Crete

5.1 Too much in the West, too Little in the East

Agriculture forms only a small part of most European economies. However, it has a major impact on the continent's landscape and ecology, and agriculture is high on the agenda of most governments.

Throughout western Europe the main agricultural trend over recent decades has been the **intensification** of agriculture. This is characterised by:

- increasing inputs of technology, particularly fertilisers, pesticides, drainage and irrigation systems, machinery and storage and processing systems;
- a decrease in the number of farm workers as farms become increasingly capital-intensive;
- a resulting increase in yields per hectare;
- a growth in the size of farms to achieve economies of scale;
- land previously unused by farmers has been reclaimed and brought into production – a process made possible by new technology;
- increasing farm specialisation in a particular crop or type of livestock.

It is these changes which have brought about the three problems now facing western Europe.

1 The intensification of farming is damaging the environment.

2 Production now exceeds demand – we are producing more food than we need.

3 The decline of the agricultural workforce is damaging the community and economy of some rural areas. When farm workers lose their jobs they may have to leave the area to find employment elsewhere.

The EU and western European governments will have to introduce new policies during the 1990s to deal with these problems – the alternative will be unacceptable environmental disruption, expensive food surpluses, and a continuing social and economic decline of some rural areas.

Eastern European governments are facing a different set of problems. Until the collapse of Communism at the turn of the decade eastern agriculture was largely state-controlled. In most cases it was suffering from inefficiency, poor management and lack of capital investment.

Inappropriate use of new inputs and new methods meant that yields did not increase as rapidly as in western Europe. The inefficiency of much of Communist agriculture along with the economic and social disruption which has accompanied the end of Communism have, in most eastern European countries, led to disruption of food supplies and, in some cases, a decline in agricultural production.

This is not a problem which western European governments can ignore. Continuing uncertainties in food supply could lead to further social and political unrest which could have repercussions in western Europe. On the other hand, if eastern European countries are successful in making their farms more efficient during the 1990s then their output would contribute to European surpluses as well as worsening environmental damage.

- With the help of Fig 5.1 explain what is meant by the 'price-cost squeeze' and why the process has led to increasing use of inputs and higher yields in western Europe.

- Select information from Figs 5.2 to 5.6 to evaluate the following hypotheses.

  a) Agriculture in north-west Europe is more capital intensive than in the rest of Europe.
  b) Agriculture is becoming more capital intensive throughout Europe.
  c) Agriculture is more productive in north-west Europe than in the rest of Europe.
  d) Output has increased more rapidly in north-west Europe than in the rest of Europe.
  e) Agriculture in eastern Europe has performed poorly since 1979.
  f) Within the EU the economies of the southern countries are more dependent on agriculture than the northern economies.

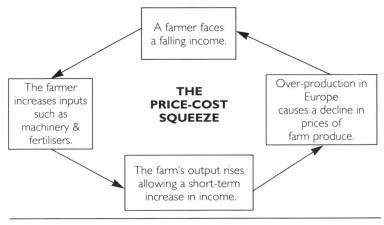

FIG 5.1 *The Price-Cost Squeeze Facing Farmers in Western Europe*

g) Within the EU northern agriculture is more efficient than southern agriculture.

h) Throughout the EU the number of farm workers is declining while farms are becoming larger.

Fig 5.3   *Changes in Agricultural Output*

Changes in agricultural output:

	Country	Agricultural output 1990 (1980=100)	Agricultural output per capita 1990 (1980=100)
North-western Europe	Austria	106	105
	Belgium/Luxembourg	119	119
	Denmark	140	138
	Finland	118	114
	France	103	99
	Germany (West)	113	110
	Ireland	117	114
	Netherlands	126	119
	Norway	103	100
	Sweden	107	104
	Switzerland	109	103
	UK	111	109
Southern Europe	Greece	103	99
	Italy	96	94
	Portugal	127	121
	Spain	119	114
Eastern Europe	Albania	113	93
	Bulgaria	91	89
	Czechoslovakia	125	122
	Hungary	105	106
	Poland	114	107
	Romania	96	91
	Yugoslavia	94	88

Fig 5.2   *Percentage of Total Workforce in Agriculture*

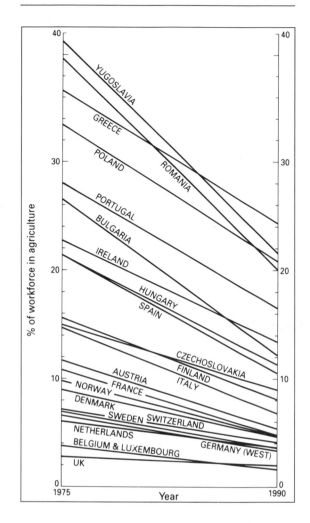

Fig 5.4   *Changes in Agriculture in the EU*

	Belgium	Denmark	Germany	Greece	Spain	France	Ireland	Italy	Luxembourg	Netherlands	Portugal	UK	EU Average
% of workforce in agriculture (1989)	2.7	6.3	5.2	27.0	14.4	6.8	15.4	9.9	3.4	4.7	20.7	2.2	7.7
Average size of farms (ha) (1989)	15	32	17	4	14	29	23	6	30	15	4	65	13
% of GDP from agriculture (1989)	2.2	4.0	1.5	15.6	5.2	3.5	10.3	4.5	2.4	4.1	6.4	1.7	3.2
Number of farm workers per 100 hectares (1987)	11	5	14	54	14	7	8	33	8	15	50	4	n/a
% change in number of farm workers 1979-87	−2%	−6%	−6%	+1%	+1%	−2%	−15%	−3%	−20%	−3%	−14%	−1%	n/a
% change in number of farms 1979–87	−20%	−30%	−17%	−5%	−1%	−22%	−3%	−2%	−19%	−11%	−17%	−3%	n/a

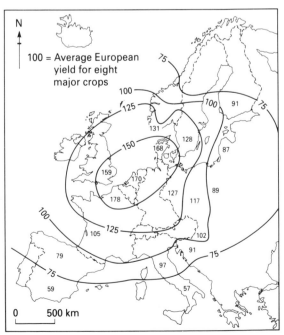

Fig 5.5   *Crops Yields*

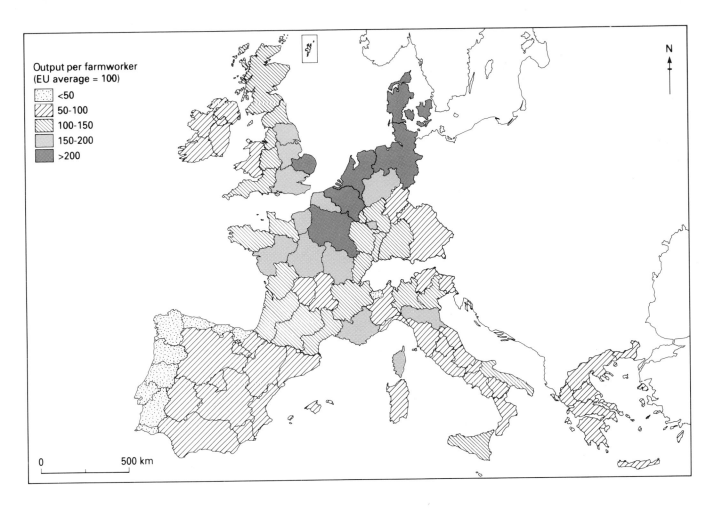

Output per farmworker
(EU average = 100)
- <50
- 50-100
- 100-150
- 150-200
- >200

0   500 km

FIG 5.6   *Labour Productivity 1986–1988*

5.2 The Common Agricultural Policy: the Need for Change

The net effect of the CAP has been, via higher prices, to transfer resources from the EU consumer to the EU producer. At the same time the CAP has led to a less efficient allocation of resources within the EU in that high prices have made the use of marginal land and labour-intensive processes economically viable.

Applied Economics, ed. A Griffiths & S Wall.

The Objectives of the Common Agricultural Policy (CAP)

The Treaty of Rome, signed by the original six members of the EU in 1957, outlined five objectives for future agricultural policy:

1   to increase agricultural production;

2   to guarantee a reasonable standard of living for farmers;

3   to stabilise food prices and food supplies;

4   to guarantee food supplies to consumers;

5   to guarantee reasonable food prices for consumers.

To understand the importance of these objectives to governments at the time it is important to remember that they were agreed only 12 years after the end of the Second

World War. Agriculture had been badly disrupted and the war had highlighted the importance of countries being self-sufficient in food supplies. Food rationing had continued for some years after the end of the war. Until 1945 agriculture was Europe's largest industry and provided a significant proportion of all jobs. In many countries farming was still a fundamental part of national life and governments depended on support from the farming population.

However, by the time of the Treaty of Rome in 1957 circumstances were changing. The economies of the six EU countries were rapidly recovering. Agriculture was declining in economic importance because of the rapid growth of industry. However, the belief that a reliable and growing supply of food was vital and should be an integral part of EU policy was firmly entrenched in the minds of politicians. In any case, the six member countries were still net importers of food.

An additional justification for the EU to actively support farmers and to intervene in the free market is that agricultural markets are inherently unstable. If the amount of food reaching the shops increases due to, for example, ideal weather conditions, prices will fall because of the law of supply and demand. However, food has a low **price elasticity of demand** meaning that consumers will not necessarily purchase more food simply because the price drops (since they can only eat a limited amount of food). As a result farmers may actually receive a lower income in a 'good year' than in a 'bad year'. There is, therefore, no incentive for farmers to boost production to guarantee reliable food supplies. Farmers may, in fact, cut production of certain crops following a price fall. This could in turn create a shortage, and therefore a price rise the following year. Such ups and downs in farm prices would make it difficult for farmers to make investment plans. This could cause long-term decline or uncertainty in food output.

An additional long-term problem for farmers is that food also has a low **income elasticity of demand** meaning that even if the peoples' incomes rise they will not buy large amounts of additional food. Over the last few decades the incomes of most workers in western Europe have risen in real terms but they have not spent proportionally more on food. The result is that farmers' incomes have fallen relative to all other workers. This again acts as a disincentive to farmers. They may be encouraged to abandon their farms and to move to urban areas to find jobs in industry. This could threaten future food supplies.

These economic arguments are used as a justification for government intervention in agriculture throughout the world, even by governments who otherwise believe in minimum state intervention in the economy. Although by the 1960s food shortages were no longer a problem in western Europe the belief of politicians that farmers should be protected from declining and uncertain incomes continued to dominate agricultural policy. Many feared that agricultural decline would lead to a collapse of the entire rural economy creating enormous social and economic problems. Others saw increasing food production as a way of boosting exports.

Within the EU there was, and continues to be, a consensus that farmers need state support.

How does the CAP Work?

The CAP aims to aid farming by:

1 preventing the prices farmers get for their products from falling below a certain level;

2 controlling imports of cheap food from countries outside the EU which could undercut EU farmers;

3 financing projects to improve agricultural efficiency, particularly in southern Europe when farm productivity and yields are low.

The cost of the CAP is met from the EU's European Agricultural Guidance and Guarantee Fund (EAGGF) which accounts for about 80 per cent of total EU expenditure. **1** and **2** above form the Guarantee section of the CAP while **3** represents the Guidance section. The Guidance Section accounts for only 3.5 per cent of total CAP expenditure.

1 Controlling Prices or Price Support

Market forces may force the price of farm products downwards. To prevent the price falling too far a price level is set by the EU called the Intervention Price. If the intervention price is reached then EU member countries guarantee to buy in produce from the farmers at the intervention price in order to maintain their income and to prevent further price falls. Since farmers are aware that the EU will always pay for any produce they are unable to sell on the open market they have been encouraged to boost production to such an extent that supply now exceeds demand. The resulting food mountains accumulated by the EU have probably contributed more than anything else to growing calls for the reform of the CAP.

A number of reforms to the CAP were made in the 1970s and 1980s in an attempt to control the size of these food mountains. These included allowing the prices farmers receive (in other words, the intervention price) to fall and imposing quotas (or compulsory limits on production) on certain products such as milk.

2 Controlling Imports

Cheap imports into EU countries would undermine the EU's attempts to maintain farmers' incomes because the price of EU produce would have to fall as well in order to compete. A levy (or tax) is imposed on all imports to raise their price to the same level as EU produce. If, on the other hand, EU farmers want to export their produce to countries outside the EU then they are paid a subsidy representing the difference between world prices and EU prices. In this way the EU has erected a protective barrier around EU agriculture and this has aroused a great deal of opposition from non-EU countries, particularly the USA.

3 Financing Improvement Projects

Although this only represents a very small percentage of total CAP expenditure it nevertheless accounts for large sums of money. Grants are given to EU member countries to support projects such as irrigation, drainage, field enlargement, new roads and other infrastructure improvements. This Guidance section of the CAP is facing increasing opposition from conservationists since large-scale habitat destruction has accompanied many of the projects.

- Explain what the quotation at the beginning of this section means.

- What does Fig. 5.7 indicate about:
  a) the importance of the CAP within the EU?
  b) the importance of price support within the CAP?
  c) the overall cost of farm support?

- Describe the pattern of monetary flows shown in Fig. 5.8. What conclusions can you make about the CAP from the graph?

The extent to which the CAP achieved its objectives up to the 1990s is open to debate but as early as the 1960s flaws in the policy were emerging. Throughout the 1970s and 1980s concerns over its operation and impact were voiced by politicians, farmers and conservationists. A number of problems which prompted these concerns can be identified.

Cost

By 1991 the CAP was costing EU tax payers and consumers £80 billion a year (or £250 per person), and the cost was still rising. Many increasingly questioned why an industry which employs only seven per cent of the EU workforce (less than three per cent in the UK) should receive such enormous quantities of public money, while other areas of economic activity received less than 40 per cent of the EU budget. In the UK comparisons were made with the government's refusal to subsidise the coal industry.

New Technology

Support prices encouraged farmers to boost output as much as possible and new technology provided the tools to do this. New types of seed, chemical fertilisers and pesticides, improved machinery, new irrigation and drainage systems and

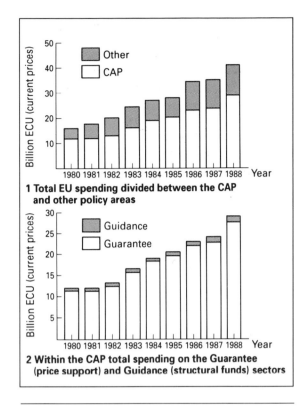

1 Total EU spending divided between the CAP and other policy areas

2 Within the CAP total spending on the Guarantee (price support) and Guidance (structural funds) sectors

FIG 5.7 *Costs of CAP*

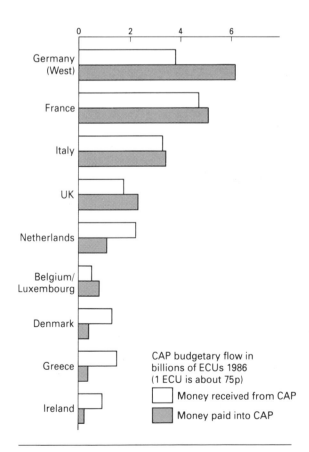

FIG 5.8 *Winners and Losers, The Guardian, 9 June 1992*

improved farm buildings all helped to increase yields. Between 1973 and 1988, for example, cereal production rose by 48 per cent. This contributed to the worsening problem of over-production and also meant that farming was increasingly capital intensive. Despite massive support less and less farm workers were needed. Rural depopulation, and the resulting economic and social decline of some rural areas, were not being prevented by the CAP.

Surpluses

The CAP price support mechanism committed member governments to buying in surplus farm produce in order to maintain farmers' incomes. The EU was then faced with a number of options to deal with the surplus.

a) Store it in intervention warehouses – an expensive process.

b) Subsidise its export to countries outside the EU – a process known as 'dumping'. This can be very unpopular in the importing countries since cheap EU food will undermine the prices being received by their farmers.

c) Use the produce for lower grade uses. For example, wine can be converted to industrial alcohol or high grade grain fed to livestock.

When French farmers' Profits were Threatened by a Bumper Harvest of Apples, They Dumped the Surplus on this Rotting Apple Mountain in Vaucluse to Prevent Prices from Falling, 6 October 1992

d) Give it away as foreign aid.

e) Destroy it.

In addition to the cost of many of these options, critics find the storage or destruction of food morally unacceptable when less developed countries and eastern European populations are faced with serious food shortages. Policies designed to reduce the size of the surpluses, such as quotas (where limits are placed on the quantities of a product, e.g. milk, each member state can produce) and set-aside (see section 5.5) have had some success but nevertheless in some cases stocks continued to grow. In 1992 grain surpluses reached 26 million tonnes and these were expected to rise to 40 million tonnes by 1993.

Unequal Benefits

Since it is the prices of farm produce which the CAP supports then it is the farmers with the largest farms and who grow the most who will receive the largest subsidies. Also, farmers operating in ideal environmental conditions will fare much better than farmers in marginal areas. Many critics see this as inequitable and difficult to justify. The EU has introduced measures to boost support to farmers in marginal areas. The EU designates 40 per cent of the UK, for example, as Less Favoured Areas where farmers are paid Compensatory Allowances such as an additional payment for each sheep or cow. Designated mountain areas also receive special allowances. However, such schemes represent a small part of total CAP expenditure.

Opposition from Outside the EU

The USA and the eastern European countries have been particularly vocal in objecting to the degree of protection and subsidy EU farmers receive. Such countries find that EU tariff barriers make it difficult to sell their produce within the EU while subsidised EU produce is 'dumped' in their own country undercutting their farmers. Opposition to CAP subsidies from the USA and less developed countries delayed agreement in the international GATT negotiations aimed at 'freeing up' world trade between 1991 and 1993.

Conflict within the EU

The CAP does not necessarily equalise the price of commodities throughout the EU. Exchange rates, for example, may result in price variations. Opposition from French farmers to cheap food imports from the UK has been violent at times.

Enlargement of the EU

When Portugal and Spain joined the EU in 1986 the weaknesses in the CAP were deepened. The two new members together increased the EU's agricultural workforce by 24 per cent, their farms were typically small with low yields and low productivity, and EU support at the time was geared to north European products such as cereals, milk and beef rather than southern products such as fruit, wine and vegetables. In order that the new members should receive an equitable level of assistance total CAP expenditure had to be considerably increased. Any future acceptance of new members in eastern Europe would pose similar problems.

Environmental Threats

Opposition to the CAP from conservationists has steadily grown over recent years and many would see this as the most important issue facing EU agriculture in the 1990s.

FIG 5.9   *Food Mountains and Wine Lakes*

Fraud

Fraudulent claims for CAP subsidies are probably occuring on a large scale and lead to the loss of millions of pounds. The EU is frequently criticised for inadequate policing of its subsidies.

- Evaluate the effectiveness of Fig 5.9 in illustrating the size of the food surpluses. Can you suggest any alternative methods of showing the quantities involved?

- Produce a table summarising the benefits and costs of the CAP for farmers and consumers. Use the following format:

	COSTS	BENEFITS
FARMERS		
CONSUMERS		

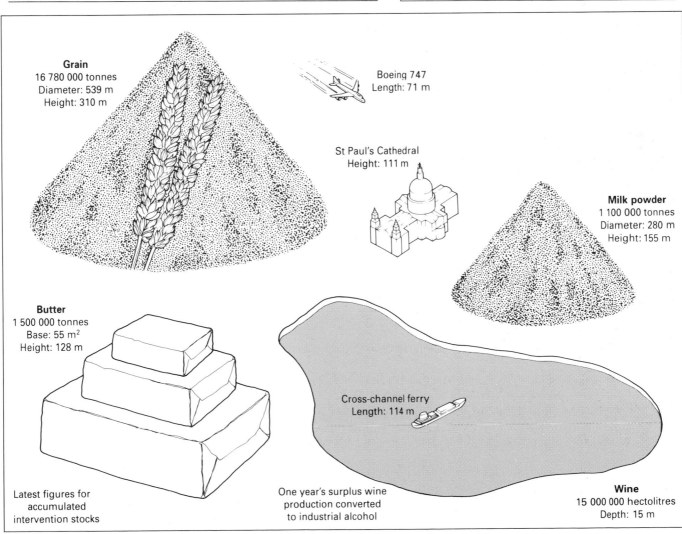

Grain
16 780 000 tonnes
Diameter: 539 m
Height: 310 m

Boeing 747
Length: 71 m

St Paul's Cathedral
Height: 111 m

Milk powder
1 100 000 tonnes
Diameter: 280 m
Height: 155 m

Butter
1 500 000 tonnes
Base: 55 m²
Height: 128 m

Cross-channel ferry
Length: 114 m

Latest figures for accumulated intervention stocks

One year's surplus wine production converted to industrial alcohol

Wine
15 000 000 hectolitres
Depth: 15 m

5.3 The 1992 CAP Reforms

These reforms represent a bitter pill for me to swallow. My father, my brother and myself will have to put about 50 to 60 acres of the farmland into set-aside. We will be paid not to crop the land, but we will have to tend the fields – to mow the weeds and grass regularly. Meanwhile, we will still need much the same amount of equipment and staff, except these costs will have to be met from the remaining land where the returns will be 29 per cent lower. This remaining land will then have to work harder simply to support those who crop it.

Matthew Dale, a British farmer.

FIG 5.10   *The Observer, 24 May 1992*

FIG 5.11a   *World Trade Talks*

Reforms to hasten the rural exodus

DAI BASSETT, the singing Welsh cattle farmer, will soon be at home on the range. The golf driving range.

Last month he and his father sold their prize dairy herd, the most productive in Glamorgan, because it could no longer provide them with a decent living. They are replacing their pasture land at Highfield Farm, Llantwit Major, with a new crop – a nine-acre driving range, complete with 20,000 golf balls, to service nearby Bridgend. An office building, coffee bar and, they hope, a 16-acre pitch and putt course will follow.

Mr Basset, 32, who has two children, spends several nights a week singing comic ditties at pub and club receptions to earn extra cash. He is also one of thousands of farmers driven by Britain's growing farming crisis to find new uses for their land.

Their numbers will be swollen by the European agricultural revolution which will follow last week's sweeping reform of the Common Agricultural Policy. This could transform the British countryside, as farmers are forced to abandon 50 years of maximising food production, creating opportunities to regenerate the landscape, provide new wilderness and expand farm tourism.

The most urgent issue facing Ministers, farmers and environmentalists is the fate of the 1.5 million acres likely to come out of production over the next couple of years; farmers will have to make up income lost by reduced grain prices by claiming set-aside compensation.

'I was getting up at 6.30am and working till six or eight at night and taking home £81 a week,' said Mr Bassett on Friday.

Even though his 41-strong herd produced the best milk yield in the county and was ranked sixth in Wales, he was forced to sell it because of eight years of deepening EC cuts in the amount each dairy farmer could produce.

He is keeping on a small herd of heifers and beef calves, but plans to spend 14 hours a day on the golf range.

He says some of his neighbours have been forced to start providing bed and breakfast accommodation, while one hires out his stables and yet another rents out caravans and go-karts. He had to drop a song called *We're Penniless Farmers Together* from his pub repertoire because his audience failed to appreciate the joke.

Across the country, arable farmer Robin Waters now tends a giant lawn. After a rent rise and a couple of bad harvests, he accepted £30,000 a year from the Government to take his 400-acre Marsh Hall Farm near Halstead, Essex, out of production. He put most of it down to grass and swapped his agricultural machinery for a huge mower, which carves a 20ft-wide swathe, to keep it trim.

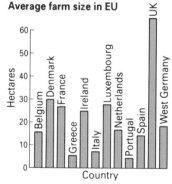

Average farm size in EU

He gets another £2,500 a year from the Countryside Commission for converting 45 acres into flower-rich ancient meadows, complete with footpaths and bridleways. He hires out his old grain stores as hangars for a neighbouring airfield, devoting himself to a second career as a steel-work fabricator.

In the last few years some 3,500 farmers have accepted government money to set up new enterprises – including farm shops, cheese-making, war games, ostrich and llama farming and even children's toy franchises – and more than 400,000 acres of land have been taken out of production in Government 'set-aside' schemes. But this is merely a foretaste.

The EC cuts will compound the severe economic crisis besetting Britain's farmers. Already they owe banks £7 billion, more than five times their total income; 35 agricultural workers leave the land every day, and a recent survey revealed that the average farmer's income had plummeted to £11,000.

The new cuts in subsidies, which will be phased in as from next year, are likely to accelerate this exodus in the short term. But it opens up new opportunities for the majority, who will adapt and stay afloat.

It is clear the reforms mark the end of decades of ever more intensive farming, born of war-time shortages and aimed at producing as much food as possible; now no funds will be used to support farmers' incomes. But it is less clear what the harvest of the new philosophy will be.

French farmers threaten to turn up heat

FRENCH farmers warned last night that they were ready to step up their attempt to blockade Paris during this morning's rush-hour as part of a wave of protests that could last several days.

Although police claimed that they had successfully countered the first day's demonstration by Co-ordination Rurale, the farmers' unofficial trade union, the movement said their actions had been a success.

The day was marked by a form of guerrilla warfare with about 30 highly mobile groups of farmers from all over France rushing from one point to another to block roads and railways.

As the groups usually dispersed before riot police arrived, there was only one significant clash, when protesters held up traffic on the Paris ring road.

After a high-speed chase police alleged that the farmers had tried to knock down their motorcyclists. Several arrests were made.

The interior minister Charles Pasqua, said the farmers had failed to achieve their goal of blockading Paris and warned them not to carry out their threat to continue mounting scattered roadblocks.

"All in all it seems to me that the least one can say is that the goals they set themselves – to block traffic around the capital – have not been met," he said.

The farmers mostly kept to their plan to stay at least 30 miles from Paris and move swiftly from one blockade to another, a change in strategy from last year when riot police easily broke up mass demonstrations.

Drivers on motorways and main roads were suddenly confronted with barricades of burning tyres or parked farm vehicles before the farmers fled after receiving instructions by telephone from their headquarters near Etampes.

But their most effective demonstrations were *"operations escargot"* in which slow farm vehicles were used to hold up traffic within and outside the city. Drivers and farmers nearly came to blows when jams stretched for several miles.

Commuters and long-distance rail travellers were also held up. At one stage, the high-speed TGV railway line to the south-west was blocked at four different places.

"It has been a very successful day," one of Co-ordination Rurale's leaders said. "There are about 10,000 farmers ready to go into action during the rest of the week to make sure the government does not back down on its resolve to oppose renegotiation of the Gatt agreement on farm products.

"The opening day was only to test the determination of the police and perfect our guerrilla tactics. Hundreds of other farmers are now ready to set up more roadblocks and hold up trains."

FIG **5.11b** *The Guardian, 16 September 1993 (above)*

FIG **5.12** *The Guardian, 17 November 1992*

Their fields are being 'set-aside' and their children have gone to search for work in the cities. Can sentiment, or barricades, save 'les paysans' and a way of life that seems out of place in the world of Gatt?

EARLY this century, the majority of the French population was still working on the land, six million in 1910. Only 20 years ago, France still had four million farms employing 20 per cent of the active workforce. Today only one million are left and that number is falling fast. Half of France's remaining farmers are already over 50 and have no heir to take over their land. Disillusioned with harsh farm life, most younger men make their way to the towns, where many of them boost France's rising unemployment figures.

The militant farmers' lobby claims the latest CAP reform package will force thousands more to leave the land. Agriculture Commissioner Ray McSharry's proposals adopted in May call for a 30 per cent drop in grain prices over the next few years and the setting aside of 15 per cent farmland to lie fallow.

Pierre Chassaigne, an agricultural estate agent in Toulouse is now dealing with five times as many properties than a few years ago. If you are tempted by the good life, there has never been a better time to pick up a farmhouse and a few hectares of *La Belle France* cheaply.

Perversely, this decline is largely due to the successful modernisation of French agriculture since the 1960s – particularly in the northern plains and round Paris – when the government first started to create larger farms. Semi-public bodies called SAFERS were set up to buy farmland on the market while another grouping, GAECS, enables farmers to jointly manage adjacent terrain. Farm sizes have leapt from an aveage 19 hectares in 1970 to 30 hectares now. Sophisticated farms of the Paris basin average 100.

Incentives and subsidies first introduced with the CAP in the 1960s and 1970s also brought enhanced productivity. The French farmer who fed seven people in 1960 now feeds more than 40. *Les paysans* see themselves as the victims of this success. The frenzy of production which eventually gave rise to EC wine lakes and butter mountains of the 1970s and 1980s also brought farm prices down. In real terms, French farm incomes are barely higher today than they were two decades ago.

Many farmers who borrowed heavily to modernise are now deep in debt. According to Credit Agricole which provided 90 per cent of the farming sector's state-subsidised loans, 7,500 of France's biggest farms now have average debts of Ffr400,000 (£50,000). Income from rented *gîtes* or the sale of quality farm produce is now vital to the farm budget and no longer merely a welcome extra. More than half of France's farmers have a second job.

The government says it is doing its best to help. France already receives the largest chunk of EC agricultural subsidy. Ecu 5.8 billion (£7 billion) in 1990, more than Britain and the Netherlands together.

Economic pressures and frustrations at the imposed changes to their lifestyle have forced the farmers onto their tractors and onto the nation's highways, hijacking English Lamb and Hungarian pork, burning hay bales in front of the prefectures.

The government is trying to highlight the opportunities provided by this shift. One solution for the surplus of unworked land is a less intensive, more eco-friendly system of land management, allowing the forest to grow back and using less chemicals. This is an approach which has found favour with two very different but increasingly powerful countryside lobbies – the *soixante-huitard* hippies who are returning to the land and the ultra-conservative hunting, fishing brigade whose fledgling political party *Chase, Pêche, Nature et Tradition* is gaining ground.

Another alternative is turning out more high class farm produce and finding new markets for *produits fermiers*, from wine to cassoulet.

Many farmers have already caught on to tourism, inviting guests to eat on the farm, converting stable blocks into charming hotels, hiring out their cattle to graze mountain pasture which becomes ski piste in winter.

But the rural revolution goes on. The village of Sos in Lot-et-Garonne lost its *notaire* in 1950, the rugby team in 1955. By 1970, the gendarmerie had gone and by 1980, the priest. In 1990, the bank closed. No amount of tourists will bring any of them back.

By 1992 the pressure for reform from both within and outside the EU had become irresistable and EU Agricultural Ministers reached agreement on a package of reforms. These included:

1 reductions of 29 per cent in the intervention price for cereals;

2 reductions of 15 per cent in the intervention price for beef;

3 a one per cent reduction in milk quotas;

4 medium and large-scale cereal farmers will have to take 15 per cent of their land out of production;

5 compensation payments to farmers to help cover the losses in income caused by measures **1** to **4**;

6 financial incentives to encourage farmers to adopt alternative uses of the land taken out of production.

Measures **5** and **6** will add £3 billion a year to the cost of the CAP in the short-term. In the longer term cuts in support prices should produce savings and slightly lower food prices in the shops.

- Which of the problems outlined in Section 5.2 will these measures tackle and which problems seem to have been ignored?

- List the social and economic consequences of the reforms which are outlined in Figs 5.10 to 5.12.

- Why do you think farmers do not believe that the 15 per cent reduction in land used for cereal production will lead to a similar reduction in cereal output?

French Farmers React

French farmers in particular have been strongly opposed to the CAP reforms and many feel they have been 'sold out' by their government and by the EU. Demonstrations by French farmers, including the blockading of roads and railways, were commonplace after the reforms were announced in 1992.

Farmers have considerable political influence in France. Although farming only employs five per cent of the labour force many people can remember when they, their family or friends worked on the land. It has been estimated that over 15 per cent of French voters are influenced by farming

French Farmers Protest Against Agricultural Reforms, The Observer, October 1992

concerns.

Some of this influence stems from farming's considerable economic importance. France's trade in manufactured goods went into the red in the late 1980s but it has a steadily increasing trade surplus in farm produce. France is now the second largest food exporter in the world after the USA.

To explain why French farmers in particular were so upset by the CAP reforms it is necessary to look at the recent history of French farming. In 1970 France had 1.6 million farms – by 1990 only one million were left. This is expected to decline to 700000 by the year 2000. In 1970 three million people worked on the land but by 1990 this had fallen to 1.5 million. Some of these reductions have been deliberately encouraged by the government to ensure French agriculture's efficiency and competitiveness. Over the same period farm productivity has increased enormously.

However these changes have not led to greater prosperity for the remaining French farmers. Between the early 1970s and the 1990s real income per farm rose by 25 per cent while wages of workers in other parts of the economy rose by 50 per cent. Nearly half of all French farmers now have a second job to supplement their income. Many smaller farmers, having borrowed heavily to invest in their farms, are now heavily in debt. In order to cut costs, less farmers are employing paid workers, so farmers and their families are working longer hours for relatively lower incomes.

French farmers are worried about the future. They are particularly angry with the EU because over recent decades they have responded to EU incentives to increase production and now they are being asked to cut output in a way which threatens their livelihood. They see any cut in the massive French Government or EU subsidies (£1.5 billion in 1991 alone) as the final straw.

- Read Fig 5.11b. Why are the farmers using these tactics? Do you think they are justified?

- Imagine that you are employed by the French Government and you have been asked to attend a meeting of farmers to convince them of the need for reform. Outline the main points you would make to the farmers.

5.4 The Threat to the Environment

The need now is to create a new countryside – no less artificial, as it will be a creation of policy – but one where wider objectives are satisfied. Just as policy-makers have begun to reappraise the meaning of 'rural' in their policies, the need now is to redefine 'farming' as more than simply 'food production'.

The Royal Society for the Protection of Birds.

EU agricultural policy is having a major impact on the rural environment in all the member countries. Farmed landscapes, which are artificial but which have evolved over hundreds or thousand of years, provide essential habitats and ecosystems. This is especially important in a continent where few wilderness areas or truly natural landscapes remain. The problem is that in large parts of Europe rapid farm modernisation has led to a reduction in wildlife habitats, damage to the visual appearance in landscapes, worsening soil erosion and pollution. Agriculture in turn is also threatened since long-term environmental deterioration will damage our ability to grow our own food.

EU policy is linked to the environmental impact of farming in three main ways.

1 Support prices (or the Guarantee section of agricultural policy) have encouraged farmers to increase production by:

a) intensification (increasing inputs of fertilisers, pesticides, machinery, and irrigation and drainage systems);
b) reclamation (reclaiming previously unused land such as moorland and wetland);
c) specialisation (concentrating on particular crops or livestock).

2 In southern Europe a greater threat is massive EU investment in farm modernisation schemes and the provision of new infrastructure such as roads and irrigation (through the Guidance section of agricultural policy). This injection of large sums of EU money is damaging the environment on a large scale.

3 The large surpluses EU policy has helped to create are providing an opportunity to cut agricultural output by reducing the intensity of production and the amount of land in production. The EU could control this process in a way which would benefit the environment.

The Impact of Price Support: a Subsidy on Environmental Disruption

Support prices have encouraged intensification, reclamation and specialisation and each can have serious environmental impacts. Intensification reduces the ability of farm land to support wildlife due to pollution and the disturbance of habitats. Reclamation destroys habitats, and specialisation creates uniform landscapes which do not provide the variety which many types of wildlife need to survive.

Support prices have been a major factor in encouraging environmental damage in northern Europe. Britain alone has lost most of its traditional hay meadows, lowland heaths, and ancient woodlands as well as thousands of kilometres of hedgerow during recent decades. The 1992 CAP reforms will moderate the environmental impact of price support but it will continue to dominate agricultural expenditure in a manner which largely ignores environmental impacts.

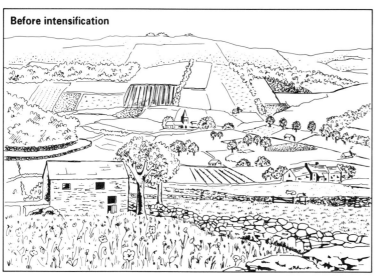

Before intensification

After intensification

FIG 5.13   *Agricultural Intensification on a British Farm*

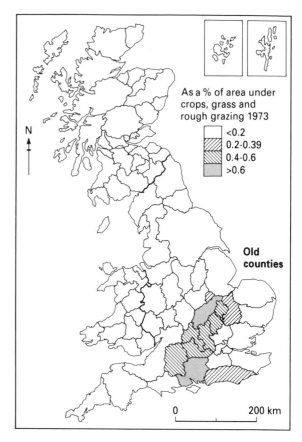

As a % of area under crops, grass and rough grazing 1973

<0.2
0.2-0.39
0.4-0.6
>0.6

Old counties

0   200 km

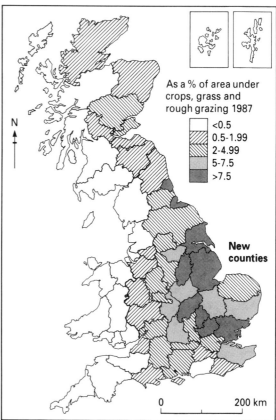

As a % of area under crops, grass and rough grazing 1987

<0.5
0.5-1.99
2-4.99
5-7.5
>7.5

New counties

0   200 km

FIG 5.14   *Changing Distribution of Oil Seed Rape in Great Britain*

- Use Fig 5.13 to describe the visual impact of agricultural intensification. Do you think the landscape has been improved or damaged by the changes?

- The CAP has had a direct impact on agricultural land use. For example, the CAP introduced high support prices for oil seed rape (well-known for its bright yellow flowers) because of a shortage of vegetable oils and protein rich livestock feed. Vegetable oils from the plant are used in cooking oils and margarine, and rapemeal, a by-product, can be used as livestock feed. Study Fig 5.14 and comment on the impact of the EU support price. Discuss the visual impact of oil seed rape on the British countryside.

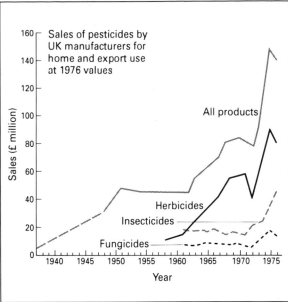

FIG 5.16   *Sales of Pesticides by UK Manufacturers*

- The use of nitrogen fertilisers can have a damaging impact on the environment. They can destroy traditional meadows full of wild flowers by allowing certain grasses to thrive and creating conditions in which most wild flowers cannot compete. They also cause eutrophication (see Section 9.5) in streams and ponds by increasing the nutrient content of the water. The high level of nutrients allows algae to multiply and the algae then deprives other aquatic life of oxygen. At its worst eutrophication can totally destroy an aquatic ecosystem. Describe the pattern of nitrogen fertiliser use in the EU shown by Fig 5.15.

- The UK joined the EU in 1973. Use Fig 5.16 to evaluate the hypothesis that 'the CAP has encouraged agricultural intensification and environmental damage'.

The Impact of Farm Modernisation: Traditional Landscapes Disappear

It is ridiculous to expect the structural funds to be concerned with the environment – they are about economic development.

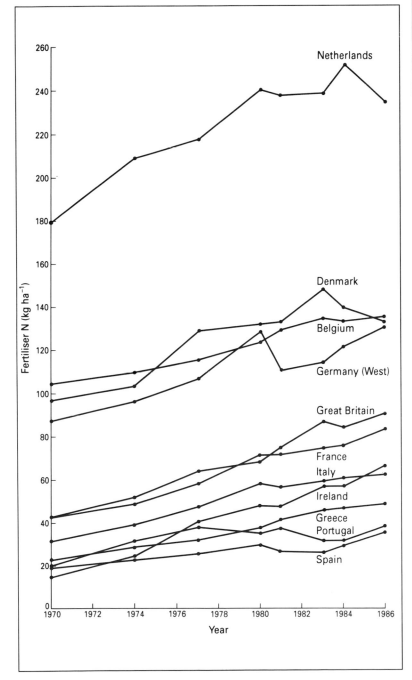

FIG 5.15   *Use of Nitrogen fertiliser in the EU*

Jean-Marie Sayler, section head of the EU's Regional Policy Directorate.

By 1993 the EU was spending £11 billion a year on attempting to narrow the economic gap between different parts of the EU. About 70 per cent of this vast sum was being spent on economic development in the so-called 'Objective One' regions covering Greece, Spain, Portugal, Corsica, Ireland, southern Italy, Northern Ireland and parts of Spain (see Section 7.7).

Additional funding and loans, £4 billion from 1986 to 1993, have been allocated through a package of measures known as the Integrated Mediterranean Programmes (IMPs). These measures are targeted at southern France, Italy and Greece. Following the entry of Spain and Portugal into the EU in 1986 the farmers in these regions would suffer greater competition from the two newcomers whose farmers grow similar types of produce.

The types of scheme funded through these structural funds include irrigation, the removal of field boundaries, drainage, pasture improvement, mechanisation, introduction of new crop types, road construction and new farm buildings. However, even in the IMPs, price support forms a large part of the package, particularly for wine, olive oil, peaches and tomatoes.

These Guidance funds are causing widespread environmental damage. Among the species of wildlife threatened are the dalmation pelicans in Greece and the imperial eagle and lynx in Spain. It is because economic change has been relatively slow in these rural areas and traditional farming methods have been maintained that such species and their habitats have survived. The EU grants now threaten their existence. In reality the EU has little control over how the money is spent since national governments design the schemes and allocate the funds on the ground. In some cases EU involvement is a well-kept secret hindering any opposition to the schemes from within the EU.

A Case Study: the Great Bustard and the Mediterranean Steppelands, Spain

If you don't like big, wide, open spaces, don't go to the Spanish Steppes! Few places in Europe rival their feeling of vastness. Beneath huge, wedgwood-blue skies, gently rolling hills and plains stretch in shades of yellow and brown to distant mauve mountains. These sierras mark the edges of the steppe but, by their very remoteness, only underline its huge extent… As the searing summer sun ascends into the huge arc of sky, the gentle lines of hills, layered to the horizon, melt into a wobbling heat haze. Circling high on the thermals, griffon vultures search for the latest casualty of the low intensity livestock farming practised over much of the steppe. Groups of lesser kestrels look for insects on the rising air currents, hunting away from their nest sites in the ancient church towers of nearby villages.

Martin Davies, Steppe in the Right Direction, Birds Magazine, RSPB, Autumn 1992.

Spanish Steppeland

FIG 5.17 *Steppelands, Spain*

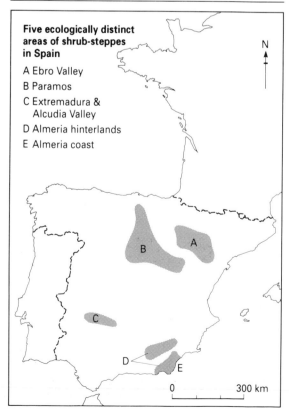

Five ecologically distinct areas of shrub-steppes in Spain

A Ebro Valley
B Paramos
C Extremadura & Alcudia Valley
D Almeria hinterlands
E Almeria coast

0   300 km

FIG 5.18 *European Population of Great Bustards*

European population of great bustards, excluding the Spanish population

Country	Number of birds 1930	1950	1970	1988
Czechoslovakia	2400	800	809	315
Germany	4000	3000	900	400
Poland	650	430	159	3
Hungary	9000	6000	3129	2365
Austria	1500	900	200	100
Romania	2500	2100	600	325
Bulgaria	200	150	30	
Yugoslavia	100	60	20	35
Russia (European)	7000	6000	3000	2980
TOTAL	27 350	19 440	8847	6500

Population estimates of great bustards in Spain

Region	Number of birds 1960	1970	1974	1977	1982
Ebro valley	1500	1000	330	99	90
Cuenca del Duero	7000	3000	3000	5492	4643
Castilla-La Mancha	6000	4500	2000	1063	1385
Extremadura	10 000	6500	5500	4120	1800
Andalusia	1000	1000	1000	508	194
TOTAL	25 000	16 000	11 830	11 282	8292

FIG 5.19 *Habitats for Great Bustards*

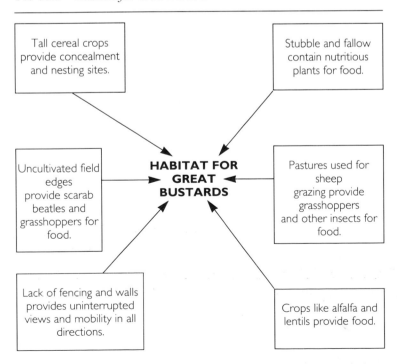

Traditional steppeland farming landscapes provide a mosaic of different environments needed by great bustards.

The Mediterranean Steppelands are a rare type of agricultural landscape found in Spain. In summer the **steppes** experience an extremely hot, dry climate – in winter it is bitterly cold. The terrain is flat or gently undulating featuring a patchwork of dry shrub areas (largely used for livestock grazing), grassland pastures, and fields used for cereal cultivation. There are few trees. Each farmer typically has a number of unfenced plots scattered among the different land types. There are five regions of steppeland remaining in Spain, each being ecologically distinctive with different altitude, rainfall, temperature and soil characteristics (see Fig 5.17).

Several species of bird of European or global significance live in these areas including the great bustard and little bustard, montagues harrier, dupont's lark and stone-curlew. They also provide wintering or 'stop-off' areas for species found in Britain such as the red kite, hen harrier and merlin.

The great bustard, for example, is a globally threatened species and most of the west European population breeds in Spain. Throughout Europe the population has steeply declined because of habitat disruption (see Fig 5.18).

The great bustards need a patchwork or 'mosaic' of different types of land use to survive, and only traditional agricultural landscapes provide such a mosaic (see Fig 5.19). These landscapes are disappearing with the aid of EU funds.

– Sheep flocks are being merged in order to save labour. This is causing more intensive grazing which is changing the vegetation cover.
– Large areas formerly used for grazing and cereal cultivation are being abandoned due to rural depopulation. Scrub is regenerating and this is reducing environmental diversity.
– Some land is being afforested reducing the openness of the landscape.
– Intensive cereal monoculture is being introduced with the help of irrigation schemes.
– Almond and olive groves are being planted on land originally used for cereals.
– Farms are being consolidated and fields are being fenced.
– New farm buildings are being erected.
– Chemical fertilisers and pesticides are being used in larger quantities.

Despite the fact that many of these 'improvements' are being funded by the EU they are actually against EU law. The EU Wild Birds Directive defines 15 protected areas in the Spanish steppes and the EU Fauna, Flora and Habitats Directive also gives protection to the steppes.

- Comment on the quote from Jean-Marie Sayler at the beginning of this section. Explain why you agree or disagree with the statement.

- Imagine you are a conservationist addressing a meeting of the National Farmers' Union. Outline the main points you would make to convince the farmers of the need to conserve rare species of bird or other wildlife.

- Study the data in Fig 5.18.
  a) Construct a line graph to show the change in the bustard populations in the five areas between 1960 and 1982. Use your graph to estimate the populations in 1988.
  b) Construct a graph designed to highlight the importance of the Spanish bustard population within Europe. Use the 1988 data from Fig 5.18 and an estimate of the total Spanish population in 1988 derived from the graph you constructed in part **a)**.
  c) What conclusions can you make from your two graphs?

5.5 Integrating Agricultural and Environmental Policies

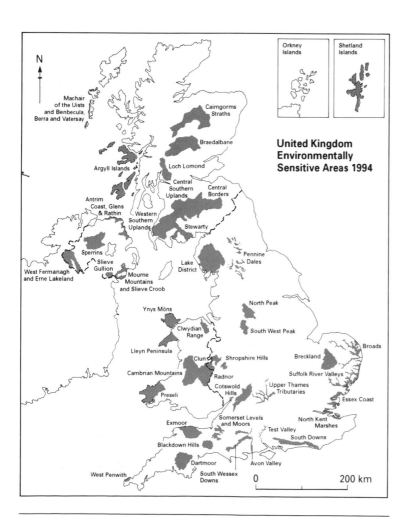

The CAP should have as one of its explicit objectives the protection of the rural environment.

Royal Society for the Protection of Birds.

A number of conservation groups, such as the Worldwide Fund for Nature (WWF) and the Royal Society for the Protection of Birds (RSPB) in the UK, have been very active in campaigning and lobbying politicians in order to persuade the EU to make the environment a priority concern of the CAP. They believe that over-production has provided an ideal opportunity to reduce the intensity of farming in a way which would enhance the environment. This section examines two EU policies which either have positive environmental impacts or have the potential to benefit the environment.

Environmentally Sensitive Areas

Since 1986 the EU has allowed member states to designate Environmentally Sensitive Areas (ESAs) in areas of high ecological or landscape value. The UK Government had 29 such areas by 1993 and an additional six by 1994 (see Fig 5.20). Farmers in ESAs can be subsidised by special payments in return for adopting less environmentally damaging production methods. Member states receive grants from the EU covering 25 per cent of

Fig 5.20 *Environmentally Sensitive Areas in the UK*

the cost (or in some cases 50 per cent). The scheme recognises the role farmers have in managing the landscape and wildlife habitats.

However, the scheme is voluntary. Member states do not have to implement ESA schemes and farmers in ESAs do not have to participate. Farmers who wish to participate can opt to have only part of their land included in the scheme.

In order to understand how the scheme operates and to evaluate its effectiveness the Cambrian Mountains ESA in Wales can be examined in detail.

The Cambrian Mountains ESA is a wild and sparsely populated upland area dissected by deep river valleys. Farming is dominated by sheep and beef production. Most of the land is used as rough grazing but oak woodland and hay meadows provide some diversity in the type of habitats available for wildlife. The area is particularly notable for its populations of birds of prey including red kite, peregrine falcon, merlin and buzzards. Twenty-three per cent of the ESA is designated as a Site of Special Scientific Interest (SSSI) by the British Government in recognition of its ecological importance. The area also has a number of archaeological and historic sites including burial mounds, cairns, and early industrial sites. The environment in the area is particularly threatened by:

— improvement of rough grazing (using fertilisers and reseeding to improve the nutritional value of the vegetation to livestock) which lowers its value for wildlife;
— overgrazing by sheep in the oak woodlands;
— coniferous **afforestation**.

The Welsh Office Agriculture Department (WOAD), the government department responsible for implementing ESAs in Wales, has the following objectives in the Cambrian Mountains ESA:

1 to encourage farmers to protect the landscape and wildlife value of rough grazing areas by limiting livestock numbers;

2 to conserve the ecology of the oak woodlands by careful management;

3 to conserve existing hay meadows;

4 to safeguard the archaeological sites in the area.

WOAD has set a number of conditions which farmers must adhere to in order to receive the ESA payments. These include:

— a ban on the installation of new drainage schemes and on the use of pesticides;
— a ban on the construction of new walls, fences or hedges. Existing hedges and walls must be maintained;
— special permission must be obtained before constructing new roads or buildings or altering existing buildings;
— lakes, ponds and streams must be conserved;
— limitations on the application of fertilisers;
— a prohibition on the ploughing, reseeding or cultivation of rough grazing land.

Some facts and figures for the Cambrian Mountains ESA

Number of farmers participating: 352
Area included in scheme: 30 160 hectares.
Percentage of total ESA included in scheme: 20%
Total ESA payments (1987–90): £1 163 000 (25 per cent of this cost met by the EU)
ESA payments per hectare: £30
ESA payments farmers believe are necessary according to a recent questionnaire: £42.50 to £100.

It is difficult to evaluate the effectiveness of ESAs because of the relatively short period they have been operating. It is also very difficult to predict what would have happened without ESAs. In a study of ESAs, Friends of the Earth (FoE) expressed the view that: *'The ESA has been little more than a holding exercise.... The existing prescriptions maintain the status quo and safeguard areas of semi-natural rough grazing. Heather moorland and other degraded habitats are not being restored and therefore wildlife populations are not recovering.'* In other words, ESAs are failing to encourage wildlife — they are merely preserving the status quo.

FoE explain this failure to enhance the environment, as opposed to merely preventing further decline, by pointing out that:
— grazing is still too intensive. Much of the rough grazing needs a 40 to 60 per cent reduction in livestock numbers but many farmers are being allowed to make reductions of only 20 to 30 per cent. In fact, two-thirds of farms have not needed to reduce numbers at all to receive ESA payments. This tendency to keep livestock numbers at the maximum permitted level is partly because the Cambrian Mountains is designated by the EU as a Less Favoured Area. In these areas farmers receive EU payments per animal — by maximising livestock numbers within the range permitted by ESA requirements the farmers are maximising their EU subsidy;
— some farmers are reluctant to participate because they argue that ESA payments are inadequate to compensate for the loss in profits resulting from ESA designation;

– some farmers only enter their more marginal land into the scheme knowing that loss of output will then be minimised. The farmers with the largest sheep flocks are reluctant to join the scheme because they would have to dispose of livestock at a loss;
– coniferous afforestation has continued in the area (often with the help of government grants) and further afforestation schemes are anticipated in the future.

On the positive side FoE found that many farmers in the Cambrian Mountains support the ESA concept and would like to see the ESAs extended as long as they remain voluntary. There is also evidence that ESA payments may be offering a more secure income to some farmers and are helping to discourage depopulation and farm decline. Generally farmers agree to ESA designation for business reasons. Environmental reasons are of secondary importance, although many accept that environmental factors should be given greater consideration.

- Why are farmers on the more marginal (or poorer) land more likely to join the ESA scheme?

- ESAs are merely 'environmental window-dressing' by the EU. In the light of the information in this chapter do you agree with this statement?

- List the advantages and disadvantages of making the scheme compulsory for all farmers in an ESA.

- Outline your proposals for the design of a government sponsored advertisement to appear in the farming press aimed at encouraging participation in ESA schemes. Think carefully about the type of people you are trying to appeal to and the type of information they will need.

Few other EU member states have designated ESAs. So far the Netherlands, Germany and Denmark have adopted the scheme, with Spain announcing two ESAs at the end of 1992 following intense campaigning by conservationists. France and Italy are also currently preparing schemes. In Germany the individual state governments, or Länder, are responsible for environmental legislation and a number of states have introduced ESAs.

The *Sociedad Espanola Ornitologia* (the Spanish bird conservation organisation) and the International Council for Bird

Cambrian Mountains ESA in Wales

Preservation have submitted proposals for ESA designation of five Spanish steppeland areas (see Section 5.4) which are particularly important as habitats for birds such as the bustard. Their recommendations have the support of the largest farmers' unions in Spain and the regional governments. One farmers' union spokesman commented:

'Certainly, the farmers recognise that they can potentially use the ESA to obtain money from Brussels, but I believe they also recognise that co-operation with conservation groups will be essential – farmers are being asked to help protect the quality of the environment on behalf of society.'

The conservationists have recommended the following management prescriptions.

– Strict limits on the extent of irrigation.
– Controls on the intensity of sheep grazing.
– Restrictions on the types of crop.
– Introduction or maintenance of crop rotation with adequate fallow periods.
– Limits on the maximum size of fields.
– Management of uncultivated strips around fields.
– Restrictions on the timing of farming activities to prevent the destruction of nests and chicks.
– Constraints on the use of fertilisers and pesticides.
– Constraints on the construction of roads, buildings, fences and power lines.
– Maintenance of buildings used as nest-sites.
– Measures to control dogs and foxes which can kill young birds.

In many cases such measures would only impose minor changes in farming methods.

In 1992 the Spanish authorities agreed to designate two ESAs (Villa Fafilia and Madrigal-Penaranda) but most of the steppes remain unprotected.

- Suggest how the ESA scheme could be modified by the EU in order to persuade more of the Spanish regions to designate the steppelands as ESAs.

Set-aside

The set-aside scheme was introduced by the EU in 1988 with the aim of reducing surpluses. All member states were obliged to implement the scheme but participation by farmers was voluntary. Farmers who were prepared to take 20 per cent or more of their land out of production for a period of five years received compensation of varying amounts depending on location and the use to which the land was put. The land taken out of production had to have previously been used for crops receiving EU price support. The set-aside land had to be left fallow, afforested or used for non-agricultural purposes such as horse grazing or golf courses.

Despite the apparent reasonable level of take up of the scheme little impact was made on the size of the surpluses. The 450 000 hectares of set-aside land represents less than one per cent of the EU's arable land and farmers tended to set-aside the least productive land and then farmed the rest of

their land more intensively.

The 1988 set-aside scheme was effectively replaced by the compulsory set-aside agreed in the 1992 CAP reforms (see Section 5.3). Under the 1992 reforms medium and large-scale cereal farmers will have to take 15 per cent of their land out of production for which they will receive partial compensation.

Conservationists are worried that set-aside will encourage some farmers to adopt new uses for their land which are not compatible with landscape conservation such as golf courses and caravan sites, while it will also encourage the belief that there is less need to protect agricultural land from housing, industrial and road developments if there is surplus which is available for non-agricultural purposes.

In 1994 the scheme was reformed. Three types of set-aside were created.

1 Rotational set-aside: farmers remove a different 15 per cent of their land each year. This has little ecological value because the period is not long enough to help flora and fauna to establish themselves.

2 Non-rotational set-aside: farmers set-aside land for a five year period. This has more value ecologically but would only have short-term benefits.

3 Ecological set-aside: farmers set-aside land for 20 years. The problem is that farmers would have to set-aside this land in addition to the 15 per cent already set-aside and they may be unwilling to do so.

- Why would the conversion of cultivated land to permanent fallow in the Spanish steppelands (see Section 5.4) probably damage rather than assist wildlife?

- Construct a table to summarise possible environmental, economic and social costs and benefits of converting arable land to **a)** a golf course; **b)** a caravan site; **c)** horse grazing and **d)** fallow land.

5.6 Farming in Eastern Europe: Learning to Cope with the Free Market

For countries in western Europe, both in and outside the EU, the main issues facing agriculture are over-production, environmental damage and the future of state subsidies. In eastern Europe the dominant issue is how to reorganise and privatise agriculture following the collapse of Communism.

The proportion of farm land owned by the state under Communism varied enormously:

Country	Land owned by State
Albania	83%
Bulgaria	96%
Czechoslovakia	83%
East Germany	90%
Hungary	90%
Poland	16%
Romania	85%
Yugoslavia	17%

Even in countries like Poland, where privately-owned farms predominated, the state made all the key decisions. There were two basic types of state-controlled farms, co-operatives and state farms. Co-operatives were made up of a number of farmers who joined together to farm the land collectively, pooling their skills, equipment and incomes. State farms were farms directly owned and controlled by the state and which employed farm workers in the same way as a factory employs workers. In both cases the central government made all the key decisions on what to produce, how to produce, what markets to produce for, and what price to charge.

The end of Communism and the policy of the new governments to introduce free market economics has created instablity and uncertainty in farming. In 1992 alone farm output in eastern Europe fell by ten per cent, although much of this decline was due to a severe drought. Also, privatisation and efficiency improvements are likely to lead to large-scale job losses and migration from rural areas. Even in fertile areas such as the Great Hungarian Plain farm productivity will have to increase considerably before eastern European farms can compete on world markets. The proportion of workers involved in agriculture is high by western European standards.

In the late 1980s farming accounted for 21 per cent of all jobs, compared with eight per cent in the EU, showing that eastern European farms are relatively labour-intensive.

Attempts to increase the efficiency of eastern farming are meeting a number of obstacles.

1 One of the major problems facing eastern agriculture is the ownership of land. Governments are under considerable pressure to return state land to its original private owners. Until this issue is sorted out long-term reforms will be difficult to implement. In the new Baltic states, for example, a land privatisation programme has already created 12 500 new farms in Latvia, 3000 in Lithuania and 4000 in Estonia.

2 Progress on privatisation has been slow in most countries. Many farm managers used to being employed by the state do not want to lose their privileges, or their best staff, to the private sector.

3 Farmers lack the capital to buy new machinery and they are reluctant to borrow the finance because of uncertainty over the future.

4 The existing infrastructure for processing and marketing farm produce is inadequate. Transport and equipment is often poor, but also the information needed for farmers and distributors to successfully operate a free market is often not available.

5 Some people doubt whether small farmers used to decisions being made by the state have the necessary managerial skills to cope with the free market. In some cases those who have acquired their own land have fared poorly and this makes others reluctant to operate as private farmers.

Even before the anti-Communist revolutions at the end of the 1980s agriculture was in a deepening crisis. The depth of this crisis, and the success with which agriculture is facing the radical economic and social changes, varies between the different countries in eastern Europe.

In eastern Germany the transition has been relatively rapid. Having merged with the wealthy West German economy, the resources have been available to finance and organise far-reaching changes in the area's agriculture.

At the time of reunification there were 850 000 people working in farming. By 1992 this figure had declined to 300 000. Of the 550 000 who left the land 120 000 found an alternative job, 105 000 were on retraining courses, 150 000 became unemployed and the rest retired.

Before reunification there were about 4500 farms in eastern Germany. By the end of 1991, 3150 of them had been privatised, having been taken over by families, private co-operatives or private companies, and split into 14 000 new farms.

These rapid reforms cost the German Government £2 billion in 1990 and £1.6 billion in 1991 mainly in price support and grants.

In other countries the transition has been less smooth. In Bulgaria, for example, urban areas have been threatened with major food shortages despite the introduction of rationing. Only those consumers using the black market are finding adequate food. Agricultural output declined by an estimated six per cent in 1990 and fertiliser use declined by 15 per cent between 1988 and 1990 (although it is difficult to be certain because the Communist government falsified statistics on output). An EU sponsored report on the agricultural situation in post-Communist Bulgaria has highlighted the following problems.

1 Livestock dying in large numbers because of inadequate fodder and untreated disease.

2 Fuel and electricity shortages worsened by the loss of oil imports from Iraq following the Gulf War.

3 Relaxation of price controls caused food prices to rise by as much as 600 per cent. 500 grammes of coffee in 1991 cost the equivalent of nine days wages for the average worker.

4 An ageing rural workforce.

5 Overcentralised and inefficient management.

6 Degradation of soil and ecosystems.

7 Over-dependance on the Russian market – a market which is unreliable following the collapse of Soviet power.

8 An unusual and severe drought in 1989 and 1990.

FIG 5.21   *The Guardian, 16 September 1993*

Albanian peasants reap spoils of chaos in land of empty shops

'IT'S quite simple,' says Shaqir Caca. 'We are just going back to the old system. It's difficult but better.'

Fifty-six years old and head of a peasant family of 12, he sits at a table groaning with the fruits of his labours – homegrown tomatoes and cucumbers, bowls of yoghurt, mounds of fresh white sheep's cheese, and glasses of raki distilled from the vines that shroud his little steading in this village on the fertile flatlands north of Tirana.

In a country desperately in need of food aid, where the shops are utterly empty and the towns going hungry, the groaning table represents a veritable feast.

Outside, the corn, beans, tomatoes, and vegetables are coming up on the three acres that Shaqir and his family farm these days. Then there are the nine sheep and three head of cattle that forage around the house – the gains of a revolution that has swept the Albanian countryside over the past month, plunging the country's farms into chaos and exacerbating the chronic food supply situation.

At first Shaqir is guarded. 'I took the first cow a year ago. Then I took another a month ago. I took it to survive. But I didn't take any sheep. I didn't steal anything.'

As he talks, the sheep he did not take can be heard bleating a few yards away as one of his sons does the shearing.

Finally, persuaded that we have nothing to do with the Tirana police, his eyes twinkle and he comes clean.

'My children were the last to take the animals. By the time they got to the co-operative, only the weak stock was left. So they got angry and took what they wanted – nine sheep, six female, one male, and two lambs.'

Down the road at the farm co-operative offices the director, Ramalan Vathi, a local communist bigwig who was once feared and is now despised, peels a handwritten list out of his desk drawer.

It itemises who took what and when. Page after page carries the names of the local peasants, their villages, and the number of animals they seized from the co-operative herds. Shaqir's family takes pride of place. With the nine sheep, they got more than any other family.

Events in Nikel are typical of much of Albania. The dislocation wrought by the swiftness of the shift from totalitarianism to pluralism has left the habitual power structures paralysed.

In this vacuum, the peasants of this predominantly peasant country are seizing the land and raiding the state-owned stockholdings, sparking a rash of family feuds over who gets what, re-opening old conflicts, and turning the once totally collect-ivised farming sector upside down.

Official figures last month showed corn production down by two thirds on last year, milk output halved, the acreage planted to cotton down by 80 per cent, and that to tobacco reduced to about half.

9 Emigration of members of the Turkish minority in eastern and south-eastern Bulgaria following ethnic unrest created a shortage of farm workers in those areas.

10 **Speculative hoarding** by producers and wholesalers.

As in the other eastern countries, farms are being privatised but the newly independent farmers will have to continue to cope with a shortage of equipment, inadequate infrastructure, and limited access to markets. In late 1990 the EU decided to aid Bulgarian agriculture by supplying technical assistance, agricultural training and finance to assist privatisation. The USA has supplied similar assistance.

The situation is even worse in Albania. Albania was the last European country to overthrow Communism (see Section 2.2). Under Communism Albania had been the poorest and most isolated country in Europe. With the collapse of the old regime the political, social and economic fabric of the country has been stretched to breaking point.

- Read Fig 5.21 on page 113:
    a) What is the 'old system' referred to in the second sentence?
    b) Why is any attempt by the new government to privatise agriculture in an organised manner likely to fail?
    c) What impact is the present chaos having on agricultural output?

The Problems Facing Farmers in Poland

Polish agriculture was unusual for a Communist country in that it was dominated by privately owned farms. Eighty-four per cent of farm land was privately owned. This was largely a consequence of the failure of the policy of collectivisation (the creation of large state-controlled farms by merging a number of private farms) in the late 1940s and early 1950s. The government was forced to accept that private farms were generally more efficient and productive than state-owned farms because they encouraged individual initiative. However, for many years the government neglected agriculture preferring to concentrate on industrialisation. By the time Communist control ended Polish agriculture faced a whole range of deep-seated problems.

1 Poland's heavy industries, particularly iron and steel, were among the most polluting in the world. Neighbouring East Germany and Czechoslovakia also 'exported' pollution into the country. The resulting deposition of sulphur dioxide, particularly in the form of acid rain, has created a number of ecologically threatened areas. In these areas the ability of the soil to maintain crop and livestock production has been damaged. It has been estimated that in Upper Silesia crop yields have been reduced by 20 per cent due to soil acidification (see Section 7.4).

2 In southern Poland in particular, inappropriate farming methods combined with steep slopes and high rainfall have caused widespread soil erosion.

3 Although only about 70 per cent as much fertiliser is used compared with western Europe the poor quality of chemicals, careless or excessive use, and poor soil management have together caused soil deterioration and river and groundwater pollution. This is particularly serious when many farms rely on groundwater extracted through wells for their water supply, both for irrigation and drinking water.

4 Farms are small and fragmented. It is not unusual for farms to comprise one hectare split into as many as 100 separate fields. Many of these will be left unused because of their distance from other fields. Mechanisation is almost impossible on such small fragmented farms.

5 Higher wages in urban areas, poor services in the countryside, and government assistance for people who moved to towns under the Communists all encouraged rural-urban migration. The younger age groups in particular have been attracted to the urban areas. Older farmers have had to run their farms without the help of the younger members of their family and productivity has been affected.

Many of the state-owned farms are now in the process of being privatised and sub-divided between new private owners. State control of prices is being withdrawn and state subsidies are being cut. But the privatisation programme has met with mixed success since 1989. Added to the problems which developed during the Communist era are new problems brought about by the transition to the free market.

- Inflation initially created uncertainty for farmers having to plan for the future. It reached a peak at the beginning of 1989 of almost 80 per cent a month although by 1993 the rate had been brought down to 2.5 per cent.
- In the first few years after the revolution inflation also led to a fall in demand for food products as consumers' wages failed to keep pace with rising prices. Farmers were sometimes left with unsold produce even though there were shortages of some types of food.
- The fall in demand and increased uncertainty forced many farmers to spend less on inputs such as fertilisers and machinery and to accept the resulting lower yields.

– The collapse of the export trade to the Soviet Union, originally the largest consumer of Polish produce, has caused a loss of income for farmers. At the same time it has been difficult to find new markets in western Europe either because of EU restrictions on food imports, or because of poor quality processing and packaging not up to the standards demanded in western Europe.

– The cost of farm inputs such as livestock feed and fertilisers has risen faster than the prices farmers obtain for their products. This has reduced farmers' profits and discouraged them from increasing output.

- Using appropriate maps in an atlas attempt to explain the location of the areas experiencing 'severe' and 'very severe' soil erosion in Poland shown in Fig 5.22.

- Fig 5.23 is an extract from a report on Poland commissioned by the Confederation of British Industry.
  a) What, according to the report, are the main factors impeding agricultural output?
  b) What factors does the report mention which may assist agriculture to become more efficient in the future?

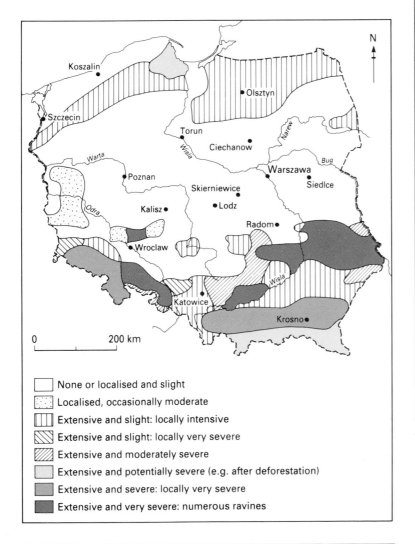

0   200 km

	None or localised and slight
	Localised, occasionally moderate
	Extensive and slight: locally intensive
	Extensive and slight: locally very severe
	Extensive and moderately severe
	Extensive and potentially severe (e.g. after deforestation)
	Extensive and severe: locally very severe
	Extensive and very severe: numerous ravines

FIG 5.22 *Extent of Soil Erosion in Poland*

THE agricultural sector has an importance to Poland's economy which is out of proportion to its output. It contributes around 15 per cent of the country's GDP, but it employs some 40 per cent of the working population. These figures hint at the inefficiency of the state-run farms and the institutions which allocate resources to the sector.

The communists' attempts to socialise Polish farming over the last 40 years were less than wholehearted: 80 per cent of the sector's total output comes from private farms. Polish farms are relatively small concerns, with an average size of 7 hectares. This is too small to benefit from economies of scale, which start to apply when a farm's land area gets to around 15 hectares. Buying and selling land in Poland is still an exceedingly difficult process, and farms are unable to evolve into efficient units in response to market pressures.

Poland is a country of great agricultural potential, with plenty of good soil and a favourable climate. Its farms are well-known in the region for the quality of their meat and vegetables, and fruit such as apples, raspberries, strawberries and currants. This potential has not been fully realised because of shortages of inputs and mis-allocation of resources. Fertilisers, machinery and spare parts are in short supply everywhere, and supplies of seeds, plant protection chemicals and animal feed are unreliable. When resources (particularly credit) have been available, greater priority has been given to the country's less productive socialised farms.

The absence of market pricing has impeded the rational development of Polish farms. In August 1990 price controls were removed, and farmers had more incentive to raise production. However, the effects of free market pricing were muted by the continued dominance of government bodies in the processing and marketing of farm produce. Private farmers can by-pass these organisations to a certain extent, but they remain partially tied, because the government bodies control the allocation of inputs like fertilisers and machinery, and they control the farmer's social security scheme.

Agricultural research services are traditionally of a high standard in Poland. However, they are poorly administered: many agencies overlap unhelpfully, while other areas have important gaps. More fundamentally, too little of the research carried out is directed towards the small farms which make the greatest contribution to overall output.

The problems raised by a transition to a market economy are not as great for farmers as for industrial enterprises: successful competition in the international market for agricultural produce tends to demand less investment in machinery and training. But liberalisation measures seem to command less support in the agricultural sector, and are proceeding more slowly there. Poland's farmers are calling on the government to protect them from foreign imports, and are pressing their demands with strikes and road blockades.

In the medium term, agriculture is one of the sectors where Poland, along with other countries in the region, has comparative trade advantages. But in the short term the picture is still highly confused.

FIG 5.23 *Doing Business in Poland, Kogan Page 1991*

The Future for Eastern Agriculture

The outlook in parts of eastern Europe seems bleak. There are, however, indications that there is enormous potential for farming. A recent report for the Confederation of British Industry (CBI) stated that Hungarian agriculture, for example, is *'one of the strengths of the Hungarian economy. The country, with good soils and an equitable climate is able to grow a wide range of crops. The country is able to feed itself two and a half times over'*. On grain production the report stated that *'the industry is, in world terms, very efficient…'*

The eastern countries need new markets for their agricultural produce if they are to earn foreign currency to finance new investment. They are looking to the EU to provide such a market and this is one reason why some eastern European countries are so enthusiastic about joining the EU (see Section 2.9). They also need expertise and training from western Europe to help them create a stable free market in farm produce. This kind of transfer of expertise is already occurring. For example, the Finnish State Agricultural Advisory Service has established training links with farmers in Estonia. The Scottish Agricultural College has been contracted by the EU to teach farm economics and business management in Polish universities.

The EU has also provided assistance in the form of 'triangular' trade. The EU buys surpluses in one eastern European country and uses them to reduce shortages in another. In one month in 1991, for example, the EU bought 45 000 tonnes of Hungarian wheat to reduce food shortages in Albania.

- If, over the next decade, the eastern European countries achieve levels of farm efficiency, productivity and output closer to those found in western Europe what problems may emerge? Use a table laid out in the way shown here to summarise your ideas.

- Complete a similar table showing the problems which could occur if eastern agriculture remains in a run-down or chaotic state.

	POLITICAL PROBLEMS	SOCIAL PROBLEMS	ECONOMIC PROBLEMS
FOR EASTERN EUROPE			
FOR WESTERN EUROPE			

Peasant Farmer, Hungary

ESSAY

1   Why does the EU intervene in agriculture?

2   'The EU's agricultural policy has done more harm than good.'
Discuss the extent to which you agree with this statement.

3   Discuss ways in which EU agricultural policy could be reformed
to aid conservation.

4   Describe and evaluate the success of existing EU policies
designed to conserve the rural environment.

5   'The problems facing eastern European farmers have nothing to
do with us.'
   Evaluate the truth of this statement.

Glossary

afforestation	The planting of forests.
capital intensive	Where machinery or equipment, rather than labour, account for most of the cost of production.
income elasticity of demand	The extent to which the demand for a particular commodity changes in response to the changes in peoples' income.
intensification	To increase the quantity of inputs (such as labour, machinery and fertilisers) being applied to each hectare of farm land.
price elasticity of demand	The extent to which the demand for a particular commodity changes in response to changes in the price of that commodity.
price support	Where the state subsidises the prices farmers receive for their produce.
speculative hoarding	Where people buy and then store commodities when they anticipate that the price of those goods will rise. They can then sell the goods at a higher price than they paid for them and so make a profit.
steppes	A level plain with few trees.
support price	The state subsidised price received by farmers for their produce.

Reviving the

ities

6

KEY
IDEAS

6.1   Some European cities are growing economically while others are declining.

6.2   Most cities in north-western Europe, and some cities elsewhere in Europe are experiencing population decline.

6.3   Many high-rise housing estates built in European cities during the 1960s and 1970s are now facing serious social, economic and environmental problems. Attempts are now being made to improve the quality of life in these estates.

6.4   In many European cities ethnic minority groups are concentrated into certain areas. In some cases ghettos have been created.

6.5   Cities in eastern Europe are likely to see particularly rapid change during the 1990s as they continue the transition from central planning to a free market economy.

6.6   Many European cities are attempting to regenerate their economy and environment by investing in new infrastructure designed to enable them to compete more effectively with other European cities. Hosting major international events such as the Olympic Games is often seen as an effective way of funding such infrastructure.

6.7   European cities, particularly in western Europe, are experiencing serious traffic congestion and associated environmental problems, particularly atmospheric pollution. A variety of policies are being implemented by European cities to manage the increases in the use of private cars and to encourage public transport.

6.8   Urban conservation has become an important issue in some European cities where the survival of historic architecture is threatened.

FIG 6.1a   *European Cities with more than 700 000 people*

City	Population '000s	Country	City	Population '000s	Country
1 Paris	8510	France	28 Zagreb	1175	Croatia
2 London	6378	UK	29 Lyons	1170	France
3 Istanbul	5495	Turkey	30 Sofia	1129	Bulgaria
4 Berlin	3301	Germany	31 Odesa	1115	Ukraine
5 Madrid	3101	Spain	32 Donetsk	1110	Ukraine
6 Athens	3027	Greece	33 Marseilles	1080	France
7 Rome	2817	Italy	34 Liverpool	1060	UK
8 Kyyiv (Kiev)	2587	Ukraine	35 Rotterdam	1040	Netherlands
9 Budapest	2115	Hungary	36 Amsterdam	1038	Netherlands
10 Bucharest	2014	Romania	37 Turin	1012	Italy
11 Barcelona	1704	Spain	38 Helsinki	994	Finland
12 Manchester	1669	UK	39 Brussels	970	Belgium
13 Warsaw	1651	Poland	40 Lille	935	France
14 Lisbon	1612	Portugal	41 Cologne	928	Germany
15 Kharkiv	1611	Ukraine	42 Riga	915	Latvia
16 Hamburg	1594	Germany	43 Zaporizhzhya	884	Ukraine
17 Minsk	1589	Belarus	44 Thessaloniki	872	Greece
18 Stockholm	1471	Sweden	45 Lodz	852	Poland
19 Belgrade	1470	Serbia	46 Zurich	839	Switzerland
20 Milan	1464	Italy	47 L'viv	790	Ukraine
21 Birmingham	1400	UK	48 Krakow	744	Poland
22 Copenhagen	1339	Denmark	49 Valencia	732	Spain
23 Oporto	1315	Portugal	50 Palermo	731	Italy
24 Prague	1209	Czech Rep.	51 Glasgow	730	UK
25 Naples	1203	Italy	52 Goteborg	720	Sweden
26 Munich (München)	1189	Germany	53 Genoa	715	Italy
27 Dnpropetrovsk	1179	Ukraine	54 Kryvyy Rih	713	Ukraine

6.1 The City League Table

Cities are concentrations of people but they are also centres of economic activity and decision making. They have a powerful influence on the economic, social and political life of Europe. The larger a city is the more potential influence it is likely to have both within its own country and internationally. Fig 6.1a shows urban areas with a population of more than 700 000. The figures shown are for conurbations or 'urban agglomerations' (where more than one town or city have merged together to form a continuous urban area).

The relative positions of the urban areas in the ranking in Fig 6.1a are not likely to change much over the next decade, although as Section 6.2 explains many cities in Europe are losing population while others are still increasing in size.

However, population is only one way of comparing the importance of cities. Another indicator of a city's power and influence is the strength and size of its economy. This is much more difficult to measure than total population, although the size and success of a city's economy will partly depend on the size of its population. Industry in larger cities is more likely to benefit from economies of scale and proximity to a large market. On the other hand, large cities may suffer from problems such as congestion and high pollution levels which can act as diseconomies by raising the costs of industry.

Any league table based on economic power may well change considerably over the next decade as eastern European cities grow in international economic importance (see Section 6.4). Also some western European cities which were originally on the **periphery** of western Europe now find themselves in the heart of Europe, such as Vienna, Berlin and Trieste, and their economies may grow rapidly.

The 1980s saw increased competition between European cities to attract investment by **multinational** or **transnational companies**, to attract prestigious international events and to attract EU finance. Section 6.5 looks at ways in which European cities are attempting to regenerate their economies so that they can compete more successfully with other cities. Some cities are in a better position to compete than others. Many of the most successful cities are located in what has been called the 'blue banana' – an area extending from London to Milan and containing cities such as Paris, Brussels, Amsterdam, Cologne, Frankfurt and Munich. These cities benefit from being located in the wealthiest and most densely populated part of Europe – the European core- and their economies are increasingly based on high-technology and information processing (or quaternary) industries. Cities on the periphery of Europe such as Dublin, Lisbon, Seville, Palermo, Athens and Thessaloniki are not in such a good position to compete.

However, there is some evidence that cities in southern Europe, traditionally a less economically developed region, are now becoming more competitive. As literacy and skill levels among southern European populations improve, and as transport and

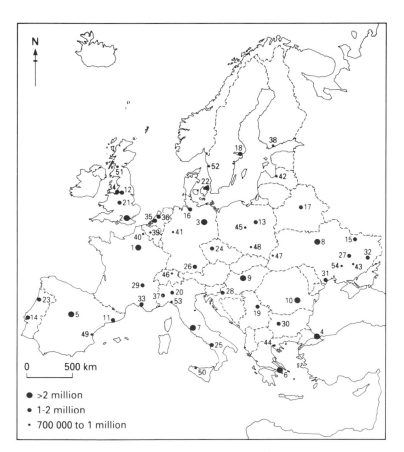

Fig **6.1b** *European Cities with more than 700 000 people*

- ● >2 million
- • 1-2 million
- · 700 000 to 1 million

0   500 km

telecommunications develop, capital is being pulled southwards by the more attractive climate and lifestyle and the lower costs of the Mediterranean regions. Cities such as Nice, Marseilles and Barcelona have been included in a 'second banana' along the Mediterranean coasts of Spain, France and Italy and including the Alpine areas around the French–Italian border (see Fig 6.2).

Various attempts have been made to rank European cities according to their economic strength or competitiveness. One such league table is shown in Fig 6.3. In this table each of the top 64 cities is given a score based on a variety of economic indicators such as total population, the numbers of multinational companies based in each city but also on indicators of infrastructure such as the skills and qualifications of the workforce, presence of major cultural facilities, trade fairs and exhibitions. The cities are allocated a Class according to their score. The table was prepared in 1989 before the Communist collapse and so excludes eastern Europe.

There is some evidence that poorer and less successful cities (mainly those dominated by traditional industries) are slipping further down the European league table while the more successful wealthier cities with strong tertiary and quaternary industries are moving upwards. In other words, the successful cities are becoming more successful and the less successful cities are slipping further behind.

FIG 6.3 *Economic Strength of European Cities*

City	ranking
Class 1	
London	83
Paris	81
Class 2	
Milan	70
Class 3	
Madrid	66
Munich, Frankfurt	65
Rome, Brussels, Barcelona	64
Amsterdam	63
Class 4	
Manchester	58
Berlin, Hamburg	57
Stuttgart, Copenhagen, Athens	56
Rotterdam, Zurich	55
Turin	54
Lyons	53
Geneva	52
Class 5	
Birmingham, Cologne, Lisbon	51
Glasgow	50
Vienna, Edinburgh	49
Marseilles	48
Naples	47
Seville, Strasbourg	46
Basle, Venice, Utrecht	45
Düsseldorf, Florence, Bologna, the Hague, Antwerp, Toulouse	44
Valencia, Genoa	43
Class 6	
Bonn	42
Lille, Nice	41
Bristol, Bordeaux, Hannover, Grenoble	40
Montpelier, Nantes, Dublin, Oporto	39
Nüremberg, Eindhoven, Bilbao	38
Palermo, Bari, Mannheim	37
Liège, Leeds, Rennes,	36
Trieste, Essen	35

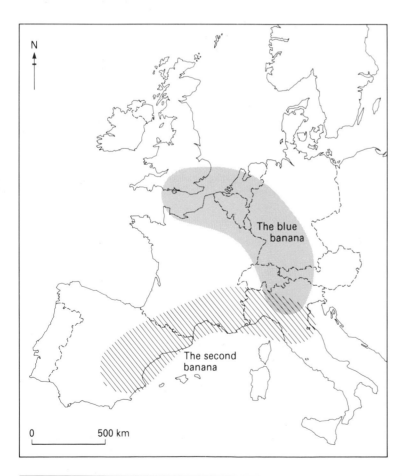

FIG 6.2 *The Blue and Second Bananas*

- One indicator of a city's economic strength and influence is the number of head offices of large companies located there. Study Figs 6.4a and b. To what extent do these maps and table support the concept of the 'two bananas' described above?

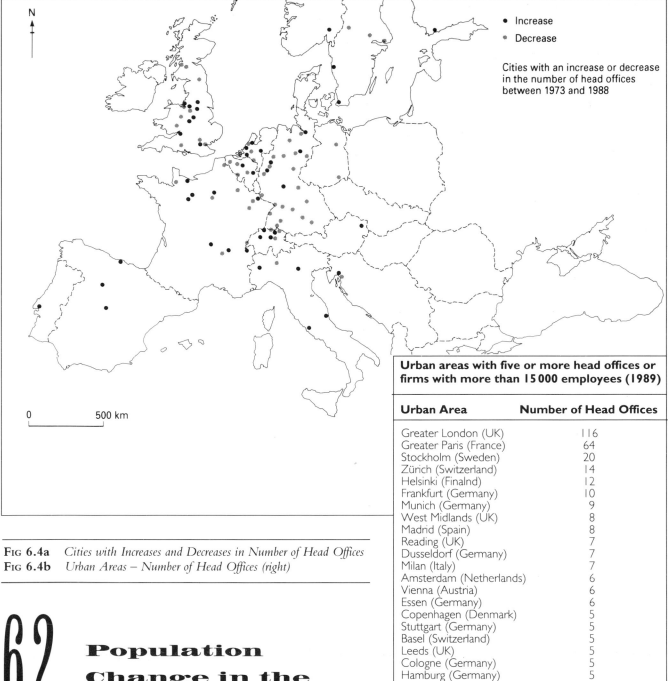

Cities with an increase or decrease in the number of head offices between 1973 and 1988

- Increase
- Decrease

Urban areas with five or more head offices or firms with more than 15 000 employees (1989)

Urban Area	Number of Head Offices
Greater London (UK)	116
Greater Paris (France)	64
Stockholm (Sweden)	20
Zürich (Switzerland)	14
Helsinki (Finalnd)	12
Frankfurt (Germany)	10
Munich (Germany)	9
West Midlands (UK)	8
Madrid (Spain)	8
Reading (UK)	7
Dusseldorf (Germany)	7
Milan (Italy)	7
Amsterdam (Netherlands)	6
Vienna (Austria)	6
Essen (Germany)	6
Copenhagen (Denmark)	5
Stuttgart (Germany)	5
Basel (Switzerland)	5
Leeds (UK)	5
Cologne (Germany)	5
Hamburg (Germany)	5

FIG **6.4a** *Cities with Increases and Decreases in Number of Head Offices*
FIG **6.4b** *Urban Areas – Number of Head Offices (right)*

6.2 Population Change in the Cities

Most cities in Europe experienced almost continuous growth for two centuries. Throughout the industrial revolution urban areas attracted manufacturing industry and population. But in the 1970s, as manufacturing industry declined in importance in many European economies, a new trend emerged. Although most cities in southern and eastern Europe continued to grow (due both to in-migration and natural increase), most large cities in north-western Europe began to experience decline. In some cases natural decrease played its part, but out-migration was the dominant reason. This process of urban population decline is known as counterurbanisation.

Counterurbanisation in North-West Europe

According to evidence from an opinion poll conducted in England in 1992, 13 million urban dwellers wanted to move out of their city to a small town or the countryside. Many said they were fed up with city life because of dirt and noise, crime, absence of community spirit, and difficulties in bringing up children. If these results are to be believed then it is not surprising that the populations of large British cities have been declining. They also perhaps provide us with a clue to the reasons for urban decline in other European countries. Undoubtedly counterurbanisation is more likely to occur when people feel that crime, pollution, deteriorating public services, traffic congestion, noise, litter, vandalism and other problems are worsening. Rural areas are often perceived to be havens of harmony, tranquility and traditional values. With increasing mobility and the development of telecommunications many rural areas are now able to offer the same quality of services as urban areas.

In fact two processes are occurring in the large cities of north-west Europe: suburbanisation and counterurbanisation. To understand these processes it is necessary to divide urban areas into three zones.

1   The city core – the built-up area of the city.

2   The urban ring – the semi-rural area around the city containing countryside, villages and perhaps small towns.

3   The urban or metropolitan region – which comprises the core and the ring. This is an area bound together by the daily flows of commuters and by movements between the two zones for shopping and recreation.

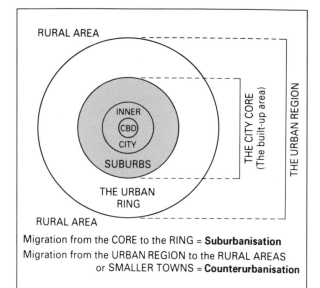

Migration from the CORE to the RING = **Suburbanisation**
Migration from the URBAN REGION to the RURAL AREAS or SMALLER TOWNS = **Counterurbanisation**

FIG 6.5   *Suburbanisation and Counterurbanisation*

Fig 6.5 illustrates the zones and the two processes of suburbanisation and counterurbanisation.

Suburbanisation is the movement of population to new suburban areas on the periphery of the city or to expanding **commuter villages** close to the city (in other words movement from the core to the ring). This is a process which has been occurring in north-western European cities for decades. In the case of suburbanisation the population of the entire urban region could continue to grow while the population of the city itself declines.

Counterurbanisation, on the other hand, refers to the decline in population of the entire urban region as people move to smaller urban areas or rural areas elsewhere.

The Paris Region provides us with an example of both these processes.

Population Trends in the Paris Region

Between 1954 and 1962 the Paris Region, known as the Ile-de-France, gained more than one million people. By the 1980s ten million people lived in the region which forms only two per cent of the total area of France. However, current estimates of the regional population for the year 2000 vary from 9.5 million to 10.5 million, indicating that further growth is uncertain.

View of the River Seine, Paris

- Study Fig 6.6a. Describe the main trends indicated in this table. Does the data in this table support the view that the Ile-de-France urban region experienced counterurbanisation during the 1970s and early 1980s?

Annual population change in the Ile-de-France region 1954–1982
Figures are in Thousands

	1954–62	1962–68	1968–75	1975–82
Natural change	+55	+67	+75	+67
Migration to/from other regions	+40	+9	−23	−61
Migration to/from other countries	+44	+54	+38	+22
Total population change	+139	+130	+90	+28

MIGRATION BALANCE BY AREA 1954–1982
Figures are in Thousands

Area	1954–62	1962–68	1968–75	1975–82
CORE				
City of Paris	−28	−46	−51	−24
Inner suburbs	+42	+10	−21	−33
Outer suburbs	+49	+59	+28	−19
RING				
Edge of urban area	+9	+20	+21	+4
New Towns[1]	+3	+5	+11	+19
Semi-urban areas[2]	+10	+15	+24	+6
Rural areas	−2	0	+5	+7

[1] = A number of new towns have been built in the ring to cater for the region's population growth.
[2] = Built-up areas which still contain pockets of countryside.

FIG 6.6a and b *Population Change in the L'Ile-de-France Region*

FIG 6.7 *The Relationship between settlement size and Population Change in France*

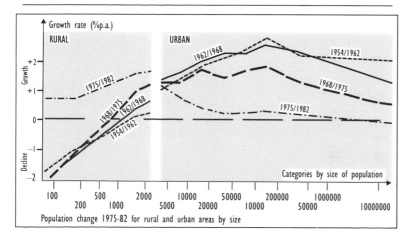

Population change 1975-82 for rural and urban areas by size

Fig 6.6a is useful for telling us something about counterurbanisation between 1968 and 1982 but it tells us nothing about suburbanisation. In order to find out if Paris experienced suburbanisation during the same period we need to break down the Ile-de-France region into smaller areas (see Fig 6.6b).

- Describe the main trends revealed in Fig 6.6b. Does the data indicate that suburbanisation occured in the Paris Region in the 1970s and early 1980s?

It is clear from Fig 6.6b that the city was losing population to other areas in the Ile-de-France. In addition to the reasons for counterurbanisation mentioned above there were a number of other reasons for this depopulation.

- Demolition of old housing, which is replaced by new housing built at a lower density.
- Average household size is declining – there are more people living on their own, more childless couples, and more single parent families. In 1968 the occupancy rate (a measure of the average number of people per room) in Paris was 0.95 persons per room. By 1982 this had fallen to 0.79. In other words, fewer people live in the same amount of housing space.
- More people want to become home owners and most new owner-occupied housing is being built beyond the city's periphery in the more rural areas. Housing is also generally cheaper in these areas. In the region's rural communities about 74 per cent of houses are owner-occupied compared with about 35 per cent in the city.
- The improvement of rail and road links to areas beyond the edge of the city has encouraged people to consider commuting from outside the city.

Counterurbanisation in France was not confined to the Paris region. Fig 6.7 shows the changing relationship between settlement size and population change. While large urban settlements were growing and rural settlements were declining during the period 1954–62, by 1975–82 rural settlements were growing and large urban settlements were showing signs of decline.

It should be emphasised that these are average growth rates. Large areas of French countryside, particularly in more remote areas continued to experience serious depopulation.

So far we have only examined the trends up to 1982. Results from the 1990 census suggest that counterurbanisation is now on the decline. The census indicates that an increased rate of inward migration to French cities is now taking place. The population growth rate for the Paris region between 1982 and 1990 was much higher than for the period 1975 to 1982 and this must be due to migration rather than natural increase.

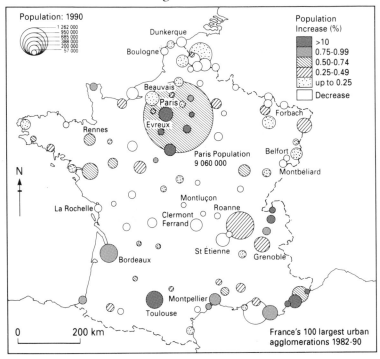

FIG 6.8 *Population Change, France (above)*

A similar trend has emerged in other large French cities although there were exceptions. Marseilles, for example, lost 2.2 per cent of its population between 1982 and 1990.

Reasons for this new migration to the cities may include:

– the growth of tertiary and quaternary industries in larger cities (including advertising, finance and research);
– the growth of new manufacturing industries such as micro-electronics and biotechnology which are concentrated in larger cities;
– the desire to be close to modern telecommunications and transport networks, such as the TGV high-speed rail lines (see Section 10.2), which are at present focused on the larger cities;
– the restoration of the old city centres attracting the middle class back to parts of the inner cities.

However, it is too early to say whether this is a long-term reversal in the fortunes of French cities or simply a short-term interruption to long-term population decline.

● Study Fig 6.8. Is there a pattern to the population changes shown on the map?

Gentrification, Rue Cremieux, Paris

Counterurbanisation in Copenhagen

Paris is not the only city to have experienced population decline due to suburbanisation or counterurbanisation in recent decades. Also, other countries, including the UK, are showing little sign of a reversal in the counterurbanisation trend. Fig 6.9 shows data for Copenhagen, the capital of Denmark.

FIG **6.9** *Population Change, Copenhagen*

Population change in Copenhagen 1950–1989		
	% Change	
Area	**1950–70**	**1970–89**
CORE		
Copenhagen City	−18.9	−24.9
Rest of Greater Copenhagen	+65.6	−4.2
RING		
Rest of Copenhagen Region	+73.1	+35.2
CORE and RING		
Copenhagen Region	+21.8	+2.2

Is Counterurbanisation a Good Thing or a Bad Thing?

There is no easy answer to this question. Many people are clearly dissatisfied with urban life and given the opportunity opt to 'suburbanise' or 'counterurbanise' – presumably these people see the trend as a good thing for themselves. However, they are not the only people affected.

The benefits of counterurbanisation for rural areas include:

– the revitalisation of village life by affluent and highly motivated newcomers. Members of the middle class who move from the cities to villages are often particularly keen to conserve the rural environment and to organise social and cultural activities in the village;
– the affluent newcomers may help to boost local businesses such as village shops or give additional support to local services such as schools;
– they often bring extra investment into the local housing stock by carrying out improvements and maintenance.

The costs of counterurbanisation for rural areas include:

– the affluent in-migrants force up house prices in the rural areas. This may put local housing beyond the reach of local people;
– the high levels of car-ownership amongst the in-migrants means that they often travel to the city or larger villages for shopping, services and entertainment rather than boosting

local facilities;
– counterurbanisation has an environmental impact. Housebuilding and increased traffic congestion are particularly noticeable. The rural area may lose the rural character which the newcomers originally found attractive. The countryside itself may become suburbanised;
– there may be social stresses between locals and newcomers with locals resenting the wealth and changes brought by the newcomers.

Counterurbanisation can also bring costs to urban areas. The city loses the younger, more skilled, affluent and ambitious residents. Therefore, the proportion of the city's population made up of disadvantaged or deprived groups (such as unemployed, pensioners, and ethnic minorities) is likely to rise. This increases the demand for public services in the city while reducing the wealth available to pay for them.

- If counterurbanisation were to become a long-term trend in the countries of north-west Europe what would be the long-term impact on **a)** cities and **b)** rural areas?

- Should planners try to discourage, encourage or ignore counterurbanisation?

- If planners decided to discourage counterurbanisation suggest three policies they could realistically implement in a large city like Paris.

Trends in Southern and Eastern Europe

Counterurbanisation is a less common trend in southern and eastern Europe.

- Describe what the data in Fig 6.9 tells us about the significance of suburbanisation and counterurbanisation in Copenhagen.

- To what extent does the data in Fig 6.10 overleaf support the following hypotheses?
  a) All Italian cities were experiencing urbanisation in the 1960s.
  b) In the 1970s northern Italian cities, which are more economically developed (see Section 3.4), were experiencing counterurbanisation. Southern Italian cities, which are less economically developed, were experiencing urbanisation.
  c) All Italian cities experienced counterurbanisation in the 1980s.

FIG 6.10   *Population Change Italy, Geography, January 1993*

Population change in Italy's major cities 1961–1991

	1991 population	% change 1961–71	% change 1971–81	% change 1981–91
Rome	2 693 383	+27.1	+1.7	−4.9
Milan	1 371 008	+9.4	−6.0	−16.1
Naples	1 054 601	+3.7	−1.3	−12.9
Turin	961 916	+13.9	−5.5	−12.8
Palermo	697 162	+9.3	+8.8	−0.4
Genoa	675 639	+4.2	−6.9	−11.1
Bologna	404 322	+10.3	−7.1	−11.3
Florence	402 316	+4.9	−1.0	−11.3
Bari	341 273	+14.5	+3.8	−8.0
Catania	330 037	+9.9	−5.4	−12.8
Venice	308 717	+4.5	−8.3	−7.2

The main reason for the continued growth of many urban areas in southern and eastern Europe in the 1980s and early 1990s was the continuing decline of agricultural employment. Compared with north-western Europe, farms are labour-intensive and less productive. As agriculture becomes more capital-intensive and productivity increases there is less demand for farm workers and so people migrate to the cities to find work. Also a low standard of living in many rural areas, combined with remoteness, encourages people to seek higher incomes and a more exciting lifestyle in the cities. It remains to be seen whether the 1990s will see counterurbanisation spread to all the cities in southern and eastern Europe.

6.3 Multiple Deprivation and Unrest in the Estates

Creating a better urban environment is the most important question that our civilisation has to tackle.

Roland Castro, French architect.

Most cities in western Europe faced a serious housing shortage in the decades immediately after the Second World War. In Paris, for example, about a third of young married couples in the early 1950s were having to live with their parents. Over 50 per cent of households had to share a lavatory. Wartime destruction, low quality housing dating from the nineteenth century and urban population growth were to blame. The construction of high-rise flats using newly developed pre-fabricated building techniques was seen as the cheapest and quickest solution. The 1960s and 1970s saw a massive building programme. Lack of space in the inner cities meant that much of this new housing was built on green field sites on the periphery of the cities.

Similarly, in the Communist countries of eastern Europe a combination of acute housing shortages and the desire to build housing estates based on Communist principles of equality and **collective living** led to the construction of massive high-rise estates. Each estate was to include neighbourhood services such as clinics, childcare facilities and community centres. Organisations sponsored by the state, such as trade unions, youth organisations and the Communist Party itself, would be active in promoting community activities. The extent to which such services were actually provided varied from city to city and country to country.

While the schemes in western Europe helped to solve the shortage of housing they did not solve the problems of economic and social **deprivation**. Many of these estates housed concentrations of unemployed people or people on low incomes. The untested pre-fabricated designs proved to be faulty and expensive to maintain. The design and layout of the estates seemed to foster a feeling of **alienation** and isolation resulting in crime and vandalism. Social facilities, like shopping and community centres, were sometimes built years after the housing was finished.

While it is true that high-rise living was often more readily accepted in mainland Europe than in Britain, and living in a flat and the renting of housing is less strongly identified with being on a low income, cities there have suffered many of the same problems as British cities.

In eastern Europe the social problems may not have been as serious until recently although the housing is often of a very low standard. Almost everybody rents a flat. Flats were allocated by the Communist authorities regardless of income or profession. This created a much greater social mix and estates were less likely to become pockets of deprivation. However, the problems may become much more serious during the 1990s. Many of the blocks were badly built. Inadequate resources, worsened by the current economic problems, means that maintenance is inadequate. Also, the transition to a free market economy is encouraging people on higher incomes to move out of these estates to more desirable housing. The growing numbers of unemployed and low income families are being left behind. Judging from the experience of western Europe this could well lead to serious social problems.

The French Estates

If the police get hold of all the drugs the estate will collapse. Hashish is all that is keeping up the walls.

A resident of a Paris estate.

The cités of the French urban periphery suffer from a negative public image that instantly associates them with rampant delinquency, immigration and insecurity, so much so that they are almost universally called 'little Chicagos'.

L Wacquant, International Journal of Urban and Regional Research,
17 March 1993.

Typical of these large high-rise housing estates built on the periphery of western European cities are the estates built around French cities such as Paris and Lyons. The *Grand Ensembles* (Large Estates) or *cités* around Paris, for example, each contain 8–10 000 dwellings and by 1969 housed about 15 per cent of the city's population. Many of these estates have now become **ghettos** containing concentrations of ethnic minority groups and the unemployed (see also Section 6.4). The more affluent residents have moved to the new and increasingly popular suburban owner-occupied houses on the periphery of the city.

Immigrant groups are particularly disadvantaged, often being poorly qualified and discriminated against in the job market. Young second generation immigrants feel particularly rejected and frustrated as victims of discrimination by employers, the police and other native French people. Drugs are a major problem on many of the estates. In the Cité Francs-Moivins at Saint-Denis, north of Paris, it has been estimated that one in four people aged 12 to 20 regularly use soft drugs.

The simmering discontent felt by many erupted in 1983 in Lyons at Les Minguettes estate in the south-eastern suburbs of the city when rioting destroyed many of the shops and community facilities. High youth unemployment in the estate was blamed. Racial tension also played a part. Thirty-three per cent of the estate's population were immigrants. But the design of the estate probably did not help. Of the 62 tower blocks (each over 15 storeys) 44 were of identical design. The residents had little respect for their environment.

The Sarcelles estate on the northern edge of Paris also became notorious in the 1960s soon after its completion. Problems included inadequate transport links to the city, incomplete shopping and community facilities, poor maintenance, lack of privacy, poor noise insulation between flats, inadequate lifts, lack of safety and security on the public staircases and a shortage of local jobs. Despite state subsidies the housing was regarded as expensive. Boredom, alienation and depression became common ailments and sufferers became known as *Sarcellites*. The problems worsened in the 1970s with growing unemployment, a growing proportion of immigrants and deteriorating buildings.

As early as 1977 the French Government tried to respond to the problems. It initiated a group called *Habitat et Vie Sociale* (Habitat and Social Life) whose job was to co-ordinate the work of different government departments in the deprived estates. At first efforts were focused on improving the physical fabric of the estates. Some of the worst tower blocks were demolished, balconies were added to flats, kitchens enlarged and the facades of the blocks brightened up in the hope that this would encourage the residents to take more pride in their surroundings.

The Dubedout Commission established after the Lyons riots began to stress the need to alleviate social and economic deprivation. The Commission pin-pointed four particular problems.

1   Extreme social **segregation**.

2   Misrepresentation in the press and in the surrounding community.

3   A high proportion of children and teenagers, and high rates of delinquency, truancy and youth unemployment.

4   Inadequate management and maintenance.

As a result of the Commission's work, education facilities and job training were improved, and attempts were made to give jobs in **rehabilitating** the estates to local people.

By 1990 the government had identified 400 priority estates or 'hotspots' which were considered to be on the verge of major social unrest and which were to receive special help. In Les Minguettes, for example, new sports facilities, shops and social centres were constructed. By the early 1990s £200 million a year was being spent on the deprived estates.

However, any idea that the commitment to allocate additional resources to the deprived estates would necessarily solve the problem had been shattered by October 1990. The Lyon high-rise suburb of Vielx-en-Velin, which has a predominantly immigrant population (75 per cent of a population of 45 000), erupted into four nights of rioting only a few days after a new sports centre had opened, containing a gymnasium, a swimming pool and a climbing wall. Many blamed the riots on the attitude of the police to immigrants, and there was evidence that a significant number of police supported the racist National Front party. It had been assumed that such investment would help to keep unemployed young people off the streets. The local council had also increased the numbers of social workers and teachers in the estate, had spent £3 million on renovating run-down flats, and provided two new libraries. During the riots 700 riot police had to be used to protect the sports centre from the rioters.

In 1993 a new round of government-sponsored improvement projects was launched. The projects formed part of the PAR initiative (*Pour une Architecture de la Réhabilitation*). This initiative is run by the Ministry of Housing and the Environment, the *Habitations à Loyer Modéré* (similar to the British Housing Associations and responsible for all **social housing** – that is housing designed for low income groups), and *Banlieues '89* (set up in the early 1980s by President Mitterrand to run government-financed experimental projects in deprived estates). The aim of PAR is to improve the quality of housing in the estates and to improve estate management and security with the help and participation of local residents. In the 1993 projects, architects from all over Europe were invited to take part in a competition to submit schemes to rehabilitate 70 high-rise estates.

One example of these projects is the Mouysset estate in the south-eastern area of Tarbes, a town to the south-west of Toulouse in southern France (illustrating that the problem is not confined to large urban areas). A group of British architects has been awarded the contract to redesign the estate.

They identified the following as the main problems in the estate:

– a bad 'public image';
– a 'fragile social climate' – in other words, there is potential for unrest;
– a poor road system in the estate – a busy dual carriageway runs close to some of the blocks causing noise and safety problems, and access to the town centre is difficult;
– poor security in the blocks.

FIG **6.11**   *The Guardian, 15 March 1993*

Mitterrand losing battle of impoverished 'banlieues'

IN A statement that perhaps he would like to forget, François Mitterrand once said that "if socialism has a future, it lies in the poor suburbs".

After more than a decade of almost continuous Socialist rule, the problems of France's impoverished suburbs, or *banlieues*, remain as pressing as ever, and the government's policy to combat them is ignored by the social workers on the ground and scorned by some of its old champions.

The inhabitants of the *banlieues* forced their way into the political eye two years ago. In October 1990, the Lyons suburb of Vaulx-en-Velin erupted in several days of sporadic rioting, sparked by the death of a young man, apparently knocked off a motorbike by a police car. The rioting was a blow to the authorities, who had just spent about £5 million on amenities for the neighbourhood, and had held up Vaulx-en-Velin as an urban renewal success story.

By the end of the 1980s, the authorities had classified around 400 *banlieues* as "hot-spots", urban areas that needed urgent investment to prevent trouble. The state was spending about £200 million on such programmes before 1990. But, as the smoke of Vaulx-en-Velin cleared, France rediscovered its half-forgotten urban problems and the government, the need to refine its policy.

The central plank of the new policy was the creation of a ministry for cities, which today has a budget of about £100 million. That appears modest compared with what was being spent two years ago, but more money comes from other ministries, such as education and housing. About £200 million is also raised from the other important reform enacted by the Socialists after the riots, a law by which wealthier towns redirect some of their state subsidies and local tax revenue to the poor *banlieues*.

With a population of 28,000, the public housing complex Val-Fourré, in Mants la Jolie, is the biggest in the Paris region. It is typical of a poor French suburb, with tower blocks built in the 1960s to house immigrant workers for the nearby factories of Renault and Simca. More than half the families are foreign, mainly from North Africa, and more than half live on state support. Unemployment is two points above the national level, at 12 per cent, but it rises to more than 20 per cent for school leavers.

Val-Fourré became the symbol of the crisis in the *banlieues* in May and June 1991. In events reminiscent of Vaulx-en-Velin, the centre of the complex was sacked by rioters after a youth of Arab origin died in a police cell. Then one night in June, a policewoman was run down and killed while trying to arrest a group of joyriders, one of whom was shot dead by police a few hours later.

Today Val-Fourré bears surprisingly few scars. The blocks of flats, recently refurbished by the state, appear in good repair. Dozens of windows sport satellite dishes, bought to pick up television from Morocco and Algeria. But a shopping centre that was brand new before the 1991 riots, sits empty and looted. A crèche and day centre, destroyed in 1991, is also empty.

Ms Metatla is not indifferent to the policies of the government, but she has no doubt that progress can be made only through local initiatives. 'The government does things like provide free holidays for young people to get them out into the countryside during the hot summers. That's fine, but we have to give people a sense of obligations as well as rights... The best way forward is for the residents to take responsibility for their own neighbourhoods and not to think that someone else will do it for them.'

In Fear and Loathing

Whole districts of Turin are withering amid rampant theft, drug addiction and poverty

THE kitchen overlooks a yard in the Corso Salvemini. A few days ago Maria Franconi opened the window and found a syringe stuck in the wooden frame. "The junkies play darts with them and use the window-frames as targets," she said. "I'm forced to barricade myself inside the house."

On a wall in the area someone has written: drugs are beautiful, death is beautiful.

Old goods wagons have been abandoned among the tangle of tracks in the Vallino goods yard behind the former Lingotto station. They are home to about 200 immigrants. It's a no-man's land. Quarrels and punch-ups happen all the time. In the past year, four people have been killed and about 20 injured on this patch.

Trains to Rome and Paris speed by metres away.

Don Andrea has been the parish priest of the church of San Remigio in the Via Millelire for seven years and he confesses to being "discouraged" because his area is dying.

He said: "Those who can do so, send their children to school elsewhere. The schools here are closing, and every day young people are taking the bus and going off in search of work." There was nowhere for people to meet. "Not a single cinema, only bars and amusement arcades, which regularly get closed down for a few days because of drug dealing."

Statistically, this is the greenest area of the city, with 25 square metres of open space per person.

Don Andrea said: "The green area they are talking about is the Colonnetti Park. But no one goes there much and it is full of litter, rubbish and syringes."

Pozzo Strada and Parella are the second-worst areas in terms of the new wave of drug addiction, with young people between the ages of 14 and 18 already on heroin. They often get together in gangs of up to 10, flaunting violence as if it were some kind of banner.

The new poverty is mainly to be found hidden away in the old buildings around Piazza della Repubblica. But there is also a problem around Cit Turin, Cenisia, Regio Parco and Borgo Vittoria. The down-and-outs include immigrants from outside the EC, elderly people, alcoholics, people who have been evicted from their homes, young people who have run away from home and ex-prisoners.

Lia Varesio from Bartolomeo e C, an association for the homeless, says there are 1,000 of them, unknown faces, heads down in search of a hot meal and a cardboard box to keep out the cold. Sister Cherubino is 78 and has been looking after down-and-outs for 56 years. She has served up more than four million meals in the kitchens of the Cottolengo. She has known tramps, delinquents, immigrants and prostitutes, "Violence and poverty are common," she said, "but things are worse today because people have no values any more."

FIG 6.12   *The Guardian, 16 April 1993*

The solutions the architects have proposed include:

- improving the 'neighbourly feel' of the estate by improving security in the blocks and improving their appearance by designing new entrances;
- improving access to the town centre and 'drawing the estate back into the town's community' by building a new road;
- moving the dual carriageway further away from the estate and creating a buffer between the flats and the road using landscaping and new garages.

The estimated cost is £1.3 million plus £330 000 for moving the dual carriageway. The cost per flat works out at about £4900.

- From the limited amount of information you have here on the proposed improvements in the Mouysset estate do you think they are likely to improve the 'fragile social climate' on the estate?

- Read Fig 6.11. What evidence is there that some people believe central government intervention to solve urban problems may not work?

Obviously such problems are not confined to France. On 4 October 1992 an El AL Boeing 747 crashed into two blocks of flats on the Bijlemeer estate on the south-eastern edge of Amsterdam. As well as the horror and the immediate consequences of the disaster the longer-term problems faced by the estate were highlighted by the media at the time. The estate had been completed in the 1970s and was typical of the pre-fabricated high-rise housing being built at that time throughout Europe. It had been planned as a 'garden suburb' with extensive landscaping and scenic waterways running between 30 ten-storey blocks of 'deck-access' flats. The first residents were people rehoused from run-down inner city housing.

However, like so many other similar estates in Europe problems soon emerged. The boring uniform and the deterioration of the blocks, mounting maintenance costs, and inadequate social facilities encouraged families on higher incomes to move out to new towns being built outside Amsterdam. An increasing proportion of the residents were low-paid workers, families with social problems or immigrants, particularly from less developed countries. More recently the estate has been used to house refugees from eastern Europe. By 1990, of the 52 000 people living on the estate, 40 per cent were from Surinam (a former Dutch colony in South America) and the Netherland Antilles, and 20 per cent from Africa and the poorer countries of southern Europe.

Current local council proposals to improve the estate involve improving the physical fabric of the estate, trying to create a stronger 'neighbourhood feel', and increasing the variety of housing available in order to attract residents from a wider range of **socio-economic groups**. The council intends to demolish some blocks and replace them with owner-occupied family dwellings.

- Using both the French and Dutch examples make a list of:
  a) the problems which characterise high-rise suburban estates;
  b) the methods being used to improve the quality of life on the estates.

- Do you think the methods being used to tackle the problems will have long-term success? Justify your answer and suggest any alternative policies you believe are necessary.

- **Multiple deprivation** is not confined to the outer city estates. Read Fig 6.12 on page 131 and list the urban problems mentioned in the article.

6.4 Unofficial Apartheid?: Ethnic Segregation in Cities

The movements of migrants into Europe since 1945 (see Chapter 4) have created ethnic minority communities in most European cities. A smaller and smaller proportion of the ethnic minority populations of European cities is made up of immigrants. An increasing proportion are second or third generation 'immigrants' – in other words people with parents or grandparents who were immigrants. Most cities are seeing a slow increase in the proportion of their populations made up by ethnic minorities either because of a) higher birth rates among ethnic minorities than in the **indigenous** population, or b) because of continued immigration, or c) because people from the indigenous population are moving out of the city to suburbs or other places beyond the city boundary.

Ethnic minorities tend to concentrate in certain parts of most European cities. The reasons for this are complex. One of the key reasons is that they are more likely to be unemployed or have low-paid jobs. Because of this they cannot afford more expensive and attractive housing and are forced to live in the areas of cheaper and less desirable housing. However, this is not the only explanation. Ethnic minorities are not found in all areas of or all types of cheap housing.

Fig 6.13 outlines the key processes that may cause ethnic segregation in cities. External processes result from actions of the indigenous population while internal processes result from actions of the ethnic minorities themselves.

The extreme case of ethnic segregation is the ghetto where the majority of the population is from an ethnic minority.

The different histories of immigration in European cities and the variations in the type of housing found in different European countries mean that there are also variations in the pattern of segregation. However, in

FIG 6.13 *Causes of Ethnic Segregation in Cities*

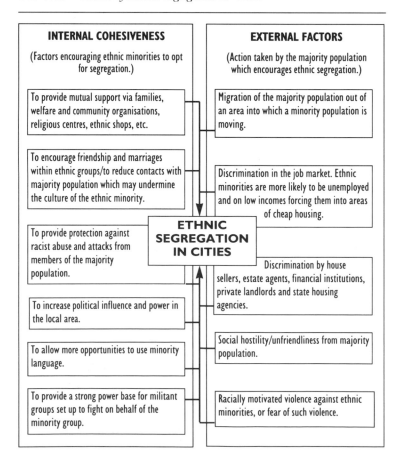

INTERNAL COHESIVENESS
(Factors encouraging ethnic minorities to opt for segregation.)

To provide mutual support via families, welfare and community organisations, religious centres, ethnic shops, etc.

To encourage friendship and marriages within ethnic groups/to reduce contacts with majority population which may undermine the culture of the ethnic minority.

To provide protection against racist abuse and attacks from members of the majority population.

To increase political influence and power in the local area.

To allow more opportunities to use minority language.

To provide a strong power base for militant groups set up to fight on behalf of the minority group.

ETHNIC SEGREGATION IN CITIES

EXTERNAL FACTORS
(Action taken by the majority population which encourages ethnic segregation.)

Migration of the majority population out of an area into which a minority population is moving.

Discrimination in the job market. Ethnic minorities are more likely to be unemployed and on low incomes forcing them into areas of cheap housing.

Discrimination by house sellers, estate agents, financial institutions, private landlords and state housing agencies.

Social hostility/unfriendliness from majority population.

Racially motivated violence against ethnic minorities, or fear of such violence.

most cities ethnic groups tend to concentrate in cheap privately rented inner city housing or in rented social housing provided by the state. This social housing is either found in the inner city or in large outer city estates such as the French cités (see Section 6.3).

- Look carefully at Fig 6.14 which shows the degree of segregation in London, Paris, Dusseldorf and Budapest.
  - **a)** Why can the maps not be compared accurately?
  - **b)** To what extent do the maps reveal ethnic segregation?
  - **c)** To what extent are the spatial patterns shown similar or different?

In the case of social housing a key role in deciding the level of ethnic segregation is played by housing managers who deal with the applications for housing. In some European countries, such as France, a quota system has been used limiting the proportion of dwellings in an estate given to immigrants or minority groups. In some cities immigrants have been excluded at least for a time from

FIG **6.14** *Distribution of Ethnic Minority Populations in Four European Cities*

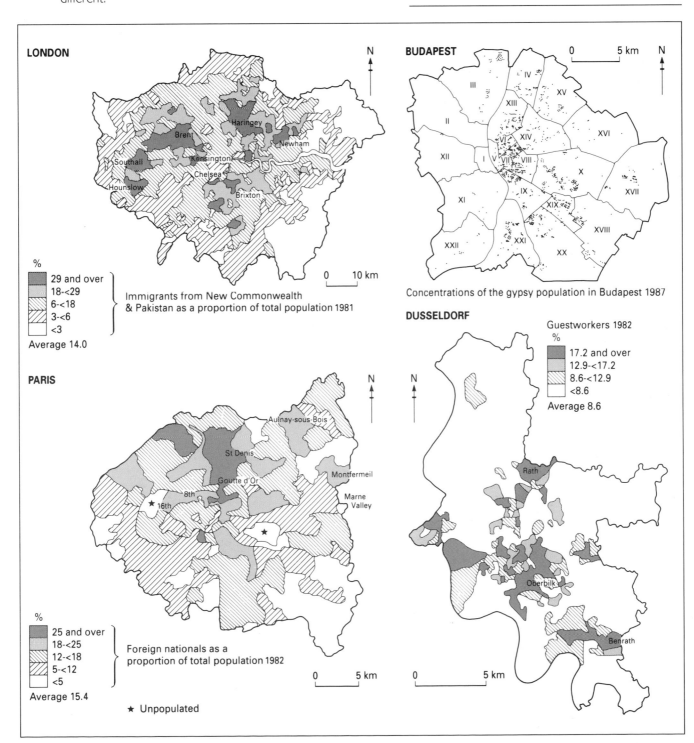

LONDON

%
- 29 and over
- 18-<29
- 6-<18
- 3-<6
- <3

Immigrants from New Commonwealth & Pakistan as a proportion of total population 1981

Average 14.0

PARIS

%
- 25 and over
- 18-<25
- 12-<18
- 5-<12
- <5

Foreign nationals as a proportion of total population 1982

Average 15.4

★ Unpopulated

BUDAPEST

Concentrations of the gypsy population in Budapest 1987

DUSSELDORF

Guestworkers 1982
%
- 17.2 and over
- 12.9-<17.2
- 8.6-<12.9
- <8.6

Average 8.6

Communist High-rise Housing in Berlin, Germany

social housing by rules requiring residence in a country for a number of years (e.g. Netherlands). Even where quota policies do not exist the idea of a 'threshold of tolerance' has been used where housing managers believe that it is sensible to limit the proportion of people from ethnic minority groups in an estate (e.g. Belgium). Where demand for housing from minorities is high and the quota system cannot be maintained 'dump estates' may be created where the estate is allocated almost totally to immigrants or ethnic groups.

Decision makers running social housing are not the only people who can control the degree of segregation. Private landlords, estate agents and managers of the institutions lending money to home-buyers can have an important influence. They may discriminate in favour of the indigenous population.

Segregation in French Social Housing

In the late 1950s and 1960s immigrants arriving in French cities found housing either in inner city slums or in *bidonvilles* – shanty towns built by the immigrants on the edge of the city. These areas were gradually demolished by the French authorities as part of urban improvement programmes and so the immigrants had to be offered alternative accommodation. Many were given housing in the new high–rise outer city estates being built in the 1960s and 1970s. By 1982, 25 per cent of families where the head of the household had foreign nationality lived in social housing, compared with 13 per cent of indigenous families. By moving immigrants into these estates the authorities hoped to encourage their integration into French society.

Many of the housing authorities in France used a threshold of tolerance concept – the idea being that above a certain level

the number of immigrants would become unacceptable to the indigenous population. 15 per cent has been the generally adopted threshold – that is 15 per cent of all households in an estate could be of foreign nationality.

In reality the situation has become more complex. For example, in the department of Seine-Saint-Denis in northern Paris about 15 per cent of all social housing tenants were foreign. However, in some individual estates the figure rises to 75 per cent. Also, foreigners are not distributed evenly within the estates (see Fig 6.15).

- Study Fig 6.15.
    a) Describe the distribution of foreign residents shown in the map.
    b) What evidence is there in the map that foreigners could have suffered from discrimination in the allocation of housing?
    c) To what extent does the map support the hypothesis 'housing policies adopted in French housing estates have encouraged segregation rather than integration of foreign households'?

There are a number of possible reasons for the uneven distribution of foreign households within such estates including:

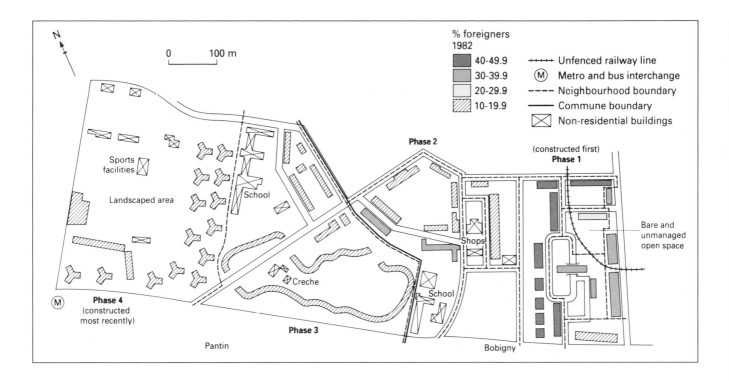

FIG 6.15 *Social Housing Estate of Les Courtillieres, Seine-St-Denis, The Planner, April 1989*

– discrimination by housing managers who allocate foreign households the less desirable housing;
– family size is generally larger in immigrant households and so families will be allocated larger flats which will be concentrated in particular blocks;
– blocks with a high concentration of immigrants may have been built at a time when particular inner city immigrant neighbourhoods or bidonvilles were being demolished and so they were used to rehouse the families affected;
– as indicated above a higher proportion of immigrants live in social housing than indigenous French households – recent movement of more prosperous French households from the older blocks to more attractive housing would make these blocks available to foreign households. In fact, it could be that the rising percentage of immigrants in some blocks could actually encourage French households to move out, a process known as 'white flight'.

Ghetto, Seine-St-Denis, Paris

6.5 Rapid Change in Eastern European Cities

Cities in eastern Europe are facing a period of rapid change. Under Communist rule urban planning was seen as a tool for building a Communist society based on equality and collective living. In reality considerable inequalities continued in Communist cities and in many ways quality of life for most people was low. Housing was often poorly built and cramped and urban pollution was a major problem largely ignored by the authorities. However, in other respects Communist cities offered benefits less common in western Europe. In some cities social and cultural facilities were widely available at a reasonable price and public transport was cheap and frequent. Low car ownership meant that traffic congestion was not a serious issue. Recycling facilities were often highly organised.

The collapse of Communist power and the transition to free market economies has led to a period of rapid change and to serious stresses and strains in many eastern cities. This section looks at two cities affected by these changes – Berlin and Prague.

Berlin: Two Cities Merge

Berlin was in a unique position. It was the only city to be divided at the end of the Second World War between western Europe under the control of the Allied Powers (USA, Britain and France) and eastern Europe under the control of the Soviet Union – later it would be divided between West Germany and Communist East Germany. This division became complete in 1961 when the Berlin Wall was built by the eastern authorities to prevent migration to the West (see Section 2.2).

Berlin was an island of Capitalism in eastern Europe (see Fig 2.3) and as such it developed its own special character. It also received special treatment and subsidies from the West German Government in order to help it flourish as an example of successful Capitalism in the heart of Communist Europe. By the time of the opening of the Berlin Wall, West German Government support for West Berlin had reached an average £2000 per person per year.

As the years passed the two halves of the city grew increasingly apart with their own incompatible infrastructures and very different standards of living. All this changed in November 1989 when the Berlin Wall was opened and the city became a united city of 3.5 million people.

As well as the wider issues of economic inequality, which the whole of the united Germany faces, the new Berlin authorities faced three particular problems.

1　How to physically unite the two halves of the city? Each half had its own public transport system, power and water distribution systems and telecommunications networks. By West Berlin standards infrastructure in the East was dilapidated and out-dated. Fax machines, for example, were unknown in East Berlin and it was very difficult to make a phone call from East Berlin to West Berlin even in 1992 due to the shortage of phone lines.

2　How to rehabilitate the tens of thousands of run-down properties in East Berlin? By western standards large numbers of houses lack basic amenities and need urgent maintenance.

3　How to redevelop the wasteland which had surrounded the wall, especially in central Berlin?

An additional factor makes these three questions crucial. Berlin is seen by many as a city in a unique economic and political position – a city which is likely to be in the forefront of growing economic and political links and trade between western Europe and the emerging free market democracies in eastern Europe. In other words, Berlin could become a trading and cultural gateway between west and east. Its potentially influential position has been strengthened by the decision to move the Federal government from Bonn to Berlin before the end of the decade. Some see it as a city which will be a magnet for massive economic investment during the rest of the 1990s. Some believe it could become the most important city in Europe growing from 3.5 million people to five million. It has been referred to as Europe's new 'centre of gravity' and as a 'world metropolis linking East and West'.

In 1989 the cost of office space was £5.50 per square metre on the Kurfurstendamm, West Berlin's prestigious shopping street. By 1991 this had increased to £33, indicating the growing demand for space in the city. In one district, Mitte, rents reached £48 per square metre, double the average in Frankfurt, Germany's financial centre.

The discussions over how to redevelop the wasteland near the wall are indicative of the controversies which could emerge over the next few years. Conservationists are arguing that the centre of the city should not be turned into an area of office tower blocks similar to the centre of Frankfurt and that the generally low-rise character of Berlin should be preserved. Developers, from both within Germany and outside including France, the UK and Japan, are more interested in exploiting the unique opportunity of building on a large area of cleared land in the centre of one of Europe's most important cities. Other companies hope to take advantage of the huge investment needed to improve eastern Berlin's out-dated infrastructure.

The current controversy is focused on Potsdamer Platz and Leipziger Platz - two areas at the heart of Berlin before the Second World War. In 1990 four companies (Daimler-Benz, Sony, Haus Vaterland and Hertie/Wertheim) bought a large share of the 50 acre site for development. Their first proposals included giant tower blocks. Sony said they intended to move their head office to Berlin but threatened to go elsewhere unless their demands for development of the area were met. Some conservationists, on the other hand, argued that the area should be rebuilt using a style of architecture similar to that which existed before the area was flattened at the end of the war. Others argued that the site was too important and historic to be taken over for use as offices and that it should contain a mixture of government, civic and cultural buildings appropriate for the centre of one of Europe's leading capitals.

A jury of architects was appointed by the Senate (city council) to choose a plan which would satisfy developers, conservationists and the Senate. When they announced their choice, a plan by a Munich firm which included offices and housing, the arguments continued. The four companies who have bought the land insisted they wanted only offices and no housing.

However, despite their initial opposition the investors have now accepted the chosen plan and in 1992 Sony and Daimler-Benz held architectural competitions for their portions of the Potsdamer Platz site.

The situation is further complicated by an EU ruling that Sony had paid too little for the site and should pay more. Also, construction of planned rail and road tunnels under the site had not yet started and development of the site may not be possible until these are complete. With the growing recession in Germany and restrictions on public spending this may delay the development for some time.

Meanwhile work is continuing on 'reconnecting' the two halves of the city. Roads have been built across the old line of the wall and two *U-Bahn* (underground railway) lines are being rejoined. The new infrastructure is proving to be very expensive. The Senate needs about £16 billion a year to run the city and of that about £2.5 billion has to be borrowed. In order to help make up the shortfall the eight per cent personal income tax allowance for Berliners and tax exemption for firms in Berlin, both introduced to encourage people and

investment to the city before 1989, will be phased out by 1995.

Despite the rapid changes since 1989 two separate societies continue to be evident in Berlin. First Class and Second Class zones, corresponding with the old west and east, remain. People from both sides of the old divide refer to the other half of the city as 'over there' (see Section 2.5).

Prague: Embracing Capitalism

People have nowhere to shop – the butchers is now a 'Bureau de Change'. The shop where we used to buy light bulbs is a wine bar. Antique shops, banks – everything for tourists. Locals out, foreigners in … and prices are through the roof.

A Prague resident.

The Communist countries of eastern Europe were centrally planned. In other words, the state made all the key decisions. In theory this gave city planners more power over the design and layout of cities than in western countries. In reality shortages of labour, equipment, materials and capital made it impossible to fulfil their plans. In any case, plans drawn up by city planners were often overridden by plans drawn up by industries or other state organisations. A decision by a state factory, for example, to increase its workforce could mean that priority would be given to building houses for the additional workers rather than to priorities drawn up by the city planners. Also, city planners often lacked the financial or legal power they needed to fulfil their plans.

The transition to free market economics taking place in eastern Europe means that city planners are having to learn to operate in very different economic, social and political conditions. Increasingly they are facing similar problems to those being experienced in western European cities.

Prague, the capital of the Czech Republic, is typical of the eastern European cities undergoing rapid change. The city, with a population of 1.2 million, is located at the heart of the continent and, as is the case of Berlin, could benefit enormously from being at a trading and political 'gateway' between eastern and western Europe. It has many of the characteristics typical of Communist cities.

For example, housing in Prague was typical of most Communist cities. Although housing systems varied from country to country there were similarities. Most urban housing was controlled either directly or indirectly by the state. Privately rented housing was virtually non-existent and owner-occupation relatively rare. After the Second World War much of the existing privately rented housing had been nationalised. Although owner-occupied housing had usually been left in the hands of private owners new private housing was made illegal in some countries and selling houses to individuals was made more difficult. Housing built by co-operatives at least partially funded by the state was common.

Rents were highly subsidised and so by western European standards housing was very cheap. This was seen by many as one of the successes of Communism. People could afford acceptable housing regardless of income.

Housing, at least in theory, was allocated according to need rather than income. In this way housing policy was seen to be aiding the creation of a classless egalitarian society.

On the other hand, flats were often small and there was little choice in housing. Since the Second World War most new housing had been provided in the form of high-rise estates on the periphery of the cities. Lack of resources and the concentration on maintaining low rents meant that maintenance was often inadequate. Pre-fabricated building techniques led to the creation of monotonous monolithic estates which are often very unpopular with residents. Prague is surrounded by large high-rise estates. Two of the biggest estates are North Town (population: 90 000) and South Town (population: 100 000).

The city has inherited a range of other problems from Communism. The central area of Prague has some of the most attractive architecture in Europe. Following the 1948 Communist revolution the authorities regarded the city's architecture as representing the hated past and it was rejected along with the overthrown political system. Many of the old buildings, particularly churches, were turned into offices, flats, warehouses or simply boarded up and abandoned. The fact that the historic core of the city survived at all was due partly to the state's decision to discourage commercial activity in the city centre. More recently the Communist authorities were careful to preserve the facades of the buildings realising their potential for attracting tourists. By the 1980s the centre of Prague looked the same as it did in the 1930s but the preservation was only skin-deep. Behind the facades the buildings were neglected. The new government is now trying to find the finance to renovate and conserve these old buildings.

Prague is also suffering from serious atmospheric pollution. The Communist regime chose to ignore the environmental damage being inflicted by state-owned housing and industry. Sulphur dioxide produced by burning brown coal, which has a high sulphur content, creates a yellow smog over the city on calm winter days. The coal is burned in the city's estate heating systems as well as in local factories. The safe daily limit is often exceeded. Unlike western cities traffic only contributes about ten per cent of the pollution although this is likely to change as a consumer society develops.

The sewerage infrastructure is inadequate and river and groundwater pollution is a growing problem. Drinking water does not meet accepted health standards.

One of the first reforms following the Velvet Revolution when Communist power collapsed, was in land and property ownership. The previous owners, or their heirs, have been given back property taken over by the government. For example, 80 per cent of inner city housing is changing hands in this way. Other housing owned by the state is being sold into private hands. Commercial property is also being privatised. During the first eight months of 1991 more than 1100 shops, restaurants and small firms were transferred into private ownership.

The phasing out of state subsidies on housing is having a profound impact on the city. The 70 per cent of Prague's population who still live in state-owned flats have faced rent increases of more than 200 per cent. A free market in housing will hit people on low incomes particularly hard, not only because they can least afford rent increases, but also because at present they may live in the most attractive areas where prices will rise the greatest. In the long term the city is likely to become increasingly segregated on the basis of income as people move to residential areas they can afford.

Prague's impressive city centre architecture has always attracted tourists but since 1989 there has been a rapid increase in the number of visitors (65 million in 1991). Money is now being invested in revitalising the historic areas of the city. New hotels are being built to meet the demand for accommodation. A new World Trade Centre is being built on a 37 ha site close to the city centre so that Prague can host international conferences and trade fairs.

Private developers are now very interested in Prague's potential. Companies from elsewhere in Europe are interested in redeveloping the buildings behind the facades in Wenceslas Square – the historic heart of Prague which attracts the most tourists. The Myslbek site, for example, has been sold to a French development company. Many people regard the company's proposals for the site as inappropriate (a ramp to a proposed underground car park, for example, will destroy a pedestrian area), but permission is likely to be granted simply because the city council needs the income such a development will bring. One international consortium of developers has proposed to build Europe's largest tower block in Prague. It would contain hotels, shops, restaurants and offices, and would cost £400 million.

The city is changing in appearance in a number of other ways. Advertising hoardings encouraging Prague's residents to buy the newly available consumer goods have appeared in their thousands. A number of existing shops have been replaced by fast-food restaurants (including MacDonald's),

western-style clothes shops, antiques shops, banks, fax shops and foreign exchange offices. The city's commercial centre is likely to expand over the next few years into the surrounding residential areas. Housing in the historic inner city will become increasingly **gentrified**.

Prague is looking increasingly like any other cosmopolitan western European city. It is also increasingly facing the same social problems as western cities.

Birmingham International Conference Centre (top), Public Art in Birmingham City Centre (bottom)

6.6 Regenerating Urban Economies

Most European cities were shaped in the nineteenth and early twentieth centuries by the Industrial Revolution. The main types of transport used (railways and canals) favoured the concentration of industry in big cities. Cities provided large local markets, large supplies of cheap labour and allowed the building of large factories (which were cheaper to run than a large number of small factories). In other words, cities allowed the new industries to benefit from **economies of scale**.

However, over recent decades these cities have seen the decline of their traditional manufacturing industries while new industries have often chosen to locate on the periphery of large urban areas or in smaller towns. This change of preferred location has contributed to the loss of population from many European cities (see section 6.1) and to the decline of many inner cities. These trends have meant that cities have had to look for new ways of attracting income and investment.

Birmingham: Attracting European Investment

Birmingham is typical of many western European cities facing these changes. In the late nineteenth century Birmingham was the UK's foremost industrial centre. The emergence of the car industry in the twentieth century meant that the city continued to prosper until the 1970s. By the early 1980s it was suffering from the combined effects of a steep decline in the British car industry and a national economic recession. In 1971 nearly 60 per cent of the city's jobs were in manufacturing. By 1981 half of these had been lost and the growth of the tertiary sector was insufficient to make up the shortfall. By the early 1980s unemployment in the city was nearly 20 per cent, rising to more than 50 per cent in some inner city areas. The scale of inner city deprivation was greater than any other English city with some of the worst urban problems in Europe.

During the late 1980s and early 1990s Birmingham City Council has attempted to build a new economic base for the city. This programme of economic regeneration is based on two key ideas.

1 The EU should be used as a major source of additional funding for economic regeneration.

2 The city should aim to attract private sector investment from the rest of Europe by becoming not just an important and well-known city within Britain but also an important European city. To create such a positive image throughout Europe it must offer a good quality of life and it must be an attractive place both for investors and skilled workers. It must also offer facilities and an infrastructure which allow it to compete with other leading European cities in attracting new industries based on new technology.

In pursuing the first key idea Birmingham City Council became possibly the most successful British city in attracting EU finance. In the early 1980s Birmingham did not automatically qualify for aid from the EU's Structural Funds (see Section 7.7) because the British Government did not see it as a region suffering seriously enough to deserve regional aid. To overcome this problem the city council began to lobby the European Commission for aid on the basis of the scale of its inner city problems. The council set up an office in Brussels in order to establish close contact with EU officials and members of the European Parliament.

The city's case was helped enormously in 1984 when the British Government declared the region an Assisted Area eligible for regional aid, giving the city access to the European Regional Development Fund (ERDF) and the European Social Fund. Between 1984 and 1987 the city received £78 million from the ERDF, and in 1988 it received an additional block of EU assistance for the period 1988–91 worth £200 million. In 1989 it was declared an Objective Two region by the EU (see Section 7.7).

In pursuing the second key idea Birmingham City Council has been actively involved in a number of projects which it believes will achieve these aims.

1 Expanding the National Exhibition Centre (NEC) and building the International Convention Centre. (In fact it was the success of the NEC in the late 1970s and 1980s in attracting representatives of European businesses that encouraged the city council to pursue the idea of attracting private sector investment from other European countries.)
2 Promoting Science Parks in partnership with the universities.
3 Investing in telecommunications and transport.
4 Redeveloping the city centre to provide improved shopping facilities.
5 Promoting the National Indoor Arena – the UK's largest indoor venue.
6 Providing a new concert hall for the internationally known Birmingham Symphony Orchestra.
7 Supporting the relocation of the Royal Ballet from London.
8 Bidding for the Olympic Games.

The NEC and International Conference Centre now provide 21 000 jobs, while visitors to the city generate a further £300 million a year. They have created a multiplier effect encouraging additional investment in tourism, hotels, restaurants and clubs. The additional visitors have prompted a doubling of Birmingham Airport's capacity with a £65 million second terminal.

The city council has also taken an interest in increasing its political influence in the rest of Europe. In 1986

representatives of the council attended a conference of European 'second cities' in Rotterdam along with Barcelona, Frankfurt, Lyons, Milan and Rotterdam, and became a founder member of the Association of Eurocities which now includes 32 European cities. The association now has a permanent secretariat in Brussels and employs a full-time Eurocities officer. This has given the cities greater political influence over EU policy. Birmingham City Council now has a 'European Steering Group' comprising senior council officers. This group has the task of furthering Birmingham's aim of attracting European investment and influencing EU policy affecting urban areas.

These approaches have not won the city council universal support. Some local people believe that the council should have allocated more resources to housing, education and other basic local services rather than ambitious high status projects.

Barcelona: Regeneration and the Olympic Games

While cities accept that a whole range of measures are necessary to regenerate the local economy, many have searched for a single catalyst project which will kickstart the local economy and boost the image of the city quickly and effectively. For some cities prestigious international sporting events have provided such a catalyst. In recent years Manchester and Berlin have bid to become a venue for the Olympic Games and Sheffield decided to host the 1991 World Student Games. The question is, do such sporting events contribute to the long-term regeneration of cities? Barcelona, in Spain, was the venue for the 1992 Olympic Games. What impact did the Games have on this city?

The city of Barcelona has a population of 1.7 million although the city is part of a conurbation of around 3.5 million people. The city lies at the heart of Catalonia, one of Spain's most prosperous regions and is Spain's leading industrial centre and largest port. Like most other western European cities it suffered from the decline of traditional manufacturing industry in the 1970s and 1980s, particularly textiles and heavy engineering. Between 1970 and 1985 the city lost 42 per cent of its industrial jobs. At times unemployment has exceeded 20 per cent. The inner city areas were particularly hard hit with the old port closing and many factories either closing down or moving out to the periphery of the conurbation.

It is also significant that Barcelona is the main city in Catalonia – a region with a distinct cultural identity and with its own Catalan language. Catalan cultural identity suffered decades of repression by the Spanish Government until the death of Franco in 1975. Since then the region has been struggling to re-establish its separate identity. The Olympic Games were seen as a method of regenerating the city economically, but also as a way of increasing its status within Europe as the capital city of an increasingly independent Catalonia and as a leading Mediterranean city.

Barcelona was not the only Spanish city using an international event as a vehicle for regeneration in 1992. Seville was the location for a 'Universal Expo' (an international exhibition) and Madrid was designated Cultural Capital of Europe for the year.

Planning for the Games was co-ordinated by the Barcelona '92 Olympic Organising Committee (COOB'92) – a consortium of Barcelona City Council, the Catalonian Regional Government, the Spanish Government and the Spanish Olympic Committee. The city council in particular saw the Games as an opportunity to revitalise the city's economy and to tackle many of the city's environmental problems. It was an opportunity to obtain massive grants from the Spanish Government to regenerate the city. Estimates of the total cost of the programme vary widely – one estimate was £165 million on sports facilities, £370 million on the Olympic Village, and £800 million on transport and telecommunications – £1.3 billion in total. Other estimates have put the total as high as £2 billion. This was urban regeneration using state funds on a massive scale, although private investment also played a part in the building of the Olympic Village and the running costs of the Games themselves.

In return for the enormous investment the city benefited from:

– a new ring road;
– an extension to the city's metro system;
– a modernised telecommunications system;
– new sewage and drainage systems;
– a facelift for many public buildings;
– a large new area of housing consisting of 2000 flats, called *Nova Icaria*, to be used during the Games as the Olympic Village, housing the Olympic teams and officials. Nova Icaria includes hotel and office blocks, a shopping mall and a conference centre;
– a programme of landscaping and environmental improvements including new squares and parks;
– a new terminal building at Barcelona Airport;
– the rebuilding of one of Barcelona's main railway stations;
– the commissioning of 'public art' such as sculptures;
– new or improved sports facilities including a new council sports complex.

Barcelona Olympic Facilities, Spain

FIG **6.16**   *Objectives of Barcelona 2000*

The objectives of the Barcelona 2000 plan

Main objective
Consolidate Barcelona as an enterprising European metropolis, with influnce over its macroregion and with a modern, socially balanced quality of life, deeply rooted in Mediterranean culture.

Strategic lines
a)   Make Barcelona one of the key centres of the macroregion.
b)   Improve the quality of life and progress for people.
c)   Support for industry and for advanced services to business.

Objectives
a)   1 Insert Barcelona in the network of Eurocities and of metropolitan centres around the world.
     2 Improve communications within the metropolitan region.
b)   3 Improve the environment.
     4 Improve, at all levels, training and research as a means of progress.
     5 Improve social opportunities for housing and training.
     6 Prioritise cultural infrastructures.
c)   7 Create basic infrastructure for advanced services, in addition to those related to transport and telecommunications.
     8 Promote technological innovation for industrial progress.
     9 Develop sectors with potential within the metropolitan area.

The magazine *Architecture Review* in 1992 expressed the view that '*Barcelona is now so thoroughly, if still incompletely, regenerated and so vibrant with all its new public places – parks and plazas, designer bars and restaurants, museums, cultural and sports centres – as well as other new facilities for education and health and all forms of commerce, that it is rather difficult to recall the city of only a decade and a half ago. It had then a shabby beauty and heady atmosphere all of its own, but was also run-down, overcrowded, and desperately short of all sorts of amenities…Now, ready for next year's more integrated Europe, Barcelona is well poised to attract all sorts of business and cultural investment…no other city has deliberately undertaken anything like such a complete and thorough regeneration of itself…*'

The scale of the programme can be seen by looking at one of the schemes, the Olympic Village, in more detail. The Village was intended to regenerate a derelict area and to form the centre-piece of a long-standing plan to open up the waterfront to the rest of the city. The site had previously been used for heavy industry. Road access has been improved, new harbour and marina facilities built (used as a base for watersports during the Games) and new beaches have been created. Three new parks have been created for a city short of public open space. Two high-rise towers dominate the development and can be seen throughout the city. In places the new ring road runs between the estate and the coast in a cutting bridged by parkland. The city council claims the scheme will create 7300 new jobs.

On the other hand, the Village flats will be far too expensive for most Barcelona residents, and for some it merely emphasises existing social inequalities within the city. There is a serious shortage of low cost housing and this is causing many young people to move out of the city while housing remains empty. Neither has the Olympics regeneration programme done anything directly to improve the desolate tower blocks in the estates on the city's periphery.

The city council is now attempting to keep up the momentum of regeneration by drawing up an Economic and Social Strategic Plan Barcelona 2000 (see Fig 6.16). The aim is to involve as many public agencies and private companies as possible in a continuing programme of regeneration. The economic regeneration strategy promoted by Birmingham City Council (see above) provided some of the ideas in Barcelona's plan.

The dominant aim of the plan is to promote Barcelona's economic importance in the macroregion containing Valencia, Saragossa and Majorca in Spain, and Toulouse and Montpellier in France – a region of 15 million people.

- Suggest two reasons why an event such as the Olympic Games is seen by local decision makers as an attractive way of 'kick-starting' urban economies.

- Suggest two ways in which this type of 'single event regeneration' can be a risky method of reviving urban economies.

- What are the main similarities and differences between Barcelona's and Birmingham's approach to regeneration?

- Read Fig 6.17 about Manchester's failed bid for the Olympic Games in 2000.
  a) What drawback for Barcelona does the article point out?
  b) Do you think the article is positive or negative about Manchester's bid? Justify your answer by using evidence from the article.
  c) What effect do you think the failure of Manchester's bid may have had on the city?

Everything to play for in Manchester

ONE hundred and fifty years ago, Manchester was Tokyo, Hong Kong and Bangkok rolled into one, a city that alternately horrified and impressed visitors from around the world. Manchester invented the Industrial Revolution and the modern industrial city; Engels came to see what it had done to the proletariat; and Schinkel the great Prussian architect came to see how it had been built. Now, like so many other big cities, Manchester is struggling to deal with the husk of its redundant 19th-century self. Coming to terms with this is a multi-layered problem, one that touches on architecture as well as the complexities of local and national politics and the cultural and social health of a city.

One of the most powerful weapons in the urban regeneration armoury has been the catalyst represented by a single spectacular event, such as the staging of the Olympic Games or of a World Fair. It's an old idea, but one that the huge success of last year's Barcelona games serves to reinforce powerfully. Such events can provide a rush of energy forcing through a host of developments that in the normal course of events might take decades to realise. It has been estimated that staging the Olympics could create 18,000 new jobs in Manchester and attract billions in new investment, much of which would have nothing to do with building stadiums or hotels.

"This is a chance to go further than Barcelona, to stage a Games that will not only bring the city alive for the duration of the Games, but leave a permanent legacy for Manchester. If you go to Barcelona now you see that many places that were so vibrant during the Games have gone back to what they were, great empty spaces. We are determined that it won't be like that,' says Jim Chapman of the local architects BDP which has played a major role in formulating the proposals.

Manchester has commissioned Norman Foster to draw up a master-plan for the major stadium site while the stadium itself has been designed by Arup Associates. While it may look a little too much like Sydney's rival stadium for comfort, with its smoke-ring roof and its forest of hi-tech masts, it is certainly an impressive piece of architecture.

Manchester is fighting hard for the Olympics, and has its imposing new airport, its metro system and its new concert hall now underway to point to. Until now the city has been prepared to settle for second best when it comes to architecture.

What Manchester and the other big cities of Britain need is the same confidence they had in the 19th century to demand the very best – wherever that comes from.

FIG 6.17   *The Guardian, 2 August 1993*

6.7 The Urban Transport Crisis

Most European cities are facing a transport crisis, particularly those in western and southern Europe where car ownership is higher. It is generally agreed that current policies are inadequate but there is widespread disagreement over how the crisis should be tackled.

Athens traffic

The crisis is the result of a number of inter-related problems.

1   The rapid growth in the use of private cars is causing widespread congestion. Gridlock (where all the traffic in part of a city comes to a complete standstill) is now a real possibility in some European urban central areas. In many cities traffic moves no faster than it did at the beginning of the century when horses provided the power. Not only is car ownership rising (Italy, western Germany and France have the highest ownership rates in Europe) but also people are using their cars for more frequent and longer journeys.

2   The rapid growth in traffic is causing serious atmospheric pollution which now poses a real threat to health. Traffic also poses other threats to the quality of the environment in urban areas – particularly noise and road accidents.

3   The growth in car ownership has led to a decline in the use of public transport. This means that public transport earns less revenue. It has become increasingly difficult to provide efficient and frequent public transport without massive government subsidies.

The deterioration in public transport means that people without the use of a car, particularly the old, the young and the poor, are finding it increasingly difficult to travel around urban areas.

4 Proposals to build new major roads to cope with the increased traffic are often met with widespread local opposition. Growing environmental awareness, particularly in north-western Europe, has strengthened the hand of anti-road groups.

FIG 6.18 *Car Pollution: Impact on Urban Areas*

Car pollution: impact on urban areas

MAIN POLLUTANTS	KNOWN HEALTH EFFECTS	OTHER ENVIRONMENTAL IMPACTS
NITROUS OXIDES (NO$_x$)	Asthma worsened. Coughs and headaches.	May accelerate erosion of stonework. Impedes tree growth.
OZONE (O$_3$)	Respiratory problems. Asthma worsened.	Damages trees. Reduces plant yields. Corrodes metals, rubber, fabrics, paint. Accelerates formation of acid rain.
VOLATILE ORGANIC COMPOUNDS (VOCs, e.g. Benzene)	Eye irritation, coughing, Carcinogenic (i.e. cancer-causing).	
PARTICULATES (i.e. smoke) e.g. Particulate carbon from diesel engines.	Lung irritation. Carcinogenic.	Reduces visibility. Encourages condensation of water vapour increasing incidence of fog. Blackens buildings.
CARBON MONOXIDE (CO)	Impedes ability of blood to carry oxygen to body tissues – people with heart and respiratory probems particularly at risk	
LEAD (when leaded fuel is used.)	May cause behavioural problems. May reduce ability to concentrate in children.	

REACT UNDER SUNLIGHT

144

The response of cities during the last decade to the crisis has varied. In Britain the response, at least by central government, has been minimal. There has been relatively little support for the development of public transport and yet acceptance that massive road-building in most urban areas is out of the question. In other countries, such as Germany and the Netherlands there has been more positive support of initiatives to discourage private cars and to develop public transport.

This section examines one aspect of the problem in more detail – atmospheric pollution – and then looks at five methods of tackling the problem – traffic calming, investment in public transport, the construction of new roads, integrated transport planning and road-pricing.

Atmospheric Pollution

Fig 6.18 summarises the main threats to the urban environment caused by vehicle emissions. It should be pointed out that the diagram does not mention the contribution traffic makes to global environmental problems. For example, vehicles emit large quantities of CO_2 which causes global warming – one of the most serious environmental problems.

The chemistry of modern urban atmospheric pollution is extremely complex. Photochemical Smog, where nitrous oxides and hydrocarbons react together to produce ozone and other pollutants, is a particularly serious problem in southern European cities which experience higher temperatures and more direct sunlight (although it is becoming increasingly serious in northern Europe as well). In reality the break up of a single molecule of a particular VOC (volatile organic compounds) may involve more than 100 separate chemical reactions, and these reactions may be speeded up by chemicals produced in other reactions. This makes the impact of growing pollution difficult to predict.

The health impact is particularly uncertain and more research is needed. There is growing evidence that nitrous oxides are a key factor in causing asthma, especially in young children. The vulnerability of individuals to pollution will vary. Factors such as age, sex, general state of health and the amount of exercise being taken will all have an effect. What is certain is that European urban

FIG **6.19** *Relative Pollution Levels*

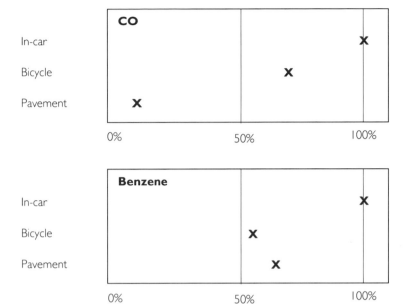

Relative pollutant concentrations experienced by motorists, cyclists and pedestrians

populations are being exposed to unprecedented levels of some chemical pollutants.

Fig 6.19 illustrates another problem with assessing the impact of vehicle pollution. Much higher concentrations of pollutants build up inside cars in traffic yet very little research has been conducted to assess the seriousness of this problem.

It should also be pointed out that the pollution created by urban traffic is not confined to cities. For example, the reactions that produce ozone may take an hour or more to occur and may still be taking place when the air mass has been travelling for up to ten hours. This means that some of the highest levels of ozone pollution are recorded in rural areas. It also means that a city in one country may be seriously adding to pollution in another country. This is known as 'transboundary pollution'.

Athens is probably suffering from traffic pollution more seriously than any other European city. A combination of high car ownership, a hot sunny climate and a large number of older cars with poor emission standards has meant that photochemical smog, known locally as the *nefos* (or cloud) frequently reaches dangerous levels.

Cities particularly badly affected by traffic pollution, such as Athens, have introduced draconian measures. Athens has imposed occasional complete bans on the use of private cars, while at other times it has rationed the use of cars by only allowing cars with odd registration numbers to be used on some days of the week and those with even numbers on the other days. The state of Thuringia in eastern Germany banned the use of private transport in early 1993 during a particularly serious pollution episode. Such strict measures may well become more widespread and frequent in the future.

- Read Fig 6.20. What, including the measures referred to in the article, can a city like Athens do in the short term to tackle this level of pollution?

FIG **6.20** *The Guardian, 2 October 1991*

City's beauty leaves honeymooners breathless

FROM the top of the Holy Hill tourists descended in droves, coughing and spluttering and cursing that they had ever come to Athens.

They had seen the Acropolis but little else. For all round the city which Melina Mercourt once likened to 'an ugly woman with great charm', the smog had cast its shadow.

As far as the eye could see, the azure skies of the Greek capital had been obscured by the ochre-coloured cloud. Beneath the haze of pollutants the Seronic Gulf had entirely disappeared. Aircraft taking off from Athens airport were lost from sight minutes after leaving the ground. All private cars and half the taxi fleet of 17 000 were banned from the city centre in an attempt to reduce the choking haze. The measures will stay in force today.

The citizens of Athens have become used to high levels of air pollution over the past 20 years. Yesterday, however, exacerbated by a freak heatwave and a lack of wind, it broke all records.

"I have never before seen such bad pollution ... at 7.30 this morning. I was still driving with my headlights on," said Panayiotis Macryiannis, a taxi driver.

As residents heeded a warning by the environment minister, Achilleas Karamanlis, to curb their movements and stay indoors, the normally congested streets emptied.

Around midday, officials at monitoring stations were saying that nitrogen dioxide levels had reached the unheard-of ratio of 696 milligrams per cubic metre of air. Ozone had hit the unprecedented mark of 490 milligrams per cubic metre of air. The state-set emergency levels are 500 micrograms and 300 respectively.

Ozone and nitrogen dioxide, mostly from car exhaust fumes, are the main constituents of the photochemical cloud that forms on warm windless days. 'Unless the government takes measures to reverse Athens' great lack of green space by planting more trees, for example, and radically cuts back on traffic circulation, this problem is only going to get worse,' said Thanassis Papaconstantinou, a leading environmental campaigner.

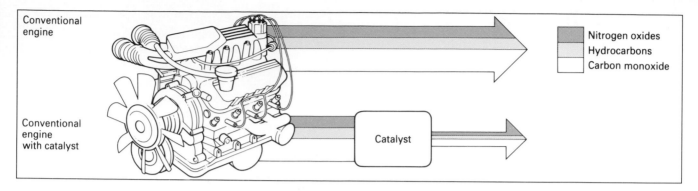

Conventional engine

Conventional engine with catalyst

Catalyst

Nitrogen oxides
Hydrocarbons
Carbon monoxide

FIG 6.21   *The Impact of Catalytic Converters on Emissions*

If the problem is so serious, what is being done to reduce the emission of pollutants from cars in the long term? To some extent policies vary from country to country but probably the most significant impact on traffic pollution will result from the 1991 EU directive which made the fitting of catalytic converters on all new cars compulsory from the beginning of 1993 (the directive also imposed new limits on diesel engine emissions). Some countries, for example Germany, had made catalytic converters compulsory before the EU directive came into effect.

Fig 6.21 illustrates the impact a catalytic converter has on car emissions. However, there are problems:

- the catalyst does not operate efficiently until it has reached a temperature of 300°C and this will take several minutes – a considerable disadvantage for short urban journeys to work;
- the effectiveness of catalysts deteriorates with age and it has been estimated that five per cent of catalysts in use will fail each year (although in the UK they will be checked in the annual MoT Test);
- the catalyst does not reduce the output of carbon dioxide – the most important greenhouse gas;
- there are concerns that the rapid increase in car ownership, accompanied by growing congestion, will quickly cancel out the improvements made possible by growing use of catalytic converters.

It is worth comparing the measures being adopted in Europe with those being implemented in California where car ownership is much higher than in any European country. By 2003 all new cars in the state must emit at least 70 per cent less VOCs and NO_x than the models being produced in 1993 (which even then were the cleanest cars in the world). Beginning in 1998 two per cent of all cars sold must have no harmful exhaust emissions at all and this proportion will increase to ten per cent by 2003. At present only electric cars are capable of meeting this standard. In addition, companies will be fined unless they offer their employees financial incentives to commute by public transport or shared cars. By comparison with these aims the 1991 EU Directive seems weak.

However, a number of European car manufacturers are investing considerable sums of money in the development of

electric vehicles. This is partly in anticipation of capturing part of the enormous Californian car market later this decade (an estimated 100 000 electric vehicles a year by 2003), but also in the belief that standards within Europe will become tougher within the next decade. Clearly, if tougher standards are introduced a manufacturer which has already developed reliable and efficient electric vehicles will be in a very advantageous position. Renault, Volvo, Peugeot, Volkswagen, Citroen and Fiat are all involved. Volkswagen alone has invested £300 million in electric vehicle research. The French Government is providing its own backing by investing £55 million in a project to trial fleets of electric hire cars in ten cities.

However, many people argue that the only effective long-term solution to the pollution problem is to limit the use of private cars and to invest in improved public transport.

- Study Figs 6.22 and 6.23. Use these graphs to write a short report on the effectiveness of catalytic converters and the extent to which they will solve the problem of urban traffic pollution.

- Why do you think some environmentalists argue that the development of electric cars is not a satisfactory solution to the problem? Is it likely to be a solution to the urban pollution problem?

FIG 6.22   *VOC/NO_x Emissions (The Impact of Speed on Emissions), opposite top*

FIG 6.23   *Changes in VOC/NO_x Emissions*

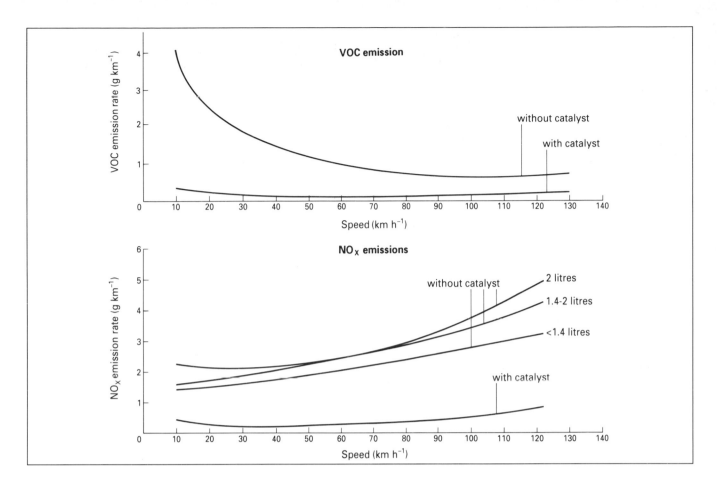

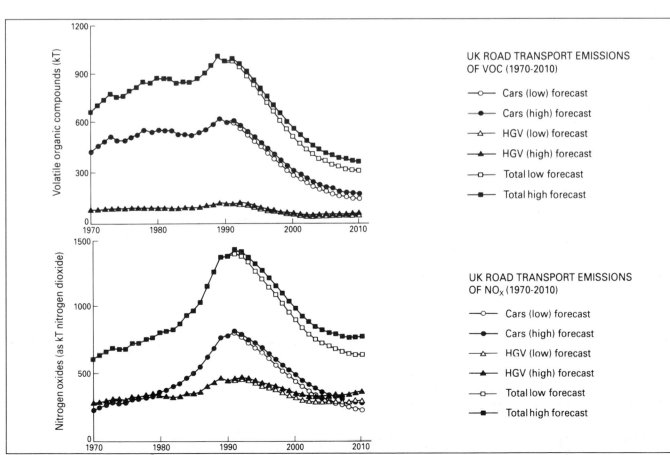

UK ROAD TRANSPORT EMISSIONS
OF VOC (1970-2010)

—○— Cars (low) forecast

—●— Cars (high) forecast

—△— HGV (low) forecast

—▲— HGV (high) forecast

—□— Total low forecast

—■— Total high forecast

UK ROAD TRANSPORT EMISSIONS
OF NO$_X$ (1970-2010)

—○— Cars (low) forecast

—●— Cars (high) forecast

—△— HGV (low) forecast

—▲— HGV (high) forecast

—□— Total low forecast

—■— Total high forecast

Road Construction

Most cities continue to construct new roads in an attempt to relieve congestion but many planners and environmentalists believe that this will never solve the problem. They refer to Down's Law which states that *'on urban commuter expressways peak-hour traffic rises to meet maximum capacity'*. In other words, new roads merely encourage more people to use cars.

One of the most ambitious road construction proposals in Europe is the one proposed for Paris involving a network of underground motorways (see Fig 6.24).

- Read Fig 6.24. Is the underground motorway a realistic solution to the transport crisis facing large European cities? Outline your views, backed up with evidence, in a written report.

Traffic Calming

Traffic calming is a term which refers to measures designed to reduce traffic speeds in urban areas. These measures involve redesigning roads to enforce lower speeds and to shift priority from traffic to pedestrians. Traffic calming may have a number of aims:

- to reduce the number and seriousness of accidents. For example, a car hitting a child at 20 mph is unlikely to result in death while at 40 mph death is likely;

- to improve the appearance of streets. Traffic calming allows flexibility in the design of streets. For example, more trees can be planted and a greater variety of paving materials can be used;

- to reduce access to cars, particularly where residential streets are used by motorists as 'rat-runs' to avoid congested main roads. This may allow traffic calming to be used in conjunction with policies to encourage the use of public transport since car journey times may well be lengthened;

- to reduce atmospheric pollution. Roads deliberately designed to prevent rapid acceleration may reduce vehicle emissions and if the amount of through traffic using a road is reduced then local pollution will also be reduced. However, the total emission per kilometre of some pollutants increases with reduced speed. In any case the impact of reduced speed varies with the capacity of the engine.

FIG 6.24   *Paris Underground Motorways*

Underground Motorway for Paris

One of the most ambitious road construction projects in Europe is for a network of underground motorways in Paris. The plan, known as Laser *(Liaison Automobile Souterraine Expresse Regionale)*, emerged in the late 1980s with the support of the Mayor of Paris, Jacques Chirac. The average speed of traffic in the central part of Paris is six mph with up to 2.8 million cars entering the city daily adding to the 1.4 million owned by inner city residents. The tunnels are seen as a radical way of tackling the congestion.

The proposed network would include 50 km of tunnels forming an underground ring road with five branches leading outwards from the ring. There would be numerous entry and exit points within the central parts of Paris. Each tunnel would be split into two levels – one level for each direction. Large vans would be banned to allow smaller tunnels. Fumes would be extracted by ventilation systems, and the traffic would be monitored and controlled by cameras and a computerised traffic control system. Laser has been designed by GTM-Enterprise – a company linked to the consortium which built the Channel Tunnel. The scheme, which would take many years if it is to reach completion, would be privately financed with revenue coming from tolls.

The 1980s saw a growing interest in traffic calming measures on an area-wide basis rather than approaching the problem on a street by street basis. The larger scale of these schemes meant that cheaper methods had to be found. The Berlin Moabit scheme was an example of this new approach (see Fig 6.25).

A speed limit of 30 kmph (20 mph) was imposed. This speed was enforced by humps, ramps, tight bends and narrowed sections of road. Because cars are travelling more slowly some road signs become unnecessary reducing 'street clutter' and lowering costs. Lower speeds also mean that traffic needs less road space. This means that more space can be allocated to parking, pedestrians, seating, and landscaping. In these area-wide schemes less emphasis is put on landscaping and use of expensive materials.

By the end of the 1980s there were still few examples in Europe of traffic calming on main roads. Most schemes on main roads have involved the reallocation of road space so that pavements can be widened, bus lanes created, or cycle lanes provided. There are a few examples of the use of ramps or humps on main roads such as Buxtehude in Germany and Ålborg and Odense in Denmark, and in many villages on main roads in Alsace in eastern France. One of the problems with obstacles like this on main roads is that they are a hazard to buses and emergency vehicles. Some towns, such as Herne in Germany, are experimenting with speed cushions which are small enough for larger vehicles to avoid but which are effective in slowing cars.

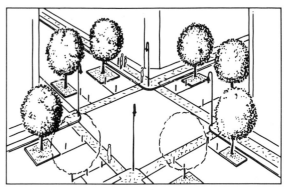
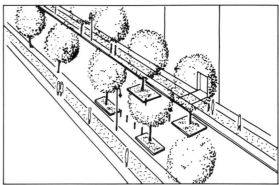
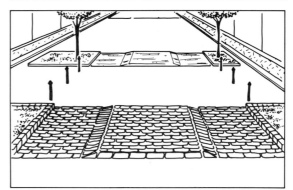

FIG **6.25** *The Berlin Moabit Traffic Calming Scheme Designs*

End of the road for cars in Amsterdam

ON THE DAY that Amsterdam voted by a narrow margin to ban cars from the city centre, I was nearly knocked off my bike.

The city centre is so small it takes minutes to cycle through. Narrow streets follow the canals over hump-backed bridges not wide enough for two cars. The slosh of the glass-topped barges touring the city canals is a reminder that seventeenth-century Amsterdam was built for river not road transport. The city council estimates that by the year 2000 traffic will have risen by 30 per cent. It says there are already some 4,000 illegal parking places and neither fines nor clamps have proved effective deterrents.

Some 20 yeas ago, in the heyday of Amsterdam radicalism, free bicycles were introduced in an attempt to shift cars off the roads. Painted white, they were left for anyone to ride short distances. But too many of the bikes were hi-jacked and sold into slavery outside the city boundaries for handsome profit.

Yesteray's referendum made history. Amsterdam has never before held a direct plebiscite. "We had to do it this way," explained Edwin van Eis of the city council. "Fewer and fewer people turn out to vote in council elections so we wanted to see if we could excite more interest by presenting a single issue." The turn-out, however, was disappointing – a lower-than-forecast 26.6 per cent.

At the town hall, converted temporarily into a polling station, the multilingual ballot paper gave citizens a choice of voting for Option A (in favour of transport policies aimed at the gradual reduction of traffic volumes) or Option B (a total ban for all but essential traffic and city-centre residents). Proposal B netted 52.9 per cent of the vote, according to results released later yesterday with 75 per cent of the ballots counted.

The Chamber of Commerce fears that a car-free centre would become a tourist museum, as business moved away. "years ago the city committed itself to a programme of underground car-park construction that it has never honoured," said a spokesman yesterday, suggesting there were solutions that the council had not bothered to explore. The results of the Dutch referendum are not binding but will influence policy. The city council will decide next month whether to act in accordance with the outcome.

Amsterdam is not the first city to try to ban cars. A similar scheme introduced for a trial period in Strasbourg (also built on a canal) has pleased all despite the initial scepticism.

FIG **6.26** *The Independent*

A more radical version of traffic calming is to ban cars completely from an area. Pedestrianised shopping streets are now commonplace in European towns and cities but area-wide bans are less common. Lübeck in Germany is one town which pioneered a complete ban on cars from its central area. Initially the ban only operated at certain times but the town is intending to make the ban complete (with the exception of cars used by disabled people and some essential commercial traffic).

- Read Fig 6.26. Assuming provision was made for commercial vehicles delivering to shops and disabled people consider the advantages and disadvantages of such a scheme.
  a) Draw up two lists under the headings 'Costs' and 'Benefits'.
  b) Draw up two lists under the headings 'Interest Groups Likely to Support the Scheme' and 'Interest Groups Likely to Oppose the Scheme'.

Improving Public Transport

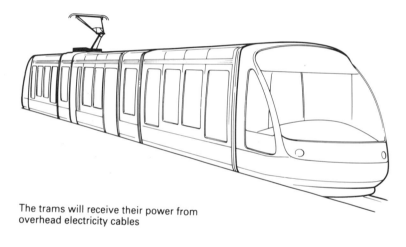

The trams will receive their power from overhead electricity cables

FIG 6.27a   *The New Strasbourg Tramway*

Some cities are concentrating limited resources on improving public transport as a way of encouraging people to leave their cars at home. In a few cases cities are building entirely new systems. For example, Manchester and Sheffield in the UK and Strasbourg in France have committed large sums of public or private sector money to building new tramway systems. A number of European cities, such as Freiburg in Germany and Zürich in Switzerland, had already shown that trams can play an important role in modern cities.

- With the help of the information on the Strasbourg Tramway (Fig 6.27a and b) compile a list of the likely costs and benefits of a tram system for any European city.

Road-Pricing

Road-pricing is the name given to charging motorists for using road space. There are two basic types being considered by a number of European cities.

STRASBOURG TRAMWAY

The first phase of the Strasbourg tramway opened in 1994 and was expected to carry about 75 000 passengers a day. The line, which is 24 km long, links suburban areas with the city centre. The trams, which are powered by electricity from overhead power lines, run at four minute intervals for much of the day. Each tram carries 290 passengers and can travel at up to 60 kmph. In some sections the tramlines run along roadways while in others they are segregated from other traffic by using the central reservations of dual carriageways or by running alongside roads. Within part of the city centre the trams use a 1.4 km tunnel. In other parts of the city centre they follow streets closed to other traffic.

FIG 6.27b   *New Strasbourg Tramway Factfile*

1   Charging motorists for entering the central area of a city. This could either be done electronically or by using toll booths.

2   Charging motorists according to the amount they travel within the central area of a city. They could, for example, be charged a certain amount per kilometre. This would have to be done electronically.

One electronic system which could be used in either case would be where motorists buy 'smart-cards' which would be inserted into a small device in the car. Detectors placed on the road side would then deduct units from the car. Once all the units were used up a new card would have to be bought.

The main aim of any road-pricing system would be to discourage people from using cars in the central and most congested area of a city. For this reason any charges would have to be high enough to act as a deterrent. They would have to make the use of a car considerably more expensive than using public transport.

Despite the complexities of installing a road-pricing system and the likely popular opposition to such a scheme, severe congestion is forcing the possibility onto the political agenda in many European cities. In 1991 an article in the economic bulletin of the German Deutsche Bank argued that road-pricing would allow the free market to regulate the amount of traffic on the roads and at the same time raise additional revenue. However the article also pointed out that *'Germans tend to regard them [charges for using roads] almost as a regression to medieval road tolls'* and would probably rigorously oppose them.

Oslo, the Norwegian capital, has the only fully operational road-pricing scheme in Europe. The system is earning £60 million a year of which about 11 per cent is spent on operating the system. The remainder is spent on improvements to the city's road network. £180 million has already been spent on a new road tunnel under the city centre which has reduced driving times across the city from 20 to 10 minutes. The aim of the city is to make motorists pay for the road improvements which they make necessary by using their cars. It is intended to suspend the system in 2007 once all the planned road improvements have been paid for. Toll gates now stand on every road into Oslo about seven kilometres from the city centre. The cost is about £1 for cars and £20 for trucks.

Motorists have the option of buying an 'electronic block' about the size of a Mars Bar which can be attached to the windscreen. These motorists can then pay their tolls in advance using a season ticket, and electronic equipment at the toll booths register that the car has passed. If they have not paid enough to cover the cost of the journey a camera automatically records their registration number and they are sent a bill which is considerably higher than the normal toll. More than 60 per cent of motorists use the electronic method so the tolls cause few hold-ups. When the scheme was first introduced traffic fell by five per cent but it has now recovered to the original volume. There is now some pressure to raise tolls during peak periods. Nevertheless, road-pricing has faced considerable opposition from some motorists who resent what they see as the high cost of driving in the city.

A scheme being considered in Stockholm, Sweden's capital, is more sophisticated. Drivers would buy a pre-programmed card allowing them to drive within the city centre for a set period. The permit would transmit a radio signal which would be monitored by electronic receivers all over the city. Automatic cameras would identify any vehicle without the necessary permit. The revenue from the scheme would be used to subsidise and improve public transport. The scheme received the backing of the Swedish parliament but popular opposition may mean that it is never implemented, or at least not within the next few years. Some people are simply opposed to government-run cameras monitoring the movements of private cars or to the fact that families on low incomes will be particularly penalised by the scheme.

- List as many points as you can against the concept of road-pricing.

- In the light of the points you have listed above do you think road-pricing is a realistic policy?

- If you were imposing road-pricing in a British city how much would you charge motorists per mile? Would you levy charges at all times? Who would you exempt from the charges? How would you cater for visitors to the city? How would you deal with motorists who tried to evade the charges?

6.8 Urban Conservation

Since 1945 virtually every European town and city centre has been a battleground between developers and conservationists. Some cities, particularly in the 1960s and 1970s, saw the complete destruction of their historic centres. Developers and planners attempted to replace obsolete street patterns and architecture with new centres designed to cater for the new demands of traffic, shopping, and office space.

As recently as the 1980s the City of London (the area of central London where banks and international financial companies are concentrated) saw a series of battles between conservationists, attempting to preserve historic architecture, and developers. The developers and their architects wanted to

create new buildings specifically designed for a rapidly growing financial sector increasingly dependent on information technology. They believed that a new type of architecture was needed to provide large open-plan offices based on the use of computers and telecommunications.

Conservationists believe that wherever possible old buildings should be preserved because they are part of our heritage and because they make our cities more attractive and interesting. They have often been supported by a general public which seems to generally prefer traditional buildings, and, in the case of the UK, by well-known personalities like the Prince of Wales.

Historic town and city centres are not only threatened by redevelopment. Many centres have been spoiled or badly damaged by growing numbers of cars. Noise, the visual intrusion of congestion and car parking, and the erosion of stonework by atmospheric pollution are a serious threat.

Probably the most well-known historic city in Europe is Venice. In many respects Venice is unusual because redevelopment has not been a real threat. The city does, however, face a number of other problems which threaten its continued existence. Venice is a test case of Europe's willingness to protect historic urban areas.

The Grand Canal, Venice

Venice: a Case Study of Urban Conservation

Venice is located on a group of islands in a shallow coastal lagoon. The first settlers arrived in the fifth century. They were fleeing from the barbarian invasions of Italy and the islands offered a good defensive site. By the late thirteenth century Venice had become an important city-state whose wealth was based on trade. For 500 years the city was Europe's most important port and one of its most powerful and influential states. Much of the wealth created by the city's merchants was spent on building a city of unique architectural importance. The builders in Venice set ground level only a few centimetres above the highest tide levels, and the buildings were built on wooden piles driven into the mud. Venice is in fact built on 118 islands linked by bridges. A network of canals, not roads, provide the main form of transport within the city. However, this architectural heritage is under threat. The city is facing an array of environmental and social problems (see Fig 6.28). Two-thirds of its buildings are in need of major maintenance. The city is rotting away.

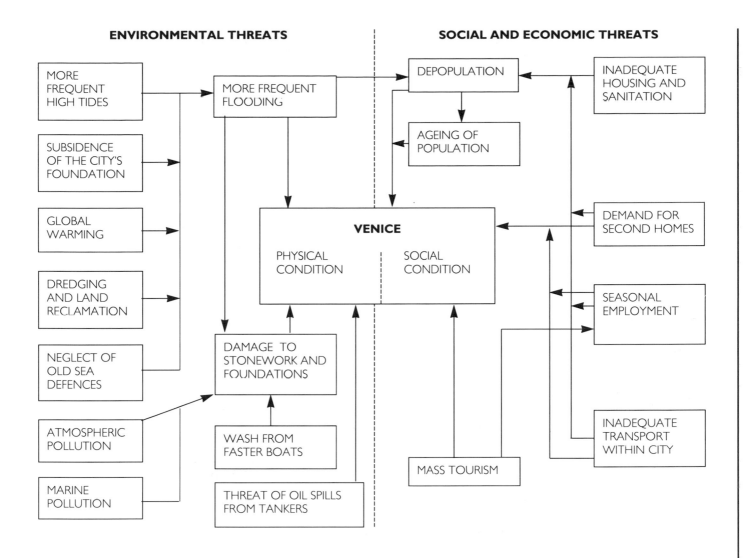

ENVIRONMENTAL THREATS

MORE FREQUENT HIGH TIDES

SUBSIDENCE OF THE CITY'S FOUNDATION

GLOBAL WARMING

DREDGING AND LAND RECLAMATION

NEGLECT OF OLD SEA DEFENCES

ATMOSPHERIC POLLUTION

MARINE POLLUTION

MORE FREQUENT FLOODING

DAMAGE TO STONEWORK AND FOUNDATIONS

WASH FROM FASTER BOATS

THREAT OF OIL SPILLS FROM TANKERS

SOCIAL AND ECONOMIC THREATS

DEPOPULATION

AGEING OF POPULATION

INADEQUATE HOUSING AND SANITATION

DEMAND FOR SECOND HOMES

SEASONAL EMPLOYMENT

INADEQUATE TRANSPORT WITHIN CITY

VENICE

PHYSICAL CONDITION

SOCIAL CONDITION

MASS TOURISM

Environmental Problems

FIG 6.28 *The Threat to the Survival of Venice*

1 High tides are occurring with increasing frequency and the flooding which results is weakening the city's foundations. The water in the lagoon rises 80–90 cm above normal sea level about 50 times a year. The homes of 10 000 people living at ground level are flooded regularly. The most serious flood was in 1966 when a rapid thaw in the Alps, heavy rain, high tides and south-easterly gales combined to cause serious long-term damage.

2 Porto Marghera on the mainland shore facing Venice is one of the biggest concentrations of industry in Italy. Atmospheric pollution, particularly sulphur dioxide, from the factories is accelerating the erosion of the city's buildings.

3 Much of the industry in Port Marghera used to obtain its water from wells. The wells were closed in the early 1970s but the resulting subsidence caused by the drying out of aquifers is still occurring. Venice has sunk by 23 cm this century. It continues to sink by one millimetre a year. This has increased the city's vulnerability of flooding. In 1908 a tide of 1.1 m above normal flooded ten per cent of Venice. In 1961 a tide of the same height flooded 36 per cent of the city. Venetians used to protect their buildings from damp by one or two courses of

impermeable stone in the foundations. Many of these foundations are now too low to protect the brick and mortar above.

4 Global warming and the resulting rise in sea levels is likely to worsen future flooding.

5 The shipping channels dug through the lagoon earlier this century to allow large ships to reach Porto Marghera have accelerated erosion in the lagoon. Erosion, together with land reclamation for industry and an airport close to Porto Marghera, have had a damaging impact on the complex natural channels in the lagoon which are only visible at low tide. These channels help to protect Venice from the full force of the tides by regulating the speed and depth of tidal water entering the lagoon.

6 Some industries dispose of their waste into the lagoon. When flooding occurs the chemicals are absorbed into the stonework of buildings accelerating their deterioration.

7 Artificial fertilisers washed off farmland around the lagoon, combined with untreated waste water from the city containing detergents, pollute the lagoon. This pollution, which is rich in phosphates causes eutrophication – the raising of nutrient levels in the lagoon causing accelerated growth of algae. The algae deprives the rest of the aquatic ecosystems of oxygen.

8 The wash from a growing number of faster boats is damaging stonework.

9 The existing sea defences have been neglected and are in a poor condition.

10 The massive numbers of tourists are accelerating the deterioration. The mayor of Venice has described the tourists as *'locusts who descend on the city for a few hours in an indiscriminate invasion, showing no real love or appreciation for the city'.*

11 An additional threat is that oil tankers regularly travel through the lagoon to Porto Marghera. An accident involving an oil spill could be disasterous both for the lagoon's ecosystem and for the city.

Social Problems

1 The population of the Venetian islands is declining as people move to the mainland settlements of Mestre and Marghera. This is partly a result of regular flooding and the feeling that the city has no long-term future, but the factors listed below also play an important part. Between 1951 and 1990 the population declined from 167 000 to 78 000. Mestre and Marghera now contain 250 000 people, despite the recent decline of traditional industries in Marghera. Local political power has shifted to Mestre.

2 The remaining population in Venice is an ageing population. The average age of resident is now higher than in any city in Europe. They are less willing or less able to pay for maintenance of buildings. The old city lacks social amenities and sports facilities for younger people and they are drawn to the mainland settlements which have more to offer.

3 Forty-five per cent of Venetian housing lacks adequate sanitation. Only people on low incomes, who have no choice, are prepared to remain in such housing.

4 With the large cities of northern Italy, Switzerland, Austria and southern Germany relatively close an increasing proportion of the houses in the city are second homes. Demand for housing by outsiders has forced rents and house prices beyond the reach of the indigenous population.

5 Mass tourism (12 million tourists a year) is making the city an unattractive place to live even though the tourists bring income and employment. Employment in tourism tends to be seasonal and low-paid. More and more housing is being converted into tourist accommodation. The city is becoming a

museum rather than a living city.

6 Cars cannot be used in the city. This means routine travel for work, shopping or entertainment is more difficult, making the city less attractive for residents.

It could be argued that the social problems listed above are a separate issue to that of conservation of the physical fabric of the city. However, one Italian city, Bologna, has already come to the conclusion that for conservation to be a success both the physical and social character of a city need to be conserved. The basis of the Bologna policy is that the city, with all its buildings and services, should be regarded as a 'public good' and not a place where property developers and speculators can make a profit at the expense of the indigenous population. Bologna has aimed to rehabilitate housing and conserve historic buildings without destroying the local community and to create an attractive environment both for residents and visitors. One author has described measures to prevent flooding while ignoring the population decline as saving Venice *'from the fate of Atlantis while condemning her to the destiny of Disneyland'.*

- Suggest reasons why the introduction of policies to halt the population decline in Venice could assist long-term conservation of the historic buildings in the city.

What is Being Done to Protect Venice?

After the flood in 1966 private organisations in a number of countries contributed £3 million for repairing buildings and works of art. In 1973 the Italian Government agreed to spend a further £200 million. This money, along with contributions from the United Nations, was to be spent on flood prevention schemes, new sources of water for the industry in Marghera, sewage treatment works and repair of buildings. Much of this money was never spent because of political deadlock in the city council over how the money should be allocated. One area of conflict within the council was over the view of some left-wing councillors that priority should be given to rehabilitating housing for low income families following Bologna's example.

Only in the 1980s was real progress made. A consortium of 21 of Italy's largest engineering and building companies was awarded the contract to build a flood protection system. Barriers will be built across the three inlets to the lagoon. Under the normal conditions these barriers will rest on the bed of the lagoon but when high tides threaten the city they will be raised to prevent tidal water entering the lagoon.

Many other smaller-scale measures are being taken including dredging of channels in an attempt to restore the lagoon's natural ability to absorb tidal variations, and the building of coastal walls round some smaller islands. The consortium has also been given the job of cleaning up the lagoon. The Italian parliament has given permission for the consortium, Veneto Regional Council and Venice City Council to borrow £1.2 billion by 1994 to pay for the work. In the main part of the city thousands of small-scale measures are planned including raising doorsteps, raising piazzas and installing syphons in drains to prevent flood water flowing up into the buildings and streets, installing damp-proof courses in buildings, dredging of canals to increase their capacity, and enforcement of speed limits on boats. The consortium already employs 800 people and continues to conduct research into the lagoon's ecosystem.

The United Nations continues to co-ordinate a programme of building and art restoration funded by organisations around the world. They are currently spending an allocation of £1.3 million. Since the late 1980s the city has considered enforcing a quota system on the number of tourists. An entry fee would be charged and entry would be refused when visitors rose above a certain number. However, the problems remain. Venice continues to be a beautiful and romantic place for visitors, but for many it is no longer an attractive place to live. There seem to be few solutions to the social problems and only the input of massive resources is likely to rescue the city from further physical decay.

FIG 6.29 *The Independent, 7 May 1992*

Venice tube scheme makes political waves

VENICE – Just as each year spring tides spill over and swamp the streets of Venice, a project periodically surfaces which makes waves in the lagoon and beyond. The latest is a proposal to build an underground railway to link the city with the mainland. Tomorrow, the city council decides whether to go ahead with the project.

There have been many proposals to sink an underground in Venice. One was envisaged in the plans to bring the Expo 2000 world exhibition to the city. "One-off solutions for one-off problems" boast the posters in the offices off the Grand Canal of Tecnomare, the engineering consultants for the original project.

The impetus for the latest version was a recent change in the law. This extended metropolitan status to Venice and its hinterland, making them eligible to apply to a government fund for urban rail systems.

The city council commissioned another firm of engineers, Zollet Engineering, to produce an updated study. It proposes a circular line, with trains on rubber wheels, which would link the islands of Giudecca, San Giorgio and San Michele to Mestre on the mainland, rather than cutting through the historic centre.

The project leader, Roberto Piccoli, a Venetian, explained the findings of his 120m lire (£55,000) study. It was not a system for tourists, he emphasised, who would still use the *vaporetti* and other water transport. "We need an underground system for three reasons. The people of Venice have a real problem of getting to and from work on the mainland. Particularly those on the Lido. It's a real voyage for them. In London or Milan, you are used to long distances for commuting. But that it is not the Venetian way. The second is to link the peripheral areas, to prevent the erosion of population. The third thing is to control access to the city, so that people can come in an ordered way."

Cynics say the real reasons for the promotion of the project by the Christian Democrat-Socialist dominated local council is the amount of money that can be made by speculators and contractors. With up to 700bn lire sloshing around, much would seep out of the system.

Leading the critics is Italia Nostra, a group that lobbies to safeguard the country's cultural and environmental heritage. In its offices off San Mark's Square, its president, Riccardo Rabagliati,

fulminated against the metro. "Venice is a city of water, an island in a lagoon. We have a marriage with the sea, not with terra firma. Venice is different from other cities. Its transport must remain by water".

The delicate structure of the buildings, constructed on top of millions of piles driven into the island, could be undermined by the metro, he said. The council should find cheaper, less risky

solutions to the provision of basic services and maintenance they had neglected for 30 years. More modern boats would create less wash, reducing erosion of the sides of the canals.

But a spokeswoman for Venice in Peril, which lobbied successfully against Expo 2000, said unless real damage were caused to buildings, she saw no reason to oppose the underground.

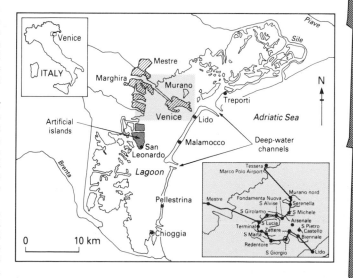

Decision Making Exercise

In 1992 a scheme to build an underground railway linking the islands with the mainland was proposed (see Fig 6.29, page 155). The proposal has already met bitter opposition from some, but not all, heritage organisations who believe the money should be spent on conservation and who argue construction work could damage the already fragile foundations of the city. The project leader, Roberto Piccoli has said:

'We need an underground system for three reasons. The people of Venice have a real problem of getting to and from work on the mainland. Particularly those on the Lido. It's a real voyage for them. In London or Milan you are used to long distances for commuting. But that is not the Venetian way. The second is to link the peripheral areas, to prevent the erosion of population. The third thing is to control access to the city, so that people can come in an ordered way.'

It is expected that such a system could cost up to £300 million to build.

There are other ways the money could be spent. Assuming adequate finance has already been allocated to new flood defences there are a number of options.

1 Additional building and art restoration.

2 Provisions of grants to home owners to improve sanitation and other household amenities.

3 Provision of new social and sports facilities for residents. This may provide a use for less important but nevertheless historic and valuable buildings.

4 Grants to industries in Marghera to improve pollution control, to farmers to limit use of fertilisers, and to improve sewage treatment around the lagoon.

- Should the underground railway system be built? Justify your answer without referring to the alternatives listed above. In other words what solutions and/or problems would arise from the project?

- Consider the options 1 to 4 above. If you have decided the railway should be built justify why the railway, not options 1 to 4, should be a priority. If you have decided the railway should not be built choose and justify another option.

Venice

1 'Europeans cities are under stress.'
To what extent do you agree with this statement?

2 Why do high-rise estates in European cities face problems?

3 Why do ghettos form in cities?

4 Why are eastern European cities facing particularly rapid change?

5 Evaluate the success of using single events such as the Olympic Games to regenerate urban economies.

6 'Traffic is the most serious threat to the quality of life in European cities'. Discuss.

7 'There is an urgent need to shift resources from private to public transport in cities.'
Do you agree? Use evidence to support your arguments.

8 'Conserving Venice is a massive waste of money.'
Discuss the extent to which you agree with this opinion.

Glossary

alienation	The process of becoming unfriendly or hostile, or feeling that you do not belong in a particular place.
commuter village	A village where many of the residents work in a nearby town or city.
collective living	Where emphasis is given to people working and living together co-operatively. Where people are encouraged to work and organise for the good of the community.
deconcentration	Dispersal or spreading out.
deprivation	Being deprived of an acceptable quality of life or standard of living.
economies of scale	Where the cost of producing each unit of output is reduced by producing larger quantities or by producing in bulk.
gentrification	The process of an area moving up-market. Where the proportion of the resident population in higher socio-economic groups rises.
ghetto	An area of severe deprivation or multiple deprivation from which people have difficulty moving. The word is usually used where the majority of the ghetto's residents are members of ethnic minorities.
indigenous	Native.
multiple deprivation	Where people are deprived in a number of different ways or where there are high levels of deprivation.
multinational company	A firm which operates in a number of countries.
periphery	The edge or boundary.
rehabilitation	To restore a building or an area to a good condition.
segregation	The separation of people according to their ethnic origin.
social housing	Housing provided and at least partially funded by the state (in other words, by central or local government). It is usually provided for people on low incomes who are unable to afford private housing.
socio–economic group	Social class, based on income, wealth, or type or status of employment. For example, Professional or Unskilled Manual are terms which can be used to describe two socio-economic groups.
transnational company	See multinational company.

The Disadvantaged Regions

KEY IDEAS

7.1 Some regions of Europe can be regarded as 'disadvantaged regions' or 'problem regions'. These are mainly regions suffering from a low level of economic development or economic decline or from severe environmental problems.

7.2 Regions in western Europe traditionally dependent on heavy industries, such as coal-mining or steel-making, are suffering from de-industrialisation. The Ruhr in Germany and Nord-Pas-de-Calais in France are typical of such regions. Various agencies are involved in trying to counteract the impact of de-industrialisation in these regions.

7.3 The former Communist countries of eastern Europe are now suffering severe de-industrialisation.

7.4 The former Communist countries of eastern Europe have inherited serious environmental problems caused by industrialisation during the decades of Communism. These in turn pose severe economic problems because of the costs of cleaning up the environment and because the lower environment quality makes it more difficult to attract investment for new industries.

7.5 Large variations exist within disadvantaged regions. For example, almost the whole of Spain is designated by the EU as a region needing regional aid, yet the type and severity of the problems vary considerably.

7.6 Peripheral regions such as the Scottish Highlands and Islands are disadvantaged.

7.7 The EU allocates considerable sums of money to aiding disadvantaged regions. This represents a significant shift of resources from wealthy regions to poor regions.

Heavy Industry in Northern Italy, Typical of those Regions Suffering from De-industrialisation

7.1 What are Disadvantaged Regions?

A disadvantaged region or problem region can be defined as an area which has difficulty competing economically or an area where the quality of life is particularly low.

Four categories of disadvantaged region can be identified.

1 The regions of western Europe suffering from industrial decline.

2 Most of eastern Europe which is facing particular difficulties because of:
a) industrial decline and the transition to market economies;
b) severe environmental problems.

3 The poorly developed regions of southern Europe.

4 Remote or peripheral rural areas where farming, the main economic activity, faces problems because of a difficult environment.

This chapter aims to give an overview of the extent of the difficulties facing some of these disadvantaged regions and of the policies being implemented to overcome these difficulties. Some of the issues stemming from these regional problems are dealt with in other chapters, particularly in the case of eastern Europe (see Chapter 2).

It is important to remember that although it is convenient to talk about disadvantaged regions it is the people living in these regions who are suffering the consequences of these disadvantages. In all the categories of region listed above the consequences for people are likely to be a lower standard of living, limited opportunities, pressure to migrate and in some cases a poor environment.

It is also important to remember that to talk about disadvantaged regions is to generalise. Within these regions there will be pockets of affluence while in affluent regions there will be pockets of poverty. To complicate the issue further it is often the case that in economically poor regions environmental quality is high, while in affluent regions the quality of the environment may be low. An individual's quality of life is affected by environmental and social factors as well as income levels.

7.2 The Old Industries Die: De-industrialisation in Western Europe

During the 1980s western industrialised societies entered a new phase in their development. Primary and manufacturing industries which had been at the heart of western economies were declining. There was a growing dependence on tertiary and quaternary activity (that is, services and knowledge-based industries). These changes have had enormous social and economic impacts. The term **post-industrial society** is often used to describe this phase of economic development.

The term post-industrial is not really very accurate because manufacturing industry is still important. In Germany, for example, about 50 per cent of the value of all goods and services produced in the country is from manufactured goods. Nevertheless, the traditional heavy industries, such as shipbuilding, coal-mining, steel-making and heavy engineering, have declined rapidly. New industries based on new technologies, such as computers, telecommunications and biotechnology, have flourished but they have not provided enough jobs to replace the dying industries.

A more useful term is de-industrialisation. Those regions or countries heavily dependent on traditional industries have experienced de-industrialisation or loss of industry. However, this term is also ambiguous because it can be defined in different ways:

- the relative decline of manufacturing output. For example, in West Germany between 1960 and 1986 the proportion of Gross Domestic Produce (GDP) created by manufacturing industry fell from 40 per cent to 33 per cent. However, this could be misleading. A percentage decline may reflect growth in other parts of the economy rather than an actual decline in manufacturing;

- the absolute decline of manufacturing output. This is more serious because it means a real decline rather than a decline relative to other parts of the economy;
- decline of manufacturing employment. For example, in Britain between 1960 and 1986 there was a loss of two million manufacturing jobs;
- declining exports and increased dependence on imports of manufactured goods. For example, since 1983 Britain has imported more manufactured goods than it exports.

Whichever definition is used, de-industrialisation is bound to have important social, environmental and economic effects especially where the decline is concentrated in particular regions within countries. Teesside in England, Clydeside in Scotland, the Basque Country of northern Spain and Nord-Pas-de-Calais in France are examples of such areas in western Europe.

Reasons why traditional heavy industries have declined include:

- reduced demand for their products as new materials and technologies are developed;
- reduced demand for their products resulting from increased competition from other countries, particularly from Japan and the rapidly industrialising less developed countries;

– automation and mechanisation have increased productivity and so for each unit of output far less workers are needed.

Until the 1990s de-industrialisation in Europe mainly affected western Europe where industry was exposed to market forces and international competition. In Communist eastern Europe traditional heavy industries were protected by the state. However, with the collapse of Communism much of eastern Europe is now experiencing de-industrialisation at an unprecedented rate as its out-dated and inefficient industries are forced to compete with the rest of the world. This issue is examined in Section 7.3

De-industrialisation in the Ruhr, Germany

Germany has the strongest economy in Europe but it has experienced a steady decline in manufacturing employment. The expansion of employment in the tertiary and quaternary sectors has not been sufficient to absorb the surplus workers. Between 1960 and 1986, 4.3 million jobs were lost in manufacturing and agriculture in the former West Germany while only four million jobs were gained in the tertiary and quaternary sectors. This de-industrialisation has been concentrated in north-western Germany. Tertiary and quaternary growth has been concentrated in the south of the country in and around cities such as Munich, Stuttgart and Frankfurt. This is due at least partly to the region's attractive image and the larger numbers of research institutions in the region.

- Study Figs 7.1a and b. Explain what graphs a and b indicate about employment change in the urban areas of western Germany.

The Ruhr region has suffered particularly badly from de-industrialisation (see Fig 7.1b). The region lies between the Lippe and Ruhr rivers in the state of North-Rhine Westphalia and contains some of western Germany's most important cities such as Duisburg, Essen, Dortmund and Bochum. These cities have a total population of 3.2 million and in fact merge with other smaller settlements to form one single urban area or conurbation housing about six million people. Other cities to the south of the Ruhr, including Cologne, Dusseldorf and Bonn, are also closely linked to the Ruhr forming a Rhine/Ruhr conurbation of about ten million people. For a century the Ruhr, based on rich local deposits of coal and iron ore, was the heavy industrial centre of Germany and the powerhouse of the German economy.

The economic 'take-off' of the area occurred in the 1870s. The discovery that the area's coking coal was ideal for iron-making, along with the political stability brought about by the unification of Germany, created the conditions which allowed the growth of the coal-mining and steel industries. Coal production reached a peak in the 1930s to 1950s and steel production reached a peak in the 1970s.

Since the 1950s the Ruhr has seen a steady decline of its industrial base. Between 1960 and 1987 the number of coal miners fell from 375 000 to 118 000 as the industry faced

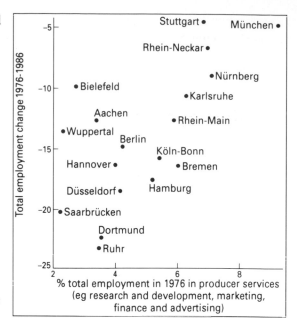

FIG 7.1a *Employment Change and the Importance of Service Industries, Western Germany 1976–86*

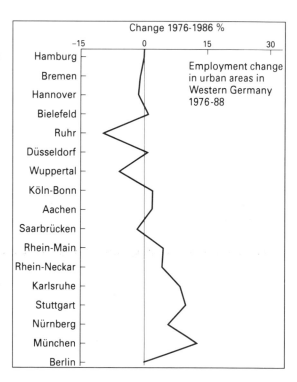

FIG 7.1b *Employment Change in the Urban Areas of Western Germany*

competition from cheaper oil, imported coal and new steel-making processes that needed less coal. Further coal-mining jobs are under threat in 1995 when the current contract to supply coal to electricity generating companies expires.

Steel-making began to decline in response to greater competition from other European countries, Japan and less developed countries. The development of new materials also reduced the demand for steel. As the steel and coal industries declined, other closely-linked engineering industries also suffered. Between 1975 and 1987 112000 manufacturing jobs were lost in the Ruhr.

These job losses encouraged people to leave the Ruhr. Between 1961 and 1988 over 550000 moved out of the Ruhr causing a nine per cent decline in the population. By the late 1980s unemployment was almost twice the average for West Germany.

- Study Fig 7.2. What does the data tell you about the economic situation in the Ruhr compared with **a)** the rest of western Germany and **b)** the rest of the EU?

Fig **7.2**   *Unemployment and GDP per Capita, The Ruhr*

| | Unemployment rate, average 1986–88 | | GDP/inhabitant 1986 | |
	Germany (6.5% = 100)	EU (10.5% = 100)	Germany (= 100)	EU (= 100)
Duisburg	180.0	110.4	105.4	121.4
Essen	170.9	104.8	125.7	144.8
Oberhausen	225.8	138.5	87.8	101.1
Bottrop	158.8	97.4	66.4	76.5
Gelsenkirchen	178.9	109.7	136.6	157.2
Dortmund	197.0	124.3	101.4	116.8
Bochum	165.5	101.5	114.8	132.2

Unlike some areas in western Europe the mining and steel industries have survived, even if they are now much smaller. Large steel companies such as Krupp and Hoesch still have their headquarters in the Ruhr. However, the closure of steel plants and coal mines has left behind large areas of derelict and polluted land. The Ruhr has a poor image and has failed to attract enough new economic activity.

In an attempt to counteract the impact of de-industrialisation, various initiatives have been launched aimed at attracting new economic development and at improving the quality of the environment. Many of these initiatives have received funding from the EU because the Ruhr is designated an Objective Two region (see Section 7.7). Between 1989 and 1991 alone the area received the following aid:

| Aid from the EU: | £130 million |
| Aid from the German Government: | £900 000 |
Aid from the North Rhine-Westphalia regional Government:	£140 million
Total	£270.9 million

The Ruhr, Germany

Such funding is aimed at supporting new industries, developing new products for the area's companies, retraining the workforce, reclaiming derelict land to provide new industrial sites and to enhance the area's environment, improving the area's infrastructure and pollution control.

Examples of the initiatives which have been taken include the following.

The Emscher Valley Park

This is a project launched by the government of North Rhine-Westphalia in 1988. The park runs along the polluted River Emscher for 70 km and is on average 10 km wide. The aim of the park is ecological, economic and social regeneration. It is not a park in the true sense of the word although restoration of the damaged and polluted environment of the area is a priority.

The Emscher Park Planning Company has been set up by the state government with about £15 million to spend on helping to launch projects in co-operation with local businesses, councils and other groups with an interest in the area. The planning company does not itself implement projects but instead allocates grants to organisations who bid for funds. A co-ordinating board runs the company, with representatives from the state government, local councils, trade unions, employers, environmental associations and other community groups.

Among the projects currently being implemented are:

- a ribbon 'landscape park' running from Duisburg to Dortmund with footpaths, cycle tracks, nature reserves, and facilities for outdoor activities;
- reclamation and landscaping of spoil heaps left from coal-mining;
- landscaping of potential sites for new businesses;
- a planned National Garden Festival for 1997;
- the creation of a Science Park near Essen aimed particularly at attracting businesses concerned with research and development in pollution control, energy conservation and reclamation. It includes private firms and research departments of Essen University;
- conservation of old buildings including preservation of the Zollverein XII mine in Essen, once the largest mine in the Ruhr;
- conversion of old buildings into community centres or arts centres. The Unser Fritz mine in Herne has been converted to a centre used by artists and musicians;
- refurbishment of old housing estates originally built by the mining companies and the planning of new housing estates using innovative designs aimed, for example, at minimising energy use.

In some respects the Emscher Park initiative is similar to the Urban Development Corporations set up in Britain to regenerate run-down inner cities but there are differences:

- in the Emscher Valley there is a greater recognition of the need for state or local council planning rather than reliance on market forces to make the key development decisions;

– rather than the co-ordinating board being appointed by central government, and being given the power to override local councils, the Emscher Valley Project aims to represent the local community, to develop a local consensus and to work in co-operation with local councils.

The Ruhr Initiative Group

This is a group set up by the former chairman of the Deutsche Bank comprising 62 local firms, including some of the largest firms in the Ruhr. The firms contribute about £120 000 a year to sponsor cultural and sporting events in the area with the aim of promoting a better image for the Ruhr.

Technology Transfer Offices

A number of these have been set up by various organisations operating in the Ruhr. They are designed to spread new ideas and technological innovations and to advise firms on how to launch new products making use of new technology. The six Chambers of Commerce in the Ruhr have set up an office in Bochum, all the universities and polytechnics in the Ruhr have one, and even the trade unions in the area have their own. The state of North Rhine-Westphalia has also founded a centre called ZENIT to co-ordinate technology transfer in the state and to advise local firms.

These and other initiatives are succeeding in creating a new image for the Ruhr and local people speak about an *Aufbruchstimmung* (a feeling of change) in the region. Nevertheless, the Ruhr still faces an uncertain future. According to one German expert on the Ruhr, *'the rebirth of the Ruhr is part fact, part myth. Measured against the hard facts of economic indicators there has been no genuine renaissance. But the notion of rebirth has become implanted in the popular consciousness and that has given the region a new dynamism.'*

There are three reasons why he says there is no 'genuine renaissance'.

1 Manufacturing industry remains the backbone of the Ruhr's economy and the onset of recession in Germany is threatening many of the local firms.

2 Up to another 30 000 jobs in steel and coal are at risk as government subsidies are cut. This in turn threatens another 50 000 jobs in linked industries.

3   The Ruhr has become a lower priority for public spending as the German Government tries to tackle the enormous problems in eastern Germany. By the standard of parts of eastern Germany the economy of the Ruhr is reasonably healthy.

- Make a list of the agencies involved in attempts to counteract the impacts of de-industrialisation in the Ruhr.

- What evidence is there that:
  a) different public and private agencies are working in co-operation to achieve their aims?
  b) the agencies are not just concerned with counteracting the economic impacts of de-industrialisation?

De-industrialisation in France

The 1980s saw increased rates of de-industrialisation in a number of French regions. The north-east, including the Paris region, experienced higher than average industrial decline. In the south and west de-industrialisation occurred more slowly than the national average, while the other regions of France experienced an average rate of decline (see Fig 7.3). Although the Paris region suffered from the loss of industry the 1980s saw Paris strengthen its dominant position in the economy generally.

In 1981 a Socialist government more willing to intervene in the free market was elected and this led to the implementation of stronger policies designed to help regions experiencing economic difficulties. In 1982, 22 regional councils were created whose prime responsibility is economic development. A system of regional development contracts signed and financed by central and regional governments is now in operation. Between 1989 and 1993 these contracts committed the national government and the regional governments to spending £6 billion and £5 billion respectively on regional economic development. Much of this money will be spent on infrastructure improvements in the regions. The largest per capita amounts have been allocated to Nord-Pas-de-Calais, Lorraine, Franche-Comté, Limousin and Languedoc-Rousillon.

The selection of some of these priority regions in the 1983–93 contracts reflects the de-industrialisation which has hit French industry during the 1980s and 1990s (while others, such as Limousin, are rural areas suffering from remoteness and poor economic development). Between 1979 and 1986 900 000 jobs were lost from French industry and these losses continue. The traditional industries such as iron and steel, textiles, coal-mining, shipbuilding, car-making and even oil-refining have all been badly hit. For example, Renault, the car company, reduced its workforce from 330 000 to 200 000 between 1979 and 1989. The areas particularly badly hit by de-industrialisation are those areas designated as 'conversion poles' by the French Government in the 1980s – that is, areas which needed to be converted to new types of industry to replace those closing down. Fig 7.4 shows the concentration of these conversion poles in the northern regions of Nord-

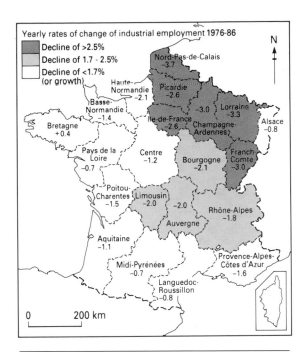

FIG 7.3   *De-industrialisation Rates by Region, France*

Pas-de-Calais and Lorraine and around the Massif Central.

The French Government's concern with de-industrialisation was emphasised when it created three enterprise zones at Dunkerque, and La Ciotat and La Seyne near Marseilles (see Fig 7.4). The zones were to operate from 1987 to 1992 and their purpose was to attract new firms to areas badly affected by the closure of shipyards. The three shipyards had been owned by NORMED, a firm employing 6800 people and heavily subsidised by the

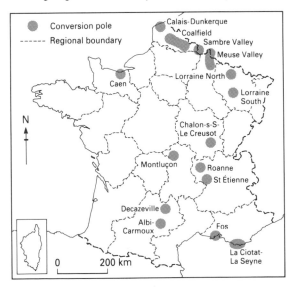

FIG 7.4   *Conversion Poles in France 1984*

government. Between 1983 and 1986 alone state subsidies to the shipbuilding industry totalled £1.5 billion. But by the second half of the 1980s there was growing pressure on the government to withdraw the subsidies. The need to cut government spending, reduced demand for new ships worldwide and competition from other shipbuilding countries particularly in the Far East had permanently cut the demand for French ships. It was becoming increasingly difficult to justify the subsidies.

The problem of the closures was compounded by the fact that all three shipyards were located in areas of high unemployment. Dunkerque is located in the region of Nord-Pas-de-Calais which has faced particularly severe de-industrialisation since the late 1970s. The last coal mine closed in 1991 and the local steel and textile industries have suffered serious decline. When NORMED announced the closure of its shipyard local unemployment already stood at over 15 per cent. In the cases of La Ciotat and La Seyne shipbuilding dominated the local economy and unemployment was already high. Both towns lie in a region experiencing rapid population growth and so there is an increasing demand for jobs.

The announcement of the closures led to violent protests by the shipyard workers – a response common to a number of industry closures in France, Belgium and Spain. The government responded by financing redundancy payments and creating the enterprise zones.

The purpose of the enterprise zones, which covered up to three square kilometres, was to attract new firms. Within the zones firms would benefit from the following:

– streamlined administrative procedures to speed up the establishing of new businesses;
– exemption from tax on company profits for ten years;
– exemption from local business taxes for three years.

Unlike British enterprise zones only manufacturing industries were eligible for help. Also, the firms locating in the zones could not be branch factories – the entire firm, including the head office, had to be in the zone.

By 1992, 145 firms had set up in the enterprise zones providing more than 4000 jobs, but this was expected to grow to more than 170 firms and 6600 jobs. This was roughly equivalent to the number of jobs lost in the shipyards. One of the largest investors is Coca-Cola with new plants both at Dunkerque and La Seyne. The decision to set up a canning factory at Dunkerque has also attracted American National Can to the zone, a company which makes metal cans.

There are probably reasons other than tax advantages for these companies choosing to locate in the enterprise zones. Dunkerque has good access to the north-west European motorway network and is close to the Channel Tunnel. In the case of the two southern zones the Mediterranean environment has a positive image which attracts firms and workers. Also, all three zones are located within conversion poles and so larger firms are eligible for regional development grants.

Masked Steelworkers in Bilbao, Spain. Protesting Against Closures and Layoffs at Tubacez Plant, The Guardian, 23 April 1993

Some concern has been expressed that the zones did not encourage the creation of new jobs but instead just encouraged existing firms to relocate. There is some evidence that this has occurred in the case of La Ciotat because it is close to Marseilles and has attracted some firms from the city. Since Marseilles is itself experiencing de-industrialisation the benefits of this are very questionable. Another problem with all three zones is that only 20 per cent of the new jobs have been taken by ex-shipyard workers. This may be because they do not have appropriate skills or it may be because they have obtained other jobs or taken early retirement.

Despite these reservations the enterprise zones do seem to have been a success and the French Government is proposing similar schemes in a number of other de-industrialising areas. However, the new schemes need EU approval and so far that approval has not been given.

FIG 7.5   *Change in Unemployment, Dunkerque*

Change in unemployment in Dunkerque and its surrounding region

	Unemployment rate	
	January 1987	January 1992
Dunkerque	15.1%	13.2%
Dunkerque hinterland (Département du Nord)	13.8%	13.2%

FIG 7.6   *Development of Enterprise Zones, France*

1987–1992

	Jobs lost following closure of shipyards in 1987	New firms in activity 1992	New jobs created 1992	Total jobs created and projected
Dunkerque	1567	33	1515	2680
La Ciotat	3036	78	1500	2265
La Seyne	2272	34	1035	1630

- Study Figs 7.5 and 7.6. To what extent does the data support the view that the enterprise zones have been a success?

- Find a source of information on British enterprise zones. What are the similarities and differences between the French zones and the British zones? Why do you think the Conservative British Government prefers the idea of enterprise zones to giving regional development grants?

- Why do you think the EU may be withholding approval of new enterprise zones?

7.3 The De-industrialisation of Eastern Europe: the Case of Eastern Germany

Even with annual transfers of up to 200 billion Marks from west to east, it is glaringly obvious that the economic process of unification has been a catastrophe. A recent study carried out by two leading economic institutes in Berlin and Kiel suggests that the de-industrialisation under way since monetary union in 1990, will continue with firms becoming less competitive because of poor products and excessive costs and pay levels. Lutz Hoffman, head of the DIW institute, has compared East Germany with Tunisia, Honduras and Sri Lanka as regards the role played by manufacturing in its economy.

David Gow, Germany Year Zero, The Guardian, April 1993.

Between the political division of Germany in 1949 and unification in 1990 two very different societies and economies developed in the two Germanies – a market economy in the west based on individual choice and a centrally planned Communist economy in the east (see Section 2.2). When the Iron Curtain was opened in 1989 and unification became a real possibility few Germans seemed to appreciate the enormous problems they faced in integrating the two parts of their country. Even in 1990 when unification officially took place the German Government did not seem to realise the size of the problem.

The scale of the differences between eastern Germany and western Germany in terms of living standards, industrial efficiency, infrastructure provision and environmental quality has meant that integration of the two parts is proving to be extremely difficult and expensive. Also, the suddenness of unification – the process took ten months from the opening of the Wall – meant that there was little time for planning and preparation.

Thanks to the post-war 'economic miracle' West Germany had become the third wealthiest economy in the world by the 1980s. Even East Germany had grown to become the tenth wealthiest economy and by the standards of eastern Europe was very prosperous. Nevertheless it lagged a long way behind the west. By 1990, output per person in East Germany was 40 per cent lower than in the west while productivity per full-time worker was 73 per cent less. For example, the East German car maker, IFA, employed 65 000 people to produce 200 000 Trabants a year. Toyota, with the same number of workers, produces four million cars a year – a productivity rate 20 times higher.

As soon as unification exposed the eastern economy to competition from the west it began to collapse. Overmanning, out-dated machinery, obsolete and unwanted products and no real marketing experience meant that it was impossible for eastern industries to compete. Within the first year of the united Germany the eastern German GDP fell by about 30 per cent with a loss of over three million jobs. By the end of 1992 more than half of eastern German's industry had closed. By 1993 eastern Germany had an unemployment rate of nearly 35 per cent. In many of the cities joblessness is now higher than it was in the early 1930s during the economic crisis which helped bring Hitler to power. Some are surprised that the level of social unrest and right-wing extremism has not been greater (see Section 4.8).

To make matters worse, as far as integration was concerned, the western economy grew during the same year by four per cent and the number of jobs increased by one million. The western economy benefited from unification in the short term simply because it opened up new markets. Most East Germans were not short of disposable income and spent a lot on western consumer goods such as cars, video machines and home computers which had not previously been available. Western firms expanded and took on more workers to meet this surge in demand.

Figs 7.7a and b show the resulting unemployment pattern by the end of 1991 and Fig 7.7c shows the impact the economic contrast between East and West Germany had on migration. Some of the highest unemployment rates are in Saxony. Saxony had been particularly dependent on traditional heavy industries which had been given priority by the central planners but whose products were no longer wanted in a market economy. Thuringia has been less badly hit because it has a greater mix of industries, is close to the prosperous western states of Bavaria and Baden-Wurtemburg, and its attractive landscape is popular with tourists.

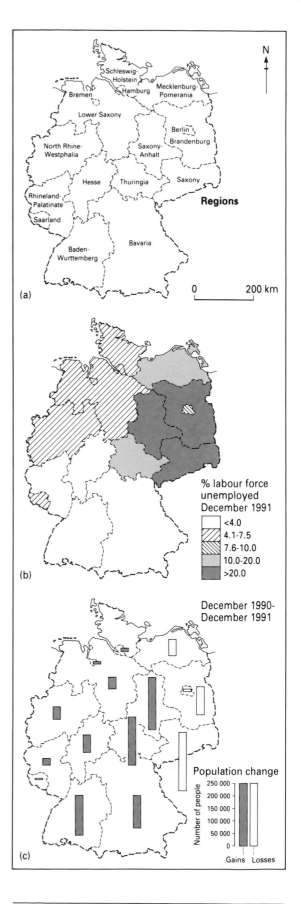

Fig 7.7 *Unemployment and Population Change in Germany 1991, Geography, December 1992*

In response to the frightening rate of de-industrialisation the five eastern *Länder* (states) and Berlin, have been designated as assisted areas by the German Government. They are eligible for £2.5 billion of grants to aid capital investment. In addition £4.5 billion of EU structural funding is available (see Section 7.7). As massive as these sums are they are far from adequate for bringing eastern Germany's economy up to the standard of the west. By the end of the decade it has been estimated that £500 billion of tax revenue paid by western Germans will need to be transferred to the east. According to one estimate £60 billion alone is needed to modernise the eastern transport system and to refurbish its run-down housing.

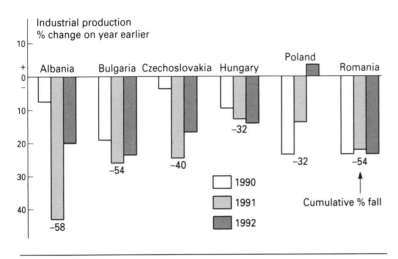

FIG 7.8 *De-industrialisation, Eastern Europe, The Economist, 13 March 1992*

There are some optimistic trends. Considerable improvements in the infrastructure are taking place and western firms are investing in the east. For example, Volkswagen and Opel-General Motors are building factories in Saxony and Thuringia and BASF are modernising a chemicals factory in Brandenburg. However, much of the new investment in the east is being spent on capital-intensive industry which will not create many new jobs.

East Germans feel badly let down and very disillusioned with the unification process. Most feel that rather than their economy being integrated with the west it has been destroyed for the benefit of the west. Chancellor Kohl's 1990 promise of 'flourishing regions' in the east within four years is now seen as hopelessly optimistic or as deliberate deception. Most politicians and experts now believe that it will take 20 years before the eastern part of the country completes the transition to a successful market economy and even then only in the larger cities will living standards match those in the west.

- The de-industrialisation of eastern Europe is not confined to Germany. Using the data in Fig 7.8 attempt to rank order the six countries in terms of the extent of de-industrialisation.

7.4 The Price of Communist Industrialisation: Pollution in Eastern Europe

Eastern Europe, it seems to me, was devastated by what I often heard described as the 'industrial megalomania' of the 1950s, when Communist governments were still trying to force into practice the hundred-year-old theory based on Karl Marx's 'Communist Manifesto'. The Industrial revolution in the west by this time was also more than a hundred years old, and hard lessons were being learned about pollution, waste, limited resources, and other matters Karl Marx never considered. The Eastern-bloc rulers, however, were blind to these problems.

Jon Thompson, East Europe's Dark Dawn,
National Geographic, June 1991.

A region suffering from economic decline or inadequate economic development can be seen as being disadvantaged and needing special assistance. The massive environmental problems now facing large parts of eastern Europe represent another sort of regional disadvantage. The scale of the ecological damage left by the Communist rush for industrialisation is such that the quality of life has been severely reduced in many areas. Economic development alone will not reduce the inequality in living conditions between western Europe and eastern Europe.

A programme to tackle environmental degradation in eastern Europe is urgently needed.

The environmental damage caused by Communist industrialisation helped to bring about the collapse of Communism in eastern Europe. During the 1970s and 1980s opposition to environmental damage was the only type of protest that most eastern European governments tolerated. Consequently, environmental or green organisations became the focus for anti-government activities and their campaigns helped to discredit and undermine Communism. However, the environmental problems remain. In fact, de-industrialisation in eastern Europe is reducing pollution levels in some areas, but on the other hand growing unemployment and economic disruption means that environmental problems may no longer be seen as a priority. There was evidence of the clash between maintaining jobs and protecting the environment as early as 1991 when the new Romanian Government temporarily closed a metals factory at Copsa Mica because of the threat that pollution from the plant was posing to the health of the local people (see below). The plant was reopened in response to the demands of the workers who feared unemployment.

The following examples illustrate the severity and the extent of the problem facing eastern Europe, although it is not usually easy to prove a link between pollution and health problems because inadequate diet, poor housing, bad working conditions and other factors all play a part.

1 In North Bohemia in the Czech Republic poorly controlled open-cast coal-mining has badly damaged the landscape. The brown coal excavated from the mines is burnt in six surrounding power stations. When the sulphur dioxide emitted by the power stations reaches danger levels sirens are used to warn people to stay inside and children at school have to wear masks. There are abnormally high levels of birth defects, miscarriages and multiple sclerosis. Coniferous forests in the area are badly damaged or dead.

2 At Copsa Mica in Hungary two factories have created appalling levels of pollution – one is a metals factory while the other makes car tyres. The whole landscape has been blackened in a 30 km radius. Vegetation, farm animals and buildings are permanently covered in black soot. 30 000 tonnes of pollutants a year from the two plants pour into the atmosphere, including lead, cadmium and sulphur dioxide. In 1990 local children were found to have double the permitted

Pollution in Hungary, near Eztergon

level of lead in their blood. Lead is a neurotoxin which damages the development of the central nervous system. The same children were found to have 'markedly worse than usual' results in IQ tests. One in three children suffer from asthma. Miscarriages and birth defects are common. Local milk and farm produce has been declared unfit for human consumption. One report put life expectancy in Copsa Mica at 43 years.

3 In the city of Baia Mare in Hungary 460 tonnes of lead a year are emitted by an ore-processing plant. Life expectancy in the area is 58 years.

4 In Slovakia a coal-fired power station relied on coal with a high arsenic content. Arsenic was being deposited on the surrounding countryside. Local children were found to have high levels of arsenic in their hair, blood and urine. Cancer is more common than normal and a higher than average number of children suffer from partial deafness.

5 The water supply to hundreds of Hungarian villages is contaminated with nitrates from fertilisers. Safe drinking water in plastic bags is supplied for young children to avoid 'blue baby syndrome' caused by a reduced ability of the blood to carry oxygen.

6 Almost one sixth of the land area of Russia is unfit for human habitation because of toxic or nuclear waste contamination. Up to 2.7 million people in Russia and the Ukraine are still living in areas affected by the 1986 Chernobyl nuclear accident – 400 000 of these are living in areas which have either been declared unfit for human habitation or areas where people have been advised to move away. 1.3 million people have been registered as suffering from diseases related to radiation exposure. All the main Russian rivers including the Volga and the Don are estimated to have between ten and

100 times the permitted viral and bacterial levels. Even by Russia's relatively lax standards 20 per cent of the drinking water does not meet the required standards on chemical content. Eighty-four towns and cities, including Moscow, have levels of air pollution which at times exceed permissible levels by at least ten times. Serious environmental problems exist even in the Russian Arctic and these have had a major impact on the Sami – the traditionally nomadic people of northern Scandinavia.

The problems are on such a large scale that eastern European governments cannot hope to tackle them on their own. Financial and technical assistance from western Europe is essential and although assistance is already being provided it is small compared with the size of the task. Some people have argued that the scale of the problem in eastern Europe has been exaggerated. There is relatively little hard data available and it may be in the interests of western politicians and opponents of Communism in eastern Europe to exaggerate the problem in order to emphasise the failure of Communism and the success of free market economies. Also, it should not be forgotten that there are many urgent environmental problems in western Europe as well. Nevertheless, there is no doubt that by western European standards an enormous and urgent problem is evident in eastern Europe.

7.5 Growth and Decline in Spain

Most of Spain is designated as an area in need of regional assistance by the EU. **Per capital GDP** is 45 per cent lower than the EU average and the unemployment rate about twice as high. (See Fig 7.9, page 172). However, within Spain there are considerable regional economic variations. To illustrate the variations three regions can be examined in more detail.

1 The northern coastal area called the Cantabrian Cornice comprising the regions of the Basque Country, Cantabria and Asturias – an area suffering from de-industrialisation.

2 The Mediterranean coast comprising the regions of Catalonia, Valencia and Murcia – an area experiencing economic growth.

3 Andalusia in southern Spain – a region which has lagged behind for centuries in terms of economic growth.

De-industrialisation in the North

This northern area is economically dominated by the Basque Country where the main economic activities are mining, iron and steel, heavy engineering and chemicals – all traditional industries which have declined. In 1960 four of the provinces in the area (each

171

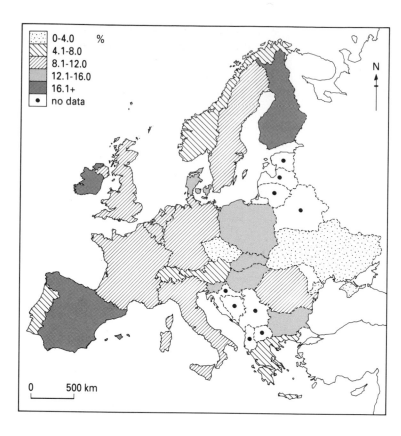

FIG 7.9   *Unemployment November 1993*

FIG **7.10**   *Regions of Spain*

As a result of the problems facing the region, Asturias in the west has been designated an Objective One region by the EU while the Basque Country and parts of Cantabria are Objective Two regions (see Section 7.7).

Growth along the Mediterranean Coast

This area produces a third of Spanish GDP, a proportion which is growing, and contributes over 40 per cent of Spain's exports. The healthy state of the region's economy is based on relatively efficient agriculture, a buoyant industrial sector and tourism.

The reasons for the region's relative prosperity are complex but include:

– proximity to other prosperous regions in southern France and northern Italy, and good transport links to north-west Europe;
– diversified industry, rather than reliance on a few key industries;
– an attractive Mediterranean climate;
– relatively good infrastructure and communications within the region;
– a tradition of entrepreneurial activity;
– success in attracting foreign investment. In the late 1980s up to a third of all foreign investment was concentrated in this region;
– the attractive image of the region, including the city of Barcelona;
– a well-qualified workforce compared to elsewhere in Spain;

Spanish region is divided into provinces) were in the top six in terms of per capita income. Now all except one are below the tenth position and two are below twentieth. Between 1975 and 1986 over a quarter of a million jobs were lost. The tertiary sector has barely grown to absorb any of the losses. The industries in the area have suffered similar problems to other industrialising areas. Changes in demand caused by the development of new materials and products, failure to compete successfully in the international market and a decline in new investment are the main problems. The area seems to be particularly unattractive to foreign investors and transnational companies. There are four probable reasons for this.

1   The distance of the area from the large and wealthy markets in north-west Europe.

2   Poor transport links along the northern Spanish coast and to the rest of Spain.

3   The poor image the area has as a result of separatism and violence by ETA, the militant nationalist group (see Section 3.3).

4   The area is probably one of the least known regions of Spain by people in the rest of Europe.

– a sense of pride in the Catalan culture and the individuality of the region.

However, the area does have problems and Barcelona in particular has suffered from de-industrialisation. Murcia and Valencia are designated Objective One regions while part of Catalonia is designated an Objective Two region. Despite these problems the area has considerable existing potential for economic growth. Farming and industry are being reorganised to take advantage of new markets. This area of Spain forms part of a larger Mediterranean region of growth whose importance within Europe will steadily increase over the next decade or so (see Section 6.1).

Andalusia: a European California?

What is certainly noticeable to an outsider is that sleepy, friendly, pleasure-seeking Seville has been dynamited out of its torpor by Expo '92 and the changes taking place round it. From being the most trying city in Spain, it has become one of the easiest in which to fix appointments and secure information.

California Dreaming, John Hooper, The Guardian, 7 February 1992.

The Spanish region of Andalusia, with 6.6 million people, has the third highest regional unemployment rate and the nineteenth lowest per capita GDP out of 171 European Union regions. Its unemployment rate is nearly three times the EU average and its per capita GDP is 40 per cent of the EU average. It has a long history of mismanagement by rural landlords and a dependence on a farming system suffering from inadequate investment. Despite this the former head of the Andalusian regional Government has boldly made the unlikely claim that it could become the 'California of Europe'.

Agriculture and tourism account for most of the region's income and the small amount of existing industry is concentrated in the west in the cities of Seville, Cadiz and Huelva. So why did the region not industrialise during the nineteenth century when much of northern and western Europe underwent an industrial revolution? Andalusia possessed many of the characteristics needed for industrialisation as long ago as the late sixteenth century. The region had plenty of capital for investment in the form of gold and silver which was imported into Spain via Seville. It had local natural resources including coal, iron, copper and lead. However, what it did lack, like much of southern Europe, were entrepreneurs needed to launch industrialisation. Andalusian society was divided between poor landless agricultural workers, who had no capital or resources, and the church and aristocracy whose wealth derived from the land and who were not interested in undermining the status quo by encouraging industrialisation. Andalusia entered a long period of relative economic stagnation.

An EU report in 1989 identified a number of weak points in the region including:

– inadequate road, rail and telecommunications links both within the region and with other regions;

– over-reliance on two economic activities – farming and tourism. Farming suffers from producing crops which are in surplus in the EU and from poor marketing. In the case of tourism there is an over-concentration on the Mediterranean coast – the potential of the Atlantic coast and inland areas has not been exploited;
– inadequate water supply infrastructure causing water shortages.
– an inadequately trained workforce (more than 30 per cent of the workforce have no educational qualifications) and a lack of support services for industry such as financial services, advice for new businesses and advice on new technology;
– environmental deterioration caused by poorly planned tourist, industrial and housing developments. Poor farming methods have also caused soil erosion and desertification.

In the past few years the region's fortunes have improved. The development of tourism on the Costa del Sol, which has been continuing for a few decades, has more recently shown signs of providing long-term benefits for the Andalusian economy. But much more importantly, Spain's entry into the EU in 1986 gave the region access to massive regional development grants. Then in 1992 Seville became the location for 'Expo '92' – an international exhibition of 'cultural and technological achievement'. The Spanish Government and the Andalusian regional Government invested very large sums of money in Expo '92 seeing it partly as an opportunity to market the possibilities of the region to the rest of the world, but also as the opportunity to kickstart the region and to turn a largely pre-industrial economy into a post-industrial economy suitable for the twenty-first century.

The city of Seville has been transformed. A new railway station, eight new bridges across the Guadalquivir river, an enlarged airport and a new 70 km by-pass were among the infrastructure improvements in the city. Seville has been linked to Madrid (400 km away) by a new dual carriageway and new motorways run from Seville to Cadiz and Huelva. Another new road links Seville to Granada. A high-speed rail link runs from Seville to Madrid and a network of fibre-optic cables has improved telecommunications within the region.

There have been criticisms of the way in which this enormous injection of funds has been spent. It can be argued that uneven development and inequality within Andalusia has been strengthened by concentrating so much investment in Seville. There are villages in the east of the region which are still without running water, electricity or road access. The benefits of the new Madrid–Seville high-speed rail link are limited by the fact that Madrid is not in turn linked to the European high-speed rail network (see Section 10.2).

With the help of these improvements to the infrastructure the regional government hopes to regenerate the economy. The region is already benefiting from industrial investment – the Spanish aircraft manufacturer CASA, has factories in Seville and Cadiz, Suzuki has a car factory near Jaen, and components for Renault and General Motors are made near Seville and Cadiz. It is hoped that these will encourage further investment and indigenous economic activity, particularly in the field of high-technology industry.

This is where it is possible, even if incorrectly, to draw parallels with California. The region already possesses a number of attractions for high-tech industry including an attractive climate, generous EU regional development grants and a relatively cheap and flexible workforce. However, the region lacks the high-tech infrastructure of research and development and highly-skilled workers found in regions like California. In an attempt to begin to tackle these shortcomings a technology park has been created in Malaga and parts of the Expo site are being offered for use in high-tech research and development.

Andalusia is designated an Objective One region for EU regional policy (see Section 7.7) and is eligible for large EU grants. Between 1989 and 1993 the region received the following assistance from the EU.

Region	Per Capita GDP EU=100	Unemployment Rate EU=100
Asturias	78	200
Cantabria	72	205
Basque Country	89	223
Murcia	66	181
Valencia	75	174
Catalonia	84	172
Andalusia	58	300

a) Would you agree that there is little evidence in the table to support the points made earlier in this section, that the northern coast is an area of decline, that Andalusia is a poorly developed area and that the Mediterranean coast is a growth area?

b) If you agree, why do you think the data does not back up the points more convincingly?

Loch Na Keal on the Island of Mull, Scotland

Communications improvements	£230 million
Support for industry	£75 million
Support for tourism	£30 million
Farming and rural development	£230 million
Development of other infrastructure	£120 million
Training and education	£80 million
Other assistance	£50 million
TOTAL	£815 million

It remains to be seen whether EU grants and Expo '92 will have been enough to create self-sustained economic development in the region.

- Using the information in this section, and any other suitable sources of information you can find, list the attractions of Andalusia you would expect to see in promotional literature designed to attract investment from other European countries into the region.

- Study the following table:

7.6 On the Periphery: the Highlands and Islands of Scotland

Without an adequate infrastructure to provide the essentials for modern living and without the opportunity to earn a reasonable living for themselves and their children, the population of large tracts of the Highlands and Islands of Scotland will be forced to leave their homeland and seek a life elsewhere.

From The Highlands and Islands of Scotland: The Case for Objective One Status, Highland Regional Council.

The Scottish Highlands and Islands form one of the most **peripheral regions** in the EU. It is remote from markets within the UK as well as elsewhere in Europe. However, the problems the region faces are not only due to its location on the edge of Europe. It also faces some of the most difficult environmental conditions in Europe. A wet, cold and windy climate combined with mountainous terrain present difficuties for most forms of economic activity and transport. The population is sparse and this in turn creates further difficulties for economic activity. There are over 50 inhabited islands making transport slower and more expensive.

On the other hand, the region has some of the most dramatic, wild and unspoilt scenery in Europe, and one of the most unpolluted environments. This makes the region an important destination for tourists and an important area for conservation.

The Highlands make up 50 per cent of the land area of Scotland, and 17 per cent of Great Britain. The region is larger than Belgium and yet only 370 000 people live there, less than one per cent of the total UK population. Average population density is nine people per km^2 compared with an average of 233 per km^2 for the whole of the UK.

Other than the local authorities such as the Highland Regional Council and the Western Isles Council, two other agencies have been

FIG 7.11   *The Highlands and Islands Enterprise Network*

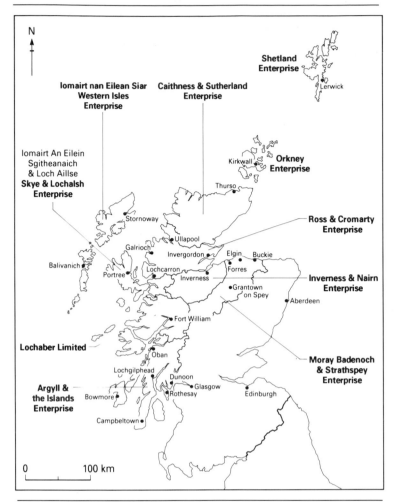

FIG 7.12   *Two Local Enterprise Companies*

LEC AREA	WESTERN ISLES ENTERPRISE (IOMAIRT NAN EILEAN SIAR)	SKYE AND LOCHALSH ENTERPRISE
Population of area	30 660	12 600
Land area	2900 km²	2700 km²
Main industries	Harris Tweed, Fishing, Fish Processing, Construction.	Tourism, Agriculture, Fishing, Aquaculture (Fish Farming).
HIE budget 1991–1992	£2.6 million (including EU Funding)	£0.8 million (including EU funding)
Private sector investment attracted by HIE projects	£5.2 million	£1.3 million
Examples of projects receiving HIE funding	a) Upgrading of an offshore fabrication yard. b) Expansion of a pharmaceutical company. c) Broadcasting projects run by the BBC and Grampian TV. d) 60 local community projects. e) Scheme to encourage local young people to become farmers. f) Gaelic language initiatives.	a) Upgrading of fish farms. b) setting up of a boat-building and repair workshop by a local company. c) Support for more than 100 local tourism-related enterprises. d) local community projects including a new swimming pool. e) Gaelic language initiatives.

particularly involved in helping the region to overcome its disadvantages – Highlands and Islands Enterprise and the EU.

- With the help of an atlas draw a sketch map of Scotland and mark on the boundary of the Highlands and Islands (see Fig 7.11). Annotate your map with labels to highlight reasons why the location and physical characteristics of the region present difficulties for transport and economic activity.

Highlands and Islands Enterprise

Highlands and Islands Enterprise (HIE) was formed in 1991 by the British Government when it replaced the Highlands and Islands Development Board (HIDB). The HIDB had been formed in 1965 as the government agency responsible for regional policy in the Highlands. It had three main aims:

1   to support **indigenous economic activity** including agricuture, fishing, industry and tourism;

2   to attract investment from outside the region;

3   to discourage migration out of the region and to stabilise the population by strengthening the economy and by improving facilities for local communities.

The HIDB could pursue these aims by:

– giving grants or loans to companies;
– setting up and running businesses;
– advertising and promoting the region;
– building factory units or other buildings to encourage new activities to locate in the region;
– funding community, sporting and cultural activities.

Although there is no doubt that the HIDB had a considerable amount of success, by the beginning of the 1990s considerable problems remained. The region's depopulation, which had been seen as one of the major issues in the 1960s, was halted during the 1970s and 1980s. However, this hides the fact that some parts of the region have continued to lose population and the 1991 census revealed that in some cases the decline is serious. Between 1981 and 1991, for example, the Western Isles lost almost ten per cent of their population.

ECONOMIC FRAGILITY

More than 30% of industrial jobs are with three vulnerable employers – two oil platform construction yards and the Dounreay nuclear research centre. These employers are likely to continue laying off workers.

ENVIRONMENTAL CONSTRAINTS

40% of the region is mountainous and useless for agriculture.
Another 50% is rough grazing. Only 1.5% is suitable for cultivation. 95% is designated as a 'less Favoured Area' by the EU.

Difficult climate increases costs of construction, transport and building.

SPARSE POPULATION

The region has the lowest population density of any region in the EU – 9.5 km^2 compared with 21 per km^2 in Alenbejo in Portugal, the next lowest.

LOWER THAN AVERAGE STANDARD OF LIVING

Average household disposable income is 85% of the British average.

Prices are 8% higher than in the rest of Britain.

Many households are dependent on seasonal jobs in tourism, forestry and farming.

THE CASE FOR OBJECTIVE ONE STATUS

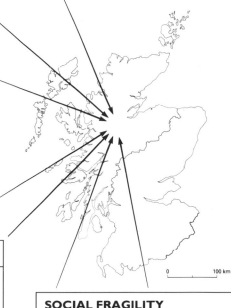

PERIPHERALITY AND REMOTENESS

Remote from population centres and markets.

Many communities rely on a single road link which is often single track.

30% of the population live on 90 islands – they are dependent on boats or ferries which increases the cost of goods in shops and raises the cost of goods exported from the region.

OBJECTIVE ONE CRITERIA

To secure Objective One status a region must have a GDP per capita less than 75% of the EU average. In 1990 the figure was 77% and falling – it had been 85% in 1987.

GDP per capita is lower than in some existing Objective One regions such as Corsica and Abruzzi in Italy.

SOCIAL FRAGILITY

Over 10% of the population, mainly on the islands and west coast, speak Gaelic. Like many other European minority languages Gaelic is declining and under threat.

FIG 7.13   *The Case for Objective One Status for the Highlands and Islands*

A Notice Outside a Gaelic Language College, Isle of Skye, showing it has Received Support From the Skye and Lochalsh LEC

Also, the activities of the HIDB were increasingly questioned by the Conservative government during the 1980s. As a public sector agency intervening in the regional economy it did not fit the government's **ideology** – the government wanted to see much more private sector involvement and more encouragement of private enterprise. So in 1991 the HIDB was scrapped and replaced by HIE.

HIE took over the responsibilities of the HIDB, but it was also given the role of running government-funded job training in the region. It was organised totally differently. Instead of a central organisation, most of the funding and most of the decision making powers were delegated to ten 'Local Enterprise Companies' (see Fig 7.11, page 176). These LECs operate as private companies although most of their funding comes from the government. This also means that to some extent the LECs compete with each other to attract investment and funding. HIE has the responsibility of supporting and overseeing the activities of the LECs.

During 1992–3 the total HIE budget was £77 million (about £195 per person living in the region). The budget is concentrated in the most fragile parts of the region where depopulation continues to be a problem and infrastructure and employment are inadequate.

Fig 7.12 on page 176 provides a closer look at two LEC areas to show the type of work being carried out by HIE.

The European Union

The EU provides regional development funds to suppport the work of agencies like Highland Regional Council, Western Isles Council, Orkney Islands Council, Shetland Islands Council, a large number of district councils and Highlands and Islands Enterprise.

During the 15 years prior to 1992 the EU had provided £240 million (equivalent to £650 per inhabitant) to the Highlands and Islands. However, when the EU's Structural Funds were reorganised at the beginning of the 1990s the region was designated as an Objective Five (b) region (see Section 7.7). This meant an 85 per cent cut in funding. The agencies working in the area were very worried that such a drastic cut in resourcing would undermine the achievements of the previous years. In 1992 they appealed to the EU Commission to be redesignated as an Objective One region which would give the region access to much larger funding, and the case they made out is summarised in Fig 7.13 on page 177. In 1993 the EU Commission decided that the region had a strong case and the Highlands and Islands became an Objective One region along with much of southern Europe and Ireland.

- Using a base map of Europe produce an annotated map to highlight the degree to which the Highlands and Islands is a remote region.

- Using the information in Fig 7.13 and the rest of this section, summarise, in no more than 300 words, the case for the Highlands and Islands needing a high level of EU support. Be as concise and persuasive as possible.

- List any arguments you can think of which could have been used by an EU Commissioner opposed to the Highlands and Islands being designated an Objective One region.

7.7 Taking from the Rich to Help the Poor: EU Regional Policy

It is the greatest shift in wealth that Europe has ever known: hundreds of billions of Ecus flowing from the richer EU regions to their poorer neighbours. Over the next six years more than Ecu 141 billion (£94 billion) will be spent on projects from new airports and motorways to the preservation of rare wildflowers – Ecu 410 (£270) for every one of the Community's men, women and children.
     The Euro-cash Deluge, Lucy Walker, The European, August 1993.

Today the future of the European Union will stand or fall on the unity of its regions.
     An EU official.

The earlier sections in this chapter have briefly described the problems facing some of Europe's regions and some of the measures being taken to overcome these problems. EU regional policy is referred to in a number of places and this section outlines the workings and aims of the policy in more detail.

There are enormous variations in the level of economic development within the EU. The European Commission believes it is essential to reduce these differences. There are four main reasons for this view.

1   One of the EU's original aims enshrined in the 1957 Treaty of Rome is to raise the standard of living of people living in all regions of the EU. The poorest regions are seen as needing special help to achieve this because they have a number of obstacles to raising standards of living which the more prosperous areas do not have.

2   Large variations in living standards could threaten the **cohesion** of the EU and cause its break up – this could lead to instability and conflict.

3   The creation of the single market at the beginning of 1993 posed a threat to the poorer peripheral regions of the EU (see Section 2.7). The **European core** (including South-East England, Belgium, the Netherlands, western Germany, the Paris region and northern Italy) is more attractive to industry than the periphery. This is because of the proximity of a large wealthy market, the availability of skilled labour, the higher quality infrastructure and the availability of facilities for research and development. The peripheral areas (such as Scotland, Ireland, Portugal, Spain, southern Italy and Greece) are a long way from the largest industrial markets and the other advantages of the core. The creation of the single market gave greater freedom to industry to invest anywhere in Europe and it was feared that the core would attract even more capital at the expense of the periphery. In other words, the rich regions would get richer, and the poor regions poorer. While it may be true that to some extent improved transport and telecommunications will overcome the problems facing the periphery most economists believe that the forces encouraging

concentration in the European core will continue to dominate.

4   The possibility of monetary union in the late 1990s (see Section 2.8) is also seen as a potential threat to poorer EU countries. Monetary union will remove some of the independence of national governments to operate their own economic policies. There is a concern that poorer countries would be unable to protect their own economic interests by, for example, changing exchange rates or interest rates. At the same time EU economic policies, under the influence of a European Central Bank, could be operated in the interests of the wealthier and more powerful economies to the detriment of the poorer peripheral countries.

●   Why do you think large variations in living standards could threaten the cohesion and stability of the EU?

●   Study Figs 7.14 and 7.15 (overleaf). To what extent does prosperity seem to be related to accessibility in the EU?

The grants allocated by the EU to assist disadvantaged regions are paid out of the EU's Structural Funds. There are in fact three Structural Funds.

1   The European Regional Development Fund (ERDF). This is the main fund specifically designed to assist disadvantaged regions.

FIG 7.14   *Regional GDP in the EU*

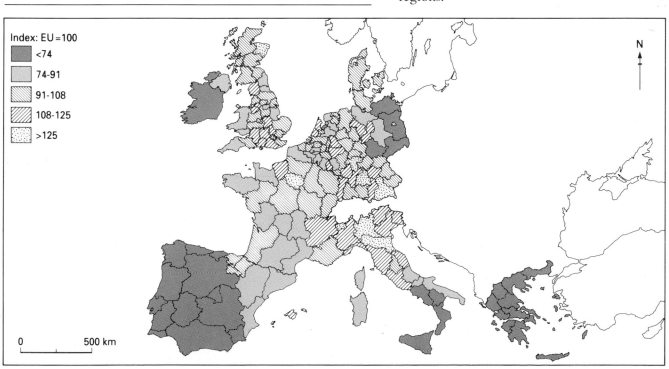

Index: EU =100
<74
74-91
91-108
108-125
>125

0   500 km

N

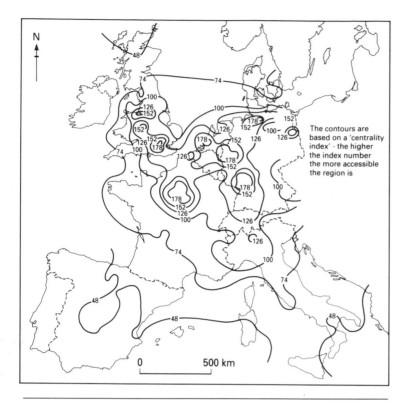

FIG **7.15**   *Accessibility in the EU*

The contours are based on a 'centrality index' – the higher the index number the more accessible the region is

2   The European Social Fund (ESF). This gives aid to specific sections of the population. In particular it assists training and employment for the unemployed, young people, women, the handicapped and migrant workers. Although about two thirds of the fund is allocated to disadvantaged regions it also finances schemes thoughout the EU.

3   The European Agricultural Guidance and Guarantee Fund (EAGGF). This funds the Common Agricultural Policy as well as schemes to improve farm productivity. The EAGGF funds agricultural policies throughout the EU and in fact only a small part of the EAGGF is specifically allocated to disadvantaged regions (see Section 5.2).

About £40 billion was allocated to these funds during the period 1989 to 1993, and during the period 1994 to 1999 this is expected to increase to about £90 billion. Spending doubled from £4.5 billion per year in 1987 to £9 billion per year in 1993 to compensate for the effects of the creation of the Single Market. The Maastricht Treaty allocates further funds to these regions.

Five key objectives have been identified for these funds for the period 1994–9.

Objective One – to promote the economic development of regions which are lagging behind by improving the infrastructure and encouraging new industries. Any region where per capita GDP is less than 75 per cent of the EU average is eligible to be designated an Objective One region.

Objective Two – to promote economic development in regions suffering from economic decline and high unemployment by diversifying the economy.

Objective Three – to combat long-term unemployment and to help people become part of the workforce, particularly women, young people and handicapped people.

Objective Four – to retrain workers so that they can adapt to changes in industry and production methods.

Objective Five – to provide the economic development of rural areas by:
a)   assisting the reorganisation of agriculture;
b)   promoting new economic activities in rural areas such as small-scale industry or tourism.

Only Objectives One, Two and Five (b) apply to regional policy because Objectives Three, Four and Five (a) apply throughout the EU. Fig 7.16 shows the regions which have been designated as Objective One, Two or Five (b) regions. Over 40 per cent of the EU's population live in one of these regions.

As the map shows, the whole of Ireland, Greece, most of Spain, southern Italy, the Scottish Highlands, Merseyside and eastern Germany are Objective One regions. Originally Objective One regions were all poor regions with relatively little industrial development and poorly developed agriculture. These regions typically have:

– low population densities made even lower by depopulation;
– a lower than average number of large towns or cities to act as centres of economic development;
– an economy dominated by agriculture which suffers from low productivity;
– a poorly educated and trained population;
– high unemployment;
– poor economic infrastructure (such as roads, railways, electricity supply) and poor social infrastructure (such as housing, schools and health services).

However, the recent addition of Merseyside and eastern Germany to this category has blurred the original definition – Objective One regions are now merely areas which need maximum help.

Objective Two regions are those which have experienced de-industrialisation such as

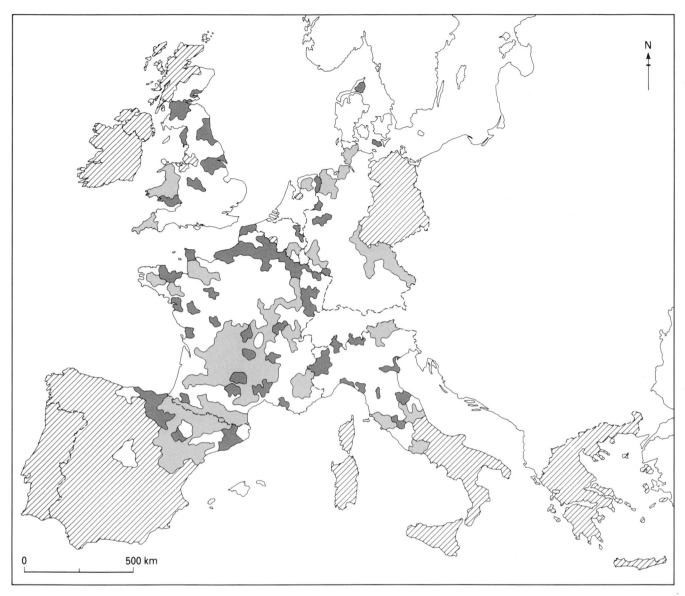

Clydeside in Scotland, North-East England, Nord-Pas de Calais in France, the Ruhr in Germany and the Basque country.

These regions typically have:

- a poor image worsened by industrial dereliction;
- high unemployment, particularly long-term unemployment;
- a declining population as people, particularly the young and highly motivated, leave the region to find work;
- a workforce whose skills are out-dated and unsuitable for new industries;
- an economy dominated by large firms involved in traditional heavy industries such as coal-mining, iron and steel, textiles, heavy engineering and shipbuilding;
- an infrastructure suitable for traditional industries but unsuitable for new industries.

Objective Five (b) regions include areas like the Massif Central in France, most of Wales, and the Pyrenees on the French–Spanish border where low incomes from farming are encouraging depopulation. These are typically areas which:

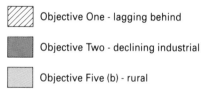

Objective One - lagging behind

Objective Two - declining industrial

Objective Five (b) - rural

FIG 7.16 *Regions Eligible Under the EU Structural Funds*

- have an environment that causes difficulties for farmers such as a short growing season or a mountainous landscape;
- are remote from large urban areas.

The way in which the three Structural Funds contribute to the five Objectives is summarised in Fig 7.17:

FIG **7.17** *Structural Funds by Objective*

	ERDF	ESF	EAGGF	Allocation 1989–93 (% of total)
Objective One	*	*	*	63
Objective Two	*	*		12
Objective Three		*		12
Objective Four		*		7
Objective Five (a)			*	5
Objective Five (b)	*	*	*	2

* denotes a contribution

Objective One is the priority and will receive 70 per cent of the Structural Funds between 1994-9, an even greater percentage than during 1989–93.

The approximate allocation of the Structural Funds by country for the period 1989–93 is outlined in Fig 7.18.

Country	Allocation 1989–93
Spain	£12 000 million
Italy	£9000 million
Portugal	£6500 million
Greece	£6500 million
France	£5500 million
UK	£5500 million
Germany	£5500 million
Ireland	£3500 million
Belgium	£800 million
Netherlands	£700 million
Denmark	£300 million
Luxembourg	£60 million

FIG **7.18** *Structural Funds by Country*

The allocation of the funds in an assisted area is decided by a partnership of local or regional authorities, the national government and the European Commission. The partnership draws up an agreed Community Support Framework which outlines exactly how the money will be spent in the region. The national governments are responsible for spending the money once it has been received from the EU.

The principle of **additionality** is applied to the Structural Funds. This means that EU funds must be matched by a similar amount of funding from the national government. Additionality is regarded as important by the European Commission because otherwise national governments may use EU aid as an excuse to cut their own spending in disadvantaged regions. If this happened there would be no additional benefit to the regions – they would receive a similar amount but from a different source. In fact there is evidence that the opportunity to obtain EU funds actually encourages national governments to spend more on disadvantaged regions.

About nine per cent of the Structural Funds are reserved for what are known as Community Initiatives which are not included in the Community Support Frameworks. There are a number of these Community Initiatives including:

– RECHAR – EU assistance to coal-mining areas suffering from mine closures;
– INTERREG – to assist areas close to national borders which have disadvantages caused by their peripheral location;
– REGEN – to promote the construction of gas and electricity distribution networks in Objective One regions;
– TELEMATIQUE – to promote the use of advanced telecommunications in Objective One regions.

- Read Fig 7.19. Explain why additionality is causing problems in the case described in the article.

It is very difficult to evaluate just how successful this massive redistribution of resources has been in reducing the gap between rich and poor regions – a process known as **convergence**. However, a number of points can be made, as follows.

1 Despite the huge quantities of money involved it represents less than 0.5 per cent of the total GDP of all the member countries. Many economists doubt that this is enough to create convergence. On the other hand, the figure is higher in Objective One regions. In the case of Ireland, Greece and Portugal EU funds represent between 2.7 per cent and 3.5 per cent of their GDP.

2 There is no evidence that convergence is occurring. Regional differences are still enormous. If the European average per capita GDP is taken to be 100 then regional GDP per capita ranges from 183 in Hamburg in Germany and Groningen in the Netherlands down to 39 in Voreio Algaio in Greece.

3 There are concerns that the funds are not being properly spent by national governments. A recent report into transport projects funded by Structural Funds stated that there were

£500m grants in danger

BRITAIN'S most needy industrial areas could lose more than £500 million of EC grants to revitalise their damaged economies because of government restrictions on local authority spending, a crisis conference heard yesterday.

Coalfield communities, which forced a revision of government thinking on European funding, should lead a new campaign to overcome government obstructions, said 250 delegates representing 120 authorities.

At issue are European Regional Development Fund (ERDF) grants, which have to be matched by local authority funding. Solutions must be found by the end of this year, or the funding could be diverted to other projects, delegates heard.

Additional EC funding is most needed in areas receiving the least industrial aid, Stephen Fothergill, director of the Coalfield Communities Campaign (CCC), told the conference in Manchester, Assistance awarded was 20 to 60 per cent to areas needing help with infrastructure and training, when 66 per cent of aid should have been awarded, he said.

In the EC Rechar aid programme for coalfield areas, only £150,000 had been allocated for South Yorkshire out of a total potential allocation of between £14 million and £16 million, he said.

Anxieties were sharpened in the run-up to Rechar 2, beginning next year, when areas in the UK could benefit from a further £125 million of EC assistance if matching local authority funding is available.

FIG 7.19   *The Guardian, 2 July 1993*

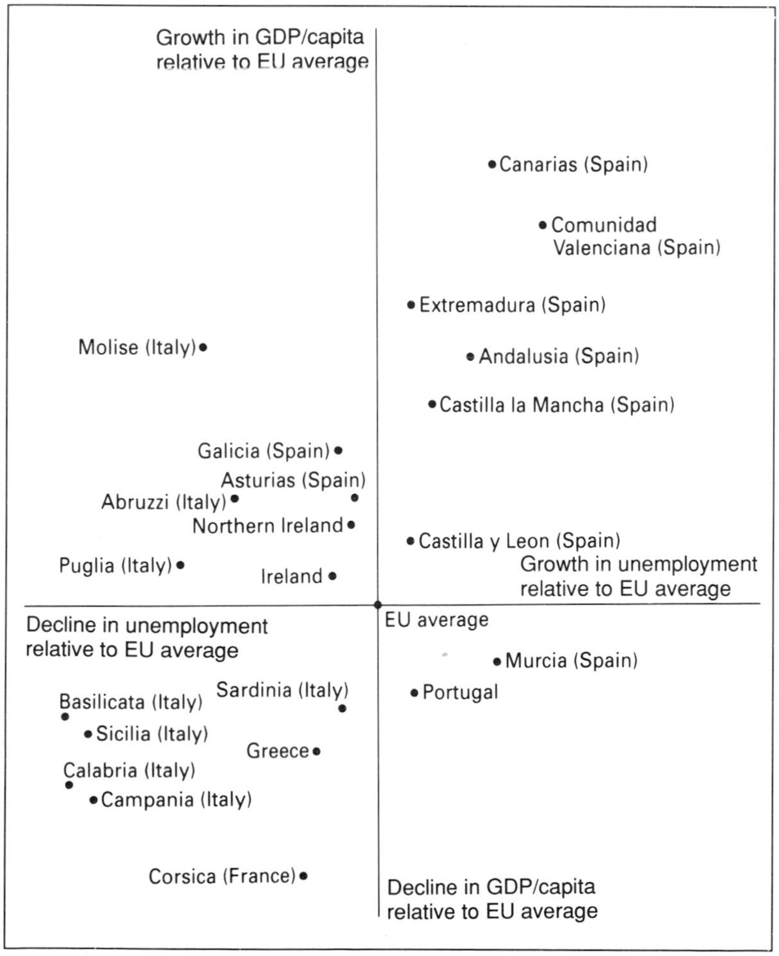

FIG 7.20   *Relative Change in Unemployment and GDP per Capita in Objective One Regions during the 1980s*

'weaknesses in the management, monitoring and control of projects'. Italy in particular has been criticised and in 1993 the European Commission tried to claw back £600 million of unspent EU grants so that they could be used elsewhere. The Commission estimated that 32 per cent of Italy's Objective One funds had not been used. The problem is caused by bureaucracy in the Italian Government, corruption, disagreements between national and regional governments and political instability.

4   There are major concerns over the environmental impact of many of the projects funded by the EU. In many cases the environmental impact of proposals is not adequately researched and in some cases EU environmental directives are ignored.

- Study Fig 7.20. To what extent does the graph support the following hypotheses?
    a) The economies of the majority of Objective One regions are growing faster than the EU average.
    b) EU regional aid is not being successful in encouraging economic growth in many Objective One regions.
    c) The above average economic growth in some Objective One regions has more to do with the success of their national economies rather than the success of EU regional policy.

- Look at Fig 7.21.
    a) Evaluate the effectiveness of the graphing technique used.
    b) Do you notice any difference in the countries receiving larger quantities of Objective One aid compared with those receiving larger quantities of Objective Five (b) aid? Can you explain any differences you identify?

- Read Fig 7.22. Scenario A assumes that the tendency for economic activity to concentrate in the European core will intensify while Scenario B assumes that the EU and national governments will intervene much more in the free market in order to speed up the development of the peripheral regions. Discuss which scenario you think is the more realistic and explain your choice.

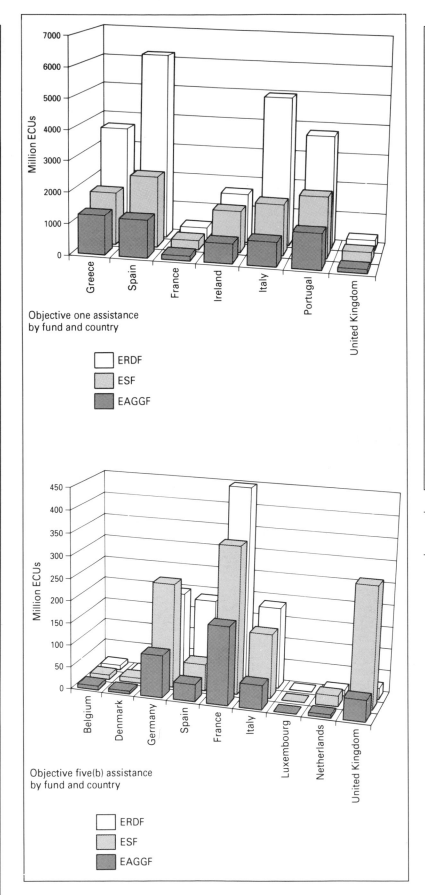

Objective one assistance
by fund and country

ERDF
ESF
EAGGF

Objective five(b) assistance
by fund and country

ERDF
ESF
EAGGF

(A) Growth scenario

The warnings that the Single European Market would result in a further spatial concentration of economic activities have proved to be correct. The high-accessibility belt from London to Milan has become a veritable megalopolis with a population of 80 million. The Channel Tunnel, the integrated European high-speed trains and the Gotthard base tunnel have increased the coherence and domination of this megalopolis, which has already in the 1990s, due to the booming east European economies, spread out its tentacles as far as Berlin and Vienna. The negative side effects are severe agglomeration diseconomies in its centres, such as exploding land prices, congestion and environmental deterioration, while the peripheral regions suffer from economic decline and depopulation.

(B) Equity senario

Soon after the introduction of the Single European Market, the European parliament realised that without a strong decentralisation policy the spatial disparities within Europe would become even greater. The result was the reform of the *European Regional Development Fund* which was given extensive powers to redirect economic activities from the agglomerations to the peripheral areas. Investment programmes such as the *Technopolis Network*, the *Remote Area Highway Programme* and the *Regional Airport Scheme* were coupled with strict land use control in urban areas, tax incentives for location in non-metropolitan regions and flat rates in long-distance telecommunication services. While some of these policies were eroded by national non-cooperation, in general they were successful, as witnessed by the new high-tech industries in traditionally agricultural regions like Macedonia or Galicia.

Fig 7.22   *Two Scenarios for the Future of Regional Policy in the EU*

Fig 7.21   *Objective One and Five (b) – Assistance by Fund and by Country*

1 Using examples define what makes a region 'disadvantaged'.

2 'The economic and environmental problems facing eastern Europe are worse than those facing any region in western Europe.' Discuss the extent to which the evidence supports this statement.

3 State intervention can help to reduce the impact of de-industrialisation. Discuss.

4 Does it matter if regions like the Highlands and Islands of Scotland decline economically?

5 Using examples, describe how the EU intervenes to aid disadvantaged regions.

6 Evaluate the success of EU regional policy using evidence from this chapter and other chapters in this book.

Glossary

additionality	The concept of EU financial aid having to be additional to financial aid from national governments and not merely an alternative to national government aid.
cohesion	The degree to which EU countries 'stick' together. The unity of the EU member countries.
convergence	The process of aligning, or reducing differences between the economic policies and economic characteristics of the EU member countries.
European core	The economic heartland of western Europe. The region of Europe where GDP per capita is highest, extending from South-East England to northern Italy.
ideology	A set of ideas which form the basis of an economic and political viewpoint.
indigenous economic activity	Economic activity carried out by firms which have emerged within a region (as opposed to economic activity carried out by branches of firms based or originating outside the region).
per capita GDP	Gross Domestic Product (a measure of the total value of goods and services produced by a country during one year) divided by the population in a country. In other words, average GDP per person.
peripheral region	A region on 'the edge' of Europe. A region remote from the core regions of Europe (see European core).
post-industrial society	A term used to refer to the social and economic characteristics of those countries which have experienced de-industrialisation.

Reactors or Wind Farms?

KEY
IDEAS

8.1 Coal continues to be a major source of energy throughout Europe. However, most of Europe's coal-mining industries are declining in the face of competition from other fuels and this has serious social and economic impacts for mining communities.

8.2 The nuclear industry throughout most of Europe is stagnating and may even decline during the 1990s. Only in France is nuclear energy widely accepted as the best option for producing electricity.

8.3 The nuclear industry in eastern Europe is in crisis due to unsafe reactor designs and inadequate funds to maintain or repair existing reactors.

8.4 Wind power has now become a commercial option in many European countries. Although it does help to reduce atmospheric pollution there is

disagreement over the environmental impact of large numbers of wind turbines.

8.5 Energy production in Europe is making a major contribution to global warming. European governments are under pressure from international agreements to reduce CO_2 emissions.

8.6 European governments are facing tough targets on reducing emissions of sulphur dioxide and nitrogen oxides in order to tackle the problem of acid rain.

8.7 Energy consumption can be significantly reduced by designing buildings which use energy more efficiently.

Pit Pony and Miner Ride the Cage to the Surface at Ellington Colliery near Newcastle for the Last Time, February 1994

8.1 The Decline of Coal

In western Europe coal-mining has been in long-term decline since 1945 and up to the early 1990s five EU countries were substantial coal producers – Germany, Spain, France, Belgium and the UK. They produced 60 per cent of the coal consumed in the EU. Coal was still used to generate 40 per cent of the Union's electricity. However since 1973 EU 'black coal' production has fallen by 30 per cent while imports have risen by 300 per cent. At the industry's peak two million miners were employed in the western European coal industry – by 1993 this had declined to 200 000.

The Decline in Britain

If October's pit closure announcement was met by anger in the UK, the common response across the Channel was one of total incredulity. Could the government with the most productive, competitive coal industry in Europe – the only one not surviving on public subsidies – really be proposing its virtual destruction and its replacement by more expensive gas-fired power?

Linda McAven, There is an Alternative, Town and Country Planning Journal, July 1993.

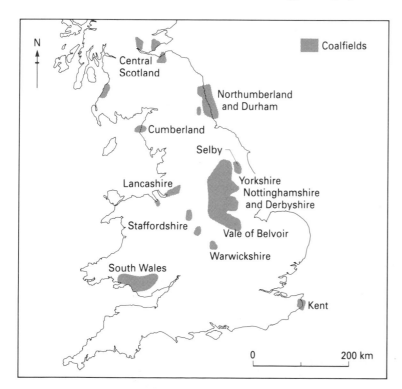

Fig 8.2 *Coalfields of Britain*

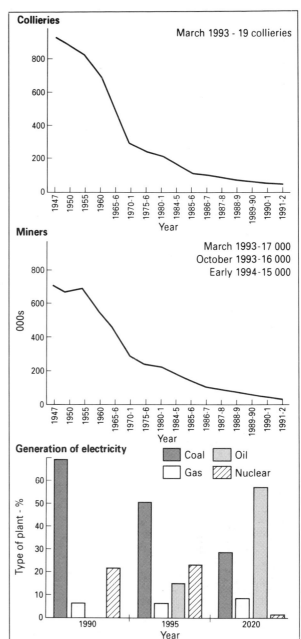

Fig 8.1 *Decline of Britain's Coal Industry*

The greatest decline has been seen in Britain despite the relatively low cost of coal production there. Fig 8.1 indicates just how severe the decline was with the number of mines declining from over 900 in 1947 to 19 in 1993 and the number of miners falling from about 700 000 in 1947 to 16 000 in 1993. Most of the remaining coalfields are located in Yorkshire, Derbyshire and Nottinghamshire – the coalfields in Central Scotland, Cumbria, Northumberland and Durham, Lancashire, Staffordshire, South Wales and Kent have lost all or most of their mines (see Fig 8.2).

This long-term decline in Britain was the consequence of a number of factors:

— greater productivity. The mining industry became more capital intensive. More automation and mechanisation enabled massive increases in the amount of coal each mine and each miner could produce in a year;
— competition from other sources of energy. In 1947 coal was used extensively in homes, in industry and in power stations. Since then the introduction of natural gas and nuclear power, and the much greater reliance on oil, have undermined the demand for coal. These energy sources are generally easier to transport, are often cleaner and at times have been cheaper. Fig 8.3 shows the extent of the decline in demand for coal;
— greater reliance on the import of cheap coal (see Fig 8.4).

These factors have applied elsewhere in western Europe as well but in the 1980s and 1990s other factors unique to Britain had an important role in the industry's decline.

1 After 1979 the Conservative government was determined to reduce and eventually remove state subsidies for the coal industry. Their aim was to sell British Coal, a state-owned industry since 1947, into the private sector. For this to happen the industry had to be made profitable and so all less productive and loss-making mines had to be closed.

2 In 1990 the government privatised the state-owned Central Electricity Generating Board (CEGB) which until then had been responsible for generating all electricity in England and Wales. Two new private sector companies replaced the CEGB – National Power and PowerGen (along with Nuclear Electric which remained in government hands). The CEGB had a contract to purchase coal from British Coal but this contract expired in 1993. The new private companies were not interested in renewing this contract. They wanted to import cheaper coal from abroad and to use natural gas in a new generation of power stations. By 1993 the bottom had fallen out of the market for coal and the government argued that the market could only support 12 mines.

3 Increasingly gas is being used to generate electricity. The 'Dash For Gas' undertaken by the generating companies in the early 1990s was a result of a) the lower cost of the fuel in the short term, b) the desire of smaller companies to enter the generating industry and they could build gas-fired power stations more cheaply and more quickly than coal-fired power stations, and c) the need to achieve targets on reducing sulphur dioxide emissions (which contribute to acid rain). Gas-fired power stations produce much less SO_2 than coal without having to invest heavily in pollution control equipment and emit half as much CO_2. Between 1992 and 1996, 20 gas-fired power stations were to come on stream.

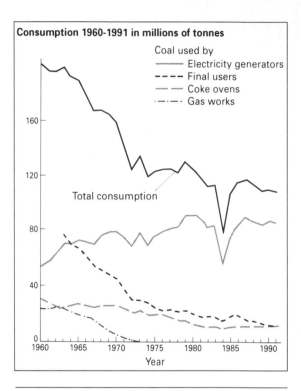

FIG 8.3 *Coal Consumption in the UK, The Guardian, 3 November 1992*

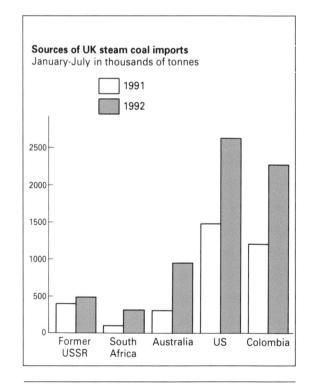

FIG 8.4 *Coal imports to the UK*

Fig 8.1 shows how electricity generation in Britain will have changed between 1990 and 2020 given current trends while Fig 8.5 shows the current programme of gas-fired power stations.

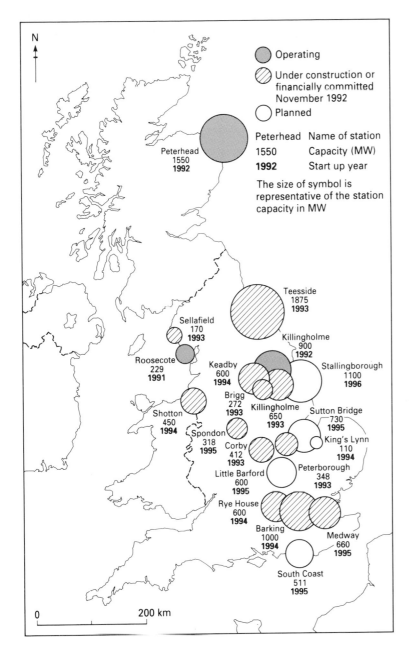

FIG 8.5 *The Location of Gas-fired Power Stations in the UK, Geography Magazine, May 1993*

The Decline in France

The French coal-mining industry is small compared to the British industry. In 1990 the top six producers in Europe outside the former Soviet Union were:

Country	Annual Production
Germany	427 million tonnes
Poland	215 million tonnes
UK	92 million tonnes
Greece	47 million tonnes
Spain	37 million tonnes
France	12 million tonnes

In fact these figures are misleading. There are two main types of coal – black (or hard coal) and brown coal (or lignite). The energy value of brown coal is about half that of black coal. More than 80 per cent of Germany's production, more than 30 per cent of Poland's, 100 per cent of Greece's and almost 50 per cent of Spain's output is brown coal. The UK, on the other hand, produces no brown coal and France produces only a small quantity. In energy terms France is the fifth largest European producer.

Since the late 1950s the French coal-mining industry has declined from an output of about 60 million tonnes to the current output of about 12 million tonnes. The number of miners declined from 300 000 to 28 000 over the same period. Production had been concentrated in three main areas – Nord-Pas-de-Calais, Lorraine and Centre-Midi. The last mine in the Nord-Pas-de-Calais closed in 1991, yet in 1950 over 50 per cent of the country's output came from the region. More than 100 mines employed 200 000 miners.

The decline of the French coal industry since the 1950s is largely due to:

- growth in coal imports. In recent years more than 60 per cent of the coal consumed in France has been imported;
- growth of nuclear power. Since the 1970s the French Government has implemented an ambitious nuclear power programme – by the early 1990s over 70 per cent of France's electricity was being generated by nuclear power stations, removing the main potential market for coal.

The large-scale mine closures have had devastating social and economic effects on local communities which have depended on the coal mines for employment for decades. It has also been claimed that the mine closures announced in 1993 alone would cost the government £1300 million in reduced income from tax, higher spending on unemployment benefits, redundancy payments, and sealing and clearing closed mines. The 1993 government decision to reduce the industry to 12 mines was met with widespread political opposition but other than a decision to keep a small number of additional mines open for the short term government policy did not change.

The ending of mining in Nord-Pas-de-Calais was also caused by the difficult geological conditions in the area. Coal seams are thin, faulted and angled making their exploitation expensive and uncompetitive. Most of France's output now comes from the Lorraine coalfield where geological conditions allow greater productivity. The Lorraine field is protected at least for the time being with the construction of a new coal-fired power station in the area.

Despite the mine closures the French state-owned coal industry (*Charbonnages de France*) continues to face financial losses. Much of this loss is accounted for by miners' pensions, redundancy payments and grants to job creation schemes for ex-miners. In Nord-Pas-de-Calais a government-sponsored organisation (FINORPA) operates to help ex-miners find work. Some miners have found work in factories, some in power stations under an agreement with Electricité de France, and some in the construction of the Channel Tunnel. Charbonnages de France continues to own housing and other property in the area so its role in the economic and social life of the area continues.

The EU recognises that areas suffering from mine closures face special problems and has created a fund called RECHAR. This fund is aimed at helping communities to survive the mine closures and at attracting new economic activities to replace mining. Between 1989 and 1993 £230 million were spent on RECHAR initiatives, mainly in Germany, France, Belgium, Britain and Spain. From 1994 British coal-mining communities alone will be eligible for an additional £125 million.

- Fig 8.6 describes the closure of the coal-mining industry in Belgium in 1992. Using the information in this article and the rest of this section produce an outline cost-benefit analysis for the closure of a country's mining industry. You will not be able to put a figure to each cost and benefit but you should be able to produce a detailed list of costs and a detailed list of benefits.

FIG 8.6   *The Guardian, 27 October 1992*

Promises made down the pits

THE SHAFT wheels and conveyor belts have stopped. The chips and beer stands next to the main entrance have gone. The cafes on the other side of the road are empty. Belgium's last coal mine, at Zolder in the north east, looks like a piece of discarded scenery, a memorial to 90 years of social and economic history of Limburg province.

The miners went underground last month for the last time to clean up and to bring the drilling equipment, electricians' tools and engines back up. A symbolic last load of coal was brought to the surface. Much of the tunnel system will be flooded. No more coal will be mined in Belgium.

Only the older generation remembers the heyday of the Limburg mines at Zolder, Beringen, Eisden, Waterschei, Winterslag and Zwartberg. The first mine was opened in 1922 and the industry reached its peak, in production and employment, in the 1950s. In 1957 some 41 000 miners cut nearly 10 million tons of coal.

But with other energy sources becoming more popular, first oil and then nuclear energy, it was downhill from the 1960s onwards. The decline was slow at first but then the cutbacks became all too

visible and a source of great tension. When the first mine was closed at Zwartberg in 1966, there were violent protests and two miners died.

The long strikes of 1970, 1985, 1986 and 1987 left their mark. No politician dared tell the miners openly that their product was too expensive and above all that there was no demand for it. No minister or member of parliament dared spark the Limburg fury. Fudging was the order of the day and promises were made which could never be fulfilled.

Because of the high turnover among miners, and the different nationalities, the traditional unions had never had much influence over them. It was always unaffiliated miners who led the strikes.

The far right tried to recruit among the miners with little success. Limburg is the one province where the Flemish Bloc and its notorious predecessors have found no support to speak of. A book called Down The Mine We're All Black explains why the different communities in Limburg always got on reasonably well. The big question is of course what will happen now that the social ties forged in the mines will disappear. It is undeniable that the Turkish and Moroccan miners and

their families are finding it most difficult to get new jobs.

In 1986 the then prime minister, Wilfried Martens, had enough of the social tension and the financial burden and ended the government's long-standing policy of mollycoddling the industry. He sent in a hatchet man, Thyl Gheyselinck, the managing director of Shell Portugal.

Gheyselinck made no bones about the fact that he knew absolutely nothing about coal mining and was only interested in closing mines in a socially acceptable manner. His direct style was appreciated, but more importantly he had some £1.7 billion to spend. He offered the unions and miners a simple choice. The pits could be kept open until 1994, or they could be closed earlier and the money could be used for redundancy payments and to create new jobs.

Despite some spluttering resistance Gheyselinck succeeded. The most generous redundancy scheme in Belgium history did the trick. Men over 50 and under 30 were quick to accept. They received a lump sum of £15 000 and a month's salary, pension rights were protected and they retained their miner's status, which entitled them to low-interest

loans and higher unemployment benefits.

Pit after pit closed without protest. Miners who wanted to stay on found work in other mines, replacing those who had taken redundancy. What problems there were concerned the redundancy terms and not the closures as such. But Gheyselinck's slogan that "creating jobs is the best value for money" did not come true. Most of the available money was spent on redundancy and pension schemes. Buying social and political peace turned out to be a very costly business; in the end there was not much left for industrial conversion and job creation.

But most of the miners have found work. Unemployment has actually fallen in Limburg despite the pit closures, largely thanks to the period of economic growth in the 1980s which coincided with the closure timetable. Some miners frittered away their redundancy pay but then found work at the Ford plant in nearby Genk or in the port of Antwerp. Others used the money to set up a dry cleaners, a driving school or a shop.

Limburg will have to do without the mines in future, but no one is sorry.

Demonstration at Plogoff, Brittany, France, 15 June 1992

8.2 A Stagnating Industry: Nuclear Energy in Western Europe

When the first nuclear power station in the world, Calder Hall in Cumbria, North-West England, began operating in 1956 the future of nuclear power looked bright. Many believed nuclear energy would safely and cleanly provide us with limitless cheap electricity. The reality has been disappointing. The development of nuclear power was partly a response to growing demand for energy in the 1950s and 1960s. Between 1956 and 1973 the demand for energy in western Europe grew by more than five per cent a year.

This rapid growth came to an abrupt end in 1973 with the sudden price rise of Middle Eastern oil. The western European economies were forced to cut energy consumption and to use oil more efficiently. The rise in the cost of oil gave added impetus to the development of nuclear power. Most European economies depended on imported oil and nuclear energy seemed an attractive alternative.

Nevertheless, the nuclear industry has consistently overestimated the speed with which it would grow and recent trends suggest that within the near future it may actually decline in western Europe. No western European country with nuclear power stations, with the exception of France, has any firm plans to build any more. Only a few nuclear stations are still under construction and even the ambitious French nuclear programme is slowing down. Austria has 'mothballed' its only nuclear station following a referendum. Sweden, which currently obtains 40 per cent of its electricity from nuclear stations, has declared its intention to close all its plants by 2010. Italy's reactors have been closed since the Chernobyl accident in the Soviet Union increased public opposition to nuclear power. No country without nuclear power is planning to build a nuclear station.

The Nuclear Power Plant at Chernobyl, Ukraine after the Explosion

The reasons for this reluctance by governments to wholeheartedly accept nuclear power are complex and include the following points.

1   In the 1970s and 1980s public unease over nuclear energy grew. This uneasiness may have arisen from a lack of understanding of nuclear power and from its association with the destructive force of nuclear weapons. People are aware that radioactivity can cause cancer and this engenders fear. This widespread unease has strengthened the hand of organised anti-nuclear groups.

2   The accident at Chernobyl nuclear power station in Ukraine (at that time part of the Soviet Union) in 1986, when a huge cloud of radioactive material was released by an explosion in a reactor hall, seemed to confirm the fears of those opposed to nuclear power. Much of the material was deposited around the nearby city of Kiev but easterly winds carried the pollution towards Scandinavia and Britain. In Britain the highest levels of radioactivity were found in North Wales and Scotland. Grazing land was contaminated and the sale of meat from sheep farms was restricted by the government. In Ukraine nine people working near the reactor were killed and many others were treated for the effects of radiation. The true death toll will never be known for certain because of the difficulties of confirming how many people have developed cancer because of the explosion, but it has been estimated that 8000 people in the Ukraine died. Inadequate safety measures at the power station were blamed for the accident but inevitably it made claims that nuclear power is safe much more difficult to accept.

3   Partly because of the introduction of more sophisticated safety measures in new reactors, the cost of building new power stations has risen. Opposition has also made the task of finding suitable sites for power stations more time-consuming and expensive. Rising costs have eroded the price advantages of nuclear power. Nuclear power stations have a reputation for exceeding expected costs. In some cases the final cost of building a power station has been double the predicted cost and in any case the capital costs of a power station are high.

4 It is difficult to find suitable sites for nuclear power stations in densely populated countries.

5 The true cost of nuclear power once the power stations have been built is also difficult to calculate. The running and maintenance costs and the cost of fuel may be relatively easy to predict but the big unknowns are the cost of closing (called decommissioning) a nuclear power station and the cost of processing or storing nuclear waste. When a plant is decommissioned it must either be dismantled – a difficult operation due to the high levels of radioactivity – or encased in concrete for hundreds of years. No commercial reactor in the world has yet been completely decommissioned and so the costs and problems are unknown.

6 Nuclear waste from power stations, including used fuel and contaminated equipment, remains perhaps the biggest problem facing the industry. No country has yet made a final decision on what to do with their high-level (the most radioactive) waste. The three main options are:

a) reprocessing to extract uranium and plutonium which can be re-used, although this still leaves dangerous waste; b) storage above ground in specially designed storage tanks and c) undergound burial. Whichever option is adopted the waste will have to be monitored for hundreds of years to prevent seepages into the environment. Sweden is developing canisters for underground storage with a design life of 100 000 years. Even in the case of underground storage groundwater could be contaminated. Finding suitable sites for waste disposal is even more difficult than finding sites for power stations. (See the article and questions on the Cumbrian underground rock laboratory). Sweden has already built an underground 'repository' for low-level and intermediate-level waste (the lower of three categories of waste based on how radioactive the material is) next to its Forsmark nuclear power station. It may be followed by a deeper high-level waste repository near Lindesberg.

FIG 8.7 *Size and Location of Nuclear Power Stations, 1990*

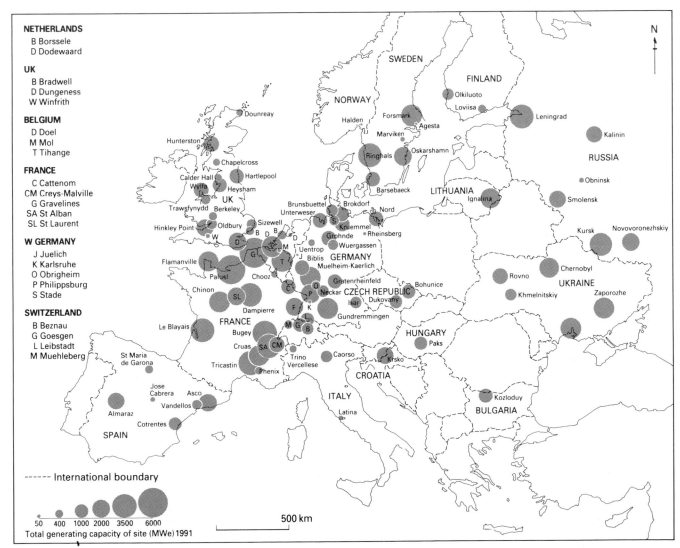

7 Other fuels, particularly natural gas and some forms of renewable energy, have become increasingly competitive over recent years and this has eroded the cost advantages claimed by supporters of nuclear power.

The extent of the cost problems facing nuclear energy emerged particularly clearly in the UK. When the British Government planned to privatise the Central Electricity Generating Board (CEGB) in 1990 they initially included Britain's nuclear stations as part of the package. However, the financial institutions interested in investing in the electricity industry were not adequately convinced that nuclear power was profitable enough. They felt that there were too many uncertainties over future costs. The government was forced to exclude the nuclear stations when they created the new privatised companies (National Power and PowerGen). Two new state-owned companies, Nuclear Electric and Scottish Nuclear, were created to run the nuclear stations. Nuclear

Electric and Scottish Nuclear receive a substantial subsidy from the government and the money for this subsidy is raised from a levy on all consumers' electricity bills. At the moment this levy, called the 'Non Fossil Fuel Obligation', increases the cost of electricity bills by ten per cent. Some of the income from the levy goes to research into renewables but most of it goes to the nuclear industry. The government is under pressure from the EU and the coal industry to end the subsidy and the levy is likely to be phased out by 1998. It is unlikely that the industry at present could operate profitably without the subsidy.

- Describe the spatial distribution of reactors shown in Fig 8.7 on page 195.

- Read Fig 8.8 which is written by a conservation group called Friends of the Lake District, affiliated to the Council for the Preservation of Rural England – one of the oldest conservation groups in Britain.

Fig 8.8   *Friends of the Lake District*

Underground Rock Laboratory in Cumbria

Going Underground
During the second half of last year proposals to develop an underground rock laboratory began to emerge, quite an unexpected change in tactics by Nirex. A rock laboratory or "Rock Characterisation Facility" (RCF) to use the correct jargon, is basically an underground laboratory to study the surrounding rock in more detail.

Nirex maintains that some form of rock laboratory had always been on the cards, albeit as a later phase in repository development, and that the new proposals have simply brought this stage forward. In this new approach, the rock laboratory has two main fuctions – to produce the final design, location and engineering specification of the repository and to provide information to help produce a convincing long term Safety Case. However the proposals as they stand pose many important planning and technical questions to which the public and the government's own advisers are demanding answers.

Planning Issues
Longlands Farm near Gosforth is the chosen location for the rock laboratory. The site, a few hundred metres from the National Park boundary, lies in an area originally proposed by Copeland Borough Council for designation as an Area of Great Landscape Value, recognising its importance as open countryside between the

Lakeland fells and the west coast. The surface structures for the numerous deep geological boreholes now being proposed for site investigation and the eventual surface development for the rock laboratory would dramatically alter the character of this area of countryside. Attractive agricultural land with trees and hedgerows would be transformed into a large industrial site with extensive levelling and hard-surfacing, substantial buildings with towers up to 30 m tall, surrounded by fencing and floodlighting.

Local people have already expressed concern at the potential effects of additional heavy traffic emerging from a new access track onto the A595 at a particularly dangerous point. Disposal of spoil, power supply lines, and effects on local watercourses and groundwater supplies are relevant issues. Clearly the environmental effects of such a development must be analysed in detail as part of an extensive Environmental Impact Assessment.

Timescales
There are, however, more fundamental questions underlying the whole scheme, many of which have been highlighted in a recent report by Environmental Resources Limited (ERL), the consultants commissioned by the County Council to take a more technical look at the proposals.

ERL have taken a look at

similar developments in other countries bearing in mind that Britain has no previous experience of developing underground laboratories. There are, however, some important differences between the experience of countries such as Sweden, Switzerland and Canada and what is proposed by Nirex here in Cumbria.

In comparison with the experience of other countries planning or constructing rock laboratories, the timetable suggested for the Longlands Farm development appears totally unrealistic. Where rock laboratories have been constructed overseas the intention has been for several years of research in advance of either reaching a fundamental decision about the option of a repository or choosing the final location of such a development. Nirex, however, has already selected West Cumbria as the prime candidate for a repository and proposes a speedy timetable in which the rock laboratory would be one of the initial stages of its full development. Conveniently, for example, ERL points out that "many of the design details of the RCF correspond directly to the specifications required for the repository ventilation shafts".

The plan is for about 13 exploratory boreholes on the site in the next few months, with an application submitted for the rock

laboratory later in the year. If permission is granted, shaft sinking would take place reaching the required depth in approximately 1996 at which stage test galleries would be drilled. Preliminary timetables however, are suggesting 1996/97 for submission of a full planning application for the radioactive waste repository itself. Not only does this timetable seem unrealistic in terms of collecting and analysing data at each stage, but it rules out any real opportunity for independent assessment of the results obtained and continuing public consultation.

There are many other technical and scientific points currently being discussed relating to the nature of the information that would be obtained and the methods used. More generally, the proposed RCF clearly represents a major commitment to the eventual development of a repository in this part of West Cumbria. At a projected cost of £120 million it is hardly intended for casual observation. Each borehole sunk into west Cumbrian rock alone costs about £5 million. With this and all our other concerns in mind, we have supported ERL's suggestion that the ECF proposals should be subject to a public enquiry. Only this way can this extremely important issue be subjected to the strict public scrutiny required.

- 'Nirex' (Nuclear Industry Radioactive Waste Executive), referred to in the article, is a state-owned company responsible for developing nuclear waste disposal facilities. Nirex has carried out research into a number of possible sites for an underground repository or storage facility but has now opted for a location close to the Sellafield reprocessing plant in Cumbria.

a) What factors do you think Nirex would have to consider when choosing a site for a nuclear waste depository?

b) Outline the purpose of the 'Rock Characterisation Facility'.

c) List the immediate impacts of the proposed RCF on the local environment.

d) Why does Friends of the Lake District believe the RCF proposal represents a commitment by Nirex to construct a repository at this location towards the end of the 1990s?

e) Is there any evidence in the article that Friends of the Lake District does not trust or respect Nirex?

Thorp: Money Spinner or White Elephant?

The challenges facing the nuclear industry across Europe are also illustrated by the issue of reprocessing.

At present used nuclear fuel is either stored under water in special cooling tanks, usually at the power station, or it is reprocessed (see Fig 8.9). As long ago as the 1970s the British Government decided to upgrade its reprocessing facilities at Sellafield in Cumbria by building a new thermal oxide reprocessing plant (THORP) at an eventual cost of £2.3 billion. The plan was that other nuclear countries, such as

Germany and Japan, would pay Britain to import used nuclear fuel for reprocessing at Sellafield and in this way Thorp would make a considerable profit as well as providing a facility to reprocess British nuclear waste. However, by 1993 when Thorp was completed the need for Thorp seemed far less certain even to many of its supporters.

The plant has faced the following problems.

– The Danish and Irish Governments called for the cancellation of the plant. They were concerned that radioactive discharges from the plant into the Irish Sea would pollute their coastlines.

– The United States Government opposed the plant on the grounds that the plutonium produced by the plant during reprocessing would increase the availability of material for the construction of nuclear weapons around the world. The US Government was becoming increasingly concerned about the proliferation of nuclear weapons and the likelihood of countries such as Iraq and North Korea obtaining such weapons.

– In 1993 there was a surplus of uranium in the world, and its price was falling, and so there was less incentive for countries with nuclear power stations to obtain their uranium from spent fuel.

– By the 1990s nuclear countries had abandoned the idea of constructing **fast-breeder reactors**. Dounreay in northern Scotland closed in 1994 and Superphénix in France closed in 1990 due to safety problems. Such reactors would have needed plutonium as a fuel and reprocessing would have provided a source. This meant that one of Thorp's potential markets had disappeared.

– There was continuing uncertainty about what to do with the waste the plant would create. By importing other countrys' waste the problem of waste disposal in Britain would be worsened. Some members of the government argued that foreign waste should only be accepted for reprocessing if countries like Germany agreed to take back the waste produced during the reprocessing of their fuel. Clearly, this would make using Thorp less attractive to the German Government.

– Storage of waste from British nuclear power stations is cheaper than reprocessing and with growing pressure on the British Government to end the subsidy to Nuclear Electric and Scottish Nuclear the cheaper

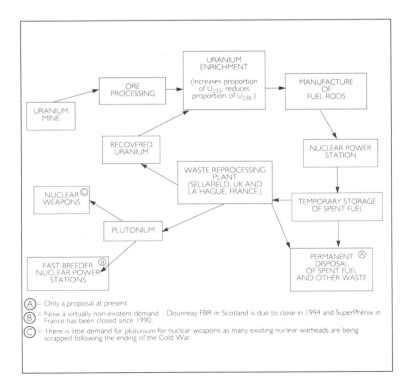

FIG 8.9 *Nuclear Fuel Cycle*

option was becoming more attractive. By 1993 Scottish Nuclear had stated its intention to store rather than reprocess.

- Even anti-nuclear environmental groups like Greenpeace and Friends of the Earth prefer storage to reprocessing because they believe it is safer.
- German nuclear power stations had a legal obligation to reprocess their fuel but by 1993 a change in German law was becoming increasingly likely. Some German power stations had already asked the French to store their waste. In late 1993 a report written for the German Government said that the higher costs of reprocessing should be avoided.

These changes in the nuclear industry around the world made it look increasingly unlikely that Thorp would make a profit but that it would become a white elephant. An article in *The Economist* magazine referred to Thorp as 'another large nuclear blunder' and argued that the plant should not be allowed to open. In fact, the British Government gave permission for the plant to start operating in 1994.

Nuclear Dependence in France

France has committed itself to nuclear power to a much greater extent than any other European country. Since 1974 the country has built 56 reactors and expects to have 60 by the end of the decade. 75 per cent of French electricity is produced by nuclear energy – a level of dependence on the nuclear industry unparalleled in any other country (See Fig 8.10). By standardising reactor design and using only one construction consortium costs have been kept to a minimum and French nuclear power stations generate electricity at two thirds the cost of, for example, German nuclear stations. France now has a surplus of electricity and some is exported to the UK, Italy and Switzerland.

Why has the French Government been so willing to support nuclear energy? There are four main reasons.

1   France lacks significant **indigenous** oil or gas **reserves**. It is highly dependent on imports of these fuels. By developing a large nuclear industry its electricity supplies are safe from any interruption to energy imports. It also helps the country's balance of payments. In 1973 France imported 135 million tonnes of oil but by the early 1980s this had been reduced to 75 million tonnes. But France does have its own uranium mines.

2   The slow and expensive **public enquiry** system which exists in some countries does not exist in France and so it is easier for the nuclear industry to ignore opposition.

3   Compared with Germany, and to a lesser extent Britain, there has been a relatively strong national consensus in support of nuclear power although it is not easy to explain why. It may be that part of the reason is that each power station has to pay a predetermined amount of money to the local community. People living or working within ten kilometres of a plant

receive a ten per cent discount on their electricity bills. Local people are often given priority for jobs during construction of the plants, and many of the power stations have been located in economically depressed areas.

There has been some militant opposition. For example, a planned reactor at Plogoff in Brittany was cancelled in 1980 following militant and sometimes violent opposition from local people. In the 1970s one man was killed and hundreds injured in protests against the construction of the Creys-Melville nuclear plant and an anti-tank rocket launcher was used in a protest against the plant but such protests are relatively unusual.

4   France has a lower population density than many western European countries and so it has fewer problems finding acceptable sites.

Fig 8.10   *Percentage of Electricity Produced by Nuclear Power*

Country	%
France	73
Belgium	59
Sweden	52
Hungary	48
Lithuania	47
Switzerland	40
Spain	36
Bulgaria	34
Finland	33
Czech/Slovak Rep.	29
Germany	28
Ukraine	25
UK	21
Russia	10
Netherlands	5

However, doubts are now growing within France over the wisdom of being so reliant on nuclear energy, particularly on one standard design of reactor. Some reactors are now reaching the end of their life and the enormous cost of decommissioning will have to be met (at least £300 million for each reactor). Some of the oldest reactors, at Chinon and Saint-Laurent in the Loire basin, at Marcoule on the Rhone and at Brennilis in western Brittany have already been partially dismantled but the highly radioactive cores remain in place. There are also signs that the

French reactors do have some inherent faults which, because they could occur in all the reactors, could prove to be very expensive. A report on nuclear safety which was leaked and later made public in 1990 outlined a number of incidents at power stations which threatened safety.

France's fast-breeder reactor, Superphénix, is currently shut down and is likely to remain so following its failure to obtain an operating licence due to faults in the reactor.

The programme has been very costly. By the mid–1980s Electricité de France owed £16 billion – making it one of the world's largest borrowers.

The nuclear programme in France is now slowing down but that has more to do with the high percentage of electricity already generated by nuclear energy and with the current surplus of electricity (some of which is exported via a cross-Channel power link to Britain) than with a reduced commitment by the government and the generating companies.

DAWN BOMB BLOWS UP ELECTRICITY PYLONS

Attack by ecologists, energy alarm in north

Two electricity pylons which carry a 380 000 volt cable from the French nuclear power station at Creys-Melville (known as Superphénix) into Italy were blown up at dawn. The pylons, which lie in an inaccessible mountain area 40 km north of Turin, were positioned 300 m apart, but more than a kilometre of cable was damaged in the explosion…this is the fourth attempt to paralyse the line bringing power from the French nuclear power station. The first two failed, the third in March this year led to the collapse of a 45 m high pylon…The police suspect the Piedmontese terrorist group *Figli Delia Terra* (Sons of the Earth). They have been spurred into action by the serious risk to north-western Italy of a Chernobyl type accident at Superphénix…The electricity line is a key connection bringing in 40 per cent of Italy's imported electricity. The terrorist attack had put the whole of the national grid in jeopardy. The electricity supply problem had been made worse by the fact that the drought of the last two years has reduced production in hydroelectric power stations to 60 per cent of normal.

FIG **8.11** *La Stampa, 11 September 1990*

Nuclear Power in Germany

The former West Germany was not so committed to nuclear power as France. A number of reasons account for this.

– With a larger population than France, West Germany had less than half the land area. Finding suitable sites was much more difficult.
– In the state of North-Rhine Westphalia, which includes some of the largest cities in western Germany, local politicians decided to resist nuclear power as a way of supporting the coal-mining industry. In any case the SPD party controls the state government and the SPD has usually adopted an anti-nuclear stance.
– There has been far more militant opposition to nuclear power in western Germany. One of the most publicised confrontations was at Brokdorf, north of Hamburg, in the mid-1970s when thousands of demonstrators and police clashed violently. In 1986 20 000 people demonstrated at the Wacksdorf construction site. On the same day an opinion poll showed that 83 per cent of western Germans were opposed to nuclear power.
– Nuclear power has been more expensive in Germany than in France, due at least partly to the lack of economies of scale.

In the early 1990s the German Government closed all the nuclear stations in eastern Germany in response to fears over safety. There is little sign that support for nuclear power in the new Germany will be any greater than in West Germany.

• **a)** Read Fig 8.11 Why, according to the information in the rest of this section, are the pylons now less likely to be sabotaged?
  b) Were the people responsible for the sabotage justified in their actions? Explain your answer.

8.3 The Threat from the East: Nuclear Energy in Eastern Europe

We have had a procession of experts. Normally they want to investigate, and to teach us something: the kind of help that produces piles of paper. We already have plenty of proposals for improving security. What we need now is money and technology, not words.

Viktor Shevaldin, Director of Ignalina nuclear power station, Lithuania, The Economist, 24 July 1993.

The Communist regimes of eastern Europe were enthusiastic about nuclear power. It helped the eastern bloc to become self-sufficient in energy, and they could rely on the Soviet Union to provide subsidised technology, expertise and fuel. They could also ignore some safety precautions because there was no need to be accountable to the public as organised opposition to government policy was illegal. Of the former Communist states only poverty-stricken and politically isolated Albania had no nuclear energy programme.

Some eastern countries are highly dependent on nuclear energy. More than half of the reactors in the world still under construction are in eastern Europe and Russia. Thirty-six are being built, mainly in Russia and the Ukraine. The Czech Republic plans to increase the amount of its electricity generated in nuclear stations from the current 27 per cent to 60 per cent by 2005.

Nevertheless, the nuclear industry in eastern Europe and Russia is now in crisis. It faces a number of serious problems.

1 The reactors are inherently unsafe by western standards. They follow a standard Soviet design and the problem has been worsened by the withdrawal of technical support since the collapse of the Soviet Union.

2 Before the 1990s most of the region's spent nuclear fuel was sent to Soviet reprocessing plants. The new governments in the former Soviet republics are now charging market prices for reprocessing and the costs are too high for east European countries, but they have inadequate storage facilities to adequately cope with the waste.

3 Most east European governments feel they have no choice but to continue to produce nuclear energy. They have inadequate alternative generating capacity and the disruption of oil, gas and coal supplies from the former Soviet Union has worsened the situation. Only Poland has scrapped its nuclear energy programme by dismantling its partly built reactor at Zarnowiec.

4 The civil nuclear industry employs 250 000 people in Russia alone. Any threat to the nuclear power programme would threaten these jobs.

The following snapshots of the situation in three eastern European countries highlight the seriousness of the crisis in the nuclear industry.

Bulgaria

Bulgaria has one nuclear power station with six reactors at Kozloduy on the River Danube with used to produce about 30 per cent of the country's electricity. In 1991 a report by the International Atomic Energy Authority highlighted serious design flaws and poorly paid and ill-trained staff at the plant. It recommended closing down the four oldest reactors describing two as unsafe. In the event the government has agreed to close them permanently once it has developed alternative sources of energy which could take a number of years. In 1992 the two newest and safest reactors were put out of operation by a fire. Electricity was rationed to a few hours a day. The situation has been worsened by disruption in supplies of electricity from Ukraine and Moldova. The construction of a second nuclear plant at Belene was halted in 1990.

Ukraine

Ukraine has inherited 14 former Soviet nuclear reactors at five sites, one of which is Chernobyl. These reactors generate 25 per cent of the country's electricity. Since 1990 there has been a moratorium on all nuclear construction but this is expected to be withdrawn in the near future. The two remaining working reactors at Chernobyl were due to close at the end of 1993 for safety reasons. However the Ukraine Government decided to delay closure and to consider building new nuclear power stations to overcome the difficulties being posed by a cut in oil and gas supplies from Russia. Ukraine needed to purchase 45 million tonnes of oil from Russia in 1993 but only 20 million tonnes was received and with the introduction of market prices for goods being traded between the former Soviet republics the price of oil has increased drastically. Since the Chernobyl accident there has been widespread fear of nuclear power among the Ukrainian population but the need for electricity overrides this fear. Ukraine's president, Leonid Kravchuk, has said that *'Ukraine cannot do without nuclear energy, for economic reasons'*. International concerns about safety at Ukraine's reactors were heightened in early 1993 when Russian nuclear experts at a conference in Switzerland reported that a reactor in Ukraine had had its safety system switched off three times in order to boost output.

Russia

Ageing oil-fired power stations provide over 80 per cent of Russia's electricity but the country's production of oil is falling (it declined by 11 per cent in 1993 alone) while a growing proportion is exported to earn desperately needed foreign currency. The head of the government's commission on nuclear and radiation safety has stated that 15 of the country's 28 reactors should be closed as soon as possible because of the impossibility of making them meet adequate safety standards. They have no containment vessels designed to prevent radiation from escaping if the reactor developed a leak, the instrumentation is inadequate, and pipes carrying coolant from the reactor are brittle.

In 1992 the Russian Government adopted a development plan for taking nuclear power into the next century. As well as extensive modernisation of existing plants it proposes 30 new reactors by 2010. Foreign engineering companies are already competing for the expected contracts. The deputy nuclear energy minister, Yevgeny Reshetnikov, has stated that in his view *'nuclear power is indispensable, so new stations must be built and those under construction completed'*. On the other hand, President Yeltsin's ecology adviser, Alexai Yablokov, describes the plan as *'ecologically, legally, economically and politically unacceptable'*.

- Read Fig 8.12. If the 'radioactive releases into the atmosphere did not exceed internationally agreed limits' why did the accident cause such concern?

FIG 8.12   *The Independent*

Russia plays down nuclear risk

A WATER leak in a nuclear reactor near St Petersburg appears to be the cause of the release yesterday of radioactive gas that resulted in considerable concern among Russian atomic energy officials fearful of another disaster similar to Chernobyl.

The station manager at the power plant initially classified the accident at level 3 – Chernobyl was a level 7 disaster – but later amended this to a less dangerous level 2, indicating there was no significant radiation exposure either to workers on the site or nearby residents. The fire at Windscale (now Sellafield), in Cumbria, in 1957 and the accident at Three Mile Island, in Pennsylvania, in 1979 were both categorised as level 5 disasters.

The Russian reactor, one of four at the plant 60 miles from St Petersburg, is of the same type as the one that caught fire at Chernobyl in 1986. There are 16 such RBMK-type reactors at five sites in the former Soviet Union.

A preliminary investigation by Russian nuclear officials suggested there was a leak in one of the reactor's 1,690 or so fuel channels where heat is used to produce steam for the turbine generators. Water cooling the uranium dioxide fuel leaked into the surrounding graphite and caused a release of radioactive iodine into the atmosphere through the plant's air filters.

Russian nuclear officials immediately shut down the reactor and promptly informed the International Atomic Energy Agency in Vienna. The incident occurred in reactor number 3 at 2.37am local time and radioactive releases into the atmosphere did not exceed internationally agreed limits, said Evgeny Ignatenko, a spokesman for the Russian Ministry of Atomic Energy.

Since the Chernobyl accident, all the operating RBMK reactors have undergone extensive modifications to correct an inherent design fault that led to the possibility of water leaks causing the reactors to produce a power surge rather than a power reduction.

Lord Marshall of Goring, chairman of the governing board of the World Association of Nuclear Operators, said that such an acceleration of power during an incident is "what you want in a bomb but not in a reactor".

Bank to bale out Bulgaria's reactors

FOUR accident-prone nuclear reactors at Kozloduy in Bulgaria are to be overhauled and kept in operation by the European Bank for Reconstruction and Development. The EBRD says it is doing this because Bulgaria cannot afford to shut them down. But a confidential report by the World Bank for the G7 summit next week indicates that the EBRD's plans for Kozloduy are riskier and more expensive than other options.

The six pressurised-water reactors at Kozloduy produce 40 per cent of Bulgaria's electricity. All six are of the Soviet VVER type. The plant's Soviet operators left in 1989, taking the operating manuals with them. Western nuclear experts who have inspected Kozloduy have been shocked by its poor safety standards.

All the water that cools the reactors is pumped from the Danube through a long, elevated canal which is damaged in places. Failure of the electric pumps or collapse of the canal could lead to meltdown. There are few barriers separating the plant's control room from the reactors, putting operators and control equipment at risk in emergencies.

In 1991, Bulgaria bowed to Western demands and shut down the plant's two oldest reactors. Last year, an electric fire put the two most modern reactors out of action, leaving just two in operation. As a result, Bulgarians now have electricity for only a few hours a day.

In June last year, the G7 group of wealthy nations agreed to spend $700 million (about £400 million) making nuclear plants in Eastern and Central Europe safe. As part of this effort, 12 industrialised countries, including Britain and the US, pledged 115 million Ecus (£90 million) last March to a Nuclear Safety Account administered by EBRD. The bank has now allocated the first 24 million Ecus of the fund to upgrading Kozloduy.

The EBRD had originally wanted Bulgaria to shut the four oldest reactors at Kozloduy by 1996, but Bulgaria refused. Ivan Sotirov, a director of Bulgaria's National Electricity Company, called the suggestion "absurd", as Bulgaria would then have to pay for imported electricity and natural gas, and build a new gas-fired station. Bulgaria restarted one of the older reactors at Kozloduy last January, and plans to start the other soon.

Last week, the EBRD agreed to spend part of its money to keep the oldest reactors at Kozloduy running for a few more years. It will also make safety improvements to bring one of the two most modern reactors back on line by 1997. Bulgaria says that with that reactor working, and if a hydroelectric project is completed by then, it will have enough electricity to shut down the oldest reactors.

The EBRD plans to have the second most modern reactor at Kozloduy back in operation as well in 1998. By then another project to build three power stations which use waste heat from factories should also be finished, and this would allow the two next oldest reactors at Kozloduy to be shut down. The schedule depends on Bulgaria getting financing for the non-nuclear projects.

The World Bank paper calculates that the EBRD's plan would be more expensive than shutting the dangerous reactors down, at least in terms of the capital investment that concerns foreign banks. The report says that it would cost $18 billion to shut down all the high-risk plants by 1995, cancel other reactors under construction, and build power plants using natural gas to make up the shortfall – all by the year 2000. By contrast, it would cost $24 billion to meet the expected demand for electricity by making safety improvements at the high-risk plants and completing the nuclear plants under construction, while building fewer gas-powered plants.

But while the cheap "low-nuclear" scenario requires less capital investment, it would cost $3 billion more a year to run, the World Bank reports. Those costs must be paid by the plant operators mainly to buy natural gas. This makes the low-nuclear option unthinkable for countries such as Bulgaria, which must import fossil fuels, unless someone else pays for the fuel.

FIG **8.13**   *The New Scientist, 3 July 1993*

- Using Fig 8.13* to help you,
  a) describe what the countries outside eastern Europe are doing to aid the nuclear industry in eastern Europe;
  b) why do you think these countries are willing to invest as much as £400 million? Try to think of more than one reason.

* The G7 group of countries referred to in the article includes the seven leading industrialised countries in the world: USA, Canada, UK, France, Germany, Italy, and Japan.

8.4 Energy from the Wind

European environmentalists and some energy experts have been campaigning on behalf of **renewable energy** for at least the last 20 years. They have consistently argued that wind, wave, tidal, solar and geothermal energy could be cost effective if only enough money had been invested in research and development. Certainly renewable energy avoids the problems of global warming, acid rain and radioactive pollution associated with conventional sources of energy. That is not to say that all renewable energy sources are environmentally friendly. Large-scale hydroelectric schemes can be very damaging to the environment (see Section 9.1) although there is no reason why small-scale hydro schemes cannot be implemented with minimal environmental impact.

Most European governments have been relatively slow to exploit renewable energy. There are a number of reasons for this:

– a mistrust of radically different technologies;
– political pressure from those parts of the energy industry with vested interests in using conventional fuels;
– the relatively low cost of coal and oil has made renewable energy less attractive. Although renewable energy sources are generally cheap to operate there are high initial **capital costs**;
– because renewable energy is at an early stage of development some of the equipment has been unreliable or inefficient.

However, international pressure to cut pollution, the development of improved technology and the failure of nuclear power to grow as rapidly as expected have encouraged many European governments to take renewable energy more seriously in the late 1980s and 1990s. Some take it more seriously than others. For example, the current German Government funding for research and development in photovoltaic cells (which convert sunlight to electricity) is about £30 million a year – double the British Government funding for all forms of renewable energy put together.

Wind energy in particular is now proving itself in a number of areas in the world. Significant amounts of electricity are now generated using wind power in California, Hawaii, Denmark, Germany, Spain, the Netherlands and India.

During the 1980s improvements in the design of wind generators meant that wind power not only became the most cost effective form of renewable energy but it also became cost effective relative to conventional sources of energy including

Wind turbines, Goonhavern, Cornwall

coal. The most recent designs allow more power to be generated at low wind speeds and avoid the problems created by high winds. They even overcome less obvious problems such as loss of efficiency caused by dead insects accumulating on the blades.

California has led the way in wind power. The state accounts for 80 per cent of wind generation in the world, equivalent to the amount of electricity generated by a medium-sized nuclear power station. The largest wind farms (the name given to large groups of wind generators feeding the national grid) have up to 600 wind generators. With a population of 30 million in an area twice that of the UK and with the world's sixth largest economy, California has become an important model for wind energy development. Nevertheless, only one per cent of the state's electricity is generated by wind after a decade of development.

About 15 per cent of the world's wind generation is in Denmark. In the 1980s the Danish Government consistently promoted wind energy by offering reductions in tax for anybody willing to invest in new wind generators. By 1990 the government felt that the commercial value had been proven and the tax incentives were phased out. 50 000 Danes, about ten per cent of the population, have invested in wind energy and about 300 new wind turbines are being installed each year. Most Danish turbines serve individual homes, farms or small businesses although there are some larger wind farms with the largest having 100 turbines.

Although wind generators produce no atmospheric pollution there are environmental costs. The main cost is the visual impact of the turbines and a secondary one is the noise they create when they are rotating. People disagree on their visual impact. Some believe that turbines can actually enhance the landscape if they are sited carefully while others believe they are an unacceptable intrusion in a rural landscape. Clearly opinion will vary depending on the size and number of turbines involved and the characteristics of the site. Unfortunately the optimum locations – hilltops and coastal areas – are often the most attractive landscapes. Wind turbines do not create a lot of noise but local residents may be used to a quiet rural environment and the imposition of new sounds into an area can be disturbing or even stressful.

Wind farms do not need to remove a lot of land from other uses. On at least two European wind farms land is cultivated up to the base of the generator towers. There are no access roads – when access is needed for heavy equipment, temporary roads are laid across the soil. At the Velling Maersk-Taendpibe wind farm in Denmark only three per cent of the land has been taken out of agricultural production.

In the UK it has been estimated that 10 000 wind turbines would be needed to generate 20 per cent of the country's electricity and that is why the visual impact of wind generators is such a potential problem. On the other hand, environmentalists argue that wind energy development should go hand in hand with extensive **energy conservation** measures so less electricity would be needed. The largest wind

development in the UK to date is the Penrhyddlan and Llidiartywaun Wind Farms which are adjacent to each other in Powys, mid-Wales. Together they have 103 turbines.

By 1993 Denmark, Germany and the UK were the leading European investors in wind energy. The European Wind Energy Association, which represents companies involved in designing and building wind generators, hopes that wind power will provide ten per cent of Europe's current electricity needs by 2030. It hopes that some of the environmental problems associated with having large numbers of wind farms will be overcome by the construction of offshore wind turbines, perhaps built on floating platforms.

- Study the photograph of the wind farm at Goonhavern in Cornwall. Evaluate its impact on the landscape.

- Using evidence in this chapter and any other ideas you may have suggest why Denmark is the leading European country for wind power.

- List the possible costs and benefits of offshore wind farms.

- Describe the pattern of wind speeds shown in Fig 8.14. Which EU countries not mentioned in this section could also particularly benefit from wind power?

- Wave power, unlike wind power, is in the early stages of development. Read Fig 8.15.

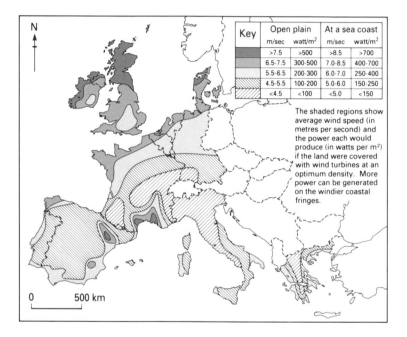

Key	Open plain		At a sea coast	
	m/sec	watt/m²	m/sec	watt/m²
	>7.5	>500	>8.5	>700
	6.5-7.5	300-500	7.0-8.5	400-700
	5.5-6.5	200-300	6.0-7.0	250-400
	4.5-5.5	100-200	5.0-6.0	150-250
	<4.5	<100	<5.0	<150

The shaded regions show average wind speed (in metres per second) and the power each would produce (in watts per m²) if the land were covered with wind turbines at an optimum density. More power can be generated on the windier coastal fringes.

0   500 km

FIG 8.14   *Europe's Wind Resource*

FIG 8.15   *The Guardian, 18 October 1993*

Glad tidings for renewable energy as Dounreay hosts world's first wave power station

THE world's first wave power station in the open sea is to be stationed off Donreay in Scotland next year and will be producing enough electricity within 12 months to light a large village.

Funding comes from the European Community after years of government cold-shouldering.

Until now schemes have been shore-based and designed primarily for research but this one, called Osprey, will stand in 18

metres of water a kilometre out and not only harvest the larger waves, which produce higher outputs, but also gain power with waves from any other direction.

The decision to go ahead with Dounreay and two other pilot schemes – at Islay in the Inner Hebrides and one by the Portuguese on the island of Pico in the Azores – will be announced this month by the EC which is putting £1.15 million into the three schemes.

The Dounreay scheme, which will feed into the national grid, will be two megawatts. It is called an oscillating water column.

As the waves rise air is pushed through an air turbine and sucked back again as the wave falls. The turbine has been designed by Professor Alan Wells, of Queen's University, Belfast, who has collaborated with a Scottish company Applied Research and Technology Ltd. This is believed

to have the backing of British Steel, GEC, Scottish Hydro, and AEA Technology.

Osprey will use the infrastructure created to service the prototype fast breeder reactor at Dounreay which is being closed down by the Government on the same site. It provides hope for hundreds of highly-skilled people whose jobs are disappearing as the nuclear element of the Dounreay site is run down.

Tilting at noisy windmills

M R ROGERS (Letters, July 12) collates modern wind farms with "beautiful traditional structures, such as windmills, sailing boats and gliders". He creates a charming picture of elegant, modern windmills, quietly whirling away, creating endless, pollution-free energy, Oh! If only it were so.

The widely-held assumption that wind farms are pollution-free is a myth and needs to be scratched. They are massive and visually out of scale with British countryside. But the over-whelming problem is the noise pollution.

There are residents within a radius of one and a half miles of Llandinam and Llangwyrafon, to name but two of the so-called wind farms which are proliferating in Wales and the West Country, who might dispute Mr Rogers'

romantic assertion. The lives of people in these areas are becoming lives of misery because of the indescribable and persistent noise caused by these massive industrial electric generating machines.

Make no mistake about it. They are an industrial intrusion on the rural environment and, as they grow in number more people will be made aware of the fact. The constant thrumming of the turbines is unremitting, 24 hours a day, seven days a week. The result is sleepless nights and nerve shattering days.

If Mr Rogers and those of like mind would care to spend a week near a wind farm, he will be glad to return to polluted London, to get a night's sleep.

One other point emerges Property values near wind farms have plummeted. Any one care to buy one of a selection of country residences; cheap but noisy?

FIG 8.16 *The Guardian, 19 July 1993*

a) Why is the EU funding this scheme?
b) Why are local people likely to welcome the scheme?
c) Using evidence in this chapter and your own ideas make a list of the costs and benefits of wave power compared with wind power.

- Read Fig 8.16.
  a) Do you sympathise with the letter writer? Explain your answer.
  b) Write a second letter in reply repudiating the points made in the letter.

Smoke from Industry, Duisburg in Germany

8.5 Global Warming

There is now almost unanimous agreement by scientists that the carbon dioxide being pumped into the Earth's atmosphere from the burning of fossil fuels is raising the temperature. The rate of that temperature increase, the variations in change between different parts of the world and the impacts of those changes are much more difficult to predict (see Section 9.6). However, there is enough agreement that global warming is a major threat for European politicians and other decision makers to seriously consider ways of reducing carbon dioxide emissions.

There are two types of policy which European decision makers are considering.

1 A tax on fossil fuels designed to encourage greater use of non-polluting sources of energy and greater energy efficiency. Such a tax has become known as a 'carbon tax'.

2 Setting maximum legal emissions of carbon dioxide to encourage the development and installation of technology designed to reduce emissions.

Carbon Tax

The EU Commission first unveiled its proposal for a carbon tax in 1992, one month before the Earth Summit meeting in Rio de Janeiro. It suggested that the tax would be phased in over a period of time but by the year 2000 fossil fuels would be taxed at a rate of $10 per barrel of oil. It said that the introduction of the tax would be dependent on the United States and Japan implementing similar action. The members of the Commission only managed to reach agreement on the tax by dropping proposals, which some members opposed, to enforce tough new laws on energy efficiency for vehicles, buildings and appliances. The main aim of the tax was to stabilise carbon dioxide emissions at their 1990 level by 2000, an aim which was reinforced by one of the main clauses in the Climate Change Convention agreed by most of the world's governments at the Earth Summit a month later.

The only country opposing the principle of a carbon tax is Britain, although some of the poorer southern EU countries want to be partly exempted from the tax for at least the first few years. By the middle of 1993 Britain's opposition to the principle of a tax, and disagreements between other countries on precisely how a tax should be implemented had prevented agreement within the EU.

In fact the aim of pegging CO_2 emissions at their 1990 level by 2000 is not a difficult one to achieve. For example, Britain's CO_2 emissions have declined by 16 per cent from a peak of 178 million tonnes of carbon in 1973 to a current level of about 150 million tonnes. Over the same period German emissions have declined by ten per cent and French emissions by about 35 per cent. The decline of heavy manufacturing industry, economic recession, the growth of nuclear energy and more energy efficient buildings, vehicles and machinery have all helped to cause this decline. Nevertheless, industrial countries are still generally very wasteful in their use of energy and there is great potential for reducing CO_2 emissions further. Many experts claim that emissions could be cut by a further 20 per cent simply by introducing energy efficiency measures which would also reduce costs for industry and householders. Unless policies designed to cut CO_2 output are implemented during the 1990s it is likely that CO_2 output will start to rise again especially with the rapid increase in the use of cars in most European countries and with the present commitment by some European governments to new road building.

There are other reasons why European countries cannot be complacent about cutting CO_2 emissions. The 1992 Climate Change Convention has a second key clause which states that countries intend to keep concentrations of CO_2 in the global atmosphere at levels below those which will cause serious disruption to the climate. The problem with this is that nobody knows what level of CO_2 concentration would cause serious climatic disruption. Rapid industrialisation and population growth in the developing countries means that global CO_2 concentrations are likely to go on rising. On current trends the Intergovernmental Panel on Climate Change (the world's think-tank on global warming) estimates that mean global temperatures will rise between 1.5°C and 4.5°C within the next century. There is also evidence that sudden and potentially catastrophic climatic changes could occur at lower levels of CO_2 than those predicted for the later twenty-first century.

There is disagreement between economists over the impact a $10 per tonne carbon tax would have. Some believe it would only make a difference if the revenue raised by the tax was all put into energy conservation and the development of alternative sources of energy. They argue that the tax itself will not increase industry's or householders' costs enough to persuade them to invest in energy-saving measures.

Fig 8.17 is based on one prediction of the impact of a carbon tax on the types of energy used for generating

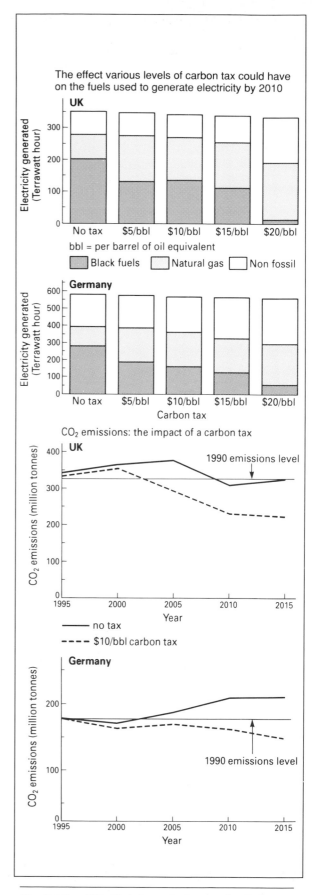

FIG 8.17 *CO_2 Emissions: the Impact of a Carbon Tax*

electricity in the UK and Germany by 2010. Both the German and British electricity generating industries are currently very dependent on coal (and lignite in the case of Germany). The experts who have made these projections also predict that it will be less costly for Germany to achieve a cut in CO_2 output than for the UK. They found that a $5 per barrel tax would be enough to achieve a 20 per cent reduction in CO_2 output from 1990 levels in Germany. To achieve a similar cut in CO_2 emissions in the UK a $15 tax would be needed. This is mainly because a significant reduction in CO_2 output could be achieved in Germany by switching from lignite (which produces a high level of CO_2 emissions) to natural gas. The coal burned in Britain produces smaller amounts of CO_2.

- Critically evaluate the methods used to illustrate the data in Fig 8.17.

- Compare the effects of different levels of carbon tax in the UK and Germany on the methods used to generate electricity.

- Compare the impact of a $10 carbon tax on CO_2 emissions in the UK and Germany.

- Assuming these projections are accurate do you think a carbon tax should be introduced? If so, what level of tax should be imposed? Use the data to help justify your answer.

- List the costs and benefits which could be created by a $10 carbon tax.

- Why is it very difficult to accurately predict the impact of a carbon tax in 2010?

8.6 Acid Rain

'Last year so many trees died that the army was called in to fell them,' he said. 'I brought an elderly German couple up here, and the old man broke down and cried. He kept saying how beautiful the forest

Spruce Forest Killed by Acid Rain, Czech Republic

used to be. He couldn't believe how it has been destroyed.'

We turned off the road onto a rough track. 'Climb up there,' he said, 'then you'll understand what acid rain is all about.' On the way up I nearly fell into a deep gulley gouged out of the mountainside by water rushing down the treeless slopes. From a high ridge I saw a forest of stark, grey, dead tree trunks extending as far as the eye could see. The feeling of desolation was overpowering. If the chimney smoke has had this effect on trees, what could it be doing to human health, I wondered?

A description of the effects of acid rain, in South-West Poland, National Geographic Magazine, June 1991.

Emissions of Sulphur Dioxide (SO_2) and Nitrogen Oxides (NO_X) from the burning of fossil fuels (mainly coal and oil) can combine with water vapour in the atmosphere to produce acidified precipitation or 'acid rain' (see Fig 8.18, page 208). Acid rain causes a number of environmental problems:

- acidified lakes and rivers cause damage to aquatic ecosystems;
- damage to forests. The damage caused by the acid rain increases the vulnerability of trees to pests and diseases;
- damage to stonework in buildings. The rate at which the stone is weathered is greatly accelerated;

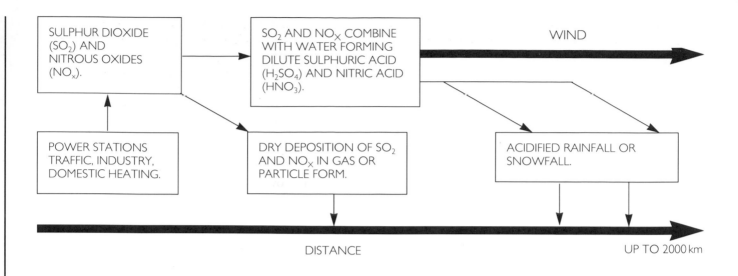

FIG 8.18   *Formation of Acid Rain*

– intensified **leaching** of soils. Acidified rainwater percolating through soil can release toxic metals such as aluminium from the soil. Aluminium washed into lakes and rivers can kill fish. Essential nutrients needed by vegetation may also be leached out of the soil.

Parts of eastern Europe have suffered particularly badly from acid rain. Reliance on brown coal or lignite which has a high sulphur content, combined with inadequate pollution control in the state-owned heavy industries which dominated the eastern economies, meant that emissions of SO_2 were particularly high.

Much of Europe's acid rain is caused by the burning of coal in power stations. The problem can be tackled in two ways.

FIG 8.19   *Sulphur Emissions*

Sulphur emissions (in kilotonnes SO_2) for Eastern European countries 1985 and 2000

	1985	2000 Scenario A	2000 Scenario B	
			Unabated	Maximum abatement
Albania	121	167	78	38
Bulgaria	1070	1555	152	11
Czech and Slovak Republic	3150	2513	1743	114
Former East Germany	5360	5048	3892	431
Hungary	1404	1529	1018	128
Poland	4300	4165	3427	425
Romania	1800	3261	2544	232
Yugoslavia	1500	2393	1093	124
Total	**18 705**	**20 631**	**13 947**	**1503**
Change	**–**	**+10%**	**–25%**	**–93%**

1   Reduce the amount of coal burned to generate electricity.

2   Reduce the emissions of SO_2 and NO_X by installing equipment designed to remove these pollutants before they enter the atmosphere.

In the 1980s two international agreements on acid rain were introduced to tackle the problem. The Helsinki Protocol signed in 1985 was concerned with SO_2 emissions and the Sofia Protocol signed in 1988 was concerned with NO_X emissions. The Helsinki Protocol called for a 30 per cent reduction in SO_2 emissions by 1993 compared with the 1980 level. When the protocol expired in 1993, negotiations began on a new agreement. This new agreement had to take into account the enormous changes which had taken place in eastern Europe since the 1985 protocol was signed. The emergence of the new democracies in eastern Europe has provided the opportunity to tackle the particularly serious problem of acid rain in eastern Europe.

Fig 8.19 shows a number of different forecasts of SO_2 emissions in eastern Europe in the year 2000. Scenario A is a forecast based on the policies of the former Communist governments and assumes no emission control measures would have been introduced. Scenario B takes into account the transition to market economies. Scenario B assumes that heavy industries will decline and energy efficient modern industries will take their place. In the case of Scenario B two forecasts are shown. 'Unabated' assumes no emission reduction measures are implemented while 'Maximum abatement' shows the maximum feasible reduction using current technology. The table indicates the enormous scale of reductions possible during the 1990s.

Target Loads for Acid Deposition

The 1993 negotiations aimed at replacing the Helsinki Protocol were based on the concept of critical loads. Critical loads refer to the maximum input of acid pollution which can be tolerated by ecosystems without causing environmental damage.

To achieve these critical loads across Europe very large reductions in pollution would be necessary. In some countries emissions would have to be eliminated completely. Because of the scale of reductions needed to achieve the critical loads they are only seen as a long-term aim. Scientists introduced 'target loads' as a basis for the 1993 negotiations. These target loads have now been agreed by ten European countries.

Early in the negotiations it had been agreed that target loads should be set so that the gap between 1980 levels of pollution and the critical load should be cut by 50 per cent. But scientists and civil servants from 24 European countries decided that even this target was too expensive. Eleven areas with the most damaged soils, forests and lakes were exempted from the targets because the sensitivity of these areas to acid pollution were lowering the critical loads which formed the basis of the negotiations. These areas include parts of Norway, Sweden, Germany and the Netherlands.

The negotiators decided that Europe as a whole would benefit as much by relaxing the targets in these areas and by giving more protection in other areas. The rest of Europe is now aiming for a 60 per cent reduction in the gap between 1980 levels and critical loads. Britain in particular would have had to cut its SO_2 emissions to 11 per cent of the 1980 levels because much of its pollution falls as acid rain on the sensitive areas of Scandinavia removed from the targets. The cost of these cuts would have been about £1200 million. Under the new targets it needs to cut emissions to 21 per cent of the 1980 level at a cost of £760 million.

If these targets are approved by European governments they will be enforced by the year 2000 in western Europe and 2005 in eastern Europe.

Some of the target reduction in SO_2 emissions can be met by switching from coal as a fuel in power stations to natural gas, nuclear energy and renewable energy. The rest of the reduction will have to be met by installing new technology to clean up emissions from power stations and other industry.

Methods of cleaning power station emissions have included Flue-gas Desulphurisation to remove SO_2 and Selective Catalytic Reduction and Low NO_X Burners to remove NO_X. All three are expensive. Flue-gas desulphurisation alone increases the cost of generating electricity from coal by between ten per cent and 15 per cent. However, one company based in Britain and the USA (Nalco-Fuel Tech or NFT) has developed a new method of removing NO_X which involves injecting urea into the furnace flames. The necessary equipment is cheap to install although it is more expensive in its long-run up-keep. However, its low capital cost is particularly attractive to eastern European companies who want to cut emissions from dated power stations and factories. The equipment has been shown to cut emissions of NO_X by about 50 per cent. NFT now has orders to install the system throughout western and eastern Europe and has more recently developed a similar system for reducing SO_2 emissions which involves injecting a slurry of slime and urea into the flames. Ironically, by doing nothing to cut NO_X and SO_2 emissions over recent decades eastern Europe is now in a position to benefit from much cheaper technologies.

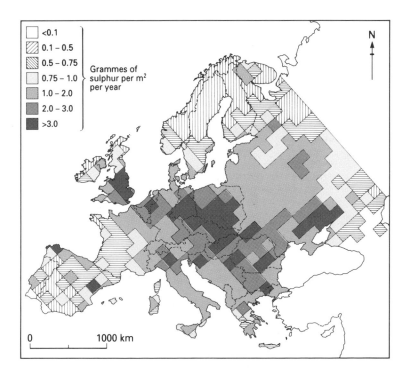

FIG 8.20 *Sulphur Deposition Target Loads, 1990*

8.7 Using Energy More Efficiently

In some western European countries, such as Britain, energy conservation has been given a relatively low priority. More thought has been given to how future demand for energy should be met than to how that demand could be reduced in order to reduce the environmental impact and cost of energy consumption. However, in other countries there has been much greater government support for research and development in energy conservation. It is possible to build a house which needs no external supply of energy at all. Three countries in particular stand out – Switzerland, Germany and the Netherlands. One of these can be looked at in more detail to illustrate the type of measures which can be implemented.

Energy Conservation in the Netherlands

In the Netherlands the official government policy of reducing fossil fuel consumption has led to the encouragement of both renewable energy and energy conservation. Under the Sustainable Building Programme adopted in 1990 higher levels of efficiency are demanded in all new buildings. Also, several Dutch energy companies now offer financial incentives for customers to invest in energy efficiency. One power company, West Friesland, gave all their electricity consumers free energy-saving light bulbs. This is seen as a profitable policy by the power company because it reduces the need for expensive investment in new power stations.

There are a number of 'showcase' examples of energy-efficient buildings in the Netherlands including the following examples.

The Town of Schiedam

Schiedam has a population of 70 000. The local council enforces particularly strict energy conservation regulations for all new buildings in the town. A new house with 100 m² of floor space must be designed to use no more than 7000 kwh (kilowatt-hours) of energy per year. By comparison, the average new house in the Netherlands uses about 11 000 kwh per year, but even this is a substantial improvement on earlier houses. The average new house in Schiedam is using 80 per cent less energy than an equivalent new house in 1975. These improvements have been achieved by improved roof, wall and floor insulation and improved double-glazing. The drawback is that these measures add about £3000 to the cost of a new house. Nevertheless other Dutch councils are now introducing similar building regulations.

Ecolonia

At the time of writing this scheme is yet to be built, but it is intended to be a national showcase for energy-efficient housing design. There will be about 100 dwellings divided into nine groups. Each group will stress one particular aspect of low energy use. For example, three groups will aim for exceptionally low energy consumption for heating, one of which will have exceptional levels of insulation, and one will have solar panels. Another group will aim for very low electricity consumption by using, for example, photovoltaic cells which convert sunlight into electricity. Another group will use building materials which need minimum amounts of energy to be produced.

Castricum

Castricum is 40 km north of Amsterdam. A house was completed here in 1989 with support from national and local government. It is at the end of a street of outwardly similar terraced houses but this one is not connected to mains electricity. The house supplies most of its own electricity using photovoltaic cells. Additional power can be supplied from storage batteries or from a mini gas-fired combined heat and power unit which both heats the house and can generate electricity very efficiently. Even some trees have been planted nearby which will reduce the house's contribution to global warming. Over the lifetime of the building the trees will take roughly the same amount of carbon out of the atmosphere as will have been produced during construction work and by the burning of gas in the house. All the household appliances have been selected to use minimum amounts of electricity. The Castricum house uses 900 kwh of electricity per year compared with 3000 in a conventional house.

- Evaluate Fig 8.21 as a method of comparing energy policies.

- How effective, according to Fig 8.21, is energy conservation?

1 Describe the extent of the decline of the western European coal industry and explain why the decline has occurred.

2 Describe the extent of the problems facing the eastern European energy industry.

3 Analyse the reasons for the contrasting levels of dependence on nuclear power found in different European countries.

4 'It is vital that western European countries financially aid eastern European countries to improve the safety of their reactors or to phase out nuclear power.' Discuss.

5 'Wind power should be used as an alternative to nuclear power.' Discuss the extent to which you agree with this opinion.

6 Evaluate the different measures which are being used and which could be used to reduce emissions of carbon dioxide and sulphur dioxide.

7 'Energy conservation is the only really satisfactory way of reducing the environmental impacts of energy production.' Discuss.

FIG 8.21 *Energy Policies*

	Visual	Health	Ecology	Climate
Coal	Moderate	Bad	Bad	Awful
Oil	Light	Moderate	Bad	Bad
Gas	Light	Light	Light	Moderate
Nuclear	Light	Modrate	Good	Light
Solar	Bad	Good	Good	Good
Wind	Bad	Good	Good	Good
Wave Power	Bad	Good	Moderate	Good
Tidal	Bad	Good	Bad	Good
Biomass	Bad	Moderate	Bad	Good
Energy Conservation	Good	Good	Good	Good

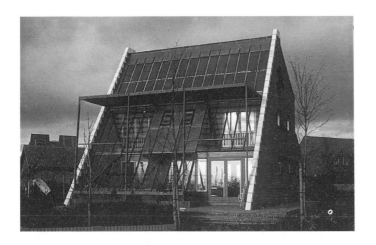

Solar House, Milton Keynes

Glossary

capital costs	The costs of purchasing plant and equipment and the costs of construction.
energy conservation	Using energy more efficiently by reducing wastage.
fast-breeder reactor	A type of nuclear reactor which uses fuel containing plutonium, and which produces more plutonium than it uses.
indigenous reserves	Energy resources located within a particular country. The term reserves is usually used to refer to fossil fuel resources including coal, oil and gas.
leaching	The process of nutrients being carried downwards through soil by percolating water.
public enquiry	A hearing at which the arguments for and against a building development are heard by a government appointed Inspector. On the basis of the evidence received at the enquiry the Inspector makes a recommendation to the government on whether or not the development should proceed.
renewable energy	A source of energy which is not finite or limited, such as wind power or tidal power.

The Rivers and the Seas: Threatened Environments

KEY
IDEAS

9.1 The construction of dams and barrages on a river can have major environmental, economic, social and political repercussions. The Gabcikovo scheme on the River Danube is an example of a renewable energy scheme which is highly damaging environmentally, economically, socially and politically.

9.2 Many rivers suffer from pollution and over-management. In the case of the Rhine these problems are now being tackled.

9.3 Wetlands, both on inland flood plains and in coastal locations, are the most seriously threatened environments in Europe. They are in danger from pollution, water extraction, farming, reclamation and other human activities. The Danube Delta is one such wetland under threat.

9.4 Irrigation and water supply schemes in the more arid regions of Europe threaten river and wetland ecosystems. Such schemes also bring social and economic benefits and costs. The Acheloos River diversion in Greece is one such scheme.

9.5 European seas such as the Baltic, North Sea and the Mediterranean are facing a variety of environmental problems. The Mediterranean in particular suffers from the effects of coastal urban, industrial, and agricultural development, tourism and river pollution.

9.6 Global warming poses an environmental, economic and social threat to the Mediterranean region although its effects are difficult to predict in detail.

The Building of the Gabcikovo Dam on the Danube, November 1989

9.1 Using Rivers for Energy: the Gabcikovo Dam on the River Danube

Two deer dive into the woods as an elderly man drags out a tree which died of thirst. 'I can't believe what they have done to a fisherman's and naturalists' paradise,' he says bitterly.

Christopher Dodd, The Damming of the Danube, The Guardian, 12 February 1993.

In 1978 the Communist Governments of Czechoslovakia and Hungary began construction work on a joint project to dam and divert the River Danube. The purpose of the scheme was to generate hydroelectricity. Austria was to help finance the scheme and, in return, was to receive most of the electricity. It was to be the biggest project of its kind ever seen in Europe and represented a major commitment of resources. Yet by the early 1990s the new democratic government in Hungary had withdrawn from the project and the dam had become the centre of an international political conflict.

The original scheme had involved two dams on the Danube, one at Gabcikovo on the border between the former Czechoslovakia and Hungary and one at Nagymaros in Hungary. Opposition to the scheme within Hungary on environmental and economic grounds helped to unify opposition to the Communists during the 1980s. Wearing the badge of the Danube Circle, an organisation opposed to the dams on environmental grounds, became a way of showing opposition to the government.

FIG 9.1 *The Hungarian Quarterly*

Different attitudes to the Gabcikovo Dam

	Hungarian Government	Slovaki Government
Perspective	Long-term perspective	Short-term perspective
Posterity	Care for future generations, their life supporting systems and basic natural resources.	Does not contemplate the situation of generations to come. 'They should care for themselves, as we do for ourselves' mentality.
Risk-management	Adoption of the precautionary principle regulating prudent behaviour in circumstances of uncertainty: according to this principle, lack of full and final scientific proof of future damage is not an entitlement to go ahead; projects should be stopped even, if there is 'only' a high probability not certainty, of damage.	Belief in the technical solution: man is master of the universe, whatever he destroys he can correct, nothing is irreversible. Mere likelihood of immense future loss is not a reason to endure a qualitatively smaller, but certain present loss.
Market economy or else	Goods with no market value (scenery, the presence of irreplaceable archeological sites, rich biodiversity) are nevertheless valuable, they deserve sacrifices, including financial ones.	Market economy dictates reasonable behaviour, tradeable services like energy and navigational improvement have priority over symbolic values.
Survival versus growth	The goal is balance with nature, sustainable existence (not necessarily development in terms of growth).	The goal is modernisation in industrial terms, growth, expansion, domination over nature.

At its peak the Hungarian Green movement, which drew much of its support from people bitterly opposed to the dams, could muster thousands of protesters to demonstrate outside the government buildings in Budapest or to link arms along the banks of the Danube in shows of defiance unusual in Communist eastern Europe. The Green movement became the centre of the movement for greater democracy which was to lead to the collapse of the Communist government in 1989 and to the new government's withdrawal from the project.

Meanwhile the new democratic government in Czechoslovakia decided to continue with the Gabcikovo dam without the Nagymaros dam and this policy was maintained by the Slovakian Government following the split in the country at the beginning of 1993. When the Hungarian Government withdrew in 1989, 90 per cent of the construction work on the Czechoslovakian part of the project had already been completed. In any case, the Slovakian Government was keen to acquire its own reliable source of energy, partly so it could become less reliant on Russian oil supplies. It also believed the scheme would accelerate economic development in the region.

Slovak nationalists argued that outside opposition to the scheme was simply an attempt to prevent the new state from acquiring its own independent energy supplies. This issue is further complicated by the fact that 580 000 ethnic Hungarians live within Slovakia and most of these in the region around the Danube diversion. Slovakia's leading water engineer described opponents of the scheme as *'paid agents working for the Hungarian Government'*. Some of the Slovakian Hungarians meanwhile accused the Slovak Government of using ecological disruption caused by the dam to 'ethnically cleanse' the region by forcing the Hungarians out of their homeland. This is unlikely to be true but it did strengthen Hungarian feelings against the dam and deepened the political dispute over the scheme. Ethnic Hungarians in the area already feel bitter about some of the policies of the new Slovakian Government such as the decision that all villages in the area must be called by their Slovakian name.

It can be argued that Slovakia's determination to continue with the project and Hungary's determination to halt it are simply the result of entirely different attitudes to development (see Fig 9.1, page 215).

The Slovakian scheme involves building a barrage across the Danube and diverting 90–95 per cent of the water in the river into a 60 km² reservoir (see Fig 9.2). From there the water flows for 25 km along a huge concrete channel to the hydroelectric power station at Gabcikovo and then a further few kilometres to where it rejoins the Danube.

Opposition to the Gabcikovo scheme is based largely on environmental grounds but economic, engineering, political and legal arguments are also involved.

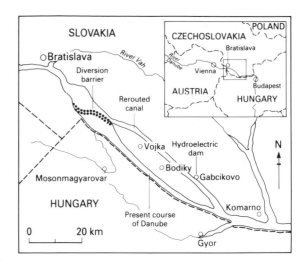

Fig 9.2 *Location of the Gabcikovo Dam*

Arguments Against the Gabcikovo Scheme

Environmental

– Adequate studies into the environmental impacts of the river diversion were not carried out by either Czechoslovakia or Hungary before construction work began.

– Reduction of the water flow in the Danube by 90–95 per cent has destroyed the aquatic ecosystems in the main river channel and in the side-channels and ox-bow lakes alongside the river. The **water table** has also been lowered in the surrounding **flood plain** (see Fig 9.3). The flood plain contained diverse **wetland** ecosystems fed by a high water table and dependent on regular flooding. The World Wide Fund for Nature estimates that 200 species of fish, 55 species of bird, red deer, otters and beavers are all threatened. The Slovak authorities claim that they are overcoming this problem by pumping water from the canal on to the flood plain but this will provide an occasional deluge instead of a steady supply of **groundwater** or throughflow.

– Studies suggest that the new reservoir and canal will not provide an attractive habitat for wildlife.

– The lowering of the water table is causing wells in the area to dry up. The Hungarian authorities claim that drinking water supplies to four million people are threatened. In some Slovak villages the authorities had to hastily lay new water mains to maintain supplies while the villagers themselves had to pay to have their houses connected to the mains. The lowering of the water table is also harming wheat and fruit farms and could damage the foundation of buildings.

– Heavy metals and other pollution in the Danube will settle in the sediment on the bed of the new reservoir where the water will move more slowly. These polluted sediments will then contaminate groundwater which is used for drinking water in both Hungary and Slovakia.

– The new concrete channel carrying the diverted water is visually intrusive. The walls of the channel are as high as a church tower.

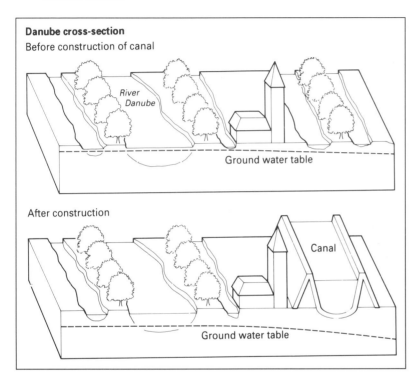

Danube cross-section
Before construction of canal

River Danube

Ground water table

After construction

Canal

Ground water table

FIG 9.3 *The Impact of the Danube Diversion on the Water Table*

Economic

– The scheme will prove to be a very inefficient way of producing electricity. The construction of new coal-fired power stations or the improvement of existing stations would be a more economic option. Alternatively, investment could have been allocated to energy conservation. It is worth pointing out that the European Bank for Reconstruction and Development has indicated its unwillingness to finance schemes like Gabcikovo because of their negative environmental impacts yet they are interested in assisting less damaging energy schemes.

– The power station will at maximum only generate eight per cent of Slovakia's present energy production.

– Where the water table has been lowered revenues from agriculture and forestry will suffer. To counteract the effect of reduced water availability considerable investment will be needed in irrigation.

– The argument that the scheme will assist economic development in the region is not very convincing. The unspoilt nature of the area offers possibilities for tourism development. Tourism would be more likely to foster an increase in investment in the area.

– It is true that the canal improves the navigability of the Danube for boats but the existing channel was adequate and could have been improved by far cheaper river management solutions.

Engineering

– The Gabcikovo Dam lies 600 m from a geological fault and the dam has not been designed to withstand possible tremors in the area.

– The dam, canal and power station have not been built to adequate safety standards.

Political and Legal

– The Slovakian scheme probably breaches international law on two counts. It breaches the 'principle of equitable utilisation', which stipulates that countries should use an international river in 'an equitable and reasonable manner', by diverting 90 per cent of the river flow and causing ecological damage in Hungary. For the same reason it probably also contravenes the 'principle of good neighbourliness' which states that countries should not carry out activities which have a significant harmful effect on the territory of another country. However, it could also be argued that Hungary's unilateral withdrawal from the scheme in 1989 was a violation of the treaty between the two countries which formed the basis of the joint construction work.

– A number of agreements determine the border between the former Czechoslovakia and Hungary as the *talweg*, or main navigation line, in the Danube. The new canal has the effect of changing the location of the talweg and therefore the border. Hungary is worried that this could sow the seeds of a future border dispute between the two countries.

– The scheme is being used as a way of expressing Slovak nationalism and an excuse for the new country to 'flex its muscles'.

The dispute between the two countries reached a peak towards the end of 1992 when the barrage across the Danube neared completion. The European Commission in Brussels acted as a mediator in an attempt to find a compromise but the parties could only agree to refer the problem to the International Court of Justice in The Hague. In the meantime they agreed to abide by the findings of an international panel of experts. The problem was that the experts failed to agree. The Slovak member of the panel wanted to divide the flow 50/50 between the Danube and the canal while the Hungarian member wanted no water at all to be diverted. The rest of the panel from the Netherlands, Denmark, Germany and Austria recommended that a maximum of 25 per cent should be diverted into the canal. They argued that by allowing some water diversion shipping could be transferred to the canal allowing the Danube to return to a more natural state. However, this would only enable two of the eight turbines in the power station to operate throwing the economics of the scheme into even more doubt.

As the barrage across the Danube neared completion police patrols were increased by the Slovak authorities in response to sabotage attempts and bomb threats. All visitors to the site were turned away.

- List the reasons why the Slovak Government decided to continue with the Gabcikovo scheme despite all of its drawbacks.

9.2 Open Sewer or River for Wildlife?: the Rhine

The Rhine drainage basin contains about 20 per cent of the EU's population and an even larger proportion of its industry. As a result the river has suffered from serious pollution. The four Rhine countries (Netherlands, Germany, France and Switzerland) have spent large sums of money, particularly since the 1970s, on attempts to reduce the quantities of toxic chemicals, heavy metals and sewage entering the river. Nevertheless, lead, phenols, arsenic, cadmium, PCBs, mercury and other pollutants continue to enter the river.

One incident in particular drew the attention of Europe to the problem facing the Rhine. In 1986 following a fire in a warehouse at the Sandoz chemical factory near Basel in Switzerland more than 30 tonnes of pesticides, fungicides, chemical dyes and mercury entered the river. Firemen had used hoses to control the fire and the water had washed the chemicals from exploding drums into the river. In one night the accident released more chemicals into the Rhine than were normally released in a year. Half a million fish were killed and many others were heavily contaminated by mercury. Snails, shrimps, water fleas, plankton and other components of the aquatic ecosystem were destroyed. The Rhine is used for drinking water and supplies had to be temporarily halted to surrounding towns and villages. Fears were also expressed that the pollutants had permeated into the groundwater around the river creating a longer-term pollution problem and that the Wadden Sea (the area of the North Sea into which the Rhine drains) would also be badly affected.

Although the Sandoz fire was clearly very serious, perhaps of even greater concern was the information which emerged after the accident. Scientists monitoring the progress of the pollution down the Rhine found high concentrations of atrazine – a herbicide which had not been stored in the Sandoz warehouse. Only later did Ciba-Geigy, a chemical company, admit to a separate spillage which they claim had occurred the day before the Sandoz fire. Within a month 12 major pollution incidents were reported involving herbicides, solvents and PVCs. The publicity caused by the Sandoz fire had brought to light the fact that significant spillages were a commonplace occurrence. Greenpeace claimed that Ciba-Geigy had in fact been releasing atrazine into the Rhine for over a year.

To some extent pollution control measures taken over the last two decades have helped. In many cases industry has been successful in reducing routine pollution levels. Major pollutants such as cadmium, mercury and toxic organic compounds have declined. For example, the large chemicals company, BASF, has cut pollution from its plant at Ludwigshafen in Germany by 90 per cent over the last 20

The Rhine, Ludwigshafen

years. Most cities on the river now have adequate sewage treatment and as a result oxygen levels in the water have significantly improved.

However, little is known about the effects of many of the remaining pollutants and many pollutants are not even monitored. Controlling emissions from specific sources such as factories can be relatively straightforward even if it is expensive (although as the Sandoz events have indicated controlling accidental or illegal emissions is much more difficult). A greater problem can be pollutants carried into the river by runoff from urban areas and fields. Widely used solvents and fertilisers, for example, enter the Rhine in this way and they are difficult to control. These pollutants from diffuse sources prevent some of the emission targets set by the Rhine countries from being met. An added problem is that the sediments on the river bed are also heavily polluted. When the river is dredged by the Dutch authorities to maintain an adequate depth for shipping the sediment now has to be stored in specially built sealed dumps rather than spread on the land.

Although it is the problem of pollution in the Rhine that has received the most publicity, another problem is the flow of water in the river. Attempts to control the flow on a large scale began in the nineteenth century. Until then for most of its length the Rhine meandered its way across a wide flood plain supporting woods and water meadows. In places the river split into a number of continually changing channels. Engineers began controlling the river by constraining it into single fixed channels. This allowed the river to be used by larger boats, prevented flooding and allowed building along the banks. In the process the ecological richness of the river was lost by the destruction of natural habitats. More recently in the twentieth century the construction of giant locks and hydroelectric schemes on the Rhine have created an increasingly artificial river.

The channelisation has also had the effect of reducing the river's length by about 100 km and increasing the speed of flow by 30 per cent.

This means that the power of the river to erode its bed and banks has been increased. As the bed of the river has become deeper so the surrounding water table has been lowered causing wells to dry up and destroying the natural vegetation of the flood plain. The time it takes for the peak flow caused by the spring snow melt in the Alps to reach areas in the lower Rhine has been halved to 30 hours. The peak flow in the Rhine can now coincide with the peak flow in some of the Rhine's tributaries like the Neckar, creating a

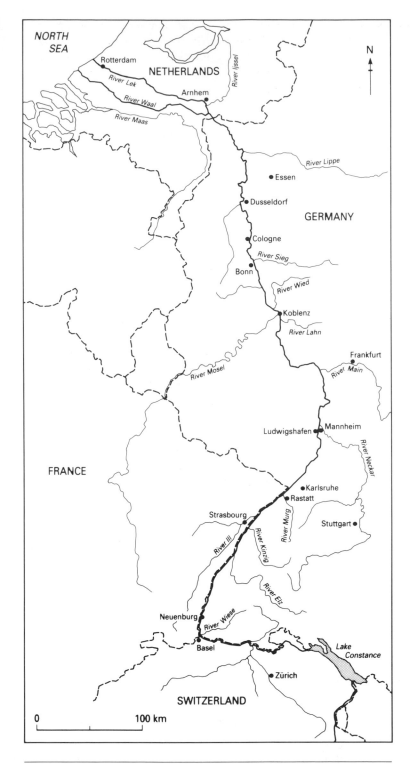

FIG 9.4   *The Rhine*

dropped in favour of encouraging ecological variety in the valley.

Engineers wanted to counteract the effect of increased erosion on the depth of the river channel by dumping gravel in the river. It was realised that the basins created by excavating this gravel from the flood plain could be used as flood retention basins to store water during peak flows to prevent flooding. This idea is now being extended to encourage the use of areas of the flood plain as flood retention reservoirs thereby regenerating the natural wetland ecosystems which used to be found in the flood plain. In Baden-Wurttemberg, for example, there are plans to install gaps in the dykes originally constructed to prevent flooding. Where human settlement would not be threatened engineers would allow flood water to flow through the gaps on to the flood plain. This in itself would not regenerate flood plain ecosystems because flooding would only occur occasionally and suddenly. But the possibility of more regular and controlled flooding is now being considered. These developments are being made possible by greater co-operation between river engineers and ecologists.

The Dutch authorities are planning to go further. Their 'Master Plan for Nature' aims to allow up to 15 per cent of Dutch farmland to be seasonally flooded in order to encourage the return of wetland ecosystems, although at the moment progress towards implementing the plan is slow. Throughout the Rhine Delta there are plans to create backwaters alongside the main channels which would be protected from the fast flowing water and the backwash of boats and which would allow wildlife to thrive. At present the fast flow and the rapid fluctuations in water level prevent the growth of large aquatic plants which can provide important habitats for wildlife. Already such measures are allowing some bird and insect species to return to the delta.

These plans indicate a growing belief that pollution control alone is not enough to revive the Rhine. It is increasingly accepted that improved management of the river flow is also essential. However, the two things do need to go hand in hand. In the Duursde Waarden wetland in the Netherlands, problems are being caused because polluted water has been allowed to flood the area and some plant species have disappeared. In another location, the Meinerswijk, the local authority is recreating a wetland area but the soils in the area are contaminated with

surge of flow in cities like Bonn and Cologne. Floods that previously were likely once in every 200 years may now occur once every 60 years. The overall effect of attempts to control the Rhine has been to create a more variable and unpredictable river.

However, attitudes are now changing. River engineers are increasingly accepting the idea that in order to manage the river successfully the old ideas on channelisation need to be pollutants. The national river authority is currently refusing permission to flood the new wetland because they fear the pollutants will be washed back into the river.

One of the main aims of the Rhine country's current Rhine Action Plan is to see the return of salmon to the Rhine by 2000. Salmon ladders are being constructed around weirs and barrages at a cost of £4 million to allow the migration of the fish up the river. The salmon will also need access to slow flowing waters where young fish can grow and these are currently few and far between. For some people the return of migrating and breeding salmon to the Rhine is seen as an important symbolic goal. Anything less would be seen as a failure.

- What evidence is there to suggest that the Rhine has been over-managed?

9.3 Europe's Most Threatened Environments: Wetlands

Wetlands are landscapes or ecosystems comprising both land and water. In the past the ecological importance of wetlands has been underrated, yet marshes, bogs, fens, estuaries and tidal mudflats are among the richest and most productive ecosystems on earth. They provide habitats for a unique range of species and can provide valuable natural resources for people. They are often rich fishing areas and can provide very fertile farmland. Wetlands cover about six per cent of the planet's land surface but they are rapidly diminishing. Large areas are being drained for agriculture or building development. Those that remain are under growing threat from pollution, water extraction, intensive agriculture, hydroelectric schemes and other types of environmental damage.

The importance of wetlands is reflected by the fact that they are the only type of ecosystem to have their own international conservation agreement. The 'Convention on Wetlands of International Importance especially as Waterfowl Habitat', known as the Ramsar Convention, came into effect in 1975. By 1990 the Ramsar Convention covered 300 000 km² of wetland in 445 different locations around the world. Unfortunately the 52 member countries often only pay lip service to wetland conservation.

The Danube Delta, Romania

Within Europe many of the wetlands under greatest threat are in the east where central economic planning by Communist governments paid little attention to ecology. Eastern Europe contains a number of vital inland freshwater wetlands, such as the Danube flood plain, and coastal wetlands such as the Danube Delta on the Black Sea Coast.

The Danube Delta Biosphere Reserve, Romania

Alan and Zameirca climbed out of the boats, up to their chests in that indescribable mix of mud, rotting weed and water, and scrambled into the reed beds to scout the route ahead… We were soon walking on the floating reed mat, cutting a path and dragging the lotcas [a local traditional type of boat] behind us. Suddenly the reeds that had closed us in for hours melted away, and we beheld the colony. The sight was unforgettable – thousands and thousands of white pelicans standing together in a dense group.

The Pelicanauts, Paul Reddish, BBC Wildlife, 1983.

Where a river enters the sea the speed of flow decreases and the highly fertile alluvial silt carried by the river is deposited. If the rate of deposition exceeds the rate at which the sediment is eroded by the sea a delta will form and gradually increase in size. Eventually an equilibrium may be reached where the rate of marine erosion is equal to the rate of deposition and the size of the delta stabilises.

Within a delta the ebb and flow of fresh and salt water leave areas alternately wet and dry. This creates conditions ideal for **invertebrates** in the mudflats and shallow water while the fertile silt helps to produce large amounts of vegetation. The channels within the delta form ideal habitats for small fish during their growing period.

FIG 9.5   *The Danube Delta and its Location*

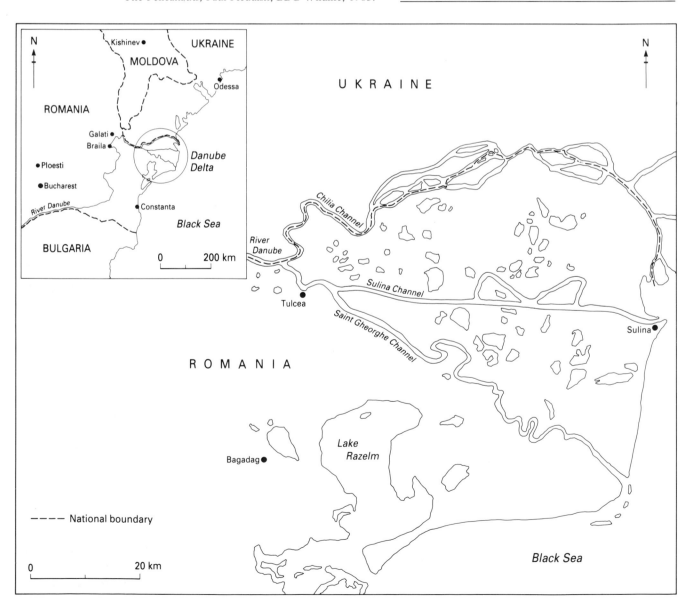

In turn the masses of invertebrates, fish and vegetation provide food and nesting sites for large populations of birds.

Deltas are fragile ecosystems and are very vulnerable to human intervention. They are also very dynamic ecosystems – they are constantly changing. Any human attempt to control the movement of water through the delta destroys this dynamism and the variety of ecosystems which make deltas such important wildlife areas.

A number of European river deltas are threatened by human activity. The Wadenzee (the delta of the Elbe, Wesser and Ems) on the North German coast, the Coto Donana (the delta of the Guadalquivir river) in southern Spain, and the Camargue (the Rhone delta) are all threatened by pollution, reclamation, industrial development or tourism.

The Danube Delta in Romania is one of the largest wetland areas in Europe. The delta covers about 5900 km². It stretches 75 km from east to west from where the Danube divides on entering the delta near to Tulcea to the present coastline. From north to south it stretches 100 km from the Ukrainian-Romanian border in the north to the Romanian lakes near the ancient Greek trading city of Istria in the south. In fact Istria's harbour was abandoned more than a thousand years ago when the growing delta finally caused the harbour to silt up. The delta is now a complex of lakes, swamps, river channels and reed beds providing a home to hundreds of species of birds and most species of European freshwater fish. The delta contains the world's largest area of reeds. The reed beds float with the help of trapped methane and are constantly shifting, changing the pattern of channels.

The delta is particularly vital for Europe's pelican population, both white pelicans and dalmation pelicans. The bird is very sensitive to disturbance. Human activity has forced the pelican population to retreat into the south-eastern corner of the continent. Between the end of the last century and 1950 the Romanian pelican population declined from millions to a few hundred. Following conservation measures the population climbed back to the current 5000. The only other nesting site in Europe has about 200. The delta is also vital to whitefront geese, red-breasted geese, duck and many other species including the white-tailed eagle.

For centuries the natural resources of the delta have been exploited by local people. Economic activities included:

– fishing;
– cattle grazing;
– cultivation of crops;
– harvesting of reeds for use as roof thatching, fencing, fodder and in a variety of traditional crafts;
– hunting of wild boar, duck, pheasant, geese, roebuck, hare, muskrat, fox, enot dog and otter for food, fur and sport;
– forestry – about four per cent of the delta is forested.

After 1955 the Communist government initiated plans to intensify the exploitation of natural resources in the delta.

– Reed exploitation was intensified between 1955 and 1965 so that the cellulose in the reeds could be used for making paper and man-made fibres. Reed-burning also became more common as a way of improving the amount and quality of sheep-grazing land. The use of reed-cutting equipment which damaged the base of the reed plants along with human disruption of the delta's **hydrology** and increasing pollution led to declining output.
– Between 1965 and 1989 fishing was intensified along with the introduction of fish farming. Intensive commercial fisheries now cover about 1600 km². From the 1960s onwards larger quotas were set by the government – quotas which the local people found difficult to achieve. Over-fishing resulted. The size of the catch decreased despite the quotas, with the numbers of the most commercially valuable species (including carp and pike) declining most rapidly. Some species have disappeared. The decline in fish stocks is not just a result of over-fishing. Land reclamation and pollution have also played a part. Even fish farm output has declined. Use of inappropriate locations, poor technology, inefficient use of energy, and poor water quality control have resulted in low yields. In many cases fish farms have been abandoned.
– Agriculture was intensified, particularly between 1982 and 1989. The first polder (an area of reclaimed or drained land) was constructed in 1940 and since then the amount of the delta used for agriculture has increased. However, yields have fallen drastically. Between 1989 and 1991 alone yields fell from an average 1000 kg per hectare to 650 kg per hectare. This recent fall has more to do with economic chaos in Romania than with environmental problems but inappropriate farming methods including overgrazing have played a part. Many polders have now been abandoned.

– Forestry only covers about four per cent of the delta but the wooded areas make an important contribution to the landscape and ecology of the delta. In some areas in order to boost timber production the naturally occurring white willows, poplars, osiers, ash and alder have been replaced by fast-growing hybrid poplars which give wooded areas a different appearance.

Management of the Delta

By the end of 1991 the delta was designated a Wetland of International Importance under the Ramsar Convention, a World Heritage Site (one of about 90 sites around the world designated for their cultural or natural importance by the United Nations) and a Biosphere Reserve (a Romanian government designation).

However, international and national protection on paper does not guarantee real conservation measures.

Romania faces more difficulties than most European countries when trying to implement conservation measures.

– The country experienced severe economic and social hardship under President Ceausescu's brand of Communism and since the revolution at the end of 1989 the country has been undergoing a chaotic period of transition. Inevitably conservation is very low on the list of priorities facing the government.
– Any attempt to produce a long-term plan for the delta is likely to meet local opposition. The concept of central government planning earned a bad reputation during Ceausecu's rule and may still attract little support.
– Romania's isolation from the rest of Europe before 1989 means that the people given the task of conserving the delta have had little contact from other countries. Also, there is no tradition of conservation within Romania. They are having to learn rapidly with the help of experts from other European countries.

The new Danube Delta Biosphere Reserve (DDBR) Authority has been given a number of broad tasks.

1 Conserving the ecological diversity of the delta.

2 Conducting research into the delta's environment and ways in which damage caused by economic activity could be minimised.

3 Co-ordinating water management to minimise ecological disruption.

4 Designating areas suitable for hunting and fishing and controlling these activities.

5 Issuing permits for exploiting the delta's resources (e.g. for reed harvesting or for fishing).

6 Ensuring shipping has adequate access through the delta.

7 Drawing up long-term plans for tourism.

8 Drawing up plans for enforcing conservation measures in the delta.

This list is very generalised and tells us little about how the Authority is going to conserve the delta's ecology in practical terms. Measures for controlling hunting and fishing have already been implemented and indicate the kind of measures likely to be introduced in the short term.

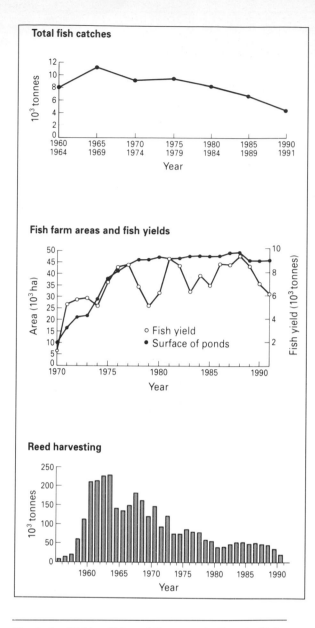

FIG 9.6 *Yields of Natural Resources in Danube Delta*

Hunting Controls

– Hunting is now confined to 26 per cent of the DDBR's area. The hunting zones are well away from important wildlife areas.
– Hunting is only permitted in groups of three or less people. Each person is allowed only five hunting days during each hunting season and each hunter is limited to shooting five birds per day. Use of automatic guns is banned.
– The hunting season has been shortened in the delta and is shorter than in the rest of Romania. The DDBR is entitled to prohibit hunting during the hunting season if it believes it necessary on conservation grounds.

Fishing Controls

– Quotas on the amount of fish which can be caught in each part of the delta are being imposed.
– Fishing nets with a larger mesh size are to be used and the minimum size of fish which can be caught is being increased.
– Fishing of some rarer species (e.g. barbel and ide) has been banned.
– Restocking of some fish is taking place. For example, 60 million fertilised pike-perch eggs have been released in the delta.

Tourism could be an important source of income for the area although at present disturbance of sensitive wildlife areas, poorly sited tourist developments and damage to water channels by fast power boats are causing problems. The DDBR Authority is currently trying to develop 'ecologically sustainable tourism' which will allow economic use of the delta's natural assets without causing long-term damage.

• List the threats to wetland ecosystems in the Danube Delta.

• 'The **productivity** of the Danube Delta ecosystem is declining.' To what extent does the data in Fig 9.6 support this statement?

9.4 Meeting the Growing Demand for Water: the Diversion of the Acheloos River, Greece

Clinging to the side of one of the most beautifully unspoilt valleys in southern Europe stands a crumbling, seventeenth century monastery. Its ancient walls covered with religious paintings, it has survived earthquakes and invasions by the Turks, and during the Second World War its secret chambers hid hundreds of refugees. But now this symbolic relic ... high up in the Pindos Mountains is finally about to fall victim to a huge hydroelectric and river diversion scheme...

Michael Bond, The Dam will drown a valley of nightingales, The European, 24 June 1993.

They are destroying this river and they have not even asked us what we think of the project. They have given us no answers. It will ruin the environment in this area and we will fight to the end to stop the dam being completed.

Member of a local council.

FIG 9.7 *Acheloos Diversion Scheme*

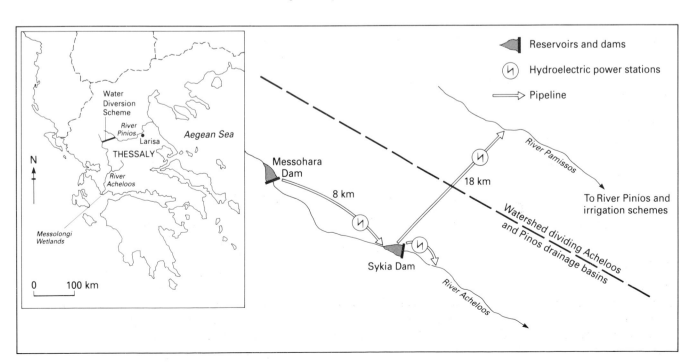

The Acheloos is the longest river in Greece. It flows from the Pindos Mountains, which form the backbone of Greece, into the Ionian Sea. Together with the River Evinos the Acheloos feeds the Messolongi-Aetoliko lagoon system, one of the largest wetlands in the Mediterranean.

The wetlands are particularly important for birds such as the white stork, spotted eagle, imperial eagle, dalmation pelican, eagle owl, griffon vulture, hen harrier, peregrine and curlew. The area forms one of 11 sites in Greece given special protection status under the Ramsar Convention although the ecological quality of the area has deteriorated over recent decades. This deterioration has been caused by:

— the construction of a number of dams in the Acheloos drainage basin which have reduced the supply of sediment to the wetlands by trapping sediment in the reservoirs behind the dams. They have also hindered fish migration;
— the use of water for irrigation and drinking water which has reduced the flow of water into the wetlands;
— chemical fertilisers and untreated sewage entering the wetlands which have caused eutrophication (increasing the quantities of nutrients in the water) which in turn has caused periodic algal blooms (the name given to the rapid growth of algae) in the lagoons forming the wetlands. Algae has the effect of depriving other organisms in the ecosystem of oxygen. At its worse it can cause mass fish deaths;
— fish farms within the wetlands have destroyed natural habitats.

FIG 9.8 *Sources of Pollution in the Mediterranean Sea (Section 9.5)*

The wetlands are now further threatened by a new project to divert the water in the Acheloos (see Fig 9.8). The project will construct two dams and an 18 km tunnel on the Acheloos to divert water into the Thessaly Plain east of the Pindos Mountains. One of the two dams, which will also be used to generate electricity, is almost complete with the help of £80 million from the EU. About 35 per cent of the water in the Acheloos will be diverted. The water would then be used for a number of purposes.

1 Irrigating an additional 3800 km² in the Thessaly Plain and supplying water to 2000 km² which are already irrigated using groundwater and an existing reservoir.

2 Supplementing water supplies to the cities of Larissa and Volos and other settlements on the Thessaly Plain.

3 Replenishing the groundwater in the overexploited **aquifers** below the Plain.

4 Increasing the flow in the Pinios River in order to dilute pollution.

5 Partially restoring Lake Karla which was drained in the 1960s to create new agricultural land, causing environmental problems.

6 Generating hydroelectricity.

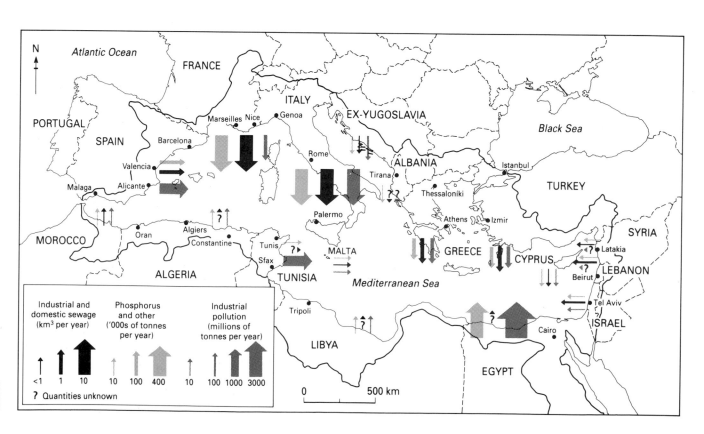

The impacts of the scheme are not confined to the wetlands but will also be felt in the upper sections of the Acheloos Valley and in the Thessaly Plain.

The Greek Government first announced its intention to proceed with the project in 1983. It has estimated that the cost of the scheme will be about £1.8 billion but that once the project is completed it will create an additional income of £0.5 billion a year from increased agricultural production, sales of electricity and sales of water.

In 1987 work began on the Mesohora Dam with the help of funds from the EU's Integrated Mediterranean Programme, although this dam could operate effectively as a separate scheme. In 1990 additional funds were provisionally allocated by the EU for the rest of the project equivalent to about 30 per cent of the total estimated cost. However, since then the decision on whether to proceed with the scheme has been postponed partly because of difficulties in negotiations with potential contractors and partly in response to opposition from both inside and outside Greece. In 1993 a new Greek Government announced that they would review the scheme, and asked a group of experts to prepare a report on the environmental impacts. Environmentalists became more optimistic that the scheme would be abandoned.

Arguments against the scheme are based on a number of probable environmental, economic, social and technical impacts.

Environmental

- The extension of irrigation in the Thessaly Plain will allow further intensification of agriculture. This, in turn, will increase levels of pollution in rivers and groundwater caused by chemical fertilisers and pesticides.
- The extension of irrigation will encourage farmers to cultivate about 700 km² of sloping land vulnerable to soil erosion.
- Further irrigation in the hot climate of Greece will cause **salinisation** of the soil.
- New crop diseases are likely to appear in the Thessaly Plain with greater moisture availability.
- The reduction of water in the Acheloos River will further reduce water supplies to the Messalongi wetlands causing encroachment of salt water from the Ionian Sea. This will damage the wetland ecosystems.
- The disruption to the flow in the Acheloos River will alter the temperature and oxygen content of the water in the wetlands. This will alter habitats and damage ecosystems.
- Only the lower 60 km (of the original 220 km) of the Acheloos River will remain. This will destroy the aquatic ecosystems and radically alter the appearance and characteristics of the upper Acheloos Valley. Species such as otter and trout are likely to disappear.
- Loss of habitats caused by the flooding of forested land to create reservoirs.
- The scheme contravenes a number of EU directives, international conventions and Greek laws on the environment.

Economic

- The crops which will benefit from more extensive irrigation on the Thessaly Plain, including cotton, tobacco, wheat, meat and dairy products, are already in surplus within the EU.
- The estimated cost of the scheme (approximately £1.8 billion) is a considerable underestimate. It underestimates the impact of inflation, the cost of irrigation infrastructure on individual farms and the cost of the interest on loans used to finance the scheme. The economic calculations on which the scheme is based also assume that all the irrigated land will be cultivated to maximum capacity. This is highly unlikely in reality and so costs will outweigh any financial gains.
- More than 1000 houses, schools, churches, and other buildings in 14 villages will be flooded by new reservoirs. These will have to be replaced at considerable cost.
- Reduced flow of water in the lower Acheloos will reduce income from agriculture in the valley.
- The EU is funding the diversion as an energy project and yet the scheme will not be a particularly efficient way of generating electricity. Similar investment in other hydroelectric projects or in energy conservation (Greece uses more energy, given the size of its population and economy, than any other developed country) would be a far more efficient use of resources.
- Reduced flow in the Acheloos will reduce electricity generation at an existing hydroelectricity plant on the river at Stratos. This was constructed in 1985–6 with the help of a grant from the EU of £50 million. The Public Power Corporation of Greece is demanding £16 million in lost revenue from the government for lost hydroelectricity.

Social

- Many people will be uprooted from areas where their families have lived for generations.
- The Thessaly farmers are among the wealthiest in Greece and yet the scheme is doing nothing for the poor farmers in Pindus, Macedonia, Epirus or Thrace. Social inequality is increasing.
- Many buildings of historic or architectural importance will be inundated by the

reservoirs, including the unique Byzantine monastery of St George at Myrophillo.

Technical

– The dams will have a life expectancy of only 50 years. Land slides and erosion will cause fairly rapid sedimentation in the reservoirs.
– The lack of water for irrigation in the Thessaly Plain is due to poor water management and not lack of available groundwater. According to experts the total water needs on the Thessaly Plain will be 2.3 billion m³ per year in 2037 while available groundwater from the plain will amount to 4.1 billion m³ per year. Much of the water is lost by evaporation or is distributed using inefficient technology.

• A total of 20 arguments are listed against the scheme. Select the ten arguments you feel are the most persuasive. Compare your selection with other members of the group. Are there any differences? If so, why?

• Why do you think the Greek Government was so keen to go ahead with the scheme despite all its drawbacks?

9.5 Sun, Sand and Pollution: Environmental Problems in the Mediterranean

The Mediterranean – Levante Beach, Benidorm

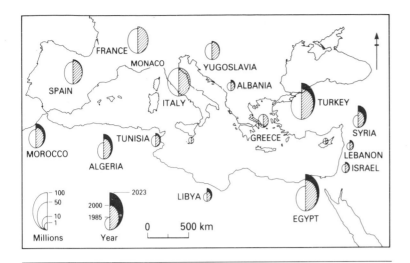

FIG 9.9 *Population Trends in the Mediterranean Region*

The Mediterranean is facing two related threats. The sea itself is under threat from pollution while its coastline is under threat from urban and industrial development. This, of course, is not only a European problem. Turkey, the Middle East and North Africa form over half of the coastline. However, eight European countries have a Mediterranean coastline – Spain, France, Italy, Slovenia, Croatia, Serbia/Montenegro, Albania and Greece.

The Mediterranean is particularly vulnerable to pollution. It is virtually land-locked so currents are weak and the tidal range is small. This means that the pollution is only dispersed very slowly. It takes 90 years for the sea's waters to be renewed completely. In fact, the amount of water lost by evaporation from the sea exceeds the inflow from the rivers entering the sea. The Mediterranean is kept 'topped up' by an inflow from the Atlantic through the Straits of Gibraltar. The pollution consists of sewage from the coastal settlements, chemicals from industry, and fertilisers and pesticides from increasingly intensive agriculture. The rivers draining into the Mediterranean, such as the Rhone, Po and indirectly the Danube, all bring pollution with them to add to the pollution discharged from the coast.

At the same time the coastline attracts people. In Spain, for example, 35 per cent of the population live along the coast compared with 12 per cent in 1900. Also, the countries

FIG 9.10 *Population in the Mediterranean Region*

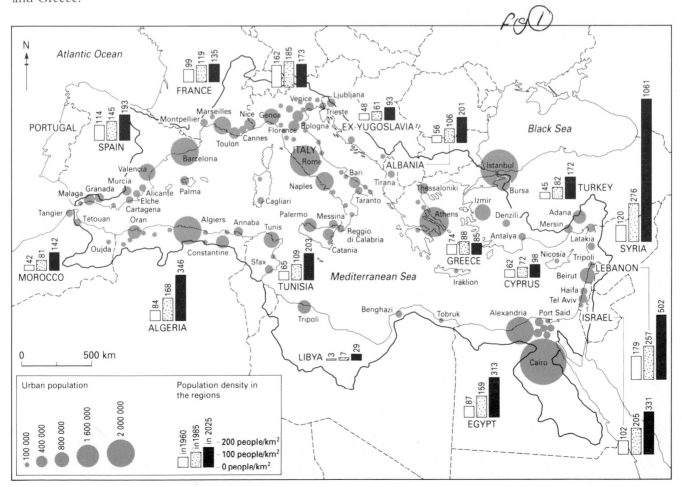

along the sea's southern coast have some of the fastest growing populations in the world. In 1950 the total population of the Mediterranean countries was 212 million. Today it is over 360 million. By 2025 it is expected to be 547 million. Algeria's population alone will increase by 30 per cent during the 1990s. The urban and industrial development associated with this rising population damages the landscape and ecology of the coast and adds to the pollution load.

To make matters worse the Mediterranean is, of course, a major tourist attraction. Over a third of the world's tourists go to the Mediterranean region. Seventy-five per cent go to France, Spain and Italy, but the fastest growth is occurring in Greece, Egypt, Cyprus and Tunisia. The ending of travel restrictions imposed by the former Communist governments of eastern Europe is likely to increase the numbers of visitors hoping to take advantage of the area's attractions. Most of the tourists come in the peak summer months when water is particularly scarce. Sewage treatment systems, where they exist, frequently fail to cope with the number of visitors. Even Athens, one of the largest cities on the Mediterranean coast, pumps all of its sewage untreated into the sea.

Although most of the pollution is discharged from the land, shipping is responsible for some. Thirty-five per cent of the world's oil trade passes through the Mediterranean and tankers pollute the sea with oil, sometimes deliberately when they illegally clean out their tanks. A third of the oil is washed up along the shore.

Governments are aware of these problems. In 1975 the United Nations through its Environment Programme, encouraged the Mediterranean countries to adopt a Mediterranean Action Plan to tackle the problems. In 1976

the Barcelona Convention for the Protection of the Mediterranean Sea committed the countries to take action to improve the situation, but there are no sanctions if governments choose to ignore their promises. In some cases the problems are being controlled but the overall prospects are gloomy, given the enormous pressures from population and development and the lack of money in many Mediterranean countries.

- Describe in detail the extent to which the information in Fig 9.8 (page 226) supports the following statement:
  'European countries discharge far more pollution into the Mediterranean than countries in the Middle East and North Africa.'

- Study the following Figs:
  a) Fig 9.9 (page 229) showing population trends;
  b) Fig 9.10 (page 229) showing urban population;
  c) Fig 9.11 showing the Mediterranean's catchment area;
  d) Fig 9.12 showing trends in tourism.
  With the help of evidence from the four maps suggest reasons why the European countries discharge more pollution into the Mediterranean than do Middle Eastern and North African Countries.

FIG **9.11**   *Mediterranean Catchment Area*

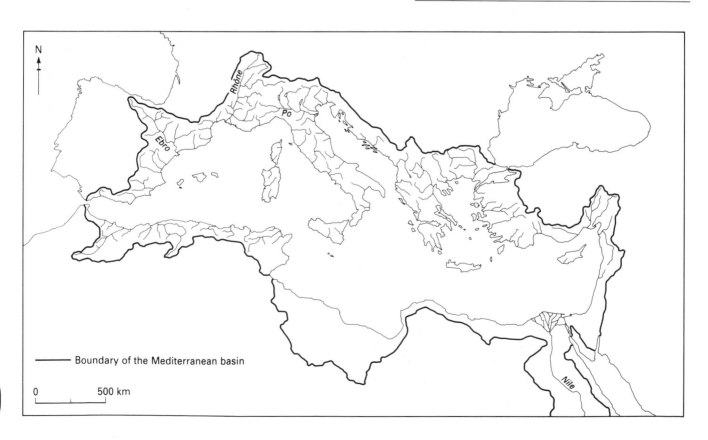

Boundary of the Mediterranean basin

0   500 km

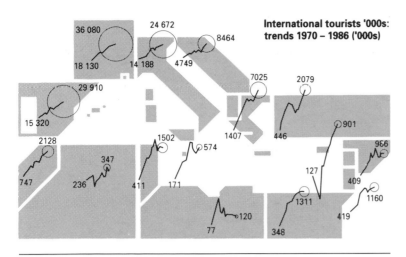

International tourists '000s: trends 1970 – 1986 ('000s)

36 080
18 130
24 672
14 188
8464
4749
29 910
15 320
2128
747
236
347
411
1502
171
574
7025
1407
446
127
1311
348
77
120
2079
901
419
409
986
1160

FIG 9.12 *Trends in Mediterranean Tourism*

FIG 9.13 *Estimates of Tourists' Annual Water Consumption in the Mediterranean Region*

	International tourism	Domestic tourism	Total
1984	222.5	346.5	569.0
2000			
A	422.7	432.0	854.7
B	592.2	742.0	1334.2
2025			
A	651.9	501.6	1153.5
B	1006.0	1535.0	2541.0

A = lowest prediction
B = highest prediction

Estimate of tourists' annual water consumption in Mediterranean countries 1984, 2000, and 2025 (millions of cubic metres)

- 'It is likely that pollution discharges will grow much more rapidly from North Africa and Middle Eastern countries than from European countries.' Is there any evidence in the maps to support this view?

- Summarise the trends indicated in Fig 9.13.

- Critically evaluate the mapping techniques used in Figs 9.9 and 9.12.

Eutrophication: an Example of Pollution in the Mediterranean

Eutrophication is a process which can occur both in freshwater lakes and in the sea. When agricultural fertilisers, sewage or detergents are washed or discharged into bodies of water the quantities of nutrients present in the water become artificially high. This can encourage the rapid growth of algae (aquatic plants with a simple structure). The high summer temperatures in the Mediterranean can accelerate the rate of growth of the algae.

In freshwater ponds or lakes the algae can seriously harm the aquatic ecosystem by depriving other living organisms of oxygen or by depriving aquatic plants of sunlight. Some types of algae also emit toxic chemicals which can kill fish. In addition, when the algae die the process of decomposition also deprives other organisms of oxygen.

A similar problem can occur in the marine environment. In recent years eutrophication has at times had a dramatic effect on parts of the Mediterranean, particularly in coastal waters and in lagoons. Many of these areas are important for fish farming and shell-fish industries as well as being important breeding grounds for fish and other marine organisms.

The coastal areas around Athens, for example, have seen algal blooms resulting from the massive amounts of sewage discharged from the city. In the Adriatic Sea to the east of Italy, algal blooms known as 'red tides', have become more frequent. The algae emit toxins which damage the marine ecosystems and can be harmful to humans. In 1988 the smell of decomposing algae drove many tourists away from the east coast of Italy with the inevitable economic impact on the tourism industry.

The Venice lagoon (see Section 6.7) has also suffered from eutrophication. The smell of hydrogen sulphide emitted by the algae, and an invasion of insects attracted by the algae were particularly serious problems in 1988. An attempt was made to tackle the problem in the short term by collecting the algae using special boats but the only real solution is to limit pollution.

9.6 Global Warming: the Threat in the Mediterranean

Global warming, and the resulting climatic changes, are seen by many as one of the most serious threats facing the global environment. A few scientists still question whether global warming is a real threat but there is now a widespread consensus among climatologists that climatic change will occur.

In 1990 the Second World Climate Conference agreed that without action to reduce emissions of the pollutants responsible for global warming temperatures would rise by between 2°C and 5°C during the twenty-first century – a rate of change unprecedented in the past 10 000 years. By 2030 temperatures will have risen by between 0.5 °C and 1.4 °C. This temperature increase will, the Conference agreed, cause sea levels to rise by between 30 cm and 100 cm by the end of next century. As these figures indicate there is considerable uncertainty over the precise rate and size of the temperature and sea level changes. There is even more uncertainty over the impact of such a temperature change on precipitation and wind patterns, and over regional variations in these changes.

Carbon dioxide and other gases in the atmosphere act like glass in a greenhouse. They allow heat energy from the sun to reach the surface of the earth but they absorb some of the heat being radiated from the earth back into space. This process raises the temperature of the atmosphere. In 1800 carbon dioxide was still at the pre-industrial level of 280 parts per million (ppm) but by 1990 the level was about 350 ppm. About 80 per cent of the CO_2 comes from burning fossil fuels (coal, oil and gas) – the remainder results from burning forests. Trees absorb CO_2 when alive but release it when they are cut down and burned.

Carbon dioxide accounts for more than 50 per cent of the 'greenhouse effect'. A number of other gases contribute to the effect, such as methane, nitrous oxides and chloroflourocarbons (CFCs), but although they are more effective as greenhouse gases they are in lower concentrations in the atmosphere. (CFCs are probably more well-known for their destructive effect on the level of ozone in the higher atmosphere. Ozone protects the earth from damaging levels of ultraviolet radiation from the sun.)

Sea levels are predicted to rise as a result of increases in temperature for two main reasons.

1 The melting of the glaciers in high mountainous areas like the Alps will increase the quantity of water in the oceans.

2 Higher temperatures will cause the water in the oceans to expand.

Rising temperatures could also cause partial melting of the Greenland and Antarctic ice caps but this is thought to be unlikely at the moment for a number of reasons, including the prediction that precipitation rates will increase in the polar areas which would keep the ice caps 'topped up'.

FIG 9.14 *Effect of Global Warming on the Hydrological Cycle*

One prediction of the effect of global warming on the hydrological cycle in the Mediterranean region

	Precipitation (mm)	Evapotranspiration (mm)	Runoff (mm)
Present	726	583	141
Future	807	620	187
Change	+81	+37	+46
	(+11%)	(+6%)	(+33%)

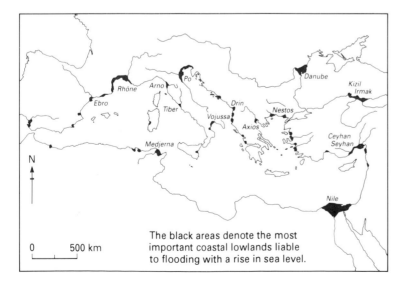

The black areas denote the most important coastal lowlands liable to flooding with a rise in sea level.

0   500 km

FIG 9.15 *Mediterranean Coastal Areas Liable to Flood if Sea Level Rises*

So what will be the impact of global warming on the Mediterranean? Climatologists predict a temperature change of between 1.5 °C and 3 °C and a sea level rise of between 12 cm and 18 cm for the Mediterranean by 2025. In some cases, where the coastline is subsiding, sea level rise could be as much as 25–40 cm. Predicting changes in rainfall and wind patterns in the region has proved to be almost impossible using current computer models but changes are certain to occur. Fig 9.14 outlines one prediction of how the hydrological cycle could be affected by the end of the next century.

A rise in the sea level could have a number of serious impacts in the region including:

- flooding of low-lying coastal areas, some of which have been used for urban and industrial development. If, as some climatologists predict, storms become more frequent then temporary, coastal flooding due to exceptionally high tides could also become more common. Fig 9.15 indicates the most important coastal areas which could flood as a result of global warming. Fig 9.16 shows one part of the Mediterranean in more detail and indicates the extent of the areas at risk;

FIG 9.16 *Coastal Areas in Greece and Turkey Liable to Flood if Sea Level Rises*

- damage to or destruction of coastal ecosystems such as wetlands either by flooding or by the infiltration of salt water;
- infiltration of salt water into the groundwater in coastal regions posing a threat to drinking water resources and to farmers dependent on irrigation;
- destruction of beaches vital for tourism;
- damage to coastal infrastructure designed specifically for the current sea level such as harbours and sea walls;
- in some areas the rate of coastal erosion could be accelerated.

Global warming would also have a number of impacts on agriculture. The higher temperatures and changed hydrological cycle are likely to alter the type of crops suitable for the region. It has been predicted that the area devoted to cereal cultivation around the Mediterranean could decline by between 8000 and 10 000 km². Cultivated land as a whole could decline by 25 per cent. In addition, there will be an impact on the productivity of the soil. An increase of

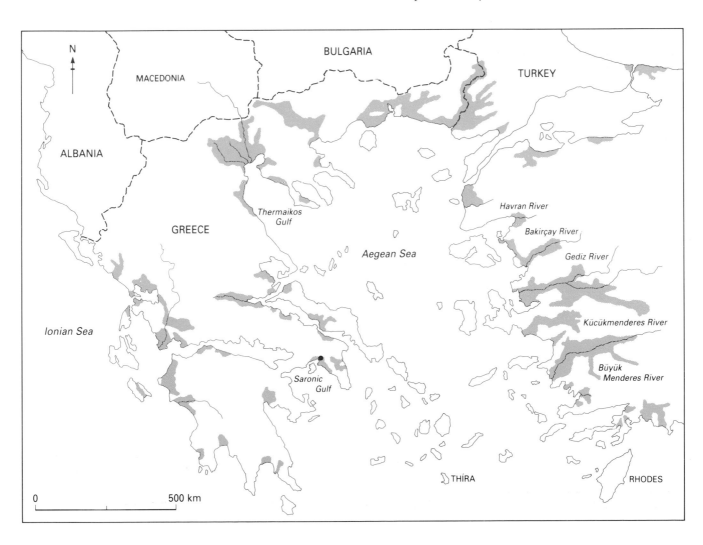

temperature of between 3 °C and 4 °C could have the following effects on soils in the Mediterranean region:

- soils will become more arid due to higher evaporation rates;
- because soils will be drier there will be more vulnerability to wind erosion;
- rainfall will percolate less easily into the drier and hardened soil and so runoff will increase. This will lead to higher rates of water erosion and in some cases lead to gullying;
- changes in the hydrological cycle could have the effect of reducing the organic content of the soil, resulting in lower fertility.

Other impacts of global warming in the region could include:

- more frequent forest fires;
- greater primary productivity, at least in the northern Mediterranean, because of the increased availability of carbon in the atmosphere which can accelerate photosynthesis.

FIG 9.17 *Impact of Climatic Change on the Environment and Society*

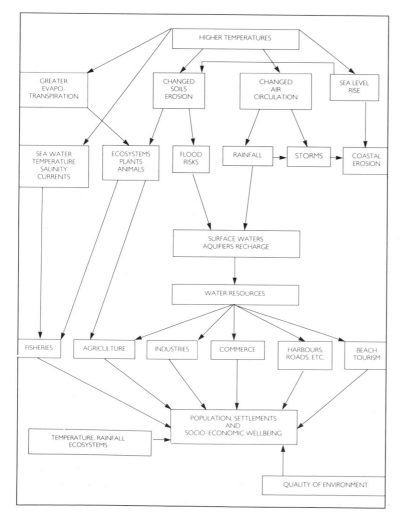

- Critically evaluate the diagram in Fig 9.17. Does it successfully illustrate how global warming could effect the environment and society? How could the diagram be improved?

The scientists involved in trying to predict the changes and their possible impacts have made a number of recommendations on what should be done to tackle the problem, assuming that some sea level rise is inevitable.

1 Limit further coastal urban and industrial development to minimise risk to human life.

2 Limit extraction of groundwater to minimise subsidence and to minimise infiltration of salt water into groundwater reserves.

3 Vital industries, such as power stations, should be located away from high risk low-lying areas.

4 Much more research is needed to improve the reliability and accuracy of predictions.

Case Study 1: the Ebro Delta, Spain

The Ebro Delta is on the Mediterranean coast of North-East Spain and has an area of 285 km². The delta forms one of the most valuable coastal ecosystems in Spain (see Fig 9.18). Its wetlands are vital to large numbers of migratory birds. The delta, which has a human population of 19 000, is also important for farming, fish farming and fishing.

The delta is already under threat from the dams which have been built on the river that feeds it. The dams retain sediment which would otherwise have been deposited on the delta. Before 1965 four million tonnes of sediment a year reached the delta – by the 1990s this had declined to 400 000 tonnes a year. Without this supply of sediment the delta started to shrink in 1970 because of erosion by the sea.

Global warming poses an additional threat to the delta. As pointed out earlier in this section, attempts to predict local climatic changes as a result of global warming are very unreliable. However, using computer models climatologists have predicted the following changes in the area containing the Ebro Delta:

- in spring cold and wet weather conditions will be more frequent;
- summers will be longer, hotter and drier;

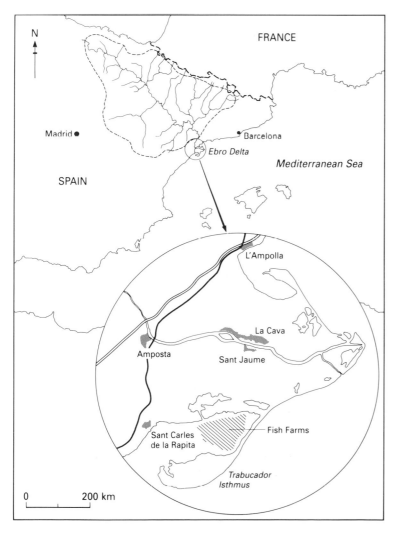

FIG **9.18** *Ebro Delta, Spain*

Rice Cultivation on the Ebro Delta, Spain

– rainfall will increase by up to 0.4 mm per day during spring and winter, and will decrease by 0.2 mm per day in the summer;
– **evapotranspiration** will increase;
– an increase in the frequency of extreme weather conditions such as storms and floods.

So what impact would these changes and a higher sea level have on the delta?

– The water balance in the delta would become increasingly negative. In other words, evapotranspiration will exceed input from the Ebro River and the irrigation systems which the Ebro feeds. This would force farmers to increase the rate at which they extract water for irrigation from groundwater reserves. This could lower the water table and threaten future water supplies for irrigation and drinking water. It would also allow sea water to penetrate into the groundwater.
– As sea level rises, draining low-lying farmland in the delta will become more difficult. Pumps will have to be used more frequently.
– Occasional flooding by the sea during storms could damage the fertility of the soil by increasing the salt content of the soil and the groundwater.

- The Trabucador Isthmus is likely to be breached by the sea. At the moment the isthmus is only 50–100 m wide and 0.5 m above sea level. This would expose the fish farms located in the bay behind the isthmus to rougher seas and this would jeopardise their activities. Also, other low-lying areas are likely to be regularly invaded by the sea causing ecological changes to wetland areas.
- Higher water temperatures in the bays around the delta are expected. Water at higher temperatures carries less oxygen and so the water is likely to become less productive for wildlife.
- Although most of the towns in the delta are located on slightly higher ground there are a small number of tourist developments on low-lying land which could be threatened by flooding. On the other hand, money is more likely to be invested in new coastal defences to protect these areas than to protect important ecological sites.

Case Study 2: the Inner Thermaikos Gulf, Greece

The Inner Thermaikos Gulf is a shallow bay of 470 km² with 160 km of coastline. In economic terms the land around the bay and the bay itself form the second most important area after Athens. The area houses a population of more than a million, 700 000 of whom live in the city of Thessaloniki. The Gulf is rich in fish and is intensively used by shipping, while the area around the bay includes 100 km² of fertile low-lying farmland.

With a possible sea level rise of 20–30 cm in the next 50 years the low-lying unprotected coastal areas, and the low-lying reclaimed farmland in the Thessoloniki Plain, could be threatened. Permanent flooding is unlikely, at least before 2040, but more frequent flooding during storms and exceptionally high tides is likely. However, after 2050 temperature increases of 2–3 °C and a sea level rise of 0.5–1.0 m, are predicted in this area. According to some scientists such a change could be catastrophic for the local economy and ecology unless radical action is taken to plan for the changes.

The impacts of climate change and sea level rise on the area predicted by scientists include:

- an increased flow of salt water into the lower tidal stretches of the rivers draining into the gulf. This would cause changes to the ecology of the rivers and the deltas;

- the flooding of coastal marshes and their conversion into lagoons. This would also have an impact on the area's ecology;
- the present sea wall protecting the city of Thessaloniki and the dyke protecting the reclaimed farmland on the Thessaloniki Plain will become inadequate. The heights of both will have to be increased;
- some low-lying industrial zones close to Thessaloniki will be threatened by flooding. Also the runways of Mikra Airport to the south are likely to be flooded;
- the tourist beaches of Emvolo, Mechianiona, Macrigialos and Methoni may be destroyed;
- increased evapotranspiration will increase demand for groundwater for irrigation and drinking water. This will cause a lowering of the water table and could allow salt water to infiltrate into the groundwater. This, in turn, could cause salination of the soil;
- growth of bacteria will be encouraged by higher temperatures, especially in areas of stagnant water. The risk of catching water-borne diseases will rise;
- some species of insects will flourish in the warmer and drier conditions. Some of these may be crop pests.

One of the more radical and expensive proposals put forward to tackle these problems is to build a dam across the entrance to the Thermaikos Bay in order to control any future sea level rise. Such a dam would have to be 4.5 km long and at least 30 m high and would have to include locks to allow ships to pass.

- Using both case studies and the rest of this section complete a list of possible impacts of global warming. Divide your list into economic, environmental and social impacts.

- Will there be any benefits from global warming for the Mediterranean region?

ESSAY

1   Using the case studies examined in this chapter, show how poorly thought out river management schemes can lead to serious environmental problems.

2   Explain why decision makers sometimes pursue river management schemes which they know will cause environmental, economic and social problems. Use examples to illustrate your answer.

3   Why is the conservation of wetlands so important and why are wetlands under threat?

4   'Unless radical action is taken, the environmental threat to the Mediterranean Sea and its coastal areas will increase.'
    Use evidence to support this statement.

5   'We are not certain what the effects of global warming will be, so no action should be taken to deal with impacts which may never happen.' Do you agree?

Glossary

aquifers	Permeable or porous rock strata containing groundwater.
evapotranspiration	The process of water being evaporated from the ground or from the surface of seas and lakes, combined with transpiration (evaporation from plants).
flood plain	A level valley floor which will be regularly flooded unless flood defences have been constructed.
groundwater	Water stored in, or flowing through, porous or permeable rock strata.
hydrology	The movement of water through the environment.
invertebrates	Animals without a backbone, such as insects.
productivity (in ecosystems)	The rate at which organic matter is produced in an ecosystem.
salinisation	The increase in the salt content of soil, usually caused by high rates of evaporation.
water table	The water table marks the dividing line between rock saturated by groundwater and the rock above it which is not fully saturated.
wetland	A landscape comprising a patchwork of land and water. Marshland, river channels and lakes form a dominant part of the landscape.

Communicatio
the Erosion of

ns:
Distance

10

KEY IDEAS

10.1 The growing dependence on cars throughout Europe is creating major environmental problems. In particular, new road construction is generating conflict between those who believe new roads are necessary and those who believe they inflict unacceptable damage on the environment.

10.2 There is now a major construction programme to expand the high-speed rail network in Europe. High-speed trains are seen as a method of strengthening European integration and of promoting economic development.

10.3 France and Britain have adopted different approaches to exploiting the opportunities offered by the opening of the Channel Tunnel. Within Britain the Channel Tunnel Rail Link has been particularly controversial.

10.4 The development of telecommunications will enable more people to work from home. Telecommunications are also being used by remote or peripheral regions to regenerate local economies and to improve the quality of life.

10.1 Out of Control?: the Environmental Impact of the Car

Traffic Jams on a Motorway in Bavaria, Germany

Personal mobility has become a vital part of European society. The affluent lifestyle most Europeans strive for is dependent on the freedom to travel easily between home, work, services and leisure. In most western European countries the average distance travelled each day has increased a hundred times this century. With the rapid growth of personal mobility over recent decades transport has become a major environmental problem. Car ownership has increased rapidly and there is considerable potential for it to increase further. At the same time use of public transport has generally declined. At the end of the 1980s the environmental problems associated with mass car ownership were largely confined to western Europe, but car ownership is likely to rise rapidly in eastern Europe during the 1990s, and so the problem will spread. In western Europe there are growing doubts over the wisdom of allowing continued, unrestrained growth in the use of cars.

When looking at the environmental problems associated with the large-scale use of cars it is useful to divide the problems into two categories:

1 problems within urban areas;

2 problems outside urban areas.

To some extent these overlap. For example, cars pollute the atmosphere whether they are in the city or travelling between cities. However, the impacts are different, as are the possible solutions. The environmental problems generated by cars in cities are examined in Section 6.7. Here the primary concern is with the overall environmental impact of cars and, more specifically, the impact of trying to meet the demand for additional road space on routes between urban areas. However, it is also worth looking briefly at the overall environmental impact of Europe's dependence on cars.

The Environmental Cost of a Car

In 1993 the Environment and Forecasting Institute, based in Heidelberg in Germany, analysed the environmental impact of cars in a new way by trying to calculate the total impact of one single car during its life. As the basis for their calculations they took a medium-sized car with a catalytic converter and assumed that it was driven 13 000 km a year for ten years. The results were as follows.

Impact during manufacture

Each car produces 25 000 kg of waste and 422 million m^3 of polluted air in the extraction of the raw materials used in its manufacture.

The transport of the raw materials to the car factory in Germany produces an additional 425 million m^3 of polluted air and 12 litres of crude oil pollution in the world's oceans.

The manufacturing process itself adds another 1500 kg of waste and 75 million m^3 of polluted air.

Impact during its ten-year life

Over ten years the car will generate:
44 tonnes of CO_2;
5 kg of sulphur dioxide;
47 kg of nitrogen dioxide;
325 kg of carbon monoxide;
38 kg of hydrocarbons;
17 500 g of material worn from the road surface;
750 g of material worn from tyres;
150 g of material worn from brake linings.

Impact from disposal of the vehicle

Each car will produce 100 million m^3 of polluted air, and together with spare parts used during its life, will produce 27 tonnes of rubbish and scrap.

In total the researchers calculate that each car, on average, is responsible for:
30 trees damaged by air pollution;
820 hours of human life lost through a fatal road crash;
2800 hours of human life damaged by a traffic accident;
200 m^2 of tarmac and concrete.

The researchers also calculated that the environmental and health costs (in other words, the externalities) of each car total £2400 per year, or £24 000 over its whole life.

It is difficult to verify these calculations and it could be argued that environmentalists have a vested interest in exaggerating the impact of a car. Also, the enormous social and economic benefits brought by each car have to be set against these costs. Nevertheless, these figures do help to highlight the often hidden costs of Europe's growing dependence on cars.

- Imagine that you have been asked to write a report to counter the arguments put forward by the German researchers. List all the economic, social and environmental benefits of cars you would attempt to include in your report. Try to categorise your ideas as much as possible.

The Environmental Impact of Roads

A good transport infrastructure is not a luxury for any country wishing to enjoy economic success and increased national prosperity. It is a necessity.

Malcolm Rifkind, former Transport Secretary in the British Government.

Connecting an economically strong region to a weak one does not necessarily help the latter. In the case of Italy, the main effect of the motorways has been to encourage…migration to the more developed areas.

Report to the European Conference of Ministers of Transport.

Massive resources are being allocated to the construction of new roads throughout Europe.

Those in favour of spending huge sums of money on new roads argue that improved roads are essential for a modern healthy economy. For example, under the Trans-European Networks plan published by the EU in 1992 roads are seen as essential for promoting European economic integration. The plan envisages 12 000 km of new motorways in the EU by 2002.

On the other hand some economists argue that there is in fact very little proof that roads generate economic growth and that the massive sums of money should be redirected to other projects.

Arguments in Favour of More Roads

1 Improved access cuts industry's costs. Lower prices can be charged for goods and so industry becomes more competitive.

2 Road congestion currently costs industry a considerable amount of wasted time. If trucks are held up in a traffic jam expensive investment and labour are not producing any returns. For example, the British Road Federation, a group which lobbies the British Government for more roads on behalf of industry, claims that congestion costs British industry £15 billion a year.

3 Industrialists list road access as one of the main factors they look at when deciding where to locate new factories or warehouses. So if an area wants to attract new investment good road links are vital.

4 Road construction in itself creates considerable employment. Construction and civil engineering firms, quarries, truck manufacturers, and firms manufacturing other essential infrastructure such as lighting are among the beneficiaries of road construction.

5 New roads are often beneficial to the environment because most divert traffic away from unsuitable roads. By-passes around villages and towns are a good example of this. Also smoothly flowing traffic is less polluting per kilometre than traffic on congested roads.

6 New roads are particularly vital to relatively remote or peripheral regions of Europe. The British Road Federation argues that if Britain is to compete effectively with mainland Europe the handicap of its island location must be removed by excellent road links to the Channel Tunnel and the ferry ports.

7 The tourism industry, a vital provider of jobs in many parts of Europe, is dependent on good access. With improved links tourists can be attracted to new areas bringing enormous economic benefits.

Arguments Against New Roads

1 Research into links between road construction, levels of unemployment and the amount of inward investment has failed to produce proof that new roads generate economic growth.

2 The main factor which attracts industry to an area is not road access but is increasingly the quality of the local environment. Industrialists are looking for attractive countryside, clean air, pleasant towns and villages, good leisure and recreation facilities and high quality services. Ironically, major road construction damages the quality of this environment.

3 Road construction is an inefficient way of creating employment. Because road construction is so capital-intensive fewer jobs are created than in, for example, house building and public transport.

4 Where new road construction does attract inward investment it often merely encourages existing industries to relocate closer to the road rather than promoting new industry. Also, roads often encourage industry to locate on green-field sites close to the road rather than promote the regeneration of existing built-up areas such as inner cities.

5 An improved road network encourages firms to centralise into fewer locations rather than having branches closer to local markets. While it may be profitable for firms to rationalise in this way it is usually done at the expense of jobs, particularly jobs in remoter areas. For example, it can be argued that improved roads linking southern Italy to the rest of Europe have merely encouraged the migration of people and economic activity northwards.

6 The construction of new roads will merely encourage more cars and trucks to use them and so any new road will very quickly reach capacity.

7 It is impossible to meet the potential future demand for road space, certainly in the more densely populated countries of western Europe. In Britain, for example, the government has estimated that the number of vehicles could grow from 24 million in 1993 to 51 million by 2025. The additional vehicles would be equivalent to a queue of parked cars nearly 200 000 km long, or a 250-lane motorway running from London to Edinburgh. The environmental and social costs of the additional road space needed to cater for these vehicles would be totally unacceptable.

This section now looks at two case studies of road construction. Both examples involve new roads constructed through areas of high environmental value although the characteristics of the environments affected are very different.

The Aspe Valley, Pyrenees, France

Case Study 1: a New Road in the Pyrenees Mountains

We are standing on a steep mountainside at the head of the Aspe valley. Before us, stretching away towards the Bearnais capital of Pau, lies scenery of chocolate box perfection. Ten metres below our feet a road bridge, so new that the tarmac still shines, collides with the bare rock face. And 50 metres back along the track which brought us here sits on olive-green jeep carrying a number of France's crack anti-riot 'gendarmes mobiles'. It is very still...Life in the Aspe valley – la 'vallée sympa' [pleasant valley] as it is called on the road signs showing a smiling bear clutching a daisy – has not been tranquil for some time. A mini civil war is raging among its dwindling inhabitants who are divided over the road scheme at the head of the narrow valley, below the Somport Pass.

Battle of Bear Valley, David Sharrock, The Guardian, 4 December 1992.

Without the tunnel we are all finished because this valley is dying. I do not want to live in a cemetery. Fifty houses have fallen empty in this village in 20 years...The bears can be saved, but if it's a choice between bears and humans in this valley it's obvious who comes first.

Jean-Pierre Lasalla, President of the Pyrenees National Park.

If they get their way and cut the tunnel there'll be juggernauts thundering through here night and day. But they'll have to drive their bulldozers right over my body.

Eric Petetin, local environmental campaigner.

In the early 1990s work began on a project to improve communications between France and Spain. It was proposed to improve the quality of the road between Pau in southern France and Saragossa in northern Spain. Between these two towns lie the Pyrenees mountains, a potential barrier to greater economic integration and stronger trading links within the EU. The EU agreed to provide £20 million from its structural funds (see Section 7.7) towards the cost of the scheme. A motorway is to be built between Pau and Oloron, and the N134 is to be straightened and widened between Oleron and a new tunnel built under the Somport Pass (see Fig 10.1, page 244).

In December 1992 construction work was halted after it was ruled that the project contravened EU and French environmental laws. Environmental campaigners believe that the pollution and noise generated by the trucks attracted to the new high-speed link would ruin the valley's environment.

What particularly concerns many conservationists is the fact that the Gave d'Aspe along with the Gave d'Ossau in France and two adjacent valleys in Aragon in Spain form part of the habitat of the only remaining brown bears in the Pyrenees. The bears were not originally mountain dwellers; they retreated there from the lowland of southern France during the nineteenth century under pressure from human interference. Two new ski resorts have recently been completed at the Somport Pass on the Spanish border, and one in the Gave d'Ossau valley in France. These have destroyed part of the bears' habitat. The conservationists also fear that the new road could in turn increase demand for additional ski resorts as more visitors are attracted by improved access. Already two million people a year visit the area.

In 1937 there were 200 bears. By 1957 there were 70, by 1983 20, and by 1988 15. By the early 1990s there were less than ten. Nobody is certain about the gender ratio of the remaining population. In any case, this number may be too small to guarantee the bears' survival without attempting to boost the numbers by importing bears from elsewhere in Europe. There are probably about 400 bears left in the whole of western Europe, with the only viable populations being in Spain and Italy. The Pyrenean bears may well die out by 2000 unless radical action is taken.

The bears have been victims of hunters, local shepherds, and human disturbance. Until a few years ago it was common for problem bears, responsible for killing sheep, to be shot or poisoned. Although bears are largely herbivorous they do need meat to supplement their diet. On average, each bear kills four to six sheep a year.

It is now illegal under French, Spanish and EU law to kill the bears under any circumstances. A compensation scheme operated by the French Government and *Fonds d'intervention Eco-pastoral* (FIEP), a French conservation organisation, now pays £150 to farmers for each sheep killed by a bear. In 1992 compensation was paid for 128 sheep. Nevertheless, it has been difficult for local people to change their traditional view of bears as pests to be eliminated. Some locals, including the mayors of a number of mountain villages, see the rise of groups determined to conserve the bears, such as *Artus* and *Groupe Ours*, as unacceptable interference from outsiders. For such organisations the bears have become a symbol of the dwindling wilderness areas in Europe.

In order to try and win reluctant support from local farmers and shepherds, FIEP provides helicopters to deliver feed and other supplies free of charge to remote pastures. They have also given shepherds mobile phones to report the presence of bears so that wardens can arrive quickly to drive the bears away from the flocks.

In 1990, 13 reserves totalling 65 km² were created by the French Government in the Gave d'Aspe and d'Ossau valleys. In the reserves, boar hunting was banned. The boar hunters can disturb or frighten bears, and frightened bears are known to abandon their young. However, some hunters continue to hunt illegally within the reserves.

Many conservationists believe that all their efforts will have been wasted if the new road is constructed. The road will cut

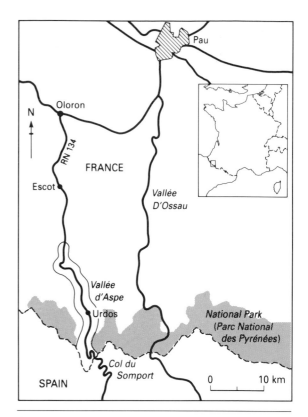

Fig 10.1 *Aspe Valley, Pyrenees, France*

the bears' territory in two and further reduce their chances of survival. Also, if a decision is finally made to introduce bears from elsewhere in an attempt to boost local numbers the new bears could well be killed by passing vehicles. At present bears frequently cross the road, which is relatively traffic-free at night.

Local opinion on the road is mixed and in some cases conflict has become violent. Some see the road as a way of reducing the valleys remoteness and discouraging further depopulation. Others see it as an unacceptable disruption of their peaceful mountain environment. The issue is made more complex by the merging of two environmental conflicts – should the bears be protected or not, and should the local environment be preserved or not? A local militia has been formed with the aim of frightening away conservationists. Car tyres have been slashed, anonymous death threats made and gunshots fired at a local conservationists' meeting place. A government bear specialist left the valley after finding his cat crucified on his cottage door. On the other side, militant environmentalists, many from outside the area and even from outside France, have disrupted construction work despite the efforts of riot police.

- Do you believe construction of the road should be prevented in order to protect the bears? Justify your answer in detail using the information in this section to reinforce your case.

- Why do you think some local people feel so strongly in favour of the road and so opposed to the environmentalists?

- Which side does the French Government seem to be on in this conflict? Which side does the EU seem to be on?

- The bears are seen by some people as a symbol of Europe's dwindling wilderness areas. Do you think true wilderness areas should be preserved in Europe? List the arguments for and against preserving areas of wilderness where human interference is kept to an absolute minimum.

- In the Haute Garonne Departement, about 200 km to the east of the bears' habitat, a number of communities are considering a plan to import bears from Bulgaria to create a well-stocked national park. Why do you think such a scheme could bring benefits to the local people? Is there a lesson here for the people of Gave d'Aspe and d'Ossau?

FIG **10.2**   *The Gap in the M3, 1993*

Case Study 2: Twyford Down, Southern England

The M3 linking London and Southampton was complete by 1993 except for a short gap near Winchester (see Fig 10.2). An existing four-lane dual carriageway, the A33 Winchester by-pass, formed the link between the two completed sections of the M3. Delays, and four or five mile queues, had become a common occurrence, particularly at one junction controlled by traffic lights.

As long ago as 1970 the proposals for a motorway route between Bar End, to the east of Winchester, and Compton, to the south of the city, had been published by the government. In 1973, following a public inquiry, a motorway route was fixed to the west of St Catherine's Hill in the Itchen Valley. At a second inquiry in 1976–7, set up to consider subsidiary road schemes associated with the motorway, the Inspector chairing the inquiry recommended that the route should be reviewed. The result was a second public inquiry in 1985 which came to the same conclusion as the first inquiry – that the

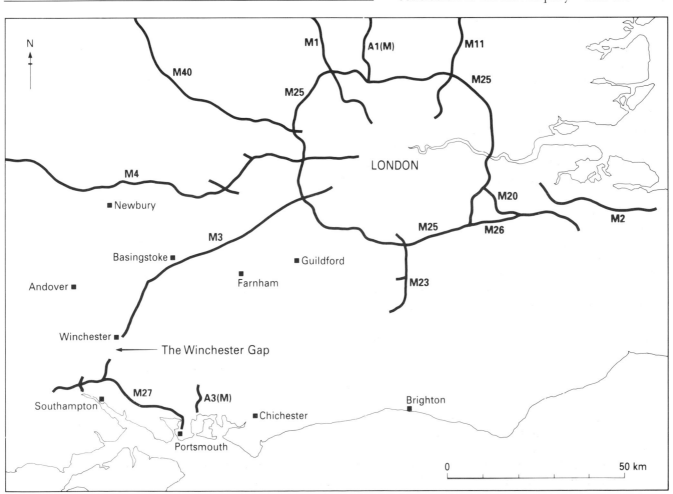

motorway should follow a route to the west of St Catherine's Hill.

However, after the 1985 inquiry concerns were expressed that the Inspector had failed to hear evidence from the Countryside Commission and English Heritage, two government agencies with responsibility for countryside planning and the preservation of historic sites. The inquiry was reopened in 1987.

Both the 1985 and the 1987–8 inquiries considered a large number of alternative routes put forward by a number of pressure groups, but all of these were basically varients of three main options (see Fig 10.3):

— a route following the line of the existing A33 to the west of St Catherine's Hill;
— a route to the east of St Catherine's Hill;
— a tunnel under St Catherine's Hill.

The Inspector argued that relying on the existing A33 dual carriageway, even with the construction of a flyover at the crossroads currently controlled by traffic lights, was not a realistic option. They believed that the future growth in traffic would mean that the road would be inadequate before the end of this decade.

Following the 1987–8 inquiry the Inspector recommended the route to the east of St Catherine's Hill with a three-lane motorway running through Twyford Down in a deep cutting, 1.5 km long, 30 m deep and 120 m wide.

In announcing the decision the Secretary of State for Transport stated that:

'Because of the adverse affects on the Winchester Water Meadows and residential areas of the city, the Inspectors recommended that the western route following the line of the existing by-pass should not be built.'

The government argued that although the scheme is environmentally damaging there would be positive environmental benefits including the removal and landscaping of the A33. They also agreed to pay for extensive archaeological excavations along the line of the motorway and to pay for the creation of a small area of chalk grassland currently used as arable land.

The decision proved to be extremely controversial and has aroused some of the most militant opposition to a road scheme seen in Europe.

Why is the Twyford Down Route so Controversial?

The removal of the Winchester by-pass and the restoration of the area as a pleasant countryside link between the main recreational areas of the water meadows and St Catherine's Hill will be a significant environmental gain to the setting of this historic city.

Cecil Parkinson, Secretary of State for Transport, 1990.

This land, all our land, is being trashed, but for what?

Member of the Dongas Tribe.

Twyford Down is a story about everyday decision making in the UK and that is a sad reflection.

Member of the Twyford Down Association.

Twyford Down Motorway Construction Site

FIG 10.3 *Three Alternative Routes for the M3 Near Twyford Down*

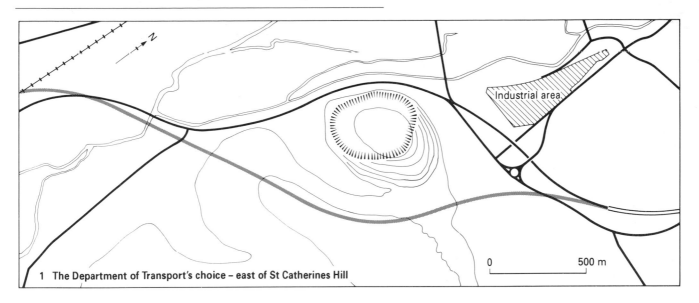

1 The Department of Transport's choice – east of St Catherines Hill

0   500 m

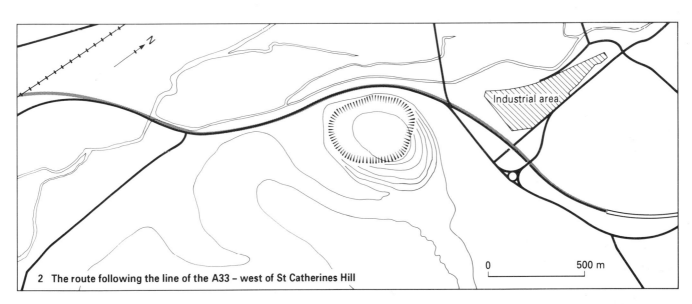

2 The route following the line of the A33 – west of St Catherines Hill

0   500 m

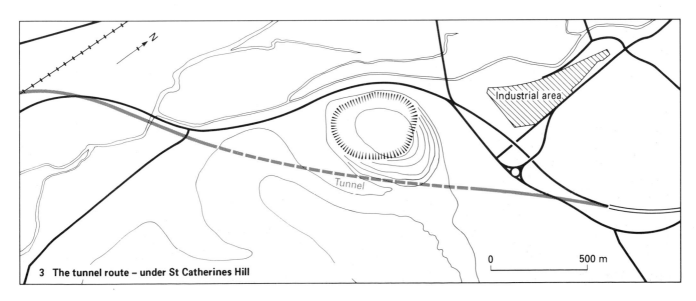

3 The tunnel route – under St Catherines Hill

0   500 m

FIG 10.4a   *M3 Routes – Costs and Benefits*

	ROUTE CHOSEN BY THE DEPARTMENT OF TRANSPORT (SIX-LANE MOTORWAY)	ROUTE FOLLOWING THE EXISTING A33 (SIX-LANE MOTORWAY)	TUNNEL ROUTE (SIX-LANE MOTORWAY)	NO MOTORWAY – RELY ON EXISTING A33 WINCHESTER BYPASS. CONSTRUCT FLYOVER AT HOCKLEY JUNCTION (FOUR-LANE DUAL CARRIAGEWAY).
COST	£36 million.	£47 million.	£128 million (plus higher maintenance costs for tunnel).	Very low.
ENVIRONMENTAL COSTS FOR WINCHESTER	Minimal.	Increased noise levels in southern Winchester. Visual intrusion of retaining wall – the motorway would cut into the lower slopes of St Catherine's Hill.	Minimal.	Existing noise levels would be maintained or increase as traffic volume rises. If flyover was inadequate to remove congestion traffic may use local roads to avoid congestion.
ENVIRONMENTAL BENEFITS FOR WINCHESTER	Considerably reduced noise levels in southern Winchester. The historic atmosphere of southern Winchester would be restored, particularly in the urban conservation areas. The closure and restoration of the current A33 route would improve the view of St Catherines Hill from Winchester, and would improve access on to the hill for local people.	None.	The same benefits as for the Department of Transport's chosen route, but noise levels would be the lowest of any option.	None.
ENVIRONMENTAL COSTS FOR PROTECTED LANDSCAPES	Two kilometres of the route is though an Area of Outstanding Natural Beauty – the route will be visually intrusive. Two hectares of St Catherine's Hill SSSI will be destroyed, and the motorway will split the remainder into two sections. 3.5 hectares of Itchen Valley SSSI will be destroyed. Destruction of parts of Hockley Down and The Dongas ancient monuments.	4.4 ha of Itchen Valley SSSI would be destroyed. Very small impact on AONB and St Catherines Hill SSSI.	Two hectares of Itchen Valley SSSI would be destroyed. Limited impact on AONB, including visual intrusion of tunnel portals and lighting at tunnel entrances. Eight hectares of land would be taken from the AONB.	None.
ENVIRONMENTAL BENEFITS FOR PROTECTED LANDSCAPES	None, although removal of A33 would allow both SSSIs to be managed as a single unit which could have ecological benefits.	No damage to ancient monuments. St Catherine's Hill SSSI maintained as a single area.	No damage to ancient monuments. No damage to St Catherine's Hill SSSI.	No damage to AONB, SSSIs or ancient monuments.
OTHER ENVIRONMENTAL BENEFITS	Reduction in congestion causing reduction in atmospheric pollution. Removal of A33 will allow improvement of footpath & bridleway routes to St Catherines Hill.	Reduction in congestion causing reduction in atmospheric pollution.	The same benefit as for Department of Transport's chosen route.	None.
OTHER ENVIRONMENTAL COSTS	1.8 million m^3 of waste to be moved. Much will be used to build embankments in Itchen Valley. Will necessitate 106 000 lorry movements, mainly off public route.	Minimal.	1.7 million m^3 of waste to be moved. Would necessitate 333 000 lorry loads – many on public roads. Delayed completion date would mean continuing congestion and higher levels of atmospheric pollution.	Increasing levels of atmospheric pollution caused by growing traffic congestion. Deteriorating road safety as traffic volume grows.
ECONOMIC BENEFITS	Will improve links between Southampton and other south coast ports with London and the south-east.	The same benefits as for Department of Transport's chosen route.	The same benefits as for Deptartment of Transport's chosen route, although the tunnel would prevent any widening to eight lanes in the future.	Flyover would improve links to the south coast (but increaisng congestion may make this only a temporary benefit).
ECONOMIC COSTS	Minimal.	Minimal.	Much higher capital and maintenance costs would reduce the amount of money available for other road schemes. Delayed completion date would mean continuing congestion would raise transport costs for industry.	Higher costs to industry if congestion continued to be a problem.
ESTIMATED COMPLETION DATE (GIVEN 1992 START)	1994.	1995.	1998.	1993.

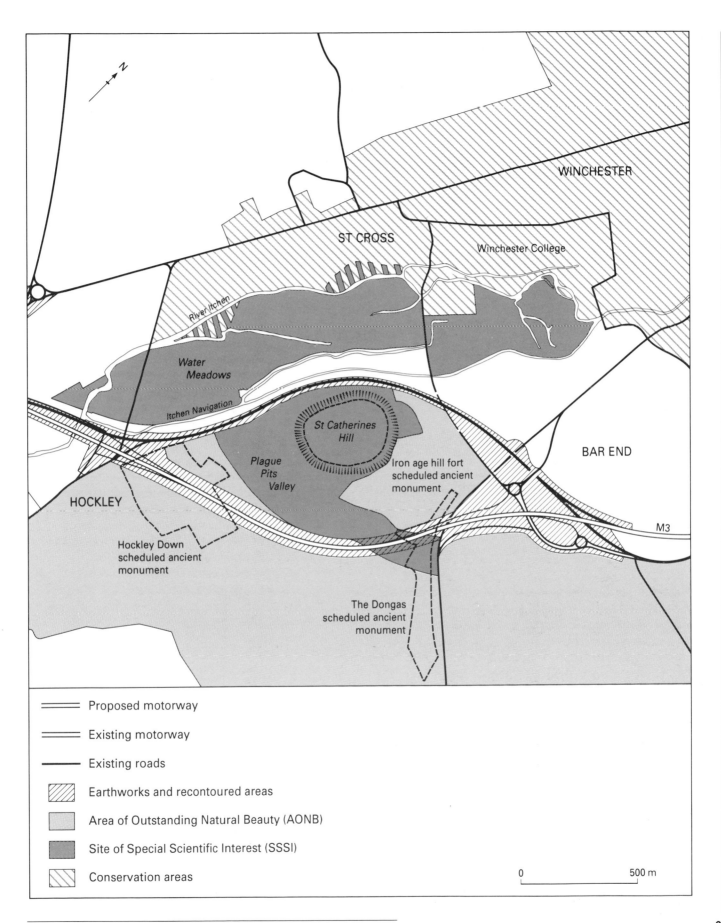

FIG **10.4b** *The Route of the M3 Through Twyford Down*

The choice of route has proved controversial because, in the view of opponents, it will cause major damage to one of the most attractive and supposedly well protected pieces of countryside in southern England.

As Fig 10.3 shows, much of the countryside to the south-east of Winchester is legally protected, as is much of the built-up area of southern Winchester.

– St Catherines Hill forms the western edge of the East Hampshire Area Of Outstanding Natural Beauty (AONB). AONBs give countryside a similar level of protection from development as do national parks.
– The Itchen Valley, including the Winchester water meadows, is a Site of Special Scientific Interest (SSSI). An SSSI is an area with particularly important or unusual ecological characteristics. This SSSI consists largely of ecologically rich unimproved meadow land.
– St Catherine's Hill is also an SSSI. This area comprises ecologically important chalk grassland. It is the habitat of a number of rare European species including the Chalk Hill Blue butterfly.
– There are three Scheduled Ancient Monuments in the area:
1   the Iron Age hill fort on St Catherine's Hill dating from the third century BC;
2   the Dongas medieval trackway system;
3   the 3000 year old prehistoric field, settlement and trackway complex on Hockley Down.
– Most of southern Winchester is an Urban Conservation Area – a built-up area with exceptional architectural, environmental, and historic value. The area includes Winchester College, one of the oldest and most well-known public schools in Britain.

Winchester College also owned part of Twyford Down and the Winchester water meadows. The government compulsorily purchased the college's land on Twyford Down for £300 000. The college appeared to have preferred this option. It was opposed to the route being built close to the water meadows and close to the college itself, despite the fact that the Twyford Down land had been left to the college by two former teachers with instructions that it should be protected from development.

Once the rest of the M3 route had been constructed it became almost impossible for the remaining section to avoid one or more of these protected areas. It has been argued that the area is a casualty of the consultation system used in motorway schemes in Britain whereby each section is treated separately. Once one or more sections of a route have been fixed it reduces the options for the remaining sections.

For most environmental campaigners the route which has been chosen is the worst possible option. Most argue that a tunnel would have been the most acceptable option, with the second choice being the route to the west of St Catherine's Hill.

An unusual coalition of politically moderate local people, national and local conservation groups (including Friends of the Earth and the Worldwide Fund for Nature) and militant environmental groups (including Earth First! and the Dongas Tribe) campaigned against the government decision, but they failed to stop the road being constructed.

At one stage even the EU attempted to halt construction work. In October 1991 the EU's Commissioner for the Environment, Carlo Ripa da Meana, ruled that the British Government was acting illegally by failing to adequately inform the public of the true environmental impact of the scheme. The government defied EU law and continued with construction work, arguing that the public had been adequately informed and that it was an internal matter which should be outside the jurisdiction of the EU. In July 1992 a new Environment Commissioner was appointed – Karel Van Miert – who had previously been Transport Commissioner. He withdrew the EU ruling and agreed with the government that adequate consultation procedures had been carried out.

Many environmental campaigners believe that this U-turn by the EU was politically motivated. The Danish population had recently rejected the Maastricht Treaty in a referendum. The EU Commission was increasingly aware that their attempts to change national government policies was seen as unacceptable interference and was causing a decline in support for the treaty in a number of countries. Some people believe that a deal was struck between the British Government and the EU – that in return for British support for the Maastricht Treaty the EU would withdraw objections to the Twyford Down and other controversial road schemes.

- Using all of the information in Figs 10.3 and 10.4 (pages 247–9) decide which route you think should have been chosen. Try to find a method of scoring or ranking each of the routes under a number of different criteria. Justify your final choice.

- What does the Twyford Down controversy tell you about:
  a) the adequacy of the public enquiry system in Britain?
  b) the effectiveness of British and EU legislation designed to protect the environment?
  c) the appropriateness of the EU intervening in British planning decisions?
  d) the significance of the scheme for future road schemes in Britain and elsewhere in Europe?
  e) the justification of direct action aimed at halting environmental damage?

- 'Twyford Down was a victim of Europe's demand-led approach to transport planning'.
  What does this statement mean? Evaluate its accuracy in the light of the information in this section.

- Read Figs 10.5 and 10.6. Comment on the two newspapers' interpretation of events. Why does the approach of the two articles to the same event differ?

Topless M-way protest

A DOZEN topless women were among protestors who stormed the controversial M3 works site yesterday.

Three hundred marchers defied a court ban to stage the demo.

They broke through a security cordon on the northern section of the site near Winchester, Hants. Five people were arrested.

The road – which links London and Southampton – cuts through Twyford Down and has already destroyed an ancient monument. Protestors admit it is now too late to stop the work.

FIG 10.6 *The Sun, 5 July 1993*

Twyford Down Protesters Invade Motorway Site

IT WAS MEANT to be a requiem but it turned out to be a party – a cheery mass trespass on the huge M3 construction site at Twyford Down near Winchester in Hampshire. The protest was mostly peaceful but there were 27 arrests.

Among the invaders yesterday were about a dozen people who had just been ordered by a High Court judge not to trespass or cause a nuisance on the Department of Transport's land where the four-mile stretch of motorway, costing £45m, is being built.

"I'm prepared to face the consequences, even it it's prison," said Reed Warbler – as he is codenamed by the Department of Transport – a full-time anti-roads campaigner.

About 500 people took part in what was billed by organisers as "a requiem for our landscape". There was meant to be a minute's silence for the destruction that the vast cutting through the chalk downland will cause to an area of countryside with high landscape, wildlife and archaeological value.

But instead of silence there was an invasion of the construction site. The security firm charged with guarding it was hopelessly outnumbered and so was the Hampshire Constabulary.

First past the chainlink fence were the New Age veterans of the Dongas Tribe, a ragged band of travellers, smelling lightly of sweat and patchouli oil, with the odd whiff of dope. They drummed and danced, chanted and hollered.

FIG 10.5 *The Independent, 5 July 1993*

10.2

The High-Speed Train Network Grows

The contribution of high-speed trains to the solution of [environmental problems] is as great as the contribution of landing a human on Mars is to the solution of Third World problems here on Earth.

John Whitelegg, The Conquest of Distance by the Destruction of Time, High-Speed Trains: Fast Tracks to the Future, 1993.

The economic fall-out of the TGV has been so important that provincial towns see super-speed links as a lifeline.

SNCF Spokesman.

An HST is defined as a train capable of exceeding 250 kmph (155 mph). HSTs can use conventional track but the relatively sharp curves, the gradients and the design of the infrastructure, such as signalling, mean that the trains cannot reach maximum speed. For that reason countries using HSTs are spending large sums of money on building new high-speed lines or upgrading existing lines.

Four European countries currently have true high-speed trains: France; Spain; Italy; and Germany. They do not as yet form a European network, but in 1992 plans were unveiled to create a network of HST lines linking the countries of the EU and extending across eastern Europe. The plans were revealed at a conference of the 12 EU railways and the railways of Austria and Switzerland. They propose an increase in total HST lines from a few hundred kilometres in 1992 to 3000 km in 1996 and 7400 km by 2000. A further 15 000 km would be suitable for speeds of 200 kmph (125 mph). An earlier, less ambitious plan, launched in 1990, had already been approved by the transport ministers of all the EU countries (see Fig 10.7).

TGV Atlantique Train in Gare Montparnasse, Paris

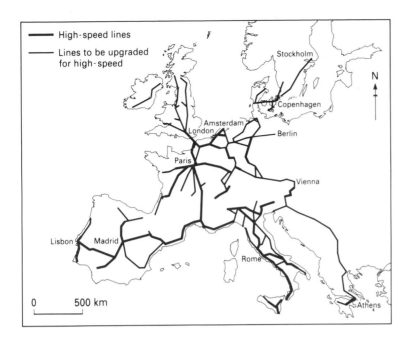

FIG 10.7 *European High-Speed Train Network, Geographical Magazine, March 1992*

The Existing Network

Probably the best known HST is the TGV (Train à Grande Vitesse) operated by SNCF, the French railway. Fig 10.8 shows the network of specially built high-speed lines in 1994. The first route from Paris to Lyons opened in 1983 while the most recent routes connect Paris to the Channel Tunnel and Brussels in Belgium. The TGV is also used on conventional lines elsewhere in France. The number of passengers using the TGV Sud-Est route to Lyons rose from six million in 1982 to 15 million in 1985 and it won over 57 per cent of the air passengers who had originally flown between the two cities.

In 1992 Spain opened its first high-speed line linking Spain to Seville in time for the Expo '92 international exhibition. A second route is planned linking Madrid to Barcelona and eventually joining up with the French TGV network.

Italy's ETR 450 HST runs on conventional track but Italy is also building new high-speed lines on which the ETR 500 train can run at up to 300 kmph (190 mph).

Germany's ICE (Inter-City Express) trains run from Hamburg in the north to Munich in the south, with plans to increase the number of trains to 150 by 1995. A number of new or upgraded lines linking most of Germany's main cities are planned for completion during the 1990s. The ICE trains try to attract business travellers by offering facilities such as video, telephones, computer terminals for making hotel and travel reservations and a conference compartment with photocopier, fax machine and typewriter. Families are attracted by the provision of a nursery on the trains.

In 1994 the German Government approved the future construction of Europe's first high-speed 'magnetic levitation' train route between Berlin and Hamburg. The 'Transrapid',

hovering above a magnetic track would travel at up to 515 kmph (310 mph) and would cost £4 billion. However, construction is not likely to begin until after 2000.

HSTs involve a massive investment. SNCF's North route, linking Paris to the Channel Tunnel, cost £2300 million (£7 million per kilometre). Germany's ICE trains cost £20 million each (representing over £30 000 per seat).

Before a truly European HST network can be created problems of incompatibility have to be overcome. For example, the German ICE trains are too heavy for French rails.

Why is the HST Network Being Built?

There are six main reasons why some governments and railway companies are committing such large sums of money to HSTs and why the EU is so keen on the concept.

European Integration

The HSTs are seen as a way of strengthening links between EU countries. For example, Lille, in northern France, to Brussels will take 35 minutes after 1996 comparied to 90 minutes at present. Lille to Lyons now takes under three hours compared with four hours and 30 minutes in 1993. HSTs have an advantage over airlines because they have direct access to city centres and are more reliable in poor weather. Also, as the network spreads, peripheral areas such as southern Spain and southern Italy, and perhaps eventually eastern Europe, will become less remote.

Regional Development

This is linked closely to the reason above, but it is argued that the HST routes will suck in investment in industry and recreation as they open up regions currently lacking good transport links. The French Government in particular sees the TGV as a catalyst for national and regional economic development.

Profit

Privatised rail companies, and governments worried about the high subsidies they are paying to the railways see HSTs as a way of making a profit. They attract more passengers,

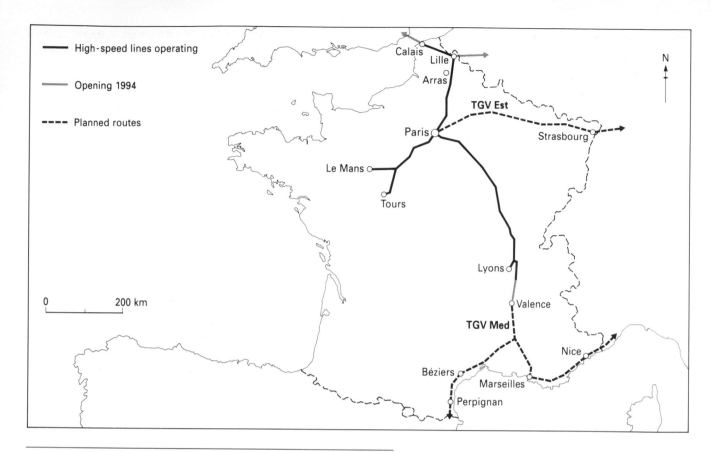

Fɪɢ **10.8** *TGV Network*

particularly business travellers willing to pay relatively high fares, and despite the massive investment involved they have been shown to be profitable.

Image

European railway companies have, on the whole, seen the use of the railways steadily decline over recent decades because of competition from private cars, lorries and airlines. This process has badly damaged the public image of railways. The situation has worsened as declining revenues and declining investment have led to a gradual running down of railway infrastructure and rolling stock. The ultra-modern image of HSTs has given the railway companies the chance to improve the image of their whole network, in effect giving European rail travel a new lease of life.

Environmental Impact

Railways produce less noise and consume less energy per passenger kilometre than either airlines or motorways. A high-speed line takes up a third of the land area needed by a motorway. For these reasons, companies developing HST networks and the EU have been able to exploit this green image to win support for their plans.

Also, rail companies argue that HST's attract passengers from motorways and airlines. This reduces motorway congestion and reduces the demand for polluting aircraft along with the need for more and more airport space.

Higher Speeds are Good

There is an assumption made by most decision makers that achieving higher speeds is beneficial in its own right – in other words, it is a sign of progress. Higher speeds are equated with greater efficiency because they save travellers' time which can then be used for more productive activities.

Arguments Against HSTs

However, HSTs are not without their critics. Some people believe that they are environmentally, economically and socially damaging. They base their views on the following arguments.

High Energy Consumption

High speeds necessitate higher energy consumption per kilometre. Even though HSTs are powered by electricity and are in themselves non-polluting they nevertheless increase atmospheric pollution at the power stations.

Environmental Damage

Although high-speed lines are not as environmentally disruptive as motorways they cause greater damage to the landscape and more noise pollution than conventional railway lines. In Germany opposition by conservationists and local people forced German Railways to put considerable lengths of its new high-speed line into tunnels, at enormous cost. This also meant that the cost of the new trains was increased because they have to be sealed and pressurised to insulate passengers from the changes in outside air pressure caused by rapid entry into the tunnels. SNCF has met opposition to proposals for a high-speed line through Provence, while in South-East England opposition to a high-speed London-Channel Tunnel link (see Section 10.3) has contributed to delays in starting construction.

Impact on Conventional Rail Networks

HSTs absorb massive amounts of capital investment which would be much better spent on revitalising and extending the existing railway networks. For example higher than expected costs in building the Madrid-Seville line in Spain contributed to the shelving of a new commuter line from Madrid to Alcala de Henares.

Greater Inequality

HSTs are mainly used by the more wealthy sections of society such as business travellers. Because they absorb resources which could have been spent on preventing the current decline of conventional types of public transport they in fact reduce the mobility of the poorer sections of society. In other words, they reinforce social and economic inequality.

Impact on Peripheral Areas

Far from sucking in capital to peripheral areas they in fact suck out capital. It becomes easier for economic activity to concentrate in the core areas of Europe, and then to use high-speed transport networks to distribute goods and services to the peripheral areas. Even if they are successful in attracting investment to areas close to the HST lines this simply increases the difficulties facing the areas which are not close to the lines.

Impact on Other Forms of Transport

HSTs do not reduce the amount of air travel or allow environmental gains. In fact the demand for air travel is so great that the airlines cannot meet present demand without dangerously overcrowding European air space. More than 30 of Europe's major airports are expected to be at full capacity by the year 2000. The airlines can fill the air space released by the reduced demand for internal European flights with new flights to destinations outside Europe.

Similarly, any extra space that may be created on motorways will simply be filled by additional road users. In total, therefore, the environmental impact of HSTs is negative.

The TGV and the Regeneration of Lille

The city of Lille in northern France has been successful in being chosen as the location of an important junction on France's emerging TGV network and as the first stop on the French side for the line from the Channel Tunnel. The TGV Nord line from Paris to the Channel Tunnel already passes through the city and by 1996 a new line to Brussels will join the Nord line in Lille. TGVs to and from Paris will use the existing station, Lille Flandres, while a new station, Lille Europe, is being built 400 m away to take the trains to and from Brussels and the Channel Tunnel. By 1996 30 million passengers a year are expected to pass through the two stations.

The city has used the development of the TGV network as an opportunity to regenerate the local economy and to redevelop the city centre. Lille has suffered considerable de-industrialisation since the 1970s with the decline of the region's traditional industries of coal-mining, steel and textiles. The city sees its key position on the TGV network as an opportunity to attract capital investment and jobs, and in fact the city successfully fought off a challenge from Amiens, which also wanted to be chosen as the location for the TGV junction. Lille will be one hour from Paris, two hours from London and 35 minutes from Brussels. The city's attitude to the TGV can be contrasted to the situation in relatively affluent Kent in South-East England where there have been campaigns against the proposed high-speed Channel Tunnel rail link (see Section 10.3).

The Lille Europe station is to be at the centre of a £1.1 billion city centre development scheme called Euralille – a scheme of a similar scale to Canary Wharf in the London Docklands and containing an international business centre, exhibition halls, hotels, offices, a shopping centre and a park. Various public sector agencies, banks, the SNCF and the Chamber of Commerce are co-operating in the initiative. 30 per cent of the finance is coming from the private sector and 70 per cent from the public sector.

- Attempt to categorise the arguments for and against HSTs into social, environmental and economic arguments.

- Suggest a method of ranking the arguments for and against HSTs to enable you to come to a conclusion on which are the strongest.

10.3 No Longer an Island: the Channel Tunnel

Channel Tunnel Terminal at Folkestone, Kent, 1994

The first proposal to construct a fixed link between France and Britain was presented to Napoleon in 1802. The concept of a Channel Tunnel is nearly two centuries old. As long ago as the 1880s, trial tunnels were being bored from the British and the French sides of the Channel. However, this work was stopped by the British Government in 1883 amid fears that a tunnel would be a threat to the defence of Britain in time of war. Fearing that a tunnel could be used by an invading army, British Governments opposed the tunnel until 1955. In fact, the defence argument was probably a smokescreen for other worries. To some the concept of a tunnel struck at the heart of a belief in the British as an island nation separate from, and different to, the rest of Europe. They believed that a tunnel would in some way change the character of Britain.

However, after 1955 support for a tunnel re-emerged both inside and outside the British Government. In 1960 a Channel Tunnel Study Group recommended that a twin rail tunnel should be built rather than a drive-through road tunnel, yet the scheme failed to progress between 1960 and the early 1980s due largely to continuing luke-warm political support in Britain (the French Government, in contrast, showed consistent support for the idea). In 1980 the Conservative government began to show stronger interest but made it clear that private sector investment must be used and not government funds. In 1981 the British Prime Minister, Margaret Thatcher, and President Mitterand of France gave a commitment to support the tunnel and in 1985 a competition was held to find the best scheme. The scheme put forward by the Eurotunnel consortium was chosen in 1986 and the tunnel finally opened in 1994.

The scheme consists of two rail tunnels and a service tunnel 50 km long linking Cheriton near Folkestone in Kent and Fréthun near Calais in the region of Nord-Pas-de-Calais. Construction work was financed by loans from banks around the world and by selling shares in Eurotunnel. Eurotunnel contracted Transmanche Link (TML), an Anglo-French company, to build the tunnel. The period of construction was characterised by disputes between Eurotunnel and TML over costs, and a series of financial crises as the total costs rose from the original estimate of £4.8 billion to £7.7 billion in 1990 and to a final bill of £10 billion in 1994. Eurotunnel had to repeatedly request further injections of money from the banks and through share offers.

The response to the decision to construct a tunnel has been very different in the two regions linked by the scheme – Kent and Nord-Pas-de-Calais. In the French region the tunnel has been generally welcomed as a catalyst for economic development, while in Kent the tunnel has either been viewed with hostility or been seen as an unavoidable development for which the costs to the county should be minimised. To understand the reasons for this difference it is necessary to compare the characteristics of the two areas (Fig 10.9).

KENT	NORD-PAS-DE-CALAIS
Largest urban areas are the Medway towns of Chatham, Gillingham and Rochester which have a combined population of 225 000.	The region has eight cities of more than 100 000 people.
70 per cent live in towns but the county is mainly suburban or rural in character.	88 per cent live in cities.
The economy relies on small manufacturing and service firms.	Traditional industries of textiles, coal and steel dominated the economy.
Although the county is not as prosperous as the rest of South-East England it was not seeking major industrial investment in the late 1980s. Unemployment is not a serious problem in most of Kent.	High unemployment caused by de-industrialisation
Unemployment in the late 1980s was 48 per cent below the EU average.	Unemployment in the late 1980s was 39 per cent above the EU average.
GDP per head in the late 1980s was three per cent below the EU average.	GDP per head in the late 1980s was 12 per cent. below the EU average.
Majority vote Conservative.	Majority vote Socialist.

- Using the information in Fig 10.9 suggest why Kent was generally less enthusiastic about the tunnel than Nord-Pas-de-Calais.

FIG 10.9 *A Comparison of Nord-Pas-de-Calais and Kent*

The information on Kent in the above table disguises some large variations in economic health. East Kent in particular is economically weak. The area is reliant on industries which are declining nationally and on a tourist industry suffering from a decreasing number of of tourists from the London area. Many of the tourists who traditionally visited the Kent seaside resorts now travel to France. Some parts of Kent have still not recovered from the closure of the local coal-mining industry. Unemployment in East Kent in the late 1980s was almost twice that of West Kent. In some towns unemployment was particularly high – for example, 21 per cent in Thanet. However, few local people saw the tunnel as an opportunity for economic development because many of the jobs in East Kent were based on the ferries and associated service industries and so were particularly vulnerable to changes brought about by the opening of the tunnel. The Kent Impact Study completed by the county council estimated that between 4300 and 6600 jobs would be lost in the ports or on the ferries, and that once the jobs created by the tunnel were taken into account there would be a net loss of between 1100 and 3400 jobs.

Kent County Council has never taken a clear stance either for or against the tunnel, although some local councils, such as Ashford Borough Council, expressed support for the scheme. Nationally in Britain the tunnel has probably had more support. The construction industry was certainly in favour while the regions in the north and west of the country saw it as an opportunity to improve links with mainland Europe and to become more competitive when trading with Europe.

- Suggest why Kent County Council never declared either support or opposition for the tunnel.

The different attitudes of the decision makers to the tunnel on the opposite sides of the Channel led to different policies.

As the table in Fig 10.10 (overleaf) indicates state intervention was minimal in Britain, other than in the area of improving road links to the tunnel, while in France strategic planning was seen to be important.

The French national and Nord-Pas-de-Calais state governments came to an agreement over how the benefits of the tunnel should be maximised very soon after the Eurotunnel scheme had been selected. The agreement, called a *protocole d'accord*, outlined a joint programme.

- Action to maximise the employment benefits of the tunnel by:
  a) co-ordinating training programmes to allow local people to benefit from jobs brought by the tunnel;

257

KENT	NORD-PAS-DE-CALAIS
Policies focused on controlling the impact of the scheme and on minimising the environmental, economic and social costs.	Policies focused on sharing out the benefits around the whole region.
There was also some desire to spread any benefits around the whole country.	There was also a desire to concentrate the benefits in Nord-Pas-de-Calais.
State intervention, particularly in the area of strategic planning, has been minimal.	The state has been keen to maximise the benefits of the tunnel by strategic planning.

FIG 10.10   *A Comparison of Policies in Kent and Nord-Pas-de-Calais*

b) informing firms in Nord-Pas-de-Calais of how they could benefit from tunnel contracts;
c) setting up retraining programmes for tunnel workers once the project was completed in 1994.

- Upgrading the regional road network by:
  a) constructing a coastal road from the Belgian frontier to Boulogne-Sur-Mer;
  b) completing the A26 motorway from Calais to Reims;
  c) constructing additional road links to the three regional ports of Calais, Boulogne and Dunkerque.

- Upgrading the rail network by:
  a) extending the TGV Nord from Lille to the tunnel (see Section 10.2);
  b) electrifying other parts of the regional rail network in order to link it to the tunnel.

- Modernising the region's ports in order to compensate for the loss of ferry traffic once the tunnel opens by:
  a) extending the container port at Dunkerque;
  b) extending the port at Calais;
  c) re-equiping the fishing fleet at Boulogne.

- Restructuring the regional economy, particularly by aiding the development of tourism along the coast.

In all, the agreement specified over £460 million of public sector expenditure between 1986 and 1994 to enable the whole region to maximise the potential benefits of the tunnel.

- List all the costs and benefits of the Channel Tunnel you can think of for **a)** Kent and **b)** Britain.

The Channel Tunnel Rail Link

Constrained by the ideology of a government which refused to sanction public investment in a dedicated rail link to the tunnel, they presided over the rail link fiasco which stands in such stark contrast to its French equivalent.

I Holliday et al, The Channel Tunnel, 1991.

A tragi-comedy in umpteen acts.

Sir Alastair Morton, Chief Executive of Eurotunnel, describing the high-speed rail link decision making process.

The differences in approach on the two sides of the Channel are particularly clear in the case of policy over constructing new rail links to the tunnel. On the British side the government, seeing the Channel Tunnel as a flagship of its transport privatisation programme, pursued a private sector approach to constructing a new high-speed rail link between London and the tunnel. It was very reluctant to commit any state funds even though British Rail is a state-owned enterprise. They believed that users of a new link should pay the full cost and not be supported by government subsidies. Since the government did not subsidise the cross-Channel ferries there was no justification, it was argued, for subsidising cross-Channel trains. There was also considerable delay and political indecision over the route the link should take both through Kent and through London. This was partly a result of the lack of an effective strategic planning agency in South-East England.

In contrast, on the French side the government was active in supporting a high-speed link between the tunnel and Paris. The government saw the tunnel as an integral part of an international transport system with the French network at its heart.

The British link will not be completed before the year 2000 while the French link was completed in time for the opening of the tunnel. To some extent the construction of a link through Kent is a more difficult task than constructing one through northern France. Kent has a much higher population density and more sensitive and vulnerable countryside, such as Green Belts, Areas of Outstanding Natural Beauty and Sites of Special Scientific Interest. Finding a consensus over a route is much more difficult. A wave of protest met BR when it announced its route options in 1988 from communities living close to the routes. Nevertheless, the delay over constructing a British link has more to do with a reluctance to invest state funds and an unwillingness to plan strategically than with environmental difficulties and local opposition.

The delays could prove to be embarrassing for the British Government. Specially designed Eurostar trains will travel from Paris at 180 mph and at 100 mph through the tunnel but when they reach Britain they will be forced to slow down to 'slot into' gaps between local commuter trains in Kent. It is possible that the existing lines in Kent will be at saturation level soon after the opening of the tunnel in 1994. There will be no spare capacity to absorb any increase in traffic generated by the tunnel in the following years. Also, there will be limitations on the number of through trains to Manchester, Leeds, Edinburgh and Glasgow.

In the meantime BR has spent £130 million on a new railway station at Waterloo to accommodate trains using existing lines from the tunnel. There is a danger that this station could become a white elephant once the high-speed link opens, although only the last 22 miles of the Waterloo tunnel route will be on slower lines by then. It will take 2 hours and 45 minutes from Waterloo to Paris compared with 2 hours and 30 minutes from St Pancras to Paris.

The government finally gave a firm commitment to start constructing the link in 1993, 12 months before the tunnel was due to open. They also announced that the £2.5 billion link would be a joint venture between the public and private sectors – a tacit admission that their attempt to rely totally on private sector investment had failed. They announced the route the link would take (see Fig 10.11) and also stated that they saw the link as a catalyst for development in the East Thames Corridor – the area encompassing the south bank of the Thames Estuary and the Medway towns. The link will terminate at St Pancras station in central London.

Conservation groups are concerned about the environmental impact of the link. The route will affect eight Sites of Special Scientific Interest, seven ancient woodlands and 15 other sites of ecological importance. One site, the West Thurrock Lagoons SSSI, is also protected by the Ramsar Convention and is of international importance for birds.

- List the points made in this section which support the view that French decision makers have supported the concept of a Channel Tunnel more strongly than the British decision makers.

- List the evidence in this section which supports the view that 'a belief in state intervention and strategic planning have allowed France to take advantage of the opportunities presented by the Channel Tunnel more effectively.'

- People living close to the route of the high-speed link in Kent and in London have shown considerable concern over the impact of the high-speed link on their communities.
  a) With the help of the information in Fig 10.12 (page 260) list the impacts you think the link will have on the communities it passes through.
  b) Which do you think would have the greatest environmental impact – a high-speed railway line or a motorway? Explain and justify your choice.

FIG **10.11** *Channel Tunnel Rail Link Route*

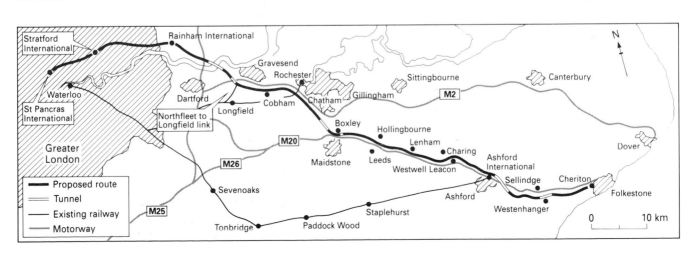

FIG 10.12   *Environmental Impacts of the Proposed Channel Tunnel Rail Link*

c) The estimated cost of the link is £2.5 billion. One of the original route proposals was estimated to cost £4.5 billion. The difference in the cost is due to the fact that more than a third of the original route was to be in tunnels. The route chosen by the government is mainly at ground level. Would a cost of £2 billion to reduce the environmental impact of the scheme have been justified? Explain your answer.

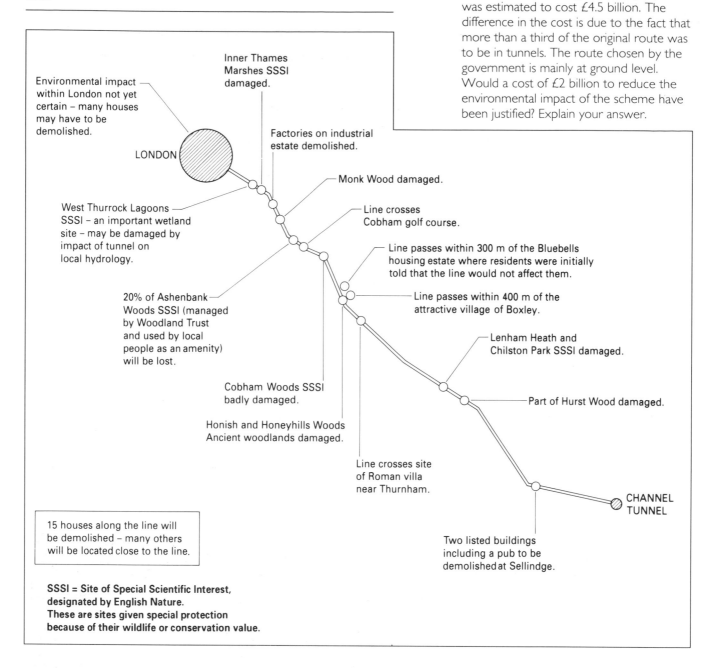

Environmental impact within London not yet certain – many houses may have to be demolished.

Inner Thames Marshes SSSI damaged.

Factories on industrial estate demolished.

LONDON

Monk Wood damaged.

West Thurrock Lagoons SSSI – an important wetland site – may be damaged by impact of tunnel on local hydrology.

Line crosses Cobham golf course.

Line passes within 300 m of the Bluebells housing estate where residents were initially told that the line would not affect them.

20% of Ashenbank Woods SSSI (managed by Woodland Trust and used by local people as an amenity) will be lost.

Line passes within 400 m of the attractive village of Boxley.

Lenham Heath and Chilston Park SSSI damaged.

Cobham Woods SSSI badly damaged.

Part of Hurst Wood damaged.

Honish and Honeyhills Woods Ancient woodlands damaged.

Line crosses site of Roman villa near Thurnham.

CHANNEL TUNNEL

15 houses along the line will be demolished – many others will be located close to the line.

Two listed buildings including a pub to be demolished at Sellindge.

**SSSI = Site of Special Scientific Interest, designated by English Nature.
These are sites given special protection because of their wildlife or conservation value.**

10.4 Instant Communications: the Impact of Telecommunications

Apart from encouraging smaller work units, apart from permitting a decentralisation and de-urbanisation of production, apart from altering the actual character of work, the [development of telecommunications, computers and other new technologies] could shift literally millions of jobs out of the factories and offices into which the [industrial revolution] swept them and right back where they came from originally: the home.

A Toffler, The Third Wave, 1980.

In Inverness, ten women sit at home answering directory enquiries calls for British Telecom, just like their workmates sitting up to 26 miles away in orderly rows at the exchange. All are teleworkers, who use telecommunications as the basis for their work. To function, a teleworker needs only a computer, a modem, some communications software and access to a telephone line. Their employer's office can be thousands of miles away – which is why Claudia Cragg, a journalist who writes for the huge Japanese publishing company Sekai Bunka, has her office in her spare room. Once there, she makes a local call to connect her to a public computer network that links to Tokyo and the rest of the world. Through it, she can contact other journalists and editors, and search databases for information, without knowing or caring about their physical location.

C Arthur, How To Give Up Going To Work,
New Scientist, October 1992

Telecommunications, particularly when combined with information technology, is reducing the effect of distance. Regions remote from centres of population can use telecommunications to minimise the problems posed by their geographical location and, at least in theory, it reduces the need for economic activity to concentrate in a particular location. It has been predicted that the development of telecommunications will have two spatial impacts in particular:

1 the development and spread of teleworking leading to the relocation of employment;

2 greater integration of peripheral and remote areas into economic activity.

In fact, the extent to which advances in telecommunications will favour remote areas is by no means certain. It seems certain that investment in new telecommunications technology will, at least initially, be

Teleworking

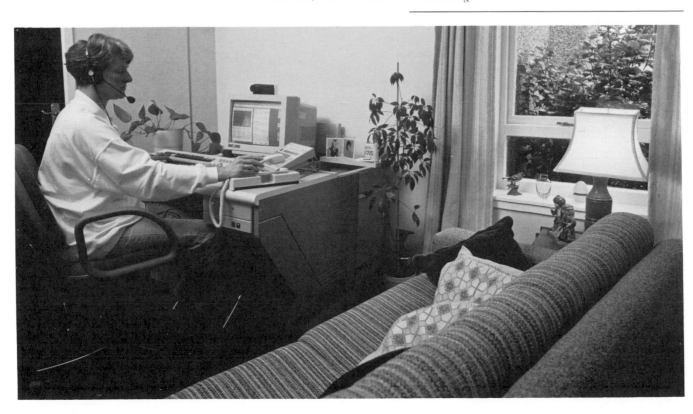

concentrated in large urban areas where high volume demand will make them profitable. This would simply reinforce the competitiveness of these areas at the expense of the peripheral areas. On the other hand, as the case study of the Scottish Highlands below shows, telecommunications can benefit remote areas. The EU has a programme to remedy deficiencies in telecommunications networks in remote and poorly developed regions for this reason.

Teleworking: a Social, Environmental and Economic Revolution?

The extract from *The Third Wave* at the beginning of this section highlights the fact that some futurologists believe that telecommunications and computers could revolutionise the way in which millions of people will work over the next few decades. Teleworking is where people work from home rather than travelling to a place of work. This is particularly relevant to office work, including occupations such as journalism, publishing, computer programming and finance and accounting. Using a computer linked to a telephone line, teleworkers can work on their own while being linked electronically to their employer, manager, or other workers.

Strategic Work 2000, a consultancy which advises British Telecom, claims that companies could save £20 000 a year in office costs and overheads per teleworker (including office rental, heating, lighting, catering, and car parking space). It says staff could save an average £750 a year in travel costs. The Henley Centre for Forecasting has estimated that up to 50 per cent of Britain's workforce have jobs which could be done on a part-time or full-time teleworking basis.

Teleworking is less widespread in Europe than in the USA where it has been estimated that over 20 per cent of the workforce have taken part in teleworking and that teleworking is growing by 20 per cent a year. It has been estimated that there are about 580 000 teleworkers in Britain in small businesses including self-employed people such as freelance writers and consultants, although many of these may only rely on the use of a telephone rather than a computer. In larger businesses it is estimated that there are 60 000 full-time and 140 000 part-time teleworkers. In 1992 another survey found that 13 per cent of companies had introduced some form of teleworking. British Telecom, who have a clear interest in promoting telework, has estimated that by the second half of the 1990s two million people could be teleworkers for at least three days a week. In the Netherlands there are estimated to be 75 000 teleworkers.

Some employers have found that teleworking can bring real advantages for them. In one survey in Britain in 1992, 75 per cent of companies involved in teleworking reported an increase in productivity by teleworkers. It also means that a firm can make use of skilled workers who otherwise may choose not to work for that firm because of, for example, the distance they would have to travel to work or because they would have to move home. The London Borough of Enfield, for example, recruited 58 teleworkers in 1989 to help administer the poll tax. In the Isle de France Region of France, regional government agencies are actively encouraging

local companies to expand telework. In the Netherlands, concern about the environmental impacts of travel to work has encouraged a number of government departments to experiment with telework. A forum made up of representatives from the government, industry and unions and called Platform Network Nederland has also been created to examine ways of expanding teleworking.

Teleworking on a large scale could bring enormous environmental gains because of the reduced need to commute to work every day – less people would need to use cars or public transport. It has also been argued that teleworking can bring enormous social benefits. People can more easily fit work around child-minding and other household arrangements. People will be under less stress because they no longer need to travel to work and they will have more freedom to choose where to live. Many more people may, for example, choose to live in rural areas. Some people have even argued that it would strengthen the family as a unit because there will be more contact between members of the family, and would strengthen communities because people would move home less frequently and so would develop a stronger commitment to their local area.

Others, on the other hand, argue that this paints a far too rosy picture. They believe that teleworking is a lonely occupation and that people miss the face-to-face contact that work usually brings. They believe that teleworkers would be less motivated than people working as part of a team in a single building. Teleworkers could be exploited by their employers because workers would be less likely to campaign collectively for better pay or conditions through a trade union. They also argue that rather than strengthening the family unit it would weaken it by increasing the potential for conflict between family members working from home. For this reason they believe that teleworking will not expand as much as some forecasters have argued and that while some occupations and some people may be suited to telework many are not.

If teleworking does continue to expand and does become a common mode of working there is no doubt that it would have very significant environmental, spatial and social effects. It remains to be seen whether the next decade will see a major shift in the location of work.

• Using the information in this section, together with your own ideas, evaluate the possible consequences of a large-scale shift to teleworking under the following headings:
   a) spatial; b) environmental; c) social; d) economic.

Telecottages: Integrating Remote Areas

At least in the short term telecommunications and information technology may have the most impact on regions geographically remote from the main centres of population and economic activity. Traditionally these areas have suffered from the effect of distance in terms of the time it takes for goods or people to travel to and from the area and in terms of the cost of these journeys. Distance has made it difficult for these areas to compete with core regions. Also, low population densities mean that many of the services found in more populous areas are not available, simply because there are insufficient people to make them viable.

Telecommunications allows remote regions to have the same access to information and the same ability to communicate as any other region. In the case of jobs involving the processing of information it makes no difference whether the worker is located on the European periphery, for example in western Ireland, northern Scandinavia, or southern Spain, or in a core region such as South-East England, Paris, the Netherlands or western Germany. It may also mean that remoter areas can have access to some of the services normally only available to urban areas.

Some of the more peripheral or remote regions of Europe are now taking full advantage of the new opportunities being provided by these technologies. The Highlands and Islands of Scotland is now in the forefront of these developments, although Sweden was probably the first country to see the possibilities.

Many areas are involved in the development of telecottages – buildings equipped with computers, desk-top publishing equipment, fax machines and phone links and which are available for use by local firms, community groups and individuals. A telecottage is a workplace-cum-training centre-cum-community centre. It provides small communities with access to information technology they could not otherwise afford. In some cases telecottages also become the base for new enterprises. In one case in France a business employing 85 people providing insurance services emerged from a telecottage.

Telecottages began in Scandinavia in 1985. By 1990 there were about 50 in Denmark, Finland, Norway and Sweden. By 1993 there were about 100. Many are located in schools and libraries. Some provide educational services, but most aim to help small businesses including farmers.

The effectiveness of telecottages in improving employment and quality of life in rural areas is being studied by a two year project called Mitre (Market Implementation of Teleworking in Rural Environments) which has received £1.6 million of funding from the EU. The rest of the money comes from academic and business organisations including Horsens

Polytechnic in Denmark, The Microelectronics Application Centre in Limerick in Ireland and the Empirica consultancy in Bonn in Germany. Below are three case studies of how these developments are being exploited within one European country – Britain.

Case Study 1: the Highlands and Islands of Scotland

One of the most advanced telecommunications networks in Europe is now in place in the Highlands and Islands. The Highlands and Islands Initiative is a partnership between Highlands and Islands Enterprise (a government-sponsored economic development agency) and British Telecom, with BT providing 70 per cent of the funding. The two organisations have jointly invested £16 million in installing advanced technology including an Integrated Services Digital Network (ISDN) – a network which will allow the use of fibre-optics to carry messages. The ISDN gives small businesses in the region the capability to link instantly to major centres of commerce and industry around the world allowing them to efficiently compete with larger businesses in the core European regions.

The ISDN allows high quality transmission of voice, text, graphics and video at high-speed. Videoconferencing is also possible (that is, holding 'meetings' between a number of people using telecommunications, including visual links, rather than actually meeting in the same place). The speed of the network means that telephone bills can be reduced. The ISDN also provides teleworkers with much greater flexibility, allowing faster and more complex link-ups between computers around the world.

HIE hopes that the initiative will either attract entire businesses to the region or encourage larger businesses to locate part of their operations in the Highlands and Islands. They hope that the new technology, combined with the high quality of the environment, the low cost of property in the region and the skilled people living in the region, will prove a major attraction for business. In this way they hope to regenerate the regional economy.

As part of the initiative British Telecom has established a computer help service at Thurso in the far north of Scotland from where advice and information is provided to BT computer users in the London area a thousand kilometres away.

In 1993 Hoskyns, an information technology services company, established an 'out-sourcing centre' at Forres, north-east of Inverness. It is expected that the centre will carry out clerical and administrative work for other companies. The project attracted £1.5 million of aid from Grampian Regional Council and HIE.

Highlands and Islands Enterprise has also been active in setting up telecottages around the region. The telecottages are called Community Teleservice Centres (CTCs). Four pilot CTCs were established on the islands of Unst, Hoy, Islay and Benbecula in 1991 (see Fig 10.15) at a cost of £240 000 – £160 000 provided by HIE and £80 000 by British Telecom. The aims of the CTCs are to raise awareness of new technology in the local areas, to provide training for local people, to provide access to new technology for local communities and to provide a location for teleworking. Although the CTCs have been initially funded by HIE, it is hoped that they will become self-financing by the second half of the 1990s. Local community groups had to apply for funding to set up the CTCs, and so much of the initial work was done voluntarily. A report evaluating the success of the CTCs published in 1993 stated that the pilot CTCs had shown that:

'computers [and] telecommunications can offer possibilities of work, income, continuing education and training, and leisure in remote rural communities. This will be very important for the future development of teleworking in the region.'

Evaluation of Community Teleservice Centres in the Highlands and Islands, The Arkleton Trust.

Case Study 2: the Kington Connected Community Project

Throughout the more remote and sparsely populated areas of rural Britain services such as education, health care, and post office services are becoming increasingly centralised in larger settlements as the authorities attempt to take advantage of economies of scale. The closure of such services poses a threat to the survival of rural and small town communities. Service decline is likely to accelerate depopulation as people move to the larger settlements in order to be closer to the services.

Kington, a small town in Herefordshire, is one community which felt threatened by these trends and a group of local people decided to take advantage of a telecommunications project launched in 1993.

The Connected Community Project is sponsored by Apple Computers and British Telecom, with the backing of the government's Department of Trade and the Rural Development Commission (a government agency with the role of supporting small-scale economic development in rural areas). The project is designed to investigate ways in which new technology can regenerate social and business activities

and create jobs and better working conditions in rural areas.

Following a competition between interested rural towns Kington was selected as the trial area for the project. £250 000 worth of equipment and expert help was provided by the sponsors and most of it is located in the project's offices in Kington High Street. Here, local businesses, individuals and community groups can receive training in the use of the equipment, prepare material on desk-top publishing equipment, communicate with any other location on the global telecommunications network, or simply try out the equipment. A Technical Director has the role of ensuring that the technology is used to maximise advantage. Funding to maintain the project has been initially provided by the local Training and Enterprise Council (TEC) and District Council. In the longer term funding will have to be found by the local community through sponsorship, earnings from contracts and commission on work distributed to local specialists in areas such as desk-top publishing and language translation. One of the Connected Community's major projects is working with local schools and offering training courses to businesses and local people.

FIG 10.13 *Part of a Kington Connected Community Project Newsletter*

KINGTON – PROUD OF ITS PAST AND CONNECTED TO ITS FUTURE

Services available at No. 2 High Street

• Training in Infomation Technology skills to local businesses, community groups and individuals;

• Obtaining and managing contracts from major companies for local teleworkers;

• Equipment hire (on and off site);

• Provision of office services to local businesses;

• Community information services including:
  – access to national databases (e.g. employment opportunities);
  – production of local newsletters, bulletins and information sheets.

The overall aim of the project is to allow people who want to work in highly-skilled and well-paid jobs to remain in the area and so to discourage depopulation. As in the case of the Highlands and Islands Initiative the Kington centre can take advantage of the ISDN telecommunications network allowing local teleworkers to communicate rapidly and cheaply throughout Britain and in the rest of the world.

The potential is enormous according to local organisers. For example, a computer database is being developed in conjunction with the local tourist information centre to give visitors up-to-date local information including the use of visual and video material. The idea of using videoconferencing technology for the benefit of the local community is also being explored. For example, 'visiting' speakers who live a long distance away could be invited to talk to local community groups. A local farmer with computer programming skills is helping to develop a system of electronic agricultural land use mapping, with the support of the Connected Community Project and a satellite equipment manufacturer. The aim is to develop a system where farmers can use a new type of hand-held computer linked to satellite technology to supply information to the European Union on farm land use. The EU demands land use information as part of their enforcement of set-aside and the system of agricultural subsidies.

It remains to be seen the extent to which the local community as a whole benefits from the project and whether it acts as a catalyst for the long-term regeneration of the local community and local economy.

FIG 10.14   *Telephones per 100 People*

Country	1980	1990
Austria	40	59
Belgium	37	55
Czech/Slovak Republics	21	27
Denmark	64	97
Finland	50	53
France	15	18
Western Germany	46	67
Eastern Germany	19	12
Greece	23	46
Hungary	12	18
Iceland	48	50
Ireland	19	28
Italy	34	56
Netherlands	52	46
Norway	46	50
Poland	10	14
Portugal	14	26
Spain	32	32
Sweden	80	68
Switzerland	72	91
UK	48	43

Case Study 3: the Antur Tanat Cain Telebureau, Clwyd, Wales

This telecottage project emerged from an investigation carried out by Clwyd County Council into ways of stemming the rise in unemployment and the out-migration of young people in rural areas. The project is based in a formerly derelict group of buildings containing a sawmill, a smithy and a pub. The telecottage now has nearly 30 computers and Antur is a recognised information technology training centre. It also supports local teleworkers and now offers computer services to other companies on a commercial basis. Services it offers include desk-top publishing and Welsh language translating. Antur is hoping to expand by setting up other telecottages elsewhere in rural Wales.

- Study Fig 10.15 (pages 266 and 267). Imagine you are a consultant being employed by the French Government and the EU to identify priority locations for telecottage development in France. Using the data in the table and the map locate five départements you believe would particularly benefit from investment in telecottages. Justify your selection. You could use a mapping technique, or any other technique you think would be appropriate.

- **a)** Comment on the trends in phone use indicated by the data in Fig 10.14.
  b) Construct a choropleth map based on the 1990 data in Fig 10.14. What does the map tell you about the likely spatial variations in the spread of teleworking in Europe over the next few years?

Département	Population		Unemployment	GDP/person
	Inhab/km² 1990	Change (%) 1980–90	% 1990	EUR=100 1989
1 Nord	441	0.9	11.7	94
2 Pas-de-Calais	215	1.9	12.0	75
3 Aisne	73	0.8	10.7	97
4 Oise	124	12.6	8.5	96
5 Somme	89	1.1	11.3	92
6 Calvados	112	6.6	9.1	99
7 Manche	81	4.0	7.3	87
8 Orne	48	−0.4	6.8	90
9 Eure	85	14.2	8.2	97
10 Seine-Maritime	195	3.2	10.4	115
11 Paris	21 537	−2.6	9.4	318
12 Seine-et-Marne	182	27.4	6.8	95
13 Yvelines	567	12.6	5.1	104
14 Essonne	601	12.0	5.3	96
15 Hauts-de-Seine	6960	−0.6	5.8	236
16 Seine-Saint-Denis	6902	4.6	9.2	108
17 Val-de-Marne	6077	1.5	6.3	112
18 Val-d'Oise	872	17.2	7.1	93
19 Ardennes	57	−2.5	11.3	85
20 Aube	48	0.5	9.0	104
21 Marne	68	3.7	9.2	116
22 Haute-Marne	33	−3.1	7.6	95
23 Côte-d'Or	56	5.5	8.0	110
24 Nièvre	34	−3.3	8.0	74
25 Saône-et-Loire	65	−1.9	8.3	100
26 Yonne	44	5.2	8.2	89
27 Cher	44	1.0	8.3	85
28 Eure-et-Loir	67	11.8	7.5	98
29 Indre	35	−3.0	9.1	90
30 Indre-et-Loire	86	6.5	9.6	99
31 Loir-et-Cher	48	4.6	7.4	108
32 Loiret	86	11.4	8.3	112
33 Meurthe-et-Moselle	137	−0.8	7.9	92
34 Meuse	32	−2.4	7.7	86
35 Moselle	163	0.7	8.0	89
36 Vosges	66	−2.4	8.4	96
37 Bas-Rhin	198	5.4	4.8	117
38 Haut-Rhin	192	4.1	4.1	108
39 Doubs	93	2.1	6.6	112
40 Jura	50	2.9	5.0	103
41 Haute-Savoie	43	0.5	7.8	76
42 Territoire-de-Belfort	224	2.6	7.9	89
43 Loire atlantique	154	7.8	10.9	99
44 Maine-et-Loire	98	6.9	8.9	89
45 Mayenne	54	3.5	5.0	94
46 Sarthe	83	2.7	8.9	92
47 Vendée	76	7.7	7.5	84
48 Cotes d'Armor	78	0.8	7.9	80
49 Finistère	125	2.2	8.6	92
50 Ille-et-Vilaine	118	8.6	7.7	99
51 Morbihan	91	6.4	9.8	84
52 Charente	57	0.7	9.5	99
53 Charente-Maritime	77	3.7	11.9	82
54 Deux-Sèvres	58	1.6	8.8	91
55 Vienne	54	3.6	8.9	88
56 Dordogne	43	2.8	9.8	82
57 Gironde	121	9.6	11.7	106
58 Landes	34	5.7	8.6	93
59 Lot-et-Garonne	57	3.6	10.5	101
60 Pyrénées atlantiques	76	5.4	10.5	104

FIG **10.15** *Social and Economic Indicators, French Départements*

| Département | Population | | Unemployment | GDP/person |
	Inhab/km² 1990	Change (%) 1980–90	% 1990	EUR=100 1989
61 Ariège	28	0.3	8.1	70
62 Aveyron	31	−2.9	5.1	77
63 Haute-Garonne	147	14.2	10.2	106
64 Gers	28	0.0	6.1	88
65 Lot	30	1.7	7.8	80
66 Hautes-Pyrénées	50	−1.0	10.0	88
67 Tarn	59	1.2	8.6	86
68 Tarnoce Garonne	54	6.3	9.0	82
69 Corrèze	41	−1.3	8.0	80
70 Creuse	24	−7.2	8.6	68
71 Haute-Vienne	64	−0.1	7.7	92
72 Allier	49	−3.8	10.4	84
73 Cantal	28	−3.2	8.4	79
74 Haute-Loire	42	0.5	7.0	78
75 Puy-de-Dôme	75	1.4	8.3	98
76 Ain	82	16.3	4.9	95
77 Ardèche	50	5.0	8.6	78
78 Drôme	63	8.9	10.0	102
79 Isère	137	11.3	7.6	103
80 Loire	156	0.9	8.6	86
81 Rhône	464	4.9	6.9	129
82 Savoie	58	9.6	6.5	111
83 Haute-Savoie	130	18.4	5.6	111
84 Alpes-de-Haute-Provence	19	12.0	8.1	94
85 Hautes-Alpes	20	10.2	7.2	108
86 Alpes-Maritimes	226	12.8	9.2	104
87 Bouches-du-Rhone	345	3.8	12.1	104
88 Var	136	19.4	12.4	82
89 Vaucluse	130	12.4	10.4	92
90 Aude	49	7.5	11.6	81
91 Gard	100	12.8	13.1	86
92 Herault	130	15.5	13.9	93
93 Lozère	14	−2.0	5.0	92
94 Pyrénées-Orientales	88	12.5	13.3	76

ESSAY

1 Many European countries are reaching a point where the costs of car use are exceeding the benefits. With the help of evidence from this chapter and Chapter 6 discuss the extent to which you think this is true.

2 Why has the construction of the M3 through Twyford Down been so controversial?

3 Compare and contrast the controversies surrounding the construction of the M3 through Twyford Down and the new motorway through the Pyrenees described in this chapter.

4 The expansion of the high-speed train network in Europe is to be welcomed. Do you agree?

5 Compare and contrast the reactions and policies of decision makers in France and Britain towards the Channel Tunnel and its associated infrastructure.

6 Describe the possible spatial impacts of telecommunications developments in Europe.

Index